CW01335689

Russian strategy in the Middle East and North Africa

Manchester University Press

RUSSIAN STRATEGY AND POWER

SERIES EDITORS
Andrew Monaghan and Richard Connolly

EDITORIAL BOARD
Julian Cooper, OBE
Emily Ferris
Tracey German
Michael Kofman
Katri Pynnöniemi
Andrei Sushentsov

PREVIOUSLY PUBLISHED

Germany's Russia problem: The struggle for balance in Europe
John Lough

Russian Grand Strategy in the era of global power competition
Andrew Monaghan (ed.)

The sea in Russian strategy
Andrew Monaghan and Richard Connolly (eds)

Russian strategy in the Middle East and North Africa
Derek Averre

Russian strategy in the Middle East and North Africa

Derek Averre

MANCHESTER UNIVERSITY PRESS

Copyright © Derek Averre 2024

The right of Derek Averre to be identified as the author of this work has been asserted in accordance with the Copyright, Designs and Patents Act 1988.

Published by Manchester University Press
Oxford Road, Manchester M13 9PL

www.manchesteruniversitypress.co.uk

British Library Cataloguing-in-Publication Data
A catalogue record for this book is available from the British Library

ISBN 978 1 5261 7581 6 hardback

First published 2024

The publisher has no responsibility for the persistence or accuracy of URLs for any external or third-party internet websites referred to in this book, and does not guarantee that any content on such websites is, or will remain, accurate or appropriate.

Typeset
by Deanta Global Publishing Services, Chennai, India

Contents

Acknowledgements		*page* vi
Introduction: the Arab Spring and Russia		1
1	Russia and the MENA region: state fragmentation, inter-state rivalries and international discord	19
2	Russia and the Syrian civil war	57
3	Russia's domestic politics and the Arab Spring	98
4	Russia, the Arab uprisings and international norms	121
5	Religion and terrorism: the challenge of the Arab Spring	147
6	A Russian strategy for the MENA region?	169
Conclusions		189
Bibliography		211
Index		265

Acknowledgements

I have spent most of my academic life in the Centre for Russian, European and Eurasian Studies, where I have enjoyed the rich intellectual support and company of many friends, colleagues and students since I came to Birmingham in 1991. Mark Youngman, Paul Richardson and Jeremy Morris were kind enough to read and comment on draft chapters of this book, offering much needed encouragement; Julian Cooper was, as always, generous in sharing data from his own impeccable study of the Russian economy, and the Manchester University Press series editors, Andrew Monaghan and Richard Connolly, at various times shared their considerable knowledge with me. Ten Russian respondents, renowned experts on foreign policy and the MENA region, were interviewed during trips to Moscow; in light of the current difficult circumstances in Russia, I decided against individual attribution, but would like to acknowledge their invaluable insights. Lance Davies (my co-author on a journal article that helped to form ideas presented in Chapter 4 of the book), David Averre, Pourya Nabipour, Tamsin Morgan and Charlie Millington aided the project with excellent research support. John Kennedy, Laure Delcour, Stefan Meister and Fatih Ekinci provided me with useful contacts. Marea Arries and Tricia Thomas have been the best administrators and friends, over a period of many years, that anyone could wish for. Two anonymous reviewers of the full draft manuscript delivered detailed and cogent comments which made revisions easy; any errors and omissions are, of course, mine alone. Rob, Humairaa, Deborah, Jen and Lillian at Manchester University Press were the most helpful editorial and production team. Finally, my love goes to Karen, David and Frances for all the joy and devilment over the years (while laughing every time I mentioned that the final draft of the book was 'just about ready'); and to my mam and dad, Derek and Margaret, who have always believed in me and who are back with us in the Land of the Prince Bishops, at last.

Introduction: the Arab Spring and Russia

> The former, traditional paradigm [of international relations] may be defined as confrontational and conflictual – the formation of opposing political-military alignments, 'zero-sum games', the need for an external enemy and the demonisation of the appropriate countries ... This mentality must change. The new paradigm must be based on cooperation. (Lavrov 2010)

The inception of the Arab Spring – sparked by the protest of Mohammed Bouazizi, a street vendor in Tunisia, against harassment by local police – caught the international community largely unawares. It came a few days before Russian foreign minister Sergei Lavrov's statement above and coincided with a period of positive, if pragmatic, relations between Russia and the leading Western powers. The US had agreed a 'reset' in its bilateral relationship with Russia, following the latter's war with Georgia in 2008; inspired by President Dmitrii Medvedev's pronouncements about the need for reform in the wake of the global financial crisis, the EU and most of its member states were pursuing Partnerships for Modernisation with Moscow. Russia's cooperative approach to foreign policy spilled over into its decision-making in the Libya uprising in 2011, the first major test of its relations with the West in the Middle East and North Africa (MENA) since the US-led intervention in Iraq in 2003. Russia echoed the West and the regional Arab states in blaming the Libyan leader Muammar al-Gaddafi for the escalating violence, warning him that failure to ensure the protection of civilians would 'be qualified as crimes with all the ensuing consequences under international law' (President of Russia 2011). The Russian leadership supported the adoption of United Nations Security Council (UNSC) resolution 1970, which deplored the Gaddafi government's gross and systematic violations of human rights and imposed an arms embargo on Libya; it subsequently abstained from resolution 1973, which imposed a no-fly zone to prevent government air strikes against opposition-held areas. With the US pressing for an arrest warrant to refer Gaddafi to the International Criminal Court, Russia supported the call for 'a fair and impartial investigation into the actions of all parties to the conflict in Libya and to bring to justice individuals involved in ... serious violations of international humanitarian law'; at the same time, Moscow expressed concern over the excessive use of force by the NATO-led coalition in its Operation Unified Protector campaign and demanded strict compliance with resolution 1973 (UNSC 2011a). At the G8 summit in May 2011, Russia accepted the collective statement that Gaddafi had forfeited legitimacy, calling for a transition that would see him step down (Martin 2022, 75).

Alarmed at the uncertainty generated by popular revolt and fearing upheaval that might spread more widely across the region, Moscow also adopted a cautious approach to the spontaneous uprisings in Tunisia, Yemen, Egypt and Bahrain, emphasising the need for a political settlement of the conflicts, even if this led to a change of leadership in some countries. Lavrov voiced Russia's recognition of the 'cardinal transformation' taking place in the MENA region, where the people were calling for 'greater democracy, a higher standard of living and well-being, unhindered access to universal human rights'; at the same time, he asserted that there should be no interference in the internal affairs of these countries, with ready-made solutions imposed from outside, but that democratic reform should be generated from within, according to their own traditions (Lavrov 2011a). Russian deputy prime minister Mikhail Bogdanov, an experienced diplomat in Middle Eastern affairs, ruled out any conspiracy theory of US plots to foment unrest which was, he argued, inspired by oppressive regimes, high levels of unemployment and corruption and other social ills (Bogdanov 2011, 12). Moscow's initial response to the Arab Spring thus appeared to have much in common with that of its Western partners.

However, the violent death of Gaddafi in October 2011 confirmed Russia's fears – shared by other non-Western powers – that the NATO-led intervention had exceeded the original UN mandate to protect the population and amounted to forcible regime change. The subsequent failure to establish effective governance in Libya, which was fragmenting into warring factions, contributed to a wider destabilisation in North Africa, generating a humanitarian crisis that spilled over into an exodus of refugees and migrants into neighbouring countries, and ultimately into Europe. These events had a decisive impact on Moscow's approach to the Syrian civil war – 'the greatest human disaster of the twenty-first century' to date (Phillips 2016, 1). Despite backing calls for President Bashar al-Assad to implement democratic reforms and restrain the use of violence by government forces against protesters, Moscow vetoed a draft UNSC resolution – the first of a series of vetoes in subsequent years – which, it believed, would lead to his overthrow. Responding to Western demands that Assad step down, Lavrov called for a non-violent resolution to the intra-Syrian crisis in which the opposition would forego radical demands in favour of negotiations with the Assad government to stabilise the situation (Lavrov 2011a). The diverging positions between Russia and Western governments were becoming more and more evident. In a UN address in March 2012 Lavrov warned against Western manipulation of Security Council decisions that could lead to external military intervention; in his words, 'hasty demands for regime change' amounted to 'risky recipes for geopolitical engineering that can only result in the spread of conflict' (UNSC 2012a).

As the Syrian conflict escalated, the inauguration of the third Putin presidency was preceded by domestic unrest in Russia surrounding the 2011–2012 parliamentary and presidential elections. The Putin leadership reacted by instituting firmer controls over domestic governance and sharpening narratives about the need to defend Russia's sovereignty against external interference in its internal affairs. Moscow's mistrust of Western intentions in Syria was reinforced by subsequent events. Ukraine's 'Revolution of Dignity' in February 2014 was depicted by Moscow as an anti-constitutional coup carried out by extremist forces and sponsored by Western governments; Russia's subsequent annexation of Crimea and support for Russophone groups in the Donbas triggered a more assertive and, as seen from the West, destabilising and even revisionist foreign policy (see Allison 2017; Gunitsky and Tsygankov 2018, 390). Russia's military intervention in Syria on 30 September 2015 to shore up the Assad government – two days after Putin, speaking at the seventieth session of the UN General Assembly, condemned the West's export of supposedly '"democratic" revolutions' that led to aggressive intervention, pervasive violence and 'total disregard for human rights' (Putin 2015a) – underscored Moscow's preparedness to challenge Western policies in regions beyond the post-Soviet space. One expert's assessment of Russia's actions reflected a common view:

> Russia has emerged as a significantly more influential and powerful strategic presence in the Middle East, reminiscent to some degree of the Soviet role during the cold war period. In relation to Syria, in particular, Russia was willing to countenance a degree of diplomatic confrontation with the West which was unparalleled since the end of the cold war. (Dannreuther 2015, 77)

But the intellectual challenge of understanding Russia's approach to the Arab uprisings goes far beyond the paradigm of Cold War confrontation, so often the starting point for analysis by Western experts. The Arab Spring has exposed deep fissures between the principles underpinning the integrity of the international system and the actions of the leading external powers. Inconsistencies in policymaking in the US have been widely criticised. Barack Obama's cautious decision-making was followed by Donald Trump's transactional approach to multilateral rules and institutions, leading to a legitimacy deficit in American leadership of the liberal international order (Ikenberry 2018, 19; see also Ikenberry 2017). As a result, US policies have exacerbated animosities in the MENA region and fuelled a contest for power between Iran, Turkey and the Arab states. Russia, displaying increasing assertiveness in foreign policy, has sought to exploit the opportunities presented by the lack of Western leadership to extend its own influence; yet Moscow, like the other external actors, has often struggled to manage the complex and rapidly shifting calculus of power and interests in the region. The humanitarian consequences of the external powers' collective failure to mitigate regional tensions have been dire. The cooperative paradigm spoken of by Lavrov in the epigraph to the present chapter has been swept away by discord and confrontation. The prospect of longer-term, and possibly far-reaching, instability in international and regional MENA affairs is reflected in Andrew Hurrell's analysis (2018, 91) of 'the return of geopolitics … and the impact of new and disruptive patterns of social and political mobilization. Today, many global governance institutions are under severe strain. Gridlock, stagnation, fragmentation, contestation, and, most recently, backlash have become the dominant frames within which to analyse global governance.'

The purpose of this book: analytical approach and key questions

The puzzles presented by Russian foreign policy in the MENA region, in the tumultuous period since the inception of the Arab Spring over a decade ago, constitute the subject matter of this book. Its fundamental aim is to examine Russia's political and security interests and its relations with regional and external actors while at the same time analysing how Russia has dealt with the insecurity within the region, in the context both of its own domestic politics and of a changing international system. At the international level, we consider how the perceptions of Russia's governing elite shape its approach to norms relating to sovereignty, the use of force and human rights and underpin its dealings with the other external powers in tackling regional conflicts. At the regional system level, we explore the challenges Russia faces in dealing with both inter-state and intra-state disputes, with power shifts involving myriad state and non-state actors; we also examine how Russia's approach to combating militant Islamist extremism in the MENA region, represented by its elites as an existential threat to the international community, is shaped by its own experience of the Islamist insurgency in the restive North Caucasus region. At the domestic level, we consider how internal political and institutional factors have influenced Moscow's thinking and decision-making in response to the uncertainties generated by the Arab uprisings, where social and economic problems deriving from weak governance have stimulated challenges to political authority.

This book addresses several key questions arising from the events described above. What particular combination of factors determined Russia's response to the Arab Spring, in particular the Syria conflict, and how do we explain the course of action taken by the Putin leadership in dealing with them? What core ideas and beliefs underpin Russian elites' understanding of the international environment and how do they influence decision-making? How do we integrate explanations of Russian behaviour into a broader and deeper understanding of recent changes in international politics, distinguishing between longer-term trends and proximate causes? How do we assess the balance of political opportunities and constraints shaping Russia's MENA policy and how does the region fit into its broader foreign policy thinking? Finally, why – contrary to many Western representations of Russia's actions in the MENA region as fundamentally adversarial – has Moscow sought to promote its interests while at the same time leaving room for accommodation with the Western powers in trying to resolve regional disputes?

In seeking to answer the above questions we argue that no single theoretical approach adequately frames the range of issues covered in this book. While we consider realists' concerns with power politics and strategic interests, which are crucial in understanding the causal factors underpinning security dynamics and alliance formation in the MENA region and Russia's purported return as a global power, we argue that Russia's role must also take account of the ideas and norms that inspire its challenge to what it perceives as the Western-dominated international order – in other words, how structural factors are translated into foreign policy through ideas embedded in state identity (see Beach and Pederson 2020, 106). Put simply, in considering theoretical explanations for Russia's foreign policy we concentrate on their practical application, assembling evidence and subjecting existing accounts to due critical analysis to account for specific aspects of change and continuity. As one leading scholar argues, identifying causal factors

> does not depend on a belief in the eternal logic of politics and insecurity as preached by classical realists, nor on the structural determinism of the neo-realists. Rather it results from the very difficult combination of recurring political dilemmas and powerful processes of historical change that are unlikely to be quickly, or easily, reversed. (Hurrell 2005, 32)

Investigating the factors determining Russia's decision-making in a complex and turbulent security environment, the role of domestic structures and institutions and the pattern of discord and confrontation with the leading Western powers presents substantive challenges that defy simple explanations. Understanding how strategic incentives affect state behaviour demands a deeper assessment of historical and contextual factors: in the case of Russia and its engagement with the countries of the MENA region over the last decade, these factors are complex, cross-cutting and subject to many variables. Indeed, the Syria intervention itself – Russia's first military operation outside of the post-Soviet space – has been described by one leading Russian expert as 'untypical' of its foreign policy (Stepanova 2018a, 37). A closer critical analysis of the empirical evidence for Russia's role in Syria and the MENA region is thus crucial in developing a more accurate understanding of its policies and ongoing engagement with regional actors and states external to the region. This has become all the more important in light of Russia's war with Ukraine, with the attendant consequences both for European security and for Russia's wider external relations with non-Western regions and countries.

This book is essentially a study in foreign policy analysis, linking an explanation of broader trends in international and regional relations with a focus on domestic determinants – culture, ideas, actors and institutions – shaping Russian decision-making. We adopt a 'pragmatist', analytically eclectic approach that focuses on the 'complexity and messiness of particular real-world situations', undertaking a wide scope of analysis in order to identify the most important aspects of the problem and attempting to capture the interactions among various causal factors that are often analysed in isolation from each other (Sil and Katzenstein 2010, 411–412; see also Darwich 2019, 31). For example, why did Moscow abstain from UNSC resolution 1973, which authorised 'all possible measures' to protect the Libyan population against an assault by Gaddafi's forces, while vetoing Western proposals for lesser measures to constrain Assad's treatment of Syrian protesters? How did Russia seek to justify its armed intervention against the opposition, after Putin had asserted that Russia would not become involved in the Syrian civil war? Why has Moscow consistently invoked the fight against Islamist terrorism to legitimise its intervention, even though Russia's governing elite professes to understand the political and social processes underpinning the MENA uprisings? Why have the negotiations to resolve regional conflicts often involved Russia's cooperation with the US, despite its exorbitant information campaign directed at Washington? What aims underpin Moscow's mediation among MENA countries with quite differing interests and ideas about the future of the region? Is Russian statecraft underpinned by a concerted strategy towards the MENA region and what are the material and political constraints it faces there? We maintain that these questions – crucial in understanding Russian policy during the Arab

Spring – can not be properly addressed without considering the broader social, historical and cultural context of Russia's internal politics and the foreign policy beliefs espoused by its political elites.

Our analytical framework draws on the model proposed by Herrmann and Ned Lebow to investigate the causes of the end of the Cold War – like the Arab Spring, a transformative moment that changed our understanding of security (see Chapter 1) – and examines four possible explanations for the evolution of Russian policy in the MENA region: first, material capabilities and structural power factors; second, the beliefs underpinning its conceptions of international society and the clash of ideas with the Western liberal democracies; third, the domestic sources of its foreign policy; and fourth, individual level explanations of agency, in other words the policy choices of the Putin leadership (Herrmann and Ned Lebow 2004, 7–8; see also Götz 2017; Dannreuther 2019). None of these explanations in isolation can account for the complex configuration of causes determining Russian policy: this book brings these explanations together to elucidate the key aspects of continuity and change, challenging existing interpretations and offering a more comprehensive appraisal of Russia's approach to the Arab Spring. The aim is to contribute to an empirical analysis of the key issues faced by Moscow, responding to the surge of interest in Russian foreign policy over the last decade, while offering a conceptually richer study that reflects the profound complexity of the challenges Russia has faced in the MENA region.

The first explanation focuses on structural factors. In Western analysis, Russia is often perceived as marshalling its economic and military capabilities in a bid to fill the power vacuum left by the muddled and erratic policies of the West, defending its 'client' states from US-led interventions and using the Middle East as an asset in geopolitical competition-by-proxy with the US (Mead 2014, 76; Stent 2016, 106). In this interpretation, Moscow favours a 'short-term, transactional approach' to assert its national interests and reduce the advantages of its adversaries in 'classically realist' fashion (Sladden et al 2017, 2, 5). As illustrated by its military intervention in the Syrian civil war, a resurgent Russia has recovered from its weakness in the 1990s to exploit the lack of Western resolve and entrench its positions in the MENA region through 'agile diplomacy backed by credible force' (Popescu and Secrieru 2018, 6; McFaul 2020, 96).

Material factors undoubtedly influence Russia's policy choices, but the above arguments leave several questions unanswered. How do we establish a clear causal link between external opportunities and constraints and the decision-making of the Russian leadership? In other words, how exactly have strategic incentives, arising from power shifts in the international and regional order, impacted its behaviour in the MENA region (see Götz 2017,

241)? Put in its simplest form, does Russia have a MENA *strategy*? We argue that, while Russia's relations with the US may plausibly be characterised as adversarial, the turbulent security environment – beset by intra-state conflicts, intensified regional rivalries and the rise of Islamist extremism – has altered established rationales and relationships, necessitating differentiated responses to policy problems and leaving room for both rivalry and cooperation. Also, when examining the fluctuating and overlapping alliances in the MENA region, we must also include non-state actors in the distribution of power 'beyond conceptualizing them as mere instruments of state units' (Soler i Lecha et al 2019, 12–13). How does Russia factor the constraints imposed by state fragmentation into its strategic thinking? Finally, while the security of nation-states remains important in understanding MENA politics, the international community has been confronted with momentous challenges posed by the devastating impact on human security arising from conflicts there (Jacoby 2015, 169–70). How does Moscow deal with humanitarian problems amid the upheaval in the region?

The second explanation considers how national beliefs and cultural identity, embedded as a set of durable perceptions about its statehood and role in the international order, influence Russia's normative approach to international affairs (see Katzenstein 1996, 6). Scholars who dispute the realist paradigm argue that 'history and culture matter, not because they determine state behavior in any mechanical way, but because they provide a reservoir of social and verbal practices out of which states' goals, purposes, and self-understandings are constructed' in order to make sense of their international environment (Götz 2017, 236; see also Weldes 1996, 277, 280). Others refer to 'principled beliefs [that] mediate between world views and particular policy conclusions; they translate fundamental doctrines into guidance for contemporary human action' (Goldstein and Keohane 1993, 9). Writers on Russian affairs have couched these ideas in terms of identities that 'generate an array of permissible and appropriate behavior and norms of how one should and should not act, and a repertoire of justifications for actions taken' (Suny 2007, 41). Russia's identity has often been constructed in opposition to the West, with the US/Europe playing the role of 'external significant others' (Hopf 2005, 227; see also Feklyunina 2018, 8–10); Russia's preoccupation with sovereignty and cultural differences has driven 'disdain and ideological resistance to "Western mentorship"', including in its approach to the Middle East (Chebankova 2017, 224, 226). In some Western interpretations, Russia's 'great power' identity is linked to status-seeking, perceived as underpinning an assertive and even revisionist foreign policy in which it revives its claims to special rights and responsibilities in a sphere of influence (Gunitsky and Tsygankov 2018, 385, 390; Clunan 2014, 286).

There is merit in each of these arguments. However, in emphasising Russia's attempts to assert its status and distance itself from the West in identity terms, Western scholarship – with some exceptions – has paid much less attention to other factors, such as its search for legitimacy in terms of norms and rule-making in a more pluralist international system of states, or how Russian perceptions of the international and regional security environment impact its strategic thinking. Russia's foreign policy in the MENA region is underpinned by distinctive ideas about political order and the exercise of power in the international system; its governing elite opposes the imposition of external standards of legitimacy and defends Russia's cultural and civilisational diversity at a time of systemic change in international society. In Chapters 3 and 4 of this book, we investigate how and why specific ideas and beliefs have influenced Russia's thinking and actions in its responses to the Arab Spring. Much of the existing literature tends towards broad-brush explanations, applied uncritically without considering contextual factors, and is of limited utility in this respect.

The third explanation centres on the influence of a country's internal politics on foreign policymaking. Charles Maier maintains that 'International orders ... have domestic socio-political corollaries ... [they] either implicitly or explicitly build upon domestic arrangements within participating countries, as well as upon the specific agreements negotiated between them' (Maier 2000, 37). In seeking to explain Russia's policy in Syria, Roy Allison argues that its commitment to a 'statist' international order that privileges the sovereignty of incumbent rulers reflects a preoccupation with its own domestic state order; this outlook is 'rooted in the structure of political power in Russia and it is shared by those in the elite who have been empowered by Putin's presidencies' (Allison 2013b, 818). Roland Dannreuther asserts that the tense political situation in Russia in 2011–2012 determined Putin's resolute stance in the Syria conflict, allowing him to consolidate his domestic support by pointing to 'perceived flaws of the imposition of Western liberal democracy and the virtues of Russia's own model of state-managed political order' (Dannreuther 2015, 77, 87). Other scholars have likened the overthrow of authoritarian governments in the MENA region to the challenge posed to Russia's conservative domestic order by the 'colour revolutions' in some of the post-Soviet countries, which have intensified Russian elites' 'profound aversion to regime change' (Cadier and Light 2016, 207). Some have gone further, maintaining that Russia's aggressive foreign policy is part of a *strategy* to preserve an autocratic Putin regime seeking external sources of legitimacy to make up for its domestic failures (Stoner and McFaul 2015, 169). In these accounts, domestic factors outweigh geopolitical imperatives (Dannreuther 2019, 739–740).

Again, these arguments deserve consideration. The Arab Spring coincided with important changes in Russia's domestic governance that had been germinating for several years, reflecting the governing elite's concerns about political legitimacy at home. However, while accepting that the Putin leadership bases its claim to legitimacy on the provision of internal order underpinned by a strong state, we challenge the argument that its approach to the MENA region is driven by a 'diversionary' foreign policy. The Arab uprisings posed no immediate threat to the Russian leadership and the evidence to support the idea that an authoritarian Putin government will inevitably back like-minded leaderships in the MENA countries is disputable (see Götz 2017, 234–235). Our analysis in Chapter 3 of this book finds little to substantiate the claim by liberal writers that there is a direct causal relationship between regime type and foreign policy; we conclude that other factors better explain Russia's intervention in Syria and reaction to crises across the MENA region. Domestic factors combine with resources available to the state and the perception of external opportunities and threats to determine responses to specific policy challenges (see Sakwa 2017, 8; Gunitsky and Tsygankov 2018, 386; Lynch 2016, 108–109).

The fourth explanation privileges the agency of Vladimir Putin over accounts that emphasise structural and societal factors. Foreign policy analysis shows that how leaders perceive and act on national interests may be a significant factor in international relations (see Beach and Pedersen 2020, 143–144). A number of recent studies have placed Putin's political methods and personal world view at the forefront of explanations of Russia's foreign policy (see Hill and Gaddy 2013), including its intervention in Syria (see Phillips 2019, 70). Michael McFaul, a prominent academic and US ambassador to Russia during the Obama administration, argues that Putin's agency, rather than a recovery in the country's economic and military power or historical and cultural determinants, offers a better explanation of recent trends in Russia's international behaviour, including his approach to the conflicts in Libya and Syria; in his words, Putin's world view plays 'a *causal* role in the conduct of Russian foreign policy' (McFaul 2020, 99; emphasis added).

In a personalised and centralised political system, where formal checks and balances are weaker or operate differently to those in more open systems, Putin's ability to impose institutional changes to consolidate his authority undoubtedly has an important bearing on Russian foreign policy planning and decision-making (Gel'man 2015, xiv). At the same time, Putin operates within a framework of political and institutional opportunities and constraints in a complex coalition of public actors and interest groups (Gel'man 2015, 35–36; Romanova 2018, 85); these actors and groups have a marked impact on foreign policy in terms of providing resources for and imposing limits on the range of policy options open to the Putin leadership (see Petrov and Gel'man 2019, 450–451). Examining the structure of decision-making and the particularistic interests of influential elites is important in terms of understanding Russia's foreign policy. Chapter 3 of this book thus investigates the role of domestic actors, institutions and interest groups in catalysing change in Russian decision-making in the MENA region, reflecting on how Putin has been able to win political support that has allowed him to prosecute a more assertive role there.

Research design and data sources

This book represents the only full-length, single-authored monograph to date on Russia's role in the MENA region since the inception of the Arab Spring. The author has drawn on a combination of primary documents and secondary open-source material in English and Russian. Primary sources include UN Security Council (UNSC) resolutions, records of its meetings, reports of the UN Secretary-General, UN General Assembly statements and other relevant documents, including UN Human Rights Council reports. Of particular interest were reports of the UN Independent International Commission of Inquiry (IICI) on the Syrian Arab Republic, established by the Human Rights Council to investigate all alleged violations and abuses of international human rights law since March 2011 in Syria. The evidence in the IICI reports is based on interviews conducted in the region and data collected and analysed from numerous sources, including communications from UN reports, governments and NGOs, though its investigations were impeded by the denial of access to Syrian-controlled territories. These sources were complemented by exhaustive coverage of Russian presidential statements and Ministry of Foreign Affairs communiqués, as well as analysis of selected official documents from the US, EU, UK, France and China. Extensive use was also made of reports from international bodies (such as the Organisation for the Prohibition of Chemical Weapons) and authoritative non-governmental organisations with a presence on the ground in the MENA countries (for example International Crisis Group, Human Rights Watch and Amnesty International), which employ rigorous methodology in their reporting and often refer to credible local sources of information.

The few book-length studies on the topic in English have limited themselves to broad empirical analysis (Kozhanov 2016; Trenin 2018b; Vasiliev 2018; Borshchevskaya 2019; Nizameddin 2013), though a number of academic articles and book chapters have investigated more closely specific aspects of Russia's role in the Syria conflict and involvement in wider MENA affairs. Several Russian policy reports have offered interesting insights into Russia's

MENA policies, including contributions written for the Valdai Discussion Club and the Russian International Affairs Council; though these bodies are closely linked with official structures, they often represent broadly independent views by authoritative scholars and commentators who offer perceptive critical analysis of Russian official thinking that adds a dimension to Western understandings of the research problem. Articles written in Russian were sourced from a keyword search of the EastView databases of Russian social science journals, periodicals and newspapers, containing extensive coverage of original Russian-language expert and media writing over the period from January 2011 to December 2022. In addition, this book draws widely on academic works that do not focus directly or exclusively on Russian policy in the Arab Spring but that contribute to our understanding of its key themes, such as Russian approaches to international law and global governance, military intervention and the doctrine of Responsibility to Protect, politics and society, military affairs and defence economy and approach to terrorism and religion. Finally, of particular importance for this study were the insights gained from interviews conducted with leading Russian scholars and experts on the Middle East in 2018 and 2019. References to these interviews in the following chapters are from written records; translations into English of interview responses, as well as of all documents sourced in the Russian original, were made by the author.

The present writer is a Russia specialist but has made considerable efforts to draw additionally on the work of recognised scholars and experts from the Middle East and North Africa, in order to incorporate regional perspectives and present a sound understanding of the broader context of Russia's policies. Studies published by the Istituto Affari Internazionali in Rome, the Euro-Mediterranean Study Commission (EuroMeSCo) network and the EU-funded MEDRESET and MENARA project consortia, which brought together experts from Europe and the MENA region to carry out on-the-ground field research, including interviews with government officials, were particularly valuable to the present study. All of the sources used in the book were chosen on the basis of the authority and reliability of experts writing for highly-regarded publishers or for recognised institutions and think tanks and were subject to appropriate critical analysis. A full list of works can be found in the bibliography.

Consideration was also given to approaching Russian officials for interview in order to obtain a first-hand account of foreign policy. However, in recent years it has become increasingly difficult to negotiate meetings with policymakers in Russia due to its tense relationship with Western governments. In the present writer's experience, Russian officials nowadays tend to stick closely to the official line in public statements and offer limited insights into the leadership's decision-making or thinking. Our efforts thus concentrated on rigorously scrutinising the extensive repository of official communiqués, speeches, articles, statements and press briefings by Putin, Lavrov and other leading officials; these were then reviewed in conjunction with interpretations of official policy voiced by our interview respondents and other experts and commentators in their published work. The rest was up to the intuition of the author in composing the analysis, to be judged by anybody who reads this book.

Challenges faced in writing this book

The first challenge – a common one when undertaking foreign policy analysis – relates to the design and scope of the study. A narrower focus, limiting the breadth of the research, might have produced a more satisfactory match between the evidence presented and the conclusions. We adopted a more comprehensive approach, drawing on an extensive volume of primary and secondary material, in order to achieve greater explanatory traction in investigating Russia's policies and allow for a definitive assessment of its role in the Middle East and North Africa over an extended period. Even so, in attempting to look beyond existing analysis and explore the extraordinarily complex dynamics of both Russian foreign policy and the politics of the MENA region, time and space constraints meant that we had to focus mainly on issues relevant to our central research questions. Ongoing topics of considerable importance in terms of Russia's involvement – such as its energy policy and military strategic planning, its multifaceted relations with Iran and Turkey, and its response to the US's approach to the region – merit more detailed examination. Indeed, Russia's involvement in the Syrian civil war, analysed in Chapter 2, is deserving of a full-length book study.

The second challenge stems from the normative approach that pervades Western writing on Russia's post-Cold War foreign policy. The consequences of Moscow's use of statecraft to entrench and extend its influence in the MENA region inevitably attract the most attention. Russian state actors are often portrayed as unashamed realists, motivated by power considerations and pursuing a purely transactional approach that disregards normative constraints on its foreign policy conduct (highlighted even more graphically by its invasion of Ukraine in 2022, the implications of which are considered in our concluding chapter). Moral sensibilities must certainly be outraged at the atrocities committed in Syria, enabled by Moscow's support for Assad. At the same time, the leading Western powers' interventions in Iraq in 2003 and Libya in 2011, their muted response to the Saudi intervention in Yemen and their own resort to statecraft to prosecute their interests are open to criticism; shifts in US policy have exacerbated the unstable political situation across the region, demanding a response from Russia. In seeking a deeper understanding of events we must take into account the international and domestic context shaping Russia's exercise of power and the different assumptions that have evolved in the minds of its elites. States must justify their actions as consistent with prevailing international law or risk forfeiting legitimacy in international society (Allison 2013a, 2); we thus examine how Russian elites' particular understanding of institutions, rules and norms impact decision-making and try to avoid simply dismissing Russia's approaches as cynical, opportunistic and unworthy of serious consideration (see Gunitsky and Tsygankov 2018, 390).

The third challenge relates to the disinformation disseminated by the Russian government and media outlets on sensitive foreign policy issues, for example on the humanitarian costs of Russia's military operations in support of the Syrian government and its rebuttal of accusations of the use of chemical and other banned weapons by Assad's forces. Russia's 'information war' – only too evident in its present conflict with Ukraine – has become a systemic factor in its external relations; difficulties in ascertaining the reliability of information sources complicate efforts to form an independent and objective analysis. Some commentators have in fact argued that the politicisation of official and media reporting represents a significant problem that goes beyond Russia's practices, criticising the biased portrayal of events on the ground by Western officials and analysts with the aim of manipulating international organisations and the media to influence public opinion and build support for the US's and European states' policies in the MENA region (Phillips 2016, 8; Ralph et al 2017; Hayward 2019; Hersh 2013; Paphiti and Bachmann 2018; Dejevsky 2018). Researchers face inevitable limitations in terms of their ability to undertake in-depth 'fact-checking' of events on the ground and achieve confident attribution based on undisputable empirical evidence. In researching this book, we have made considerable efforts to cross-refer official Russian government accounts with research by independent experts and authoritative organisations to obtain a clear and credible account of the causes and effects of Russia's actions. Examining how and why disinformation is used to justify Russia's policies constitutes an important aspect of our analysis.

We have tried to keep these questions firmly in mind, aiming to avoid the biases present in Western commentary on Russia while at the same time subjecting the latter's claims to due critical analysis; our presentation of Russia's foreign policy in the MENA region is intended to form the basis for a deeper understanding of its role in the Arab Spring and not as a justification of the arguments that Russian elites appeal to when defending these policies. The aim throughout is to offer an objective and reasoned explanation of how Russian thinking, in all its complexity and ambiguity, informs its policy preferences and actions. Whether or not we have succeeded in doing so is left to the reader to decide. A personal appraisal of the moral failings and lack of integrity of Russian – and indeed Western – actions, particularly in the appalling conflict in Syria, is offered in the concluding chapter.

Structure of the book and content of chapters

Chapter 1 explores Russia's involvement in the contemporary political and security affairs of the MENA region in the context of its broader foreign policy thinking. It opens by examining the causes of the Arab uprisings and goes on to consider how Russia has dealt with the challenges posed by the fragmentation of political authority, emergence of non- or quasi-state actors and intensification of regional rivalries, responding to the perceived dual threat to stability of militant Islamism and Western intervention inspired by the notion of democratic transition. This is followed by a close analysis of Russia's political and diplomatic engagement with the MENA states in a reconfigured regional order – in particular the key powers, Iran, Turkey and Israel – and the principal external actors, namely the US, Europe and China. How does Moscow negotiate transactions with regional and external power-brokers to safeguard its core interests? We conclude the chapter by challenging the argument, prevalent in the existing literature, that Russia's actions are primarily and deliberately designed to undermine Western interests in pursuit of strategic pre-eminence in the region: we argue that, in the context of enduring regional rivalries and intra-state hostilities barely constrained by international institutions, Russia's policies have been largely reactive, motivated by specific limited goals and aimed at diversifying its links with MENA leaderships in order to manage regional conflicts and pursue incremental improvements in relations.

Chapter 2 focuses on the Syrian civil war, international responses to the initial crisis and Russia's involvement through successive phases of hostilities. We examine official Russian narratives about the causes and consequences of the Syrian uprising, highlighting the differences between Russia and the Western powers that have frustrated international efforts to resolve the conflict. We then go on to analyse in detail Russia's diplomatic and military support for the Assad government and its pivotal role in the various multilateral negotiating formats aimed at securing a resolution of the civil war, in particular the UN-sponsored Geneva talks and the trilateral Astana format led by Russia, Iran and Turkey. We explore the thinking behind its military intervention in Syria, which changed the regional security calculus and raised fears over further interventions by Russia to consolidate its positions in a region of perceived strategic importance. We argue that, despite its extravagant claims about its strategic successes, Russia faces considerable constraints in dealing with disorder and instability spilling over into the wider region and has sought international support from the Western powers in order to resolve the conflict and limit its future military engagement in Syria. We conclude by assessing the implications of Russia's Syria intervention for its future foreign policy practice, not least in the context of Moscow's prosecution of its war with Ukraine.

Chapter 3 addresses the question of how Russia's domestic politics has shaped its policies in the MENA region and to what extent its involvement there has in turn influenced internal developments in Russia. We examine how the governing elite under Vladimir Putin has sought to consolidate a strong domestic state authority by manufacturing a distinctive national identity, reasserting Russian statehood and reinforcing societal cohesion to insulate the country against externally promoted liberal ideas. We go on to consider to what extent its approach to the Arab Spring, privileging order and stability over legitimate demands for social change, is an expression of its preoccupation with its own domestic order and concerns over Western challenges to its legitimacy. We question assertions, prevalent in the literature, that Moscow's intervention in Syria can be explained by the need to rally domestic support for the Putin government and that the ascendancy of Russia's authoritarian leadership inevitably translates into the use of coercive power and diplomatic heft to sustain illiberal regimes; we argue that Russia is not preoccupied simply with defending like-minded governments against Western designs and that other factors better explain Russia's intervention in Syria and its approach to crises in individual countries across the region. Drawing on writing by leading Russian political scientists, we trace how domestic politics has been translated into changes in bureaucratic structures and identify the political, economic and security actors driving Russian policy in the MENA region, showing how the rising personalism in foreign policy decision-making under Putin and the decline of auxiliary political institutions have compromised its effectiveness and cohesion. Finally, we consider the part played by public debates and media commentary in Russia in shaping its policies in the region.

Chapter 4 investigates how Russia's recent involvement in the MENA region has influenced its role in a changing international order. We examine how Russia's cultural and historical beliefs and distinctive vision of the international system of sovereign states are reflected in its attitudes to international law, often in opposition to Western approaches. Drawing on the work of leading international relations and legal scholars, as well as Russian presidential and foreign ministry documents, we offer a critical analysis of how Russia articulates its normative position on issues of sovereignty and humanitarian intervention, the use of force and responsible protection of populations in order to defend the legality and moral rightness of its policies in the context of its military intervention in Syria. We conclude by highlighting two key trends in Russian foreign policy: first, how Russia's search for international legitimacy in terms of rule-making is bound up with its need to secure its international status, consistent with its ideas of the emergence of a multipolar world, and how it exerts diplomatic power to make strategic use of normative arguments in pursuit of its wider political and security aims in challenging the Western-led 'rules-based' international order; and second, the implications of Russia's decisive shift away from engagement with the West over liberal approaches to responsible protection norms and the provision of humanitarian assistance.

Chapter 5 explores the evolution of Russia's response to the rise of political Islam in the context of both the Arab Spring and its domestic campaign to quell the Islamist insurgency in the North Caucasus. We analyse how Russia has promoted reductive narratives about the 'fight against terrorism' in order to instrumentalise the threat of transnational militant Islamism and justify its intervention in Syria. We go on to examine how the Russian state's handling of insurgency and protests in Syria and the broader MENA region has been shaped by domestic debates over the threat posed by extremist Islamism in Russia. We focus on Moscow's response to the challenge posed by Islamic State and other extremist groups, particularly in the context of the return of Russian-speaking 'foreign fighters' from Iraq and Syria to Russia's Muslim-populated regions. We then consider how Russia, which identifies itself as a secular, multi-ethnic and multi-confessional country, addresses the religious aspects of its national identity, and how the increasing prominence in terms of cultural and civilisational values of the Russian Orthodox Church impacts Russian society's approaches to domestic Islam and its engagement with the Arab countries. Finally, we examine the role of the Chechen leader Ramzan Kadyrov and the challenges he poses both to Russia's relations with the Islamic world and to Russian governance in its Muslim-majority North Caucasus region.

Chapter 6 assesses Russia's economic and security interests in the MENA states and how they have shaped specific aspects of its military and trade policies. Drawing on defence/economic data from authoritative Russian and Western sources, we analyse Russia's deployment of military power in the Syria conflict and consider to what extent this reflects a broader militarisation of its foreign and security policy; we go on to examine Russia's trade with the MENA region and ask whether it represents a core priority in its external economic policy. We challenge the common Western notion of a 'resurgent' Russia that seeks to maximise its geostrategic influence in the MENA region by committing expeditionary forces for the purposes of power projection, in competition with the other external powers; we argue that, while the limited Syria intervention has had a substantive impact on Russia's military planning and while Moscow's economic and security interests have incentivised a more pronounced presence in the wider region, there are considerable external and domestic constraints on Russia's foreign policy ambitions deriving from both the unstable security environment and Russia's own limited military and economic resources. Finally, we consider how Russia's MENA strategy is encompassed within its broader foreign policy thinking and practice and how the Putin leadership marshals its resources to achieve its objectives. We conclude that, though a more influential future role in MENA affairs cannot be ruled out, the limited structural power at Russia's disposal is out of proportion to the longer-term political-military and economic investment that a commanding strategic presence in a conflict-prone region would require.

The concluding chapter revisits the key arguments in the book, outlined in our introductory framework and followed up in successive chapters, to draw conclusions about how the complex and multidimensional conflicts in the MENA region have influenced Russia's relations with both regional actors and the Western powers. We identify the key driving factors explaining Russia's actions and consider how its more active engagement in the region has impacted regional security affairs and how the rapidly evolving events there have in turn influenced its own thinking and practice. We challenge some of the key assumptions in the academic and expert literature pertaining to Russian foreign policy in the Arab Spring and consider how its experiences are likely to shape its future role in the regional and international order. We conclude with, first, a personal assessment of the collective failures of both Russia and the Western powers to mitigate the humanitarian consequences of the MENA conflicts, their diverging approaches to international order and the implications for future multilateral cooperation; and second, by examining how Russia's experience of the Syria conflict has influenced its actions the present war in Ukraine, particularly in terms of Moscow's resort to military instruments to achieve its political and security objectives, and how the war may ultimately exacerbate the longer-term challenges currently faced by Russia.

1

Russia and the MENA region: state fragmentation, inter-state rivalries and international discord

> War, with its own internal logic, special mentality, principles and priorities, is beginning to penetrate the fabric of global politics with ever greater intensity. Clausewitz's formula is beginning to work in reverse, with politics being the continuation of war by other means. (Kortunov 2018)

Introduction

The Arab Spring has been called a 'critical juncture' or 'revolutionary moment' – an open-ended struggle fraught with uncertainties and the potential for massive upheaval, involving political emancipation and a crisis of authority that challenged dominant thinking about the region; its impact on political and social structures resembles in some respects the transformative historical developments in Central and Eastern Europe in the late 1980s, changing how we think about order and justice (Gerges 2014, 1–2; see also various contributions to Monier 2015). The Arab uprisings originated in internal disputes between government and opposition forces, as well as among non-state groups, inflaming long-standing rivalries between the leading regional states and exacerbating the transnational threat posed by Islamist extremism and religious sectarianism. State breakdown and civil conflict – leading to territorial fragmentation in some MENA states, and in others the imposition of harsh authoritarian measures to quell internal opposition with attendant violations of human rights – have combined with deep structural problems and social dislocation to pose long-term challenges to the external powers in dealing with the resultant disorder. One leading expert on the region argues persuasively that 'the failure of current security paradigms requires a comprehensive re-think of the regional and global environment' (Fawcett 2015a, 49).

How has Russia responded to this 'revolutionary moment'? Russia's actions during the Arab Spring have been widely presented in Western commentary as consciously designed to undermine Western positions and contest US influence. There is little doubt that Moscow has sought to maximise opportunities arising from the power shifts in the region and entrench its involvement in a bid to shape MENA security and economic affairs in its favour. At the same time, its policies have often been reactive, constrained by the unpredictable and fast-moving politics in countries facing diverse challenges; moreover, it has engaged in active diplomacy and dialogue with parties to regional conflicts, sometimes in cooperation with the US and its allies. Far from making a power grab in the pursuit of geostrategic gains or acting as a 'spoiler' in impeding Western designs, Russia has been forced largely to undertake crisis management to deal with the complex problems generated by the political and institutional disorder in the MENA region.

This chapter explores the principal causes and effects of the Arab Spring and how Russia negotiates the shifting alliances and rivalries that mark the regional security system and shape the external powers' involvement in MENA countries. The next section focuses on how structural processes that led to the Arab uprisings collided with agency factors to inspire collective action that challenged incumbent authorities. The fragmentation of political authority, exacerbated by ethno-confessional divides and the emergence of non-state or transnational actors – some of which have acquired governance functions that threaten the integrity of established state structures – have combined with inter-state rivalries within a thinly institutionalised region to present a number of potentially long-term challenges to the international community. The third section examines Russia's own responses to these tumultuous political and security developments and its elites' understanding of the changes that the Arab Spring has brought about. The remaining sections analyse Russia's relations with regional states and its diplomatic engagement with other external actors, primarily the US, EU and China. The concluding section highlights the main trends of Russia's MENA policy and the constraints imposed by the regional security environment.

Our analysis throughout uses the term Arab Spring, popularised in Western commentary, though we recognise that it misses the diversity of processes across the MENA region, where the terms *thawla* (revolution) or 'Arab Awakening' are often used (Monier 2015, 5). In referring to the Middle East and North Africa (MENA) – rather than the Arab World, the Southern and Eastern Mediterranean or the Levant – we draw on the inclusive definition used by the MENARA research consortium that encompasses historical and cultural factors relevant to the emerging post-Arab Spring regional order; this definition includes the Arab countries and the three non-Arab states which play central roles in that order, Turkey, Israel and Iran (Soler i Lecha et al 2019, 8–9). On occasion, we disaggregate the greater MENA region into the Middle East and North Africa. We use the term Islamic State to cover the various iterations of the movement's name, unless otherwise called for. The term Muslim is used to describe those who practise Islam, and Islamic to designate movements or groups; Islamist is employed to refer to political Islam, without identifying any specific political movement, with the designation extremist or militant Islamism denoting violent political thought or action.

The Arab Spring

The challenges to political authority and territoriality in the Arab Spring were 'the result of very complex historical and political processes [that] generally also reflect the contentious legitimacy of the state and of political rule' (Del Sarto 2017, 769); these processes are compounded by religious, ethnic, sectarian and tribal identities as well as socioeconomic, demographic and environmental problems (Stivachtis 2019, 32). The transnational 'contagion' effect that characterised the uprisings meant that causal changes across the region were 'loose rather than tightly mechanistic' and subject to many variables, including specific local grievances (Whitehead 2015, 19). Differing political cultures and socioeconomic structures produced varying outcomes. The spontaneous mobilisation of citizens led to militarised rebellion in Egypt, and to a lesser extent in Tunisia, Morocco, Algeria, Jordan and some of the Gulf states, and ultimately to a protracted civil war in Syria, Yemen and Libya, but a common feature was the deepening of mistrust among political actors and an inability to institutionalise political transition (Gerges 2014, 8). Repression unleashed by incumbent governments in response to unrest reinforced the sense of collective insecurity and injustice and made popular demands for 'effective citizenship, personal agency, and government accountability' non-negotiable (Anderson 2014, 52; see also Whitehead 2015, 23). Unifying figures or coordinated emancipatory movements across the region have been largely absent, compounded by the lack of an effective regional organisation or strong leadership that might manage the transition to more just and equitable governance (Fawcett 2017, 792). The outcomes – the transformation of the Arab countries from below, or the resilience of authoritarian power structures limiting pluralism and tightening control – are still subject to 'interpretative uncertainty' (Falk 2016, 2322; Kamrava 2018, 57).

The political and economic factors that led to mass protests were compounded by the agency of state leaderships and insurgent leaders. A prime example is Syria. The first wave of protests there did not advocate Islamist rule, being primarily aimed at arbitrary and corrupt governance, but repression by Assad's forces turned some groups in the region to Islamism and in some cases violent extremism (Fares 2015, 149–50). One authoritative scholar argues that 'both the military and the Islamists, illiberal and undemocratic, have a vested interest in perpetuating the autocratic status quo', sustaining socioeconomic hierarchies and leaving a 'weak secular and liberal segment caught in the middle' (Gerges 2014, 24). Further problems have been caused by the emergence of local militias and transnational armed groups, particularly Islamist movements, split along sectarian or local loyalty lines and supported by regional states (Salamey 2015, 115–16). The emergence of these non-state or transnational actors, who exercise state-like capacities and control over territory, weaponising resources while providing services to sections of the population (Alaaldin 2019, 5–6), highlights the erosion of hierarchical state-centred forms of order at both the domestic and international level and 'the shift from statist to "post-statist" geopolitics in the region' (Kamel ed. 2017, 87–88; see also Kaldor 2013, 95–96). Paradoxically, despite the fragmentation of territory in some states resulting from internal conflict and ethno-confessional divisions, there is evidence for the persistence among warring factions of the idea of a unitary state and national identity (House of Lords 2017, 65; Alaaldin 2019, 5).

Shifts in the political priorities and strategic requirements of actors external to the region have also exacerbated the repressive trends in MENA states. The US-led coalition's 2003 intervention in Iraq generated a 'deepening disillusionment among the citizenry [over] the failure of these recently independent Arab states to uphold the sovereign integrity of the country in response to post-colonial Western intrusive designs'; it also contributed to the deepening of Sunni–Shi'a rivalry, intensifying the competing regional ambitions of Iran and Saudi Arabia, as well as to the growth of extremist Islamism and sectarianism that led to large-scale violence in Syria and Yemen (Falk 2016, 2323; see also Aras and Yorulmazlar 2016, 2265; Shumilin 2021, 51). In its 'war on terror' after 9/11, the US promoted national security practices which in many cases led to the reinforcement of centralised power, violations of due criminal process and restrictions on civil liberties and ultimately the securitisation of political Islam. As American policy since the inception of the Arab Spring has wavered and Washington's political leverage has declined – though the extent of its decline is open to question, as discussed later in this chapter – its policies have been refocused to fight Islamic State and support its Gulf allies in countering the spread of Iranian influence, while providing weapons and intelligence to militias and 'deploying new tools and techniques to foster and wield influence over hybrid actors and networks ... [US] military power and modes of engagement with the region have been reconfigured to match the networked and self-organizing patterns of these emerging forces' (Hazbun 2017, 35).

In the past, Western orientalists often emphasised the dominant anti-liberal traits in Islamic cultures, associating religious and patrimonial practices in the Arab world with authoritarianism and the obstruction of individual liberties and democratic constraints on power; support by external patrons for the coercive security apparatus of Arab states was justified by their strategic importance, prioritising stability over liberty and thereby undermining the capacity of mass movements to establish accountable governments (Salamey 2015, 111–112). The Arab uprisings against existing power structures challenged the Western 'exceptionalist' narrative of an Arab world existing 'outside the "box" of modernity, democracy, legal rationality, civility' (Sadiki 2015, xxxiii; see also Aras and Falk 2015, 322–323). Western policymakers and experts tended to perceive the protests in terms of a new 'wave' of democratisation; however, they were marked by a complex interplay of identities and a fragile societal consensus, despite their potentially empowering and transformative impact and connection to universal human rights (see Aras and Falk 2016, 2253–2254). Authoritative scholars of the MENA region have warned against expecting an 'unhindered linear transition to representative rule ... the democratic wave is far from irreversible' (Ayoob 2014, 403; see also Salamey 2015, 112–113). In any case, the Arab Spring did not bring an end to external intervention into the affairs of the region's states. The Western powers continued to promote democratic and liberal human rights norms that purport to define legitimate statehood, even though internal conflicts meant that weak states struggled to maintain effective sovereignty and territorial control. In the case of the intervention in Libya by a US-led coalition of largely Western forces, the results were damaging and made external actors wary of staking their interests on emergent counter-elites that they could neither evaluate nor control (Whitehead 2015, 24).

The Arab Spring has thus posed fundamental challenges to the external powers, which were used to dealing with the 'die-hard regime cronies and affluent oligarchs' of regional states who emphasised citizens' responsibilities to respect law and order rather than citizenship rights (Kamrava 2018, 4, 113–114). Countries where the challenge to incumbent governments was weaker, such as Morocco, Algeria, Tunisia and Jordan, have experienced the restitution of authoritarianism or continuation of illiberal trends, despite the formal trappings of democracy. Other states, in which personalistic leaderships hold sway and the effectiveness of the state has weakened, have witnessed 'the multiplication, fragmentation, partial hybridization and/or polarization of sectarian, tribal or ethnic markers of identity that have become plural and often antagonistic in their expressions and claims' (Boserup and Colombo 2019, 26–27). The situation has been exacerbated by the involvement of the regional powers in internal conflicts as well as by the entrenchment of militant Islamist groups, especially those linked with Al-Qaeda and Islamic State, adept at forming tactical alliances with local tribal militias, businesses, religious leaders and protest movements (Dixon and Lawson 2022, 2137; Lounnas 2018a, 2–3). Developments in Iraq, Syria and Egypt (after the short-lived ascendancy of the Muslim Brotherhood) disappointed the expectations of popular movements that Western support for political transition would be forthcoming: 'a new balance was established, whereby the Western case for peaceful transition was replaced by the acknowledgement of realities on the ground' (Aras and Yorulmazlar 2016, 2265). The resilience of established elites, buttressed by Western support for authoritarian leaderships in countries where they have longstanding strategic interests, has defied the legitimacy deficit that many of them suffer from.

Fundamental structural and agency factors – widespread poverty, armed conflict, a crisis of political authority, the weakness of formal institutions, a lack of social cohesion and fragmentation of identities, the configuration of national elites and the shifting interests of powerful external patrons – thus combine to explain the turmoil the MENA region has experienced (Boserup and Colombo 2019, 29–30; Kamrava 2018, 68–70; Phillips 2016, 3). A recent extensive survey of the opinion of experts from the Middle East, US, EU, Russia and China found that these factors, rather than a deficit of democracy or human rights, are the main drivers of instability (Fusco 2021, 5–6). Following a long period of limited balancing among regional powers during the 'American era' in the Middle East, the conflicts generated by the US-led invasion of Iraq and the Arab Spring have led to the rise of a new arrangement of states projecting power in an attempt to reshape the regional system around their own interests (see Hazbun 2018, 2). Inter-state rivalries have intensified, so that 'a new reality based on internationally backed spheres of influence is emerging' (see Barnes-Dacey 2017).

This new context of conflictual state–society and inter-state relations raises a number of questions about Russia's involvement in the MENA region. How does Moscow perceive the changes taking place there and how do they influence its broader foreign policy thinking? How does it address demands for political change while at the same time dealing with incumbent authorities fearful of domestic upheaval and guided by the 'logic of regime survival' (Darwich 2019, 8)? How does it negotiate transactions with other external and regional power-brokers to safeguard its core interests? What is the nature of the trade-off between human rights and good governance on the one hand and the need for order and stability on the other?

Russia's responses to the Arab uprisings

Fundamental notions about the contemporary international system were firmly embedded in Russian foreign policy thinking well before the inception of the Arab Spring, reflecting a deep-seated preoccupation with critical challenges facing Russia arising from structural shifts in the international order, the increasing militarisation of international relations, the emergence of new disputes and security threats and the fracturing of international security mechanisms (Averre 2008, 30–31). These ideas have been unambiguously set forth by Lavrov. In an increasingly conflictual international environment, Western claims to 'own "the monopoly on the truth"' and attempts to impose unilateral solutions, sometimes through coercive methods – enforcing sanctions, sponsoring coups, fomenting regional conflicts and even engaging in direct military interventions – run counter to 'objective processes' towards 'polycentrism' and the redistribution of global power and influence (Lavrov 2016a). Systemic change, leading both to the reduced influence of the US and its Western allies and to the greater prominence of regional states and non-state/transnational actors in international security, requires Russia to defend its own interests and reinforce its claim to a greater international role as an independent sovereign power.

The scale and nature of the Arab Spring events appeared to validate Russia's views. At the same time, Moscow's early response was cautious, mirroring international support for legitimate civil protests and condemning violations of international humanitarian law by incumbent governments. Russia initially supported the transition in Tunisia and abstained from UNSC resolution 1973 authorising intervention in Libya, rather than vetoing it; it adopted a wait-and-see approach to the crisis in Bahrain, as well as in Yemen before accepting the transfer of power from the Saleh government. In Egypt, Moscow's acceptance of the overthrow of Hosni Mubarak in 2011 and the election in 2012 of Mohamed Morsi's government, supported by the Muslim Brotherhood, was followed by prompt recognition of the Abdel Fattah al-Sisi administration after it removed Morsi from power. Even though its backing for the Assad government in Syria was much stronger and its concerns over the impact of his possible overthrow on regional security more pronounced, Russia's representative at the UN, Vitalii Churkin, asserted that 'we are not advocates of the Al-Assad regime', criticising the authorities' suppression of protests while at the same time arguing that 'a significant number of Syrians do not agree with the demand for a quick regime change' given concerns over instability (UNSC 2011b, 4).

Assessments by prominent Russian experts generally concurred with those of specialists from the MENA region, focusing on domestic factors – poor governance, the legitimacy deficit of many incumbent leaderships and the mobilisation of the younger generation with the aid of new means of communication – to account for the protests (see Naumkin et al 2016, 3–4; Vasil'ev 2011; Issaev and Shishkina 2020, 99). In an article written shortly after the protests began, Evgenii Primakov – the former Russian prime minister and foreign minister and a leading academic Arabist, who has had a profound influence on current Russian foreign policy thinking – dismissed talk by Western commentators of a 'clash of civilisations' with the Arab world, pointing to the political and socioeconomic rather than the religious nature of the protesters' demands. He warned that

> the dialogue between civilisations is being driven into an impasse by the forcible attempts to spread into [the MENA region] the model of democracy that is accepted in the West, without taking account of the civilisational, traditional and historical features of the Arab world and the mentality of its people ... the forcible imposition of democracy is not only the distinguishing feature of the American expansion in the Middle East but also its ideological justification. (Primakov 2011)

Other Russian scholars concurred, arguing that attempts by outside forces to impose external solutions on complex problems were counterproductive for two reasons; first, alien civilisational models imported from abroad are associated by local populations with repression by authoritarian leaders, and second, efforts by external actors to influence progressive change are seen as a challenge by the governing Arab elites to their own power (Baranovsky and Naumkin 2018, 10; Naumkin et al 2016, 3).

Moscow's opposition to forcible 'regime change' under the banner of democracy promotion was to become a leitmotiv of Russian thinking. Unsettled by the overthrow of Gaddafi in Libya, Russia soon began to frame the rapidly escalating conflicts to correspond to its core perceptions of the international environment. The Arab Spring was depicted less in terms of a democratic transition and more as a result of internal divisions which threatened to undermine state institutions and escalate into a struggle between secular state forces and radical Sunni Islamism, generating internal sectarian conflicts among powerful sub- and non-state actors supported by external patrons (Lavrov 2013f, 2013g; see also Averre and Davies 2015, 820; Dannreuther 2015, 80). Moscow's fears focused on the emergence of a pan-regional militant Islamism exacerbated by the overthrow of authoritarian secular governments – subsequently borne out by the emergence of Islamic State – threatening wider regional security and spreading into Russia's North Caucasus (see Chapter 6). In Moscow's eyes, this threat was best dealt with through cooperation within an international counter-terrorist coalition.

As the Syria conflict escalated, Russian interpretations of the political significance of the Arab Spring began to differ more and more from those of the liberal democracies. Naïve talk in the West about democratisation and promoting human rights in Syria was 'kindergarten stuff', according to Lavrov, who claimed that Western approaches risked intensifying support for the armed opposition and would lead to the erosion of government control and attendant humanitarian casualties, and ultimately to regime change and civil war (MFA, 2012). He argued that, faced with the threat of state collapse in MENA countries, the external powers should encourage political dialogue between the incumbent authorities and opposition groups, sponsoring constitutional reform and, where possible, peaceful transition and stable development. Russia's insistence on locally owned, inclusive political processes began to develop into a forceful narrative: official statements have consistently maintained that the unilateral imposition of supposedly progressive Western models and liberal human rights norms risked undermining the traditional spiritual and moral foundations of countries, exacerbating cultural and religious contradictions (Averre and Davies 2015, 828; see Chapter 4). In a quite extraordinary article, the Russian Ambassador to Saudi Arabia declared that Russia, acting in concert with other states sympathetic to its outlook, should respond to the 'inevitable reformatting of the region' by positioning itself 'as an opponent of both globalist projects – the worldwide caliphate and the neoliberal "global village"' (Ozerov 2016, 86; see also Dannreuther 2019, 733).

Russia's understanding of the nature of the Arab uprisings thus focused on a dual threat to stability: the spread of militant Islamism and external Western intervention inspired by the false premise of 'democratic' transition. This thinking has underpinned its legal arguments and had a significant impact on its broader foreign policy (Allison 2017, 520–521). It has had particular resonance in Syria, the crucible in which Russia's MENA policy has been forged. As analysed in more detail in Chapter 2, Western governments' attempts to legitimise their position on Syria by criticising Russian vetoes at the UN – arguing that Russia was on the wrong side of history by supporting Assad – were bitterly rebutted by Lavrov, who rejected the politicised nature of their positions and advocated instead a 'comprehensive and logical' approach based on traditional international law (Lavrov 2013a). Indeed, Russia's position on Syria both underscored its status as an autonomous power capable of defending its global and regional interests and at the same time signalled a strategic shift in its outlook, hastening its departure from the post-Cold War system in which the West had ignored Russia's interests and tried to marginalise its influence on the international stage (Naumkin et al 2016, 28).

Russia's involvement in the MENA region

In the decade prior to the Arab uprisings, Russia had gradually developed relations with the principal regional organisations, signing a memorandum of understanding with the League of Arab States (LAS) in 2003 and gaining observer status at the Gulf Cooperation Council (GCC) in 2005. However, the rapid escalation of militant Sunni Islamism and internal sectarian, tribal and ethnic conflicts in the fragile post-Arab Spring environment – prompting overt or covert interventions by the regional powers in Libya, Syria, Yemen and Bahrain and initiating a scramble to ensure that any new alignment of forces would meet their respective interests – has weakened these organisations (Makdisi 2017, 105). They have generally been ineffective in terms of institutional design and organisation, lacking the capacity to promote a genuine regional order due to deep-set rivalries and engendering 'more geopolitics as usual' (Fawcett 2015b, 134, 145; House of Lords 2017, 62–3). Moreover, none of the respective memberships of the GCC and the LAS – as well as the Organisation of Islamic Cooperation (OIC), which brought the non-Arab states Iran and Turkey into a regional framework (Fawcett 2015a, 45) – represents the entire region.

The LAS initially endorsed NATO's intervention in Libya and supported a Gulf initiative for the transition of power in Yemen, as well as mediating in the Syria crisis. However, its ability to resolve the most intractable problems – ending the Syrian civil war, checking the spread of Islamic State, mitigating the deteriorating security situation in post-Gaddafi Libya, and tackling the renewed conflict in Yemen and the Israel–Palestine question – has been limited and its membership split on key issues, notably the fate of Assad in any 'transition' in Syria (Isaac 2015). The GCC, under Saudi leadership, has depicted the Levant sub-region as an Iran-sponsored 'Shia crescent', incorporating Syria, Iraq and Hezbollah, which is attempting to undermine Arab interests; in response, the Gulf monarchies have strengthened links with Sunni Iraqi tribes and financed Sunni militias and Al-Qaeda proxies in regional conflicts (Calculli 2015, 62, 69–70). Disputes among the Gulf states – Saudi Arabia, the United Arab Emirates (UAE) and Qatar – have also compromised regional cooperation. None of the major regional powers has managed to secure a sufficient following to become a regional leader; their policies 'have been piecemeal and localized, driven by their strategic interests ... Their involvement therefore has checked any efforts to create region-building efforts in the Mediterranean space' (Ehteshami and Mohammadi 2017a, 119).

This challenging security environment prompted Russia to renew its efforts to deepen ties with the Arab states, both bilaterally and through the Arab-Russian Cooperation Forum, established in 2013 at foreign minister level, and the Russia-GCC Strategic Dialogue at ministerial level. Russia has also engaged in multilateral diplomacy over the Syria conflict with the Saudi-convened Riyadh group and the GCC, which has run parallel to the

Geneva peace talks. Moscow's central aims are to pursue energy and investment interests, as well as to reduce the Gulf states' support for militant Islamist groups in Syria and stem the return of foreign fighters to the North Caucasus; these fora also provide a platform for Moscow to build support for its opposition to Western attempts to establish a 'unipolar world' (Lavrov 2022a). As discussed later in this book, Russia has stepped up its proposals for a concept of collective security in the Gulf region, bringing regional states and institutions together with key external actors to explore prospects for confidence-building measures, transparency and cooperation in counter-terrorism, arms control and nonproliferation and joint approaches to emerging security challenges (Lavrov 2018a, 2020b).

As a result, Russia has become much more embedded in the politics of the MENA region. However, Moscow faces a plethora of challenges arising from the altered political and security map that has tested its 'agile diplomacy' to the limit. The shallow regionalism and complex rivalries that characterise relations among its states have produced a 'significant qualitative change in the regional Middle East system, now increasingly defined as a multipolar system lacking norms, institutions or balancing' (Hazbun 2018, 2). This fragmented regional environment has placed considerable constraints on Moscow's, and indeed the other external powers', ability to influence events. Moscow's guarded response has been to diversify its partnerships across the region and pursue incremental improvements in relations in a bid to carve out an independent regional policy.

At the same time, power politics has dictated Moscow's policy of investing considerable political capital in its relations with the region's most powerful states, the non-Arab countries Iran, Turkey and Israel. Regional experts have identified the Tehran–Ankara axis – based on the shared desire of Iran and Turkey to prevent Kurdish separatism and curb Israeli power, common economic and energy interests and considerable soft power resources – as the linchpin of Middle Eastern politics in the coming years (Ayoob 2014, 402; Akbarzadeh and Barry 2017, 980–982). Despite tensions between the two states – both are bidding to extend their influence in the region and support proxy forces on opposing sides in the Syrian civil war – Iran's strategic resistance to Western involvement and Turkey's partial rebalancing of its foreign policy away from the West have altered the political map of the Middle East. Russia has capitalised on their greater influence by incorporating them into the trilateral Astana format, established to resolve the Syria conflict (discussed in more detail in Chapter 2), and in bilateral relations. Russia's increasing security engagement with Israel, driven largely by the need to mitigate growing Israel–Iran tensions stemming from Tehran's involvement in the Syrian civil war, forms its third key relationship in the region.

Iran

A defining dynamic in the Middle East is the growing challenge posed by Iran, which supports Shia forces against Sunni Arabs – backed up by local allies and armed proxies in Syria, Iraq, Lebanon and Yemen – and pursues 'asymmetric "strategies of opposition"' aimed at maintaining an 'axis of resistance' against US and Israeli predominance (Wastnidge 2017, 156; ICG 2018a, i–ii). At the same time, in trying to resolve the contradictions between the multiple identities in the modern Iranian state – nationalism, traditional Shi'ism, 'Third-Worldism' and non-confessional revolutionary Islamism (Khomeinism) – its ruling elites have followed a pragmatic foreign policy strategy in which the survival of the state and its ruling elites take precedence over ideological purity (see Posch 2017). This approach is shaped by two factors: first, domestic pressures deriving from socioeconomic and demographic changes and, second, the perception of mounting security threats against Iran stemming from both Sunni Islamist extremism and regional rivalries with Saudi Arabia and Israel, both concerned about the challenges posed by Tehran's perceived bid for regional supremacy. Iran's power projection, maximising resources in order to mitigate its isolation and achieve strategic depth, has inspired its extensive military support for Syria, albeit at a heavy cost in lives and resources; despite the differences between Syria as a secular Arab state and Iran as a theocratic pan-Islamist power, they share 'visions of regional autonomy and reduced foreign penetration of the Middle East' (Ahmadian and Mohseni 2019, 341–342; Barzegar and Divsallar 2017, 40, 45). Tehran's support for the Houthi rebels in Yemen's civil war has also unsettled the Gulf Arab states. The designation 'West Asia' instead of Middle East, used by Iranian elites to describe the country's geopolitical location, and their preference for the term Islamic Awakening rather than Arab Spring, suggest an attempt at creating an alternative world order based on 'antihegemonic perspectives and critical geopolitics' to challenge dominant Western discourses (Ehteshami and Mohammadi 2017b, 92, 95), creating 'a deep ideological chasm between a Western and an Islamic conception of world order and international relations' (Tajbakhsh 2018, 49).

Prior to the inception of the Arab Spring, Russia's relations with Iran were problematic, with Moscow joining multilateral sanctions over its nuclear material enrichment programme and refusing to deliver on a contract for S-300 missile defence systems. The situation changed markedly with their military collaboration in Syria, based largely on a shared desire to frustrate US attempts to remake the Middle East by interfering in the domestic governance of its states, as well as to stem the tide of Sunni Islamist extremism and avoid territorial divisions in Syria and Iraq. Russia's intervention in Syria with air support, heavy weaponry and intelligence-sharing – following extensive consultations with Tehran – was complemented by Iran's and Hezbollah's commitment of ground forces and financial support to Assad, and by closer policy alignment of both Russia and Iran with Iraq. Russia–Iran relations are now supported by contacts at head of state and foreign and defence ministry levels and by increasing military-technical cooperation. Combined Russian and Iranian military support for Assad has been described as post-revolutionary Iran's 'first political-security partnership … with another world power that was only possible due to the new understanding in Tehran about the nation's power dynamics and limitations' (Barzegar and Divsallar 2017, 51). Indeed, some Russian experts imitate Iranian elites in referring to West Asia or Western Asia to describe Iran's location, reflecting the shifting geopolitical configuration of the region in Russian foreign policy thinking (Kuznetsov 2019, 125–126; Makhmutov and Mamedov 2017).

Moscow has also provided substantial diplomatic support for Tehran by opposing US-inspired resolutions against Iran in the UN Security Council and supporting the Joint Comprehensive Plan of Action (JCPOA), instituted during the second Obama administration to monitor Iran's nuclear material enrichment activities, a crucial element in nuclear nonproliferation (discussed later in this chapter). Donald Trump's withdrawal from the JCPOA in 2018 and imposition of extensive unilateral sanctions – since maintained by the Biden administration, drawing criticism from Moscow as well as from its European signatories – have escalated Iranian retaliation, threatening to undermine regional stability (see Rouhi 2018). Lavrov has repeatedly asserted that Iran is abiding by the terms of the JCPOA and accused the US of yet again undermining multilateral disarmament agreements to punish 'undesirable' states (Lavrov 2020a; see also Tajbakhsh 2018, 42), by placing pressure on Russian and European firms which fear the loss of business with the US if they do not respect the sanctions (Alcaro and Dessì 2019, 8–9). Lavrov has dismissed US accusations of state-sponsored terrorism by Iran, demanding proof and stating that 'there is no such concept in international law' (Lavrov 2018a). Russia continues to deepen its economic and energy cooperation with Iran, welcoming it as the newest member of the Shanghai Cooperation Organisation, and bilateral talks continue with the Ebrahim Raisi administration on a new inter-state treaty to formalise relations.

At the same time, Moscow faces a number of challenges in sustaining its compact with Tehran. Russia's search for a political settlement in Syria, both to stabilise the regional order and secure its own interests there, conflicts with Iran's ambitions to build on its military successes and create an arc of influence from Iraq through Syria to the Mediterranean, thereby threatening a stable regional balance of power (see Shumilin and Shumilina 2017, 121; Chulov 2021). Both Syria and Iraq have become an arena of confrontation between Tehran and other regional powers. Iran's efforts to build political-military and intelligence structures and strengthen the network of Shia militias in Syria – a 'deep state', partly independent of the Assad government, to entrench its influence and maintain strategic deterrence against the US, Saudi Arabia and Israel (Antonyan 2017, 340) – is also a challenge to Russia's own influence there. In response, Russia is cooperating with Israel and deploying its troops along the Israeli border in south-west Syria to contain the Iranian presence (Khatib and Sinjab 2018, 23).

There is also a potential dispute between Iran and Russia over the Syrian Kurds; Moscow has advocated a degree of decentralisation in Syria as part of constitutional reform while Tehran opposes a de facto Kurdish autonomous region in north-eastern Syria, fearing the encouragement it could give to its own Kurdish minority (Kausch 2018, 79–81). Though a more coherent Kurdish-oriented policy may provide Moscow with more leverage in the region, the risk of worsening relations with Iran, Turkey and Iraq may preclude this (Geranmayeh and Liik 2016, 6; Mamedov 2019, 11). Russia's support will also be tested in the event of Iranian non-compliance with the nonproliferation obligations imposed by the JCPOA and a generally harder line adopted by the Raisi administration. Trade in military goods is inhibited by Iran's inability to pay for large Russian armaments supplies, as sanctions continue to hit the economy. Overall bilateral trade turnover remains modest compared with Iran's trade with its regional neighbours and China, and many Iranian business elites favour closer relations with the EU (Zamirarad 2017, 14).

The convergence of tactical interests driving the Russia–Iran partnership to preserve the Assad government and limit US influence across the Middle East thus clashes with their differing aims for the longer-term future of the region. Russia wants to avoid an escalation of tensions and minimise disruption of its security and trade relations with Israel and the Arab Gulf states, and for this it needs US diplomatic support. These differences militate against an alliance with Iran; as a former Iranian ambassador to Moscow has stated, despite the establishment of high-level ties 'we cannot have *strategic* relations. In some areas, our objectives are in conflict' (Amirahmadian 2016, 17, emphasis added). Iran has not joined the international criticism of Russia's war with Ukraine and has supplied Moscow with drones for combat operations – together with military advisers, according to Ukrainian sources – but has offered neither unequivocal support for the invasion nor more potent military hardware. There is still mistrust in Tehran over Moscow's intentions; one MENA expert – drawing on interviews with Iranian sources – argues that 'Tehran sees a persistent danger that Moscow takes foreign policy decisions without considering the long-term consequences [with] neither the capacity nor the will to relate them to strategic planning which would satisfy its great power status' (Zamirirad 2017, 26).

Turkey

Turkey's long-held aspirations to be the MENA region's political-military and economic powerhouse and a leader of the global Islamic community faced a much more complex and challenging security environment with the inception of the Arab Spring, the growing penetration of militant Islamist forces and the rise of the Kurdish People's Protection Units (YPG) (see Coşkun 2015; Dalacoura 2021, 1125). President Recep Tayyip Erdoğan's previously positive relations with Assad, shaped by shared concerns over Kurdish separatism and the emergence of extremist Islamism amid the post-2003 destabilisation of Iraq, veered sharply towards hostility due to Syria's attacks on Sunni opposition groups. In response, Ankara stepped up its military involvement in the civil war through support for the anti-Assad Syrian National Council and Free Syrian Army; its objective was to reshape the power balance to replace Assad with a mainly Sunni Islamist elite, as well as to prevent a threat to Turkey's territorial integrity in the shape of a Kurdish nationalist autonomous territorial structure that might assume state-like authority (Okyay 2017, 830, 834). Ankara also launched a diplomatic offensive condemning the human rights atrocities committed by Assad's forces and urging the international community to intervene to unseat him, as well as opening its borders to Syrian refugees – thereby allowing the passage of anti-Assad fighters and opening a transit route for extremist Islamist forces (Akbarzadeh and Barry 2017, 985). Damascus retaliated to the increasing power of Turkish-supported extremist Islamist groups in Syria by allowing the Kurdish Syrian Democratic Union Party (PYD), affiliated to the Kurdistan Workers' Party (PKK) which is seeking independence from Ankara, to take over part of the Kurdish-inhabited area on the border with Turkey (Hinnebusch 2015, 15). The PKK and its political affiliates – the YPG, Women's Protection Units and the PYD – went on to control large areas of the Syria–Turkey border, declaring a federal region in northern Syria (ICG 2017a). Turkey and Iran were also on opposite sides in the Yemen crisis, where Ankara supported the Saudi position, intensifying the danger of Sunni–Shia sectarianism (Akbarzadeh and Barry 2017, 989). Turkey's relations with Iraq and Egypt also deteriorated due to Ankara's sponsorship of Iraqi Sunni elements, some of them linked with Islamic State, and support for the Muslim Brotherhood in Egypt (Coşkun 2015, 195–196).

Two events have shaped Turkey's regional policies in the recent period. The first relates to its domestic politics. The attempted coup in July 2016 against the Erdoğan government prompted a crackdown on the opposition and suppression of civil rights, thereby souring relations with the West and undermining Turkey's already difficult accession talks with the EU, exacerbated by the pressure of refugee flows into Turkey (Elitok 2018; Akbarzadeh and Barry 2017, 990; Blockmans 2016a). The coup attempt provided a pretext for the increased securitisation of the long-running Kurdish issue, fed by Erdoğan's concerns over terrorist attacks by the PKK. Turkey's military forays into Syrian areas where the US military is deployed in the fight against Islamic State antagonised Washington, which has been helped materially by Kurdish forces; Erdoğan also condemned the US's refusal to extradite the alleged leader of the coup attempt, Fethullah Gülen (see Aras and Falk 2016, 2256; Pearson et al 2018).

The second event was Russia's military intervention in Syria. Russian air power, supported by Iran and Hezbollah on the ground, revitalised the Syrian army's ability to repel Turkey-backed rebel forces, threatening to place Moscow and Ankara on opposing sides in an escalating civil war. The situation was compounded by the Turkish air force shooting down a Russian fighter aircraft in November 2015, apparently in response to air attacks by Russian forces on Turkish-aligned Syrian Turkmen rebels in northern Syria (Williams and Souza 2016, 48). The incident was depicted by Moscow as a planned provocation and resulted in a period of estrangement, with Russia placing extensive sanctions on trade with Turkey and deploying S-400 air defence systems to Latakia, restricting Turkey's access to Syrian air space. Erdoğan ultimately had little choice but to issue a public apology to Russia and engage with Moscow and Tehran over Syria, joining the Astana format to manage hostilities. In return, the Putin leadership voiced its firm support for Erdoğan's crackdown in response to what Moscow called the 'unconstitutional' coup attempt (Allison 2017, 539). Putin's support contrasted with cooling relations between Turkey and the West, which is concerned over Erdoğan's increasing illiberalism and the erosion of civil rights. Moscow subsequently accepted Ankara's position that allowing PKK bases in the Kurdish-held Syrian territory would pose a threat to Turkey's security.

Putin's support for Erdoğan following the attempted coup – interpreted by some as reflecting a shared authoritarian political culture that privileges state sovereignty over liberal values in defiance of Western encroachment (see Bechev 2018, 96–97) – has since led to more extensive cooperation. This benefits Moscow insofar as Turkey offers benefits in bilateral trade and also opens a channel to improve Russia's relations with Sunni Gulf elites. Ankara's focus has shifted, moderating its hostility to Assad and mounting a campaign to prevent the Kurds from launching attacks along its border with Syria. Moscow allowed Ankara access to Syrian air space for its military incursion into the border region to clear the area of Islamic State and the YPG, lasting from August 2016 to March 2017 under Operation 'Euphrates Shield', and in 2018, under Operation Olive Branch, to take over the Afrin enclave from the YPG; in return Ankara left the way open for Moscow to prosecute its own offensive against the Syrian opposition (Rüma and Çelikpala 2019, 80–81; Dalacoura 2021, 1131–1132; Bechev 2018, 98). Despite Turkey's censure of Russia's role in the siege of Aleppo and air strikes on the Turkish-backed Syrian opposition groups in Idlib, agreement was reached in Sochi in September 2018 on the establishment of a demilitarised zone, though there are ongoing tensions there (discussed in more detail in Chapter 2).

Turkey's participation in the Astana process has been accompanied by a marked improvement in reciprocal trade, tourism and investment with Russia, comprising increased gas deliveries from Russia through the Turkish Stream pipeline and cooperation on nuclear power; a higher level of Turkish exports to Russia has filled the demand gap left by Western sanctions over the war in Ukraine. Turkey is now by far Russia's main trade partner in the region and economic cooperation continues apace. Moscow's supply of S-400 air defence systems to Ankara in 2019 led to Turkey's removal from the US programme to supply its F-35 fighter jets, a potentially important step both for bilateral and wider international security relations, with Ankara appearing set on balancing between Washington and Moscow (Öniş and Yılmaz 2016, 84). Moreover, Ankara's assistance to Iran in circumventing US sanctions has contributed to their cooperative relationship in the Astana format.

Russia–Turkey relations have the potential to shape events in the MENA region in the face of less active US and European involvement. To date, they have managed to pursue their strategic interests while managing differences. However, any notion of Ankara pursuing a strategic realignment towards Moscow must be kept in perspective. Turkey's ongoing military campaign against the Kurds and the Syrian government forces reflects serious tensions on the ground, leading to fierce clashes in 2020 in Idlib and other northern Syrian provinces. Moscow has tried to restrain further Turkish campaigns to extend its control across the Turkey–Syria border. In Libya, Turkey's military support to the UN-backed Tripoli government clashes with Russian support, mainly using private military contractors, for forces allied with Field Marshal Khalifa Haftar (ICG 2020a). Trust between Moscow and Ankara is provisional, with Lavrov openly expressing concern about fundamental differences over the Azerbaijan–Armenia conflict, Russia's annexation of Ukraine and Cyprus (Lavrov 2020f). Anti-Russian rhetoric has periodically been disseminated in Turkish nationalist political and media circles (Rüma and Çelikpala 2019, 75). Turkey, wary of isolating itself from the West and jeopardising a long history of NATO membership, has been vocal in support of Ukrainian sovereignty, criticising Russia's invasion of Ukraine in February 2022 and supplying military hardware to Kyiv; at the same time, it has tried to mediate between the two sides and strike an agreement for the export of grain and fertilisers, refraining from joining the West's sanctions regime against Russia. Moscow and Ankara face a constant struggle to manage tensions in an unpredictable wider regional security environment.

Israel

Russia's relationship with Israel represents yet another delicate balancing act. Despite problems that predate the Arab Spring – Russia's refusal to designate Hamas as a terrorist organisation, regularly hosting its representatives in Moscow, and Israel's accusations that Russia was providing Assad's forces with missiles which were being used by Hezbollah (Shumilin and Shumilina 2017, 117–118) – common economic interests and the presence of the large Russian Jewish diaspora in Israel, together with military and intelligence cooperation and a shared interest in fighting extremist Sunni Islamism, have combined to improve relations (see Katz 2018, 103). Putin's personal relationship with long-time Israeli leader Binyamin Netanyahu has deepened their understanding of each other's national security priorities, allowing both a degree of latitude in dealing with regional crises, despite the US's pro-Israeli, pro-moderate Arab and anti-Iranian position on regional affairs. Israel's initial reluctance to impose sanctions on Russia over its invasion of Ukraine, despite joining the vote at the UN General Assembly condemning the invasion – prompted by domestic revulsion at Moscow's prosecution of the war – reflects its recognition that closer reciprocal relations suit Israel's national interests.

At the same time, two interlinked problems – Iran's increasing regional power projection and the conflict in Syria – pose a potentially enduring challenge to the Russia–Israel partnership. As mentioned earlier, Syria has become part of Iran's axis of resistance against Israel alongside a more powerful Hezbollah and the Yemeni Houthis (Ehteshami and Mohammadi 2017b, 96), with Israel also accusing Tehran of financing and organising Hamas in the Gaza Strip. In 2019 the Trump administration recognised Israel's claims to the contested Golan Heights, where Israeli and Syrian troops have been under the supervision of the UN Disengagement Observer Force since 1974, in contravention of international agreements; the area remains a potential zone of military escalation, with regular violations reported. The likely long-term presence in Syria of Iranian forces increases the risk of inter-state confrontation between Iran and Israel. Continuing attacks by the Israeli air force on Hezbollah and Iranian positions have numbered as many as a thousand over eight years of conflict, drawing criticism from Moscow for violating UNSC resolutions, though without altering the substance of Russia–Israel cooperation. Israel consented to return areas in the southern de-escalation zone, bordering the Golan Heights and Jordan, to the partial control of the Syrian Army in return for a Russian undertaking to restrain the presence of pro-Iranian Shiite forces on the border with Israel (Barmin 2018a, 9), but the agreement has reportedly been ignored by Iranian and Syrian forces. Hezbollah has also launched attacks on Israel from Lebanon. Netanyahu repeatedly warned Putin about the deeper penetration of Iran's Islamic Revolutionary Guard Corps and its proxy forces into Syria, exacerbating the perceived threat posed by Iran's nuclear programme and missile capabilities (see Boms 2017, 331–333). At the same time, Tehran is unlikely to make concessions which would be perceived – both internationally and within Iran – as reversing its strategic gains in Syria and Iraq (see Aksenyonok 2018).

Recent events thus threaten Russia's goal of bringing Israel into a wider Middle Eastern settlement. Israel appears intent on managing the threat posed by Iran and Hezbollah using limited military strikes and cyber operations against Syria (see Malmvig 2017); Moscow has sought to reassure Israel and avoid impeding its operations as long as this does not endanger Russian soldiers or destabilise Assad's regime (Lund 2019, 30). Frequent meetings between Putin and Netanyahu have underpinned efforts at deconfliction; the shooting down of a Russian aircraft off the Syrian coast in September 2018 by Israeli forces drew a muted response from Moscow, which emphasised the importance of their historical ties. At the same time, the recent Abraham Accords between Israel and the UAE, Bahrain, Morocco and Sudan, together with Israeli attempts to normalise its relations with other Arab states in the face of perceived threats from Iran, may well exacerbate divisions and preclude lasting stability in the Middle East in the face of ongoing internal Arab conflicts and US acceptance of Israel's increasingly nationalist outlook and claims of sovereignty over Palestinian settlements. Tripartite talks in 2019 between Russia, the US and Israel on the challenge posed by Iran and Syria made limited progress, unsurprisingly given Moscow's limited ability to restrain Tehran. Russia is continually forced to adjust its mediation in response to shifting circumstances.

The Arab states

The upheaval across much of the Arab world and Russia's intervention in Syria have compelled Moscow to diversify its links beyond the key relationships with Iran, Turkey and Israel to the Arab states. In the wake of the 2011 protests in Bahrain, quickly suppressed with the help of Saudi military intervention, the Gulf Arab leaderships reconsolidated power through domestic coalition support, control over natural resource rents and the backing of powerful external actors. At the same time, Saudi Arabia's attempts to broker a deal in Syria failed. Fuelled by its regional rivalry with Iran and fearful of the latter's expanding influence, Saudi Arabia became increasingly hostile to Assad and began to push for his overthrow, supporting rebel groups in Syria along with Turkey and Qatar (see ICG 2017c, 12–14). Saudi and other Gulf Arab authorities framed the protests in Syria in sectarian terms, as the work of Shia forces acting for Iran, with wider consequences for the region as it transformed 'a fundamentally domestic event into a new regional cold war' (Kamrava 2018, 63–64).

Russia's attempts to repair relations with the Gulf Arab monarchies were stepped up in an attempt to parley on all fronts, playing down their support for Syrian opposition groups and steering clear of involvement in their internal disputes, notably the Saudi/UAE antagonism with Qatar due to its sponsorship of the Muslim Brotherhood (see Naumkin 2017a). Moscow's increasingly frequent bilateral high-level contacts with the Gulf states, alongside diplomatic links with the Organisation of Islamic Cooperation within the OIC/Russia Islamic World Strategic Vision Group, have focused on security dialogue as well as cooperation over trade and investment, particularly in the energy sphere (discussed further in Chapter 6), with the aim of underwriting a more stable regional environment conducive to Russia's interests. Helped by the Biden administration's strained relations with Riyadh, the Gulf Arabs are open to developing closer economic and, up to a point, political relations with Russia, showing reluctance to join the US sanctions regime and introduce a cap on oil prices – potentially damaging to Russia – following the invasion of Ukraine. Tentative Saudi attempts to improve security dialogue with Tehran also offer Moscow an opportunity for mediation.

Early in Yemen's civil war, the GCC launched an initiative – backed up by UNSC resolution 2014 in October 2011 – aimed at securing a political settlement between the Houthis, supported by Iran and buoyed by the forces of former President Ali Abdullah Saleh, and the Saudi/UAE-backed government of Abdrabbuh Mansur Hadi. The initiative ultimately proved fruitless and conflict ensued. The Saudi coalition's military intervention in March 2015, Operation Decisive Storm, at the invitation of the internationally recognised Yemen government and supported by the US and other Western powers and aimed at restoring the Hadi government – authorised by UNSC resolution 2216 – has only driven the Houthis closer to Tehran and contributed to escalating humanitarian atrocities. The Houthi rebel occupation of the capital, Sana'a, and a Saudi/UAE blockade have since devastated much of the country. Deep-seated elite rivalries have marginalised civil society and all but eroded state governance in favour of the interests of various armed militias and tribes, exacerbated by external intervention. The risk of longer-term state collapse is complicated by the local presence of Al-Qaeda and the Southern Transitional Council independence movement. Piecemeal reconciliation efforts through the December 2018 Stockholm agreement, and the November 2019 Riyadh agreement between the Hadi government and the Southern Transitional Council, eventually culminated in an agreement in December 2020 to create a new coalition government. A truce was announced in April 2022, with GCC-led talks leading to a transfer of power and the formation of a new Saudi-backed presidential council. However, the fragmentation of power across the Yemeni 'chaos state' persists, with economic and humanitarian pressures threatening further conflict (Salisbury 2018; ICG 2020c).

Experts have pointed to the lack of understanding of the conflict in the West, arguing that the Houthi northerners mistrust the US's and UK's political mediation efforts due to their role in supporting and arming the Saudi-led coalition (Salisbury 2016). Russian commentators have argued that, in contrast, Moscow may be able to carve out a role 'as a country that adheres to international law, respects sovereignty and demonstrates zero tolerance to neo-colonialist scenarios ... open[ing] up the prospects for establishing contacts with all the major actors in Yemen, which is the key to settling the crisis' (Serebrov 2017). Russia's approach has largely conformed with this assessment, criticising the Saudi-led intervention as having no basis in international law while playing down Iran's support for the Houthis (Buys and Garwood-Gowers 2019, 25). At the same time, it backed the GCC and supported demands for the Houthis to reverse their takeover of government institutions and cease occupation of Sana'a in favour of a peaceful inclusive political transition as mandated in UNSC resolution 2201. Influenced by its burgeoning relationship with the UAE, which backs the Hadi government, Russia voted in February 2022 for UNSC resolution 2624 that for the first time referred to attacks by the 'Houthi terrorist group', with the UAE abstaining from the draft UNSC resolution condemning Russia's invasion of Ukraine. But overall Russia has limited influence on the ground in Yemen and relies heavily on diplomatic engagement with the regional powers (see Naumkin 2018).

Russia also faces complex challenges in Iraq in the context of unresolved Shia–Sunni tensions, the Kurdish independence issue, Iran's penetration into Iraqi security structures and the persistent presence of Islamic State. The incomplete political and institutional reconstruction of Iraq, following the US-led intervention in 2003, has generated periodic political crises and sectarian fighting (see Collombier et al 2019). Domestically fragile, with numerous armed groups operating outside state control, Iraq risks being drawn unwillingly into US-Iran antagonism (see ICG 2019a). Moscow has gained some leverage by supplying Iraq with weaponry at short notice in 2014 to stem a surge by Islamic State when the US refused to do so; Moscow now has closer institutional ties with Baghdad and agreed that it could host the joint information centre, comprising Russia, Iran, Syria and Iraq, set up to combat terrorism in the region. There is further scope for Russia to train and equip Iraq's military and security forces and supply armaments, and in bidding for oil and gas development tenders, with $13 billion reportedly having been invested to date by Russian energy majors. The Iraqi leadership has welcomed Russia's 'sober and pragmatic approach to relations' – a leitmotiv for Russian policy across much of the Middle East – as an external power that supports incumbent state leaderships and non-interference in the internal affairs of sovereign countries (see Mamedov 2019). Yet Moscow recognises the limitations to its political influence in Iraq relative to that of Iran and the US, and indeed of Saudi Arabia through its cultivation of Shiite groups there, with China also making rapid gains in economic influence.

The outlook remains similarly unstable across much of North Africa. In the violent aftermath of Gaddafi's overthrow, the inability of the new Libyan government to establish order and the lack of coherent international leadership in terms of rebuilding the state have jeopardised transitional arrangements. Various groups have assumed control of parts of the infrastructure and economy, reducing the chances of restoring a strong, legitimate central authority with functioning security structures. Institutional divides and continuing conflict have increased corruption and created the *de facto* privatisation of state resources, with armed groups carving out networks involving individuals from business, politics and the state administration, obscuring the distinction between state and non-state and legitimate and illegitimate activities. International attention is focused on the confrontation between Fayez al-Sarraj's Government of National Accord (GNA), backed by Islamist authorities in Tripoli, and the Arab Libyan Forces (ALF, formerly the Libyan National Army) headed by the powerful Haftar, who has gained control over crucial oil fields and ports in the east of the country. As elsewhere in the region, the conflict has drawn in both regional and external actors in a complex permutation of provisional coalitions. Turkey's increased support for the GNA, along with Qatar, has generated opposition among some of Libya's Arab tribes. Russia has joined Egypt, Saudi Arabia and the UAE, as well as France, in backing Haftar's ALF as a potential contributor to a peace settlement, despite his military campaign against Tripoli. Moscow has allowed Wagner Group private military contractors to operate alongside Haftar's forces, seeking a political – and potentially in the longer term military – foothold to further its economic interests, particularly in the energy and infrastructure sectors (Souleimanov and Abbasov 2020, 83).

The suggestion of some commentators that Moscow is seeking independent leverage to secure its interests by sponsoring Haftar, a powerful military figure, in a 'proxy' war ignores substantive constraints on Russia's policy. Russia has tried to balance support for Haftar – who is accused of recruiting mercenaries to commit war crimes against the population and who faces opposition in both the west and east of the country – with improving relations with the GNA to safeguard Russian oil interests and engage with other influential groups in Libya (Lukyanov and Mamedov 2016; Alaaldin 2019; Lounnas 2020, 40–41; Charap et al 2019, 15). Moscow's efforts have been directed more at negotiating between rival forces to promote a national dialogue to stabilise the conflict-torn country, thereby enhancing Russia's authority as a mediator in cooperation with Europe and the US – in the words of one Russian expert, a '"strategic equidistance" approach that … Putin might explore further in the future' (Barmin 2018b, 11; see Lund 2019, 38). Moscow officially declared its support for a political process based on the Plan of Action proposed by the then UN Secretary-General's Special Representative for Libya, Ghassan Salamé (MFA 2019c).

Prior to the Berlin Conference on Libya in January 2020, Russia, with Turkey's support, hosted talks between al-Sarraj and Haftar in Moscow. However, it subsequently abstained on UNSC resolution 2510, which called for a nationwide ceasefire and enforcement of the Libya arms embargo, arguing that there was no prior consent on the part of the conflicting parties. The ceasefire agreed in Berlin did not hold, mainly due to Haftar's recalcitrance, and external actors – including Russia, which has reportedly deployed military equipment, including fighter jets, to defend Haftar's positions (ICG 2020d) – continue to supply arms to the parties to the conflict in violation of the UN arms embargo. A ceasefire was agreed in October 2020 and an executive was set up to form a new Government of National Unity in February 2021, but disagreement over a new constitution remains. Elections scheduled for 2021 were postponed amid controversy over the presidential candidature of Haftar and Gaddafi's son, Saif al-Islam, both accused of war crimes. The situation has been complicated by rivalry between two governments, both claiming legitimacy, one under the new prime minister of the Government of National Unity Abdul Hamid Dbeibeh, based in Tripoli – who condemned Russia's invasions of Ukraine – and the other led by Fathi Bashagha, backed by Haftar and the Tobruk-based parliament, and favoured by Moscow. Armed violence continues and external patrons have intensified their involvement; any political settlement establishing a stable and unified Libya may only come after further protracted military hostilities (see ICG 2020a, 2020b). Russia is intent on having a say in any final Libyan agreement but wants to avoid more extensive military commitments and, far from securing a client state, has limited sway over internal power-brokers.

After the brief period of Morsi's rule in Egypt, the military reasserted itself as the dominant force in Egyptian politics. The Putin government moved quickly to cement relations with the authoritarian al-Sisi leadership, which continues to dominate a political system reliant on patronage and bedevilled by mistrust between Islamists and secular forces and between political elites and society (Kamrava 2018, 54–58). The improving relationship between Russia and Egypt was aided by a decline in US influence. Cairo is suspicious of US engagement with the Muslim Brotherhood, and Washington withheld arms deliveries and discontinued the nascent US–Egypt Strategic Dialogue in response to al-Sisi's domestic human rights record. Moscow has enacted its own Partnership and Strategic Cooperation Agreement with Cairo, with close consultations established at defence and foreign minister levels to further security and counter-terrorism cooperation and reciprocal support for the Syria peace process (Lund 2019, 28–30). They also have similar approaches to Libya and the intra-Palestinian dialogue. Bilateral economic cooperation shows marked successes, with Russia investing $8 billion in Egypt. As well as Russian interests in gas extraction and grain exports, nuclear power plant, transport and energy engineering contracts have been signed, as well as arms deals – estimates suggest worth around $2 billion – covering fighter aircraft, helicopters, guided missiles and air defence systems. Security links include joint military exercises, which may portend the use by Russia of Egypt's military infrastructure (Barmin 2018b, 9). At the same time, Egypt came under Western pressure for its position on the Russia–Ukraine war, which prompted Cairo – along with the majority of MENA countries – to back the UN General Assembly resolution ES-11/4 condemning the Russian invasion and demanding the withdrawal of Russia's forces; the US subsequently agreed to provide F-15 fighter jets to Egypt. Also, Egypt depends on grain imports from Russia and Ukraine, long-term disruption of which could cause internal unrest. Bilateral Russia–Egypt cooperation continues but, as with other MENA countries, may well be affected by the increasing volatility of the international environment.

After the initial Arab Spring protests in Algeria, Morocco and Tunisia, the authorities responded by suppressing criticism to varying degrees while amending constitutional provisions and co-opting elements of the opposition in order to maintain regime stability (Kamrava 2018, 64–67). Moscow is looking to its longer-term goals there, namely avoiding a spillover of instability from Libya and developing new markets in its areas of comparative advantage. Moscow may also be planning to gain access to warm-water ports in Algeria, Morocco and Tunisia, possibly prefiguring a naval presence in the Western Mediterranean (Barmin 2018b, 4–5). Despite its concerns over the 2019 street protests in Algeria, Moscow did not endorse President Abdelaziz Bouteflika's bid to retain power, insisting the political crisis was a domestic matter. Moscow's preference for a negotiated settlement suggested that it wanted to prevent both a breakdown of order that might encourage Islamist forces and a successful popular revolution that might tip the country towards liberal democracy, seeing state-controlled incorporation of the opposition as the most effective way to contain the latter's influence (Ramani 2019b). Algeria's support for Russia's position on Libya is an additional factor. Algeria has been the second or third biggest customer for Russia armaments in recent years, making it an important economic partner. The two countries signed a Declaration of Strategic Partnership in 2021; it was notable that Algeria abstained from UNGA resolution ES-11/4, attesting to the closeness of their political and trade relationship. Current Russian economic and political cooperation with Morocco and Tunisia is limited, though they are important regional interlocutors in the talks over Libya. Morocco initially tried to distance itself from Western pressure to condemn Russia's invasion of Ukraine, motivated by the need for Russia's support in conflicts in the Western Sahara, though it did eventually vote in favour of UNGA resolution ES-11/4. The suspension of parliament in Tunisia – generally regarded as the most progressive Arab state – and the deployment of the army by the country's president in July 2021 demonstrate the extent of the unresolved political and socioeconomic problems across the region.

A recent Chatham House study, drawing on extensive interviews with policy practitioners and experts, offered a positive assessment of Russia's diplomatic adeptness in managing its relationships with the MENA states and its potential to play a leading mediation role in regional conflicts (Vakil and Quilliam 2021, 63). As Russia's leading academic authority on the Middle East, Vitalii Naumkin, has argued, Russia's fundamental aim is to stabilise the region and ensure a balance of interests in order to obtain reciprocal security guarantees and pursue its legitimate trade interests (Shestakov 2016). Progressive agendas for change do not figure highly on Moscow's agenda; its approach is largely transactional. At the same time, Russia's ability to further its influence in regional MENA affairs – largely hostage to shifting alliances and divisions – depends heavily on local dynamics. Any notion of Russia acting strategically to control events for geopolitical gain is misleading: the security interests of regional states, domestic challenges faced by their governments, shifting rivalries and tactical alliances within a weakly institutionalised region – fraught with potential conflict escalation and ethno-confessional tensions – shape an environment which calls for crisis management rather than power plays.

Russia and the US

The US emerged from the first Gulf War in 1991 as the pre-eminent external power in the MENA region, extending its military presence and diplomatic reach in an effort to build a *Pax Americana* and resolve some of the key disputes there. However, ongoing problems – the failure of the Israel–Palestine and Israel–Syria peace processes and Arab opposition to normalising relations with Israel – were soon accompanied by new ones: the challenge of Al-Qaeda, 9/11 and the subsequent war in Afghanistan, the material and reputational costs of the disastrous 2003 Iraq invasion and persistent tensions surrounding Iran's nuclear programme and more assertive regional strategy. President George W. Bush's proposals for a Greater Middle East initiative in 2004 – part of a strategy aimed at expanding political rights and societal participation in Muslim countries to reduce the appeal of Islamist extremism – foundered on regional governments' concerns about the lack of consultation and attempts to impose Western values and models, differences among liberal Arab reformists and the desire of European countries to see a more gradual programme of societal change (Ottaway and Carothers 2004, 2). Washington made little headway in sponsoring an effective institutionalised multilateral regional security system. The Arab uprisings produced a new political dynamic, one that challenged the external powers to respond to demands for change while negotiating transactions with regional governments and power-brokers to safeguard their interests.

The Arab Spring was initially hailed by Barack Obama as a breakthrough. In a keynote speech in May 2011, he pledged economic support and engagement with civil society in exchange for progress on democratic reform (The White House 2011). Despite his assertion that the protests represented a wave of demand for democratic change, deserving of support from the liberal democracies, his approach was pragmatic, recognising the deep-seated structural shifts taking place. Obama himself had opposed the Iraq campaign and was even prepared to explore engagement with Iran and Syria. A former senior US security official has described how a hesitant Obama's backing for the NATO-led intervention in Libya was 'a 51–49 decision', dependent on support from regional states and on condition that the US would only provide intelligence and reconnaissance assets and would not put boots on the ground (Fishman 2022, 116–117; see also Martin 2022, 20). However, senior administration officials disagreed about political developments in key MENA countries, creating a dysfunctional foreign policymaking system. Obama's cautious approach was widely perceived as inadequate (Quandt 2014, 418–419, 422; see also Goldberg 2016); the need to balance values and strategic interests led to the US's 'selective' response to democratisation across the MENA countries and a 'deepening gap between strong rhetoric and timid policy practices' (Isaac and Kares 2017, 24, 25; ICG 2017c, 23). Expectations that the US would intervene to support protesters against repressive measures and engage in nation-building 'were based on the old order, not the new post-American Middle East of the Obama era' (Phillips 2016, 233).

Influenced by the experience of Libya, Obama's restraint was manifest in his approach to the Syria conflict (see Bowen et al 2020). While delivering warnings to Syria and Iran about the consequences of their actions, he refused to commit large-scale forces to 'somebody's else's war' (cited in Docherty et al 2020, 264). The US ambassador to NATO – when Assad's crackdown on the opposition had been going on for almost a year – commented that 'there has been no planning, no thought, and no discussion about any intervention into Syria … There needs to be a demonstrable need, regional support, and sound legal basis for action … None of them apply in Syria' (cited in Buckley 2012, 93; Bowen et al, 814–815). As conflicts in Libya, Syria and Yemen were leading to state fragmentation, and while political developments elsewhere in the region were reinforcing sectarian and confessional divides amid a growing threat from Islamist extremism, the US's approach graduated into containment, with military action limited to air strikes against Islamic State positions and arming elements of the Syrian opposition. Even though Obama had asserted that the use of chemical weapons by Assad's forces represented a 'red line', the chemical attack in Ghouta in August 2013 was resolved through an agreement brokered by Russia and the US to sponsor Syria's chemical disarmament (discussed in more detail in the next chapter), which effectively meant impunity for Assad against large-scale US intervention. Obama's reticence was widely criticised by its traditional partners in the region for allowing the humanitarian costs of the Syria conflict to escalate, with the result that they became more assertive in pursuing their own interests and more prepared to use military force to achieve them (Mueller et al 2017, 5; Hanania 2020, 174–175).

The increased agency of regional leaderships has frustrated US efforts to contain crises and respond effectively to repressive state control by authoritarian leaders (see Boserup et al 2017, 8). Secretary of Defense Ashton Carter asserted that US strategy had begun to focus on its own core security concerns: countering Islamic State and other militant Islamist movements, nuclear non-proliferation, stemming Iran's 'malign influence' in the region, capacity-building with regional allies – notably Israel and the Gulf Arabs – and securing energy flows (Carter 2017, 13–14; see also Mueller et al 2017, 2). US security policy in the region has increasingly been questioned by the Gulf states, a problem only partly resolved at a US-GCC summit held in May 2015 pledging closer defence and security cooperation (The White House 2015; Shumilin 2018; Mueller et al 2017, 6–7). The incoming Trump administration stepped up coercive US sanctions against Iran, since maintained by Biden, but effectively continued the Obama-era policy of limiting US military operations in the Middle East (Gause 2019, 11–12). Rather than seeking to rebuild the regional order and mediate between rival forces, the US has fuelled disputes – among the Gulf states, between Israel and the Palestinians and between conflicting parties involved in Syria, Libya and Yemen – by choosing sides while avoiding closer engagement. Despite ongoing military support to Iran's regional opponents, in particular Israel and Saudi Arabia, US equivocation under Biden is seen as allowing Tehran to extend its regional influence. Indeed, the survey of experts and practitioners referred to earlier in this chapter found that the US is perceived as the most destabilising actor in the Middle East, much more so than Russia, despite its professed attachment to liberal values (Fusco 2021, 9). Uncertainty over the extent of the US commitment to the region – in terms of both security and support for human rights – persists (see Aksenenok 2022). Indeed, recent surveys carried out in Arab countries, including those with traditionally close relations with Washington, have found that the popularity of the US has declined relative to that of Russia.

What of Russia's response to US policies in the region? As suggested earlier in this chapter, conventional thinking ascribes Moscow's more assertive approach to a desire to 'fill the vacuum' left by the decline in US influence and 'intimidate the West' (Weiss and Ng 2019); its MENA policy 'is subordinated to the Kremlin's global strategy towards Washington' (Rodkiewicz 2019; see also Alaaldin 2019, 7). A closer examination of Russia–US engagement in the Syrian civil war suggests a different picture. While firm in its opposition to Western-inspired regime change and seeking to promote itself as an influential actor alongside the US, Moscow was intent on maintaining close contact at the operational and tactical level to ensure deconfliction; it was more concerned about the incoherence of Washington's policy than obstructing US interests. Official Russian statements, albeit often overshadowed by mutual recriminations, have signalled considerable frustration at inconsistent US decision-making that vitiated progress in resolving the conflict. Lavrov accused Washington of dragging its feet in the battle against Islamic State and of failing to deliver on its commitments, saying that 'we do not see an overall [US] strategy' (Lavrov 2016b).

At the time when Lavrov and US Secretary of State John Kerry were engaged in intensive diplomacy over Syria, Ashton Carter – echoed by other senior military figures such as General Philip Breedlove – declared that the key security threat was posed by Russia and that the transatlantic community had to prioritise deterrence (Carter 2016, 57; Sakwa 2017, 205). Despite Trump's declared aim of securing a deal with Russia in Syria, his administration's 2018 National Defense Strategy defined the central challenge to US security as the '*reemergence of long-term, strategic competition*' with the 'revisionist powers' China and Russia (US DoD 2018, 2; italics in original). One account describes how, having discounted direct military involvement in the Syrian civil war, some officials at the State Department and National Security Council were exploring ideas for intelligence sharing and joint targeting of terrorist groups with Russia, while at the same time 'Carter and other Pentagon officials were steadfastly opposed to any cooperation in the fight against the Islamic State … The Pentagon's arguments carried the day with Obama' (Weiss and Ng 2019; Wilhelmsen 2019, 1105, 1110). A fractured US strategy, exacerbated by the deep mistrust of Russia in its defence and security establishment, has undercut constructive political-military engagement in the MENA region. The result was that Moscow sought increasingly to exercise diplomatic, and subsequently military, leverage outside of the framework of cooperation with Washington.

Yet Washington retains an unrivalled military presence across the Middle East, a critical geopolitical region that may again become a key focus for US military planners in the case of increased threats to its regional interests posed by Iran's 'axis of resistance' and a resurgence of Islamist terrorism (see Wood 2019, 163–165). US involvement in the Iranian nuclear talks is crucial if a credible and durable agreement is to be reached. A strategic shift in most MENA countries away from Washington towards Russia and China is unlikely. In spite of increased regional agency in security affairs, MENA states still depend on the involvement of the principal external actors acting as security guarantors or mediators through the UN or in other formats. While Russia's intervention in Syria showed its readiness to use coercive power to strengthen its hand in conflict negotiations, Moscow recognises the need for the US to commit its own military forces to maintain a stable balance of interests in the region. Leading Russian experts have argued that Russia's policy in Syria was firmly aimed at accommodation with the US (House of Lords 2017, 36; interviews #1, #7, #8). Some US policy analysts even recommended that Washington should seek partnership with Russia over post-conflict stabilisation in Syria, leveraging Moscow's relations with Iran and cooperation in the battle against terrorism (Parasiliti et al 2017, 5, 13). A senior UK official responsible for MENA policy acknowledged that any diplomatic settlement in Syria will require some kind of regional accommodation with Russia (House of Lords 2017, 38). Russian officials have established 'diplomatic back channels' to engage US cooperation on post-conflict reconstruction and refugee return to Syria; contacts at the operational level between US and Russian defence, security and intelligence agencies in Syria and talks between the US and Russia over rules of engagement have mitigated the risks of military escalation (Shumilin 2018, 2–3). Moscow's diplomatic contribution to brokering a political agreement in

Libya within the framework outlined by the UN Support Mission there will also be important.

However, further progress towards a settlement of the Syria conflict has achieved little to date. Russia–US engagement over other key security challenges – Libya, the Iranian nuclear deal, Tehran's regional strategy, militant Islamism – remains limited, despite common interests in some areas. Moscow's policies, hitherto not so much unremittingly damaging to US interests as seeking to address the shortfall left by its equivocation and lack of policy coherence, founder on a reciprocal lack of trust, a shifting global balance of power and – increasingly shaping the thinking of security planners – a resurgence of great power rivalry. Russia's uneasy engagement with the US, alternating between cooperation and acrimony, is being reshaped by increasingly differing perceptions of a fundamentally changed regional political and security environment. The war in Ukraine, the US sanctions regime against Russia and Moscow's uncompromising response have only exacerbated mutual hostility and may well have a long-term adverse impact on cooperation in the MENA region.

Russia and Europe

The European Union's engagement with the MENA region through the Barcelona Process-Euro-Mediterranean Partnership (EMP), established in 1995 to encourage political and economic governance reform in its southern neighbourhood, achieved limited results due to a 'hesitant' Common Foreign and Security Policy and conflicting priorities of the EU member states (Stivachtis 2018, 111). The US coalition's intervention in Iraq in 2003 – supported by the UK, Italy, Spain and some central European states but not by France and Germany – accentuated internal EU divisions at a time when the leading MENA countries were increasingly pursuing independent policies to deal with a worsening security environment (Colombo and Huber 2016, 17). While further EU initiatives – the Union for the Mediterranean, established in 2008, and the 2011 Partnership for Democracy and Shared Prosperity – promised greater attention to democratic development and support to civil society in the Arab countries, they achieved little more than the EMP (see Özçelik 2019, 51–52). The Arab uprisings surpassed 9/11 in terms of the challenges posed to Europe; the emergence of vibrant civil societies resisting coercive state control and apparently yearning for democratic governance to replace pro-Western dictatorships prompted an EU response that was mainly limited to political dialogue. Underdeveloped crisis management strategies appeared out of touch with events on the ground as the conflicts escalated (Colombo and Huber 2016, 18). Incumbent MENA governments, fearing threats to their hold on power, were mostly unable or unwilling to accede to the EU's political conditionality demands; Brussels' attempts to export its own democracy norms to the region allowed little room for manoeuvre during negotiations (Stivachtis 2018, 115, 121; Dark 2018, 14). Even though the EU continues to provide support to civil society through human rights and democracy programmes and is the main donor of humanitarian aid for refugees, in the absence of reform in the region and a broader vision of post-conflict structures, it struggles to foster inclusive political processes and democratic citizenship (Youngs 2018).

In Egypt, Brussels adopted a pragmatic position, accepting Morsi's election but subsequently opting to maintain relations with al-Sisi after his military takeover. After Gaddafi's overthrow, the EU established EUFOR Libya, a military operation to support humanitarian operations, and the EUBAM Libya civilian border assistance mission under the Common Security and Defence Policy to monitor the effects of migration flows. It has also supported moves to establish a government of unity. However, one authoritative assessment, based on extensive interviews in Brussels, concluded that these instruments did not address core issues or add up to an effective foreign policy; securing its borders against irregular migration and illicit trafficking began to dominate the EU's concerns (Colombo and Huber 2016, 24–27). The EU's role in supporting UN mediation in Yemen was undermined by the UK's and France's military support for the Saudi-led coalition (ICG 2017c, 29). In Syria, the EU reacted to Assad's crackdown by freezing the draft bilateral Association Agreement and imposing sanctions and an arms embargo. At the same time, it joined the International Syria Support Group (ISSG) and adopted a communication supporting a political solution to prevent regional destabilisation and address the humanitarian consequences of the conflict (European Commission/HR CFSP 2013), as well as a counterterrorism/foreign fighters Strategy for Syria and Iraq in October 2014, part of a broader regional strategy adopted in March 2015. However, European intervention has mainly been in the hands of the member states and Brussels has had little direct involvement in negotiations over a political resolution of the civil war. Brussels has been ambivalent over what constitutes an inclusive transition, and internal EU divisions – with the UK and France continuing to push for Assad's removal, while Germany and Eastern European states supported the idea that Assad should be part of a transition – have undermined the possibility of an effective resolution of the conflict (ICG 2017c, 29; Colombo and Huber 2016, 32; Youngs and Gutman 2015). According to one authoritative source, Moscow has told Europe 'to stop clutching onto the fantasy that playing the sanctions and reconstruction card can still achieve the regime change that eight years of war failed to deliver' (ICG 2019c, i).

The EU has thus steered clear of a political role commensurate with its extensive economic and security interests in its southern neighbourhood, even though crisis response is seen as a top priority (Council of the European Union 2015). Brussels lacks institutionalised procedures for mainstreaming its approach to external conflicts into policy programming (Bøås and Rieker 2019, 11–12, 14; see also Dark 2018, 10). The emphasis on regional stability and 'state and societal resilience' in the 2016 EU Global Strategy signals that the EU is prioritising the migration issue, part of its own internal security concerns, disregarding broader strategic challenges and 'supporting the status quo of repressive regimes in the region' (Debuysere 2019, 1–2; Schumacher 2020, 188, 194; Youngs and Gutman 2015; Blockmans 2016b, 1–2). Deepening divisions with Turkey – a pivotal player in the MENA region – are a major problem for Brussels. The EU–Turkey migration agreement of March 2016, a response to the growing Syrian refugee crisis, became bound up with bilateral negotiations on visa liberalisation for Turkish citizens, attracting criticism for adding a political dimension to humanitarian issues; EU leaders have also prioritised national security over its humanitarian responsibilities by linking migration with the terrorist threat so that 'the support it has provided has been limited and falls short of meeting its own human rights criteria' (Senyücel and Dark 2019, 74).

The increasing activism of the other external actors and major regional powers presents an additional challenge to Brussels (see Ehteshami, Huber and Paciello 2017, 5). Even prior to the Arab Spring, UN diplomacy was being shaped increasingly by Russia and other non-Western states, with the EU's approach to human rights receiving less support; as a result, the EU 'often seems defensive where it should be visionary' (Gowan and Brantner 2008, 1, 3). Europe's variable relationship with the Trump administration obstructed Brussels' preferences for a liberal rules-based order where diplomatic solutions brokered by consensus prevail. Evidence from elite survey research in nine Mediterranean countries suggested that, in a deteriorating post-Arab Spring security environment, the EU's regional influence will remain modest, as it struggles to adjust to a 'multipolar region driven by power politics', prioritising its own security at the expense of fostering development and democracy in the MENA region (Dark 2018, 7–8, 10–11).

There has been little effective engagement between Russia and the EU over the Arab Spring. Brussels ultimately plays only a supporting role to the US and Russia in the hard bargaining needed to manage and resolve conflicts (Dark 2018, 9). EU policy in Libya – with its own member states split, not least over the migration crisis in the central Mediterranean – has lacked coherence as influential regional actors have aggressively pursued their interests (Schumacher 2020, 195). Despite its considerable potential in post-conflict reconstruction, the EU asserted in its Strategy on Syria, adopted in April 2017, that it will only contribute to rebuilding Syria when a 'comprehensive, genuine and inclusive political transition' has taken place (Council of the European Union 2017). The EU has unsurprisingly been highly critical of Russia's role, particularly its support for the Assad government; while European elites do not see Russia as a credible power-broker and believe that Moscow will need external support to stabilise Syria, they recognise that the EU can generally do little to counter Russian influence across the region (Lovotti and Ambrosetti 2019, 75–76). The Strategy on Syria called attention to Russia's responsibilities to international humanitarian law as a co-chair of the ISSG, while continuing to support the UN-led political process outlined in the 2012 Geneva communiqué and UNSC resolution 2254 (Council of the European Union 2017). However, it has failed to provide incentives for the warring parties to reach a political settlement that could attract the backing of Russia and the other major external powers (ICG 2017b). Lacking a wider political vision for a resolution to the conflict, Brussels faces pressure to acquiesce to Assad remaining in power and deliver reconstruction assistance in order to sustain its local governance and civil society support programmes (Youngs 2018). Meanwhile, Moscow will want preferential treatment in lucrative reconstruction contracts, given its investment in supporting Assad.

One area of common interest in Russia–EU relations, despite differing views on regional issues, is the Iranian nuclear programme. The EU played a leading role in coordinating the JCPOA negotiations, endorsed by UNSC resolution 2231 in 2015 and conducted in the E3 (Britain, France and Germany) + 3 (US, China and Russia) format (otherwise referred to as the P5+1). Brussels has a strategic interest in exerting diplomatic pressure to try to mitigate tensions between the US and Iran and broker a mutually acceptable multilateral solution to the nuclear issue, as well as further trade relations with Tehran (Alcaro and Dessì 2019; Ehteshami and Mohammadi 2017b, 96–97; Barnes-Dacey 2017, 6). Despite its long history of nuclear cooperation with Iran in building the Bushehr facility and supplying enriched uranium, Russia had supported UNSC resolution 1929 in June 2010 authorising a fourth round of sanctions on Iran over its nuclear activities and suspended the sale of its S-300 missile defence system to Tehran, demonstrating its commitment to multilateral nonproliferation efforts. Following Trump's withdrawal from the JCPOA, Russia tried to convince the remaining E3+3 signatories to abide by the terms of the JCPOA and where possible circumvent heavy US sanctions, while seeking to broker a compromise (Rodkiewicz 2019). Brussels also maintained its commitment to the agreement and tried to facilitate negotiations, despite Iran's gradual resumption of uranium enrichment activity beyond the mandated limits and concerns that its regional power projection threatens European trade and security interests with Israel and the Arab Gulf states. The EU and Russia – neither of which want to be embroiled in trade disputes with the US over Iran – face the problem of pooling diplomatic efforts to minimise the impact of sanctions on the Iranian economy and keep Tehran from abandoning the JCPOA, which would most likely lead to escalating military action by the US, supported by Israel (see Thomson and Shah 2020). The future of the nuclear agreement depends heavily on powerful domestic constituencies in the US and Iran, with widely divergent positions over regional issues unresolved.

As stated earlier, France and the UK are Europe's most active players in MENA regional security and, alongside the US, Russia's most vocal antagonists at the UN over the Syria conflict. France responded to the potential strategic vacuum left by Obama's policy of strategic retrenchment by becoming more activist through small-scale military interventions, while seeking to increase its influence in Euroatlantic structures (Cadier 2018); it was instrumental in endorsing NATO's Libya campaign and advocated a forceful response to the August 2013 chemical weapons attack by Assad's forces in Ghouta. However, Russia's military intervention in Syria in September 2015 and the terrorist attacks in Paris a few weeks later – claimed by Islamic State as retaliation for French strikes on its forces in Syria and Iraq – triggered a heated debate over the prioritisation of threats. Some French politicians were in favour of closer cooperation with Russia to fight terrorism; on becoming President, Emmanuel Macron also sought diplomatic support from Moscow in his bid to persuade Iran to return fully to its JCPOA commitments in exchange for dialogue with the US on its nuclear and missile policies (see Thomson and Shah 2020, 6–7). Macron's 2017 Strategic Review of defence and national security reasserted the importance of national and European strategic autonomy in the face of Russia's military presence on France's eastern and northern flanks and its dominant influence, alongside Iran and Turkey, in the Middle East. However, Russia's invasion of Ukraine in 2022 has reinforced France's search for Western unity over Moscow's aggressive actions in Europe and its wider neighbourhood; one expert has concluded that 'French activism abroad is becoming increasingly Americanized, regionalized and preferably performed with respect for international law' (Crone 2017, 56; French Republic Presidency 2017, 23, 56–58).

The UK joined France in promoting the Libya intervention. An official UK report was damning about Prime Minister David Cameron's 'failure to develop a coherent Libya strategy' that 'drifted into an opportunist policy of regime change', with its attendant consequences of state collapse and the spread of Islamist extremism (House of Commons 2016, 3, 10–12; see also Martin 2022, 63). The UK's inconsistent behaviour in condemning and acting on government violence in Libya, while making only muted comments on abuses in Bahrain, Egypt, Tunisia and Yemen, was perceived by many as double standards: '[its] use of human rights language was ... a cover for national self-interest rather than genuine concern for global norms [and] had an impact in later failures to achieve an international consensus on how to react to the Syrian civil war' (Leech and Gaskarth 2015, 139). In Syria, the Cameron government advocated 'exceptional measures' up to and including military action, despite a lack of international support other than by France, to deter the Assad government from using chemical weapons after the Ghouta attack (Buys and Garwood-Gowers 2019, 18). However, the refusal of the UK Parliament to grant approval for military action in August 2013 reflected the general 'British confusion and disarray in Syria [and] the contradictions in international policy on President Bashar al-Assad' (House of Lords 2017, 93). The UK consistently echoed the US and France in condemning Russian policy and pressing for Assad's departure, but its lack of engagement with Moscow to explore possibilities for a political solution – reflecting a general downturn in bilateral relations – has resulted in a signal failure to match policy goals with outcomes (see Ralph et al 2017).

Russia and China

China's role in the Arab Spring has drawn Western attention primarily owing to its diplomatic alignment with Russia in vetoing draft UNSC resolutions designed to curb Assad's excesses in the Syria conflict – reflecting a shared commitment to authoritarian values and willingness to oppose interventions in illiberal states seen in the West as lacking legitimacy – as well as to its support for the JCPOA in opposition to the US. China's industrial, financial, trade and investment muscle, with the One Belt One Road (OBOR) initiative underpinning its rapid economic expansion into the MENA region, is another source of concern to the Western powers. An economic partnership between China and the Arab states comprising energy, including nuclear, infrastructure construction and trade/technology cooperation was initiated in 2014. Some MENA countries are in a network of infrastructure projects spanning 60 countries as part of the OBOR initiative, underwritten by generous loans funded by the Asian Infrastructure Investment Bank in Beijing (Milosevich 2019, 45). China's 2016 Arab Policy Paper publicised its strategic bilateral partnerships with eight Arab countries (Chinese Government 2016); as of 2020 this had increased to 13, building on the China-GCC Strategic Dialogue forum established in 2010. MENA countries have become China's biggest supplier of crude oil, accounting for close to half of its consumption, with the region constituting almost 7 per cent of China's trade turnover in the 2014–2019 period. Its export/import trade with the Middle East exceeds that of the US and it may soon overtake the EU as the Middle East's main external trading partner (Sidło 2020, 34–35).

More significantly, Beijing declares its aim to 'enhance the sharing of governance experience with Arab states', underpinned normatively by respect for state sovereignty and non-interference in internal Arab affairs and in practical terms by fighting terrorism and promoting conflict resolution (Chinese Government 2016; see also Xinhua 2018). One expert argues that, in developing its 'soft power' approach, 'China's economic success and rise as an alternative to the US in the region is increasingly featured in Arab intellectual discourse, to the extent where it has in some quarters been embraced as an alternative to the US model' (Alaaldin 2019, 9). While taking care not to disturb the regional balance of power between the Gulf states and Iran, Beijing also concluded a twenty-five-year economic and cooperation agreement with Tehran in March 2021 that apparently includes military/military-technical cooperation and intelligence-sharing, prompting Israel to seek China's support in halting Iran's nuclear programme and mitigating the influence of Iran-backed Hezbollah forces in Lebanon (Alaaldin 2019, 10; Vakil and Quilliam 2021, 6–7). China has also held three trilateral naval exercises with Iran and Russia since 2019.

China's interests are thus being pursued through a strategy – part of a 'systemic' approach, developed over the past decade, that represents China as not just a Pacific but also an Asian power (Antipov 2014) – central to which is the avoidance of political conditionality in trade and interference in the MENA countries' internal affairs, while fostering stability to protect its energy, trade and construction projects (see Liangxiang 2020, 16). This extends to a security role. Its involvement in joint anti-terrorist efforts in Syria and Iraq, prompted by concern over returning Uighur fighters to Xinjiang autonomous territory, and mediation in regional conflicts have become more prominent, along with participation in maritime security and anti-piracy missions; in 2016 it appointed a special representative for Syria to engage in peace negotiations and despatched 300 military training officers (Larin 2018; see also Lons et al 2019). Top-level bilateral contacts with Egypt and Saudi Arabia, as well as ongoing dialogue with Iran, Israel and Turkey, indicate an expanding presence that includes a naval base in nearby Djibouti and arms supplies to the region (Moran 2017).

China may be content at present with a lower profile in the MENA region, playing down suggestions of rivalry with Russia or the US and avoiding becoming embroiled in regional disputes that may adversely affect its economic interests. At the same time, while not an absolute priority for

Beijing, MENA countries appear to be increasingly important in terms of long-term trade and investment prospects underwritten by security cooperation. Although Russia prizes China's diplomatic support – reflected in the declaration of a 'no limits' friendship immediately prior to the invasion of Ukraine – Moscow will have to take account of Beijing's increasing economic, and to an extent political, influence in the region. As one Chinese expert concludes, as 'Beijing recalibrates its foreign policy in line with its status as a great power, it is likely that Beijing's involvement in the region will deepen in the years to come' (Chen 2018, 83, 86).

Conclusions

Three factors combine to shape Russia's MENA policy a decade on from the inception of the Arab Spring. The first is the turbulence afflicting the region. Little progress has been made in addressing the underlying causes of the multiple conflicts; the deficit of authority and legitimacy of many state leaderships in the MENA countries, weak regional institutions, corrupt and non-transparent governance, poverty and lack of social cohesion, and sectarian violence fed by external patrons, all preclude any organising principle for a stable regional security environment. Amid the fantastically complex alliances and rivalries, lasting political solutions are difficult to achieve given the multiple conflicting goals of the protagonists. The second factor is the increasing agency of the regional powers and the commensurate decline of Western authority. Failed attempts to resolve the internationalised civil wars in Libya, Syria, Yemen and Iraq have shown that none of the external actors can exercise effective influence without taking account of power arrangements within and between the leading MENA states. Even the US – for decades the most powerful external player – has a lesser capacity to control not only its increasingly assertive adversaries but also its regional allies (see Mueller et al 2017, 8). For Europe, the dilemma between tackling the root causes of conflicts by promoting democratic citizenship and human rights on the one hand, and the need to deal with authoritarian governments to maintain order and protect Europeans' own interests on the other, remains unresolved. The third factor is the inability of the external powers to address regional challenges collectively, as they 'evidently perceive security differently. With such competing visions of regional security, and an absence of strong leadership and direction, the result has been a period of unparalleled instability, making efforts to create any viable security architecture ever more elusive' (Fawcett 2015a, 42). At the same time, the reconfigured regional order is still embedded in wider structural shifts in global trade and changing social forces (Boserup et al 2017, 9).

Western commentary tends to represent Russia as adopting 'the role of spoiler ... the urge to derail America's course increasingly prevails over the pragmatic calculation of risks and benefits' (Baev 2015, 9). One authoritative scholar suggests that all the great powers 'are starting to use MENA conflicts, notably in Syria, to fight their own proxy wars ... there are too many "spoilers" to make a settlement of the Arab civil wars easy or likely anytime soon' (Hinnebusch 2016, 146). However, we have argued in this chapter that the notion of Russia exploiting the US's retreat by building proxy alliances in strategic competition misses vital aspects of its policy. Moscow does exercise its diplomatic heft and procedural influence at the UN to curb Western interventions in the region; it uses all available means to promote its security and trade interests there. At the same time, mindful of the challenges it faces, it has calculated that its interests are best served by diversifying its links with regional leaderships and pursuing incremental improvements in relations while mediating in regional conflicts (Naumkin 2018). Its ambitions are tempered by the need to establish legitimacy and credibility among the countries of the region.

Russia's war with Ukraine has added an additional layer of uncertainty to the volatile politics of the MENA region. With Russia increasingly isolated from and distrusted by the West, will it prioritise relations with countries in Asia and the global South and seek to entrench itself further in their economic and security affairs? Or, with the war impacting energy flows, social stability and food security, will Russia's positions in the MENA region be undermined as states turn more to the West and China for trade, reconstruction and humanitarian assistance? To what extent will the US and Europe be prepared to compartmentalise their opposition to Russia over Ukraine and draw on Moscow's influence with the MENA states to address critical issues in the region? Might Russia revert to playing a spoiler role there if the West is perceived as undermining its trade and security interests? The situation is unpredictable; to use a metaphor reflecting the epigraph to this chapter, Moscow faces navigating its way through a minefield without a map, with the consequences of the Ukraine war inhibiting its ability to manage regional affairs to its own advantage. A final question is whether the war will embolden Russia to try to expand its nascent strategic positions in the MENA region or whether it will be forced to limit its engagement there. This question is central to its continuing involvement in the Syrian civil war, the subject of the next chapter of this book.

2

Russia and the Syrian civil war

> Today, the Central Museum of the Armed Forces of Russia hosted a ceremony for the donation of a painting by outstanding Spanish battle artist Augusto Ferrer-Dalmau dedicated to Russian peacekeeping activities in Syria. (Maria Zakharova; MFA 2019b)

With demonstrations having already broken out in Tunisia in December 2010 and in Egypt, Yemen and Libya in January to February 2011, limited protests flared up in Syria in February. On 6 March fifteen teenagers were arrested for writing anti-government slogans on the walls of a school in Dara'a. The demonstrations against their punishment, largely peaceful and unarmed, called for greater political freedom, economic reforms and an end to corruption. On 18 March government forces killed three demonstrators at a mass rally. The protests spread and demands for the resignation of Assad intensified. His government announced a series of political and legal reforms in March and April and launched an attempt to initiate dialogue with the population in the most restive areas. However, it was clear that Assad would not relinquish power, as from late April the use of force by the army intensified, prompting demonstrators to arm themselves to defend their cities. In July, defectors from the armed forces set up the Free Syrian Army in opposition to Assad and were joined by various militias.

Even though all the major external powers called on the Assad government to end the violence against protesters, differences between the approaches of Russia and the leading Western states to the crisis soon emerged as the conflict became increasingly internationalised. The US representative at the UN complained that 'these brutal acts are those of neither a responsible Government nor a credible member of the international community'; while calling for an investigation into the violence and for the guilty to be brought to justice, the Russian representative stated that 'the process of democratic reforms proclaimed and being earnestly implemented by the leadership of Syria is worthy of support', warning that 'a real threat to regional security, in our view, could arise from outside interference in Syria's domestic situation, including attempts to promote ready-made solutions or to take sides' (UNSC 2011c; see also Issaev and Shishkina 2020, 99).

By summer 2012 the Syria conflict had acquired the dimensions of a civil war, as opposition-held areas were subjected to air strikes by government forces. Opposition groups, some of them sponsored by regional actors, began to put aside ideological differences and fight alongside Salafi jihadi movements to defend Sunni civilians against government repression (Lister 2017, 8; ICG 2016b, 1fn). International efforts to mediate were thwarted by the Assad government's intransigence and splits within the opposition. At the same time, divisions among the leading external powers hardened. The Western position was reflected in the unequivocal warning by the UK's UN representative that the Assad leadership faced the same fate as Gaddafi:

> The developments in Libya should give all Governments reason to pause before using violence against their own people. The international community will ensure that responsible individuals within such Governments are held to account, either in their own courts or in international courts such as the International Criminal Court (ICC). Impunity is no longer tolerable ... the Government of Syria ought to be aware that the eyes of the world are upon it. (UNSC 2011d)

In response, the Russian government intensified its diplomatic support for the incumbent Syria authorities against what it depicted as a divided opposition, warning of the threat of Islamist terrorism and the risk of destabilisation of the wider region that external intervention would cause.

The scene was set for a major internationalised civil war which has devastated large parts of the country and impacted significantly on regional security. A leading Syria scholar has written of its wider implications: 'Syria is the pivotal Arab state ... when it is divided, as now, it becomes an arena for the struggle of external forces, all seeking to shift, through it, the regional balance of power in their favour' (Hinnebusch 2012, 111). A Russian expert concluded presciently that the 'existential' battles between Assad's largely Alawite government and Sunni Islamist militants, and between the government and secular democratic opposition forces supported by the West, would last for many years: 'Russia and the US will hold endless negotiations about the restructuring of Syria ... The whole region will undergo reformatting' (Kuznetsov 2015).

This chapter briefly introduces the causes of the Syrian civil war before going on to take a closer look at the three key phases of Russia's involvement. The first phase covers the period from the start of hostilities up to Russia's military intervention in September 2015, examining the UN-sponsored Geneva process and attempts to resolve or moderate the conflict; it also investigates the crisis caused by the Syrian government's use of chemical weapons in August 2013. The second phase considers the reasons for Russia's military intervention – a critical juncture in the course of the conflict – and analyses events culminating in the ceasefire in December 2016 that ended the siege of Aleppo. The third phase analyses the Astana process involving Russia, Turkey and Iran, the continuing political deadlock in the later stages of the civil war and the further use of chemical weapons by Syrian forces. The penultimate section raises some key questions about Russia's intervention in Syria, leading to conclusions that consider the wider implications of the conflict and Russia's future role in the MENA region.

The causes of the Syria conflict

Chapter 1 of this book showed how the turbulent regional context was crucial in shaping the course of the Syrian civil war: 'To understand the international response to the Syrian crisis, the impact of the Arab Spring must be considered … no foreign-policy maker was ever dealing with Syria in isolation, but rather as yet another strand of what appeared a sudden and confusing regional transformation' (Phillips 2016, 60). Libya and Egypt were initially of more concern to actors external to the region. Assad's measures to suppress the protests did not initially seem to pose a major threat and the international reaction to the unrest was muted. But as the violence intensified, Assad's attempt to 'modernize authoritarianism' by managing pressure for popular participation, while balancing among domestic constituencies to retain power, failed; real social reforms were few and far between and the moderate opposition was marginalised, as a result of which localised protests escalated into a widespread uprising aimed at unseating the government (Hinnebusch 2012, 95; see also Phillips 2015, 370–371). With hierarchical power structures in Syria more institutionally embedded within the state system – prominent Alawis in Damascus had long since built patronage networks among Christian and Druze minorities and were largely backed by the urban business community and military elites (Falk 2016, 2328; Buckley 2012, 90) – the cohesion of the governing elite's support base was ultimately to be decisive.

Ethnic and religious factors also played a major role. Many of the protesters were Sunni, empowered by the rising tide of Sunni movements across the region and by funding from Saudi Arabia and the Muslim Brotherhood in exile. In August 2011 the Western-backed anti-Assad Syrian diaspora established the Syrian National Council, formed of secular intellectuals and the Muslim Brotherhood, but they were unable to form a unified internal leadership. Faced by this broad-based opposition – moderate Syrian nationalists, Islamists, Sunni jihadi forces tied to Jabhat-al-Nusra, Jaysh al-Islam, Ahrar al-Sham and Islamic State in Iraq and the Levant, as well as Kurdish groups defending their own regions (UNGA 2014, 6; IICI 2021, 2–3) – the Syrian government began to lose swathes of territory and its military began to collapse. In response, Assad mobilised foreign Shia forces to fight alongside pro-government militias formed from Alawi, Christian, Shia and Druze minorities, armed from the early days of the uprising; their ranks were swelled by the Shabiha, a militia of irregular combatants and criminals which frightened minorities by warning of the threat of Sunni jihadi protesters (Khatib and Sinjab 2018, 14). Although sectarian identity was not initially a principal cause of the uprising in Syria, the Assad leadership 'aggravated sectarianism to rally its Alawi core' (Hinnebusch 2012, 110). Antagonism between Sunni groups and the Shia 'Resistance Axis' became a primary mobiliser for violence and the main vehicle for external interventions:

> it was perceived that the outcome of the 'new Struggle for Syria' would tilt the power balance in favor of one or the other of the rival camps ... Saudi Arabia, Turkey, Qatar and Iran, all intervened with arms, fighters and financial aid to governments or insurgents ... the effect of sectarianization was far more damaging, deepening and prolonging civil wars and creating anarchy. (Hinnebusch 2016, 142–143; Hinnebusch 2012, 111; see also Darwich and Fakhoury 2016, 712–713, 720–721)

Phase 1: Russia's diplomatic involvement in the Syria conflict: the Geneva process

As highlighted earlier in this book, Russia's initial reaction to the turmoil in Syria was to recognise the need for reform and an end to government violence against the protesters. At the same time, Lavrov stated that the situation did not represent a threat to international peace and security and thus should not be on the agenda of the UN Security Council (Lavrov 2010c). Russia backed a Security Council statement on 3 August 2011 condemning the government's human rights violations and the lack of serious reforms (UNSC 2011e), but later that month objected to a UN Human Rights Council (UNHRC) vote to launch an investigation into crimes against humanity; Russia and China refused to discuss a draft resolution circulated by the Western powers that warned of sanctions on Assad, releasing a joint statement urging the international community not to interfere in Syria's internal affairs (Charbonneau 2011; Phillips 2016, 68). A coordinated announcement by the US, UK, France, Germany and Canada – prompted by public pressure to act – demanded that Assad stand down. The EU issued a similar statement (European Union 2011).

As one expert argued, 'regime change in Syria was now official Western policy and, with the campaign in Libya still under way, many wondered whether an assault on Syria might be next' (Phillips 2016, 76). The Western powers had initially claimed that the Libya intervention was limited to the protection of civilians and did not have regime change as the ultimate goal, but after Gaddafi's overthrow some of the leading participants in the operation were frank in acknowledging that there was effectively no distinction between intervention for humanitarian purposes and regime change (see Martin 2022, 38–39, 59). In the same way, the Western powers' representation of the Syria uprising as part of a tide of reform sweeping across the region formed a central part of their narrative to delegitimise the Assad government, justifying calls for him to stand down. Russia responded by pointing to the baleful consequences for wider regional security of the Libya intervention and Gaddafi's demise. As Lavrov later remarked, 'we … expressed clearly to our [international] partners that we would never, under any circumstances, issue similar mandates for the resolution of conflict situations without knowing the scope and aims of the use of force' (MFA 2013a). He claimed that Russia's position was not prompted by a desire to protect Assad but was motivated by concerns over instability that could spill across borders arising from the possible disintegration of Syria as a sovereign, independent, multiconfessional and multiethnic state (Lavrov 2013g). The Syria conflict had in fact begun to impact neighbouring states. There was a mass influx of refugees into Iraq (400,000 by the end of 2014, according to the UN), which was still facing sectarian conflict a decade after the 2003 US-led invasion and was soon to be hit by the rise of Islamic State. Libya was also affected by refugees fleeing from Syria through the Egyptian border.

Moscow's aim was thus to frustrate the policies of Western states and regional actors intent on Assad's removal by emphasising the dangers of state breakdown and terrorism, reasoning that, even though Assad bore some responsibility for the protests, political transition through inclusive dialogue was the key to alleviating conflict and resolving differences between the warring groups. On 4 October 2011, Russia, along with China, vetoed a draft Security Council resolution (submitted by France, Germany, Portugal and the UK) that condemned human rights violations by the Syrian authorities and demanded access for human rights monitors and humanitarian agencies under article 41 of the UN Charter authorising non-coercive measures to respond to threats to peace and acts of aggression. Russia's representative to the UN, Vitalii Churkin, again spoke out against government repression of peaceful demonstrations but highlighted the violence by the extremist opposition, urging the international community to respect the sovereignty and territorial integrity of Syria and condemning the threat of sanctions that could exacerbate the conflict and destabilise the region; in response Western rhetoric was scaled up, with the US representative asking whether the Security Council 'will stand with peaceful protesters crying out for freedom or with a regime of thugs with guns that tramples human dignity and human rights' (UNSC 2011b).

As peaceful protest escalated to organised armed resistance, international efforts to address the conflict were stepped up. The UNHRC established the Independent International Commission of Inquiry (IICI), mandated to investigate alleged human rights violations. The League of Arab States (LAS) called in October 2011 for the protection of civilians and an end to the violence, subsequently imposing sanctions on Syria and suspending its membership when the Assad government failed to rein in its attacks and engage in talks about a political transition. The LAS also formed a monitoring mission in December and an Arab ministerial committee to liaise with the Assad leadership but, with Saudi Arabia withdrawing its participation in January 2012 in the face of continuing violence and petitioning the external powers to put pressure on Assad, the mission was soon discontinued. Russian initiatives to bring together government and opposition negotiators in Moscow also failed. A second UNSC draft resolution on Syria in February 2012, submitted by a much wider group of countries including some MENA states, aimed to achieve a ceasefire, reinforcing demands on Assad to cease all violence and protect the population; it was again vetoed by Russia and China. The US complained that the draft supported an Arab League plan that Assad himself had agreed to uphold and began to talk about 'crimes against humanity' perpetrated by 'desperate dictators': Assad's 'killing machine continues effectively unabated' (UNSC 2012b, 5–6). In February 2012 the informal Friends of Syria group, composed of the Western powers and leading MENA states, launched an initiative to explore a solution to the conflict, but disagreements within the group meant that it had little direct impact (Phillips 2016, 113–114).

Churkin, evidently under intense diplomatic pressure at this time, echoed the appeal for an end to violence and announced that Lavrov and Mikhail Fradkov, head of Russia's Foreign Intelligence Service, would visit Damascus on 7 February to try to further the political process; at the same time, he reiterated Russia's rejection of calls for regime change in Syria (UNSC 2012b, 9). The Lavrov/Fradkov mission – which came late in the day, when the conflict was already spiralling – failed to persuade Assad to initiate meaningful dialogue with the opposition on a new constitution and allow the LAS to resume its efforts to stabilise the situation. This proved to be a turning point: even though the two draft resolutions vetoed by Russia had not made any reference to a Chapter VII resolution authorising the use of force, or even formal UN sanctions apart from urging states to exercise restraint over the sale of arms to the Syrian government, the guarantee that

Moscow would veto any formal condemnation of the Syrian authorities meant that Assad had limited incentive to compromise. The fighting continued to escalate amid reciprocal accusations of bad faith between Russia and the Western powers at the UN.

At the same time, sufficient consensus was achieved with the appointment by the UN and the LAS of Kofi Annan as their joint Special Envoy to Syria. Annan's six-point plan was accepted by Damascus, and the Security Council in April 2012 unanimously approved resolution 2042, which called on all parties to cease armed violence and authorised an advance party of thirty unarmed observers to monitor the fragile ceasefire. A further Russian-sponsored resolution (2043) called upon all parties to bring an immediate end to the violence and human rights violations, secure humanitarian access and facilitate a Syrian-led political transition; it established a UN Supervision Mission in Syria (UNSMIS) to monitor the ceasefire over ninety days. However, by May the fighting had resumed, with neither the government nor opposition forces respecting the six-point plan.

The Geneva I Conference on Syria, convoked by Annan and held on 30 June 2012, was attended by Lavrov, US Secretary of State Hillary Clinton, Chinese Foreign Minister Yang Jiechi and British Foreign Secretary William Hague. It sought a consensus among the leading external powers – neither the Syrian government nor opposition figures were present – and produced the Final Communiqué of the Action Group for Syria, hailed as a road map for a negotiated transition. The Communiqué reiterated the importance of fulfilling the six-point plan and called for 'the establishment of a transitional governing body *[which] could include members of the present Government* and the opposition and other groups' and the preservation of Syria's military forces and security services (UNGA 2012; emphasis added). The opposition and its Western supporters interpreted the road map as a call for Assad's immediate departure. The US, UK and France, with the support of Germany and Portugal and the approval of the LAS, immediately prepared another UNSC draft resolution under article 41 to enforce non-coercive sanctions against the Syrian government if it did not implement the six-point plan, which Russia and China again vetoed. The French representative at the UN asserted that 'It is now clear that Russia merely wants to win time for the Syrian regime to crush the opposition'; Churkin responded by dismissing the resolution as opening the way for later external military intervention, even though it made no mention of this (UNSC 2012c). Annan himself had rejected foreign intervention, arguing that any further militarisation of the crisis would only exacerbate the conflict – 'we have to be careful that we don't introduce a medicine that is worse than the disease' – and noting that the General Assembly had issued a resolution emphasising that any intervention 'should be Syrian led and Syrian owned' (cited in Blair 2012), as mentioned in the Final Communiqué. This established a pattern repeated throughout the early years of the civil war: the external and regional powers proved 'unwilling to prioritise ending the conflict over their own wider geopolitical agendas' (Phillips 2016, 101–102).

Part of the problem lay in Annan's flawed peace plan itself. The plan urged Assad to make most of the concessions and offered him few incentives to accept a transition that would effectively transfer power to the opposition: 'confusion over [Annan's] mandate encouraged the opposition to treat Assad's departure as a precondition for, rather than an end result of, negotiations' (Hinnebusch and Zartman 2016, 1). Facing pressure from Western and some Arab states to deliver progress on a conflict that by this stage had claimed several thousand lives, Annan resigned on 2 August. The failure of attempts to reach agreement on the draft resolution reflected the limitations of the major powers' influence to steer the talks towards peace. In particular, Annan had overestimated Russia's leverage over Assad. Lavrov himself later admitted that 'Assad is not going to move. He said this publicly and he would not listen to us, to the Chinese, to the Iranians, to no one' (Lavrov 2013g). With the Assad leadership paying little heed to external calls for political negotiations, the other main regional powers – Turkey and the Arab Gulf states – were divided in their approach to consolidating the opposition, most of which rejected a negotiated solution. The promise of the Geneva I conference – 'when it was still potentially possible to roll back the damage done by the conflict and constitute a pluralist settlement within a working state' (Hinnebusch and Zartman 2016, 12; see also Akpinar 2016) – thus went unfulfilled.

With the major powers split over the fate of Assad and the Syrian opposition implacable in its insistence that he stand down, Russia's diplomatic efforts became more intensive. At a high-level meeting of the UN Security Council on the Middle East, shortly after the Geneva Communiqué was signed, Russia announced the establishment of the Russian-Arab Cooperation Forum and began to take steps to consolidate support for its position among the BRICS group (Brazil, Russia, India, China and South Africa), supposedly in a bid to achieve consensus in the Security Council. Lavrov reiterated Russia's view that 'a significant share of responsibility for the continuing bloodshed rests upon those States that are instigating Bashar Al-Assad's opponents to reject the ceasefire and dialogue and at the same time demanding the unconditional capitulation of the regime', asserting that the primary goal should be the fight against terrorism (UNSC 2012d, 14).

Official Russian statements also emphasised the fragmented nature of the opposition and declared that it did not represent a coherent political force capable of replacing Assad in a transition. Moscow criticised a draft resolution adopted by the UN General Assembly describing the National

Coalition of Syrian Revolutionary and Opposition Forces, formed of the Syrian National Council and other anti-Assad groups, as the 'legitimate representative' of the Syrian people, instead presenting them as 'a heterogeneous group formed under active external patronage' while pointing to evidence of atrocities by Islamist extremists integrated within the opposition (cited in Averre and Davies 2015, 819–820). This statement was not without foundation. One source cites an interview with Lakhdar Brahimi, Annan's successor as Special Envoy, who said that he 'felt the Russian analysis was correct but was tasked with producing a process that would – initially or eventually – remove Assad' (Hinnebusch and Zartman 2016, 17). The US recognised the National Coalition in December 2012, but in fact its legitimacy and influence within Syria were limited.

Brahimi had inherited an increasingly difficult mediation situation. His efforts focused on trying to find common ground between the US and Russia but made little progress towards agreement on the status of Assad in a transition. The major world powers met in the G8 format at Lough Erne in June 2013, with Putin – recently elected to a third presidential term – in attendance. The Lough Erne communiqué recommitted the parties to achieve a political resolution based on a vision for a united, inclusive and democratic Syria, endorsing a decision to expedite a second Geneva conference on Syria to implement fully the Geneva Final Communiqué. This included *inter alia* sponsoring a UN-supervised cessation of hostilities, bringing parties together to negotiate an agreement, guaranteeing humanitarian access to conflict locations, achieving the release of arbitrarily detained prisoners and respecting the right to peacefully demonstrate (UNSC, 2012b). The G8 repeated the Final Communiqué calls for the establishment of a transitional governing body formed by mutual consent and urged all sides to respect international humanitarian law, 'noting the particular responsibility of the Syrian authorities in this regard'; it also referred to the growing threat of terrorism and sectarian violence, as by this time Islamic State and the al-Nusra front had emerged as serious military forces (G8 2013).

No appreciable progress was made in Lough Erne in resolving the divisions between the external powers, however. This was reflected in the Friends of Syria statement only a few days later, which – despite calls in the Geneva and Lough Erne communiqués for the preservation during the transition of Syria's military and security services – rejected any role for Assad and his associates in the transitional governing body; the Friends of Syria were committed to 'change the balance of power on the ground' by providing 'all the necessary materiel and equipment to the opposition … in order to enable them to counter brutal attacks by the regime and its allies and protect the Syrian people' (UK Government 2013). There was thus a notable disjunction between the West's purported commitment to a political resolution and its support for the armed opposition, as Annan himself had acknowledged (see Hinnebusch and Zartman 2016, 6).

The G8 Communiqué touched on an additional point which was to become a central issue in the conflict. It condemned the use of chemical weapons (CW) in Syria – several instances of which had been alleged in the previous months – and called for access for a UN team, drawing on the expertise of the Organisation for the Prohibition of Chemical Weapons (OPCW) and World Health Organization, to carry out an investigation. Obama had asserted in 2012 that the use of CW represented a 'red line' beyond which Assad may face 'enormous consequences' (The White House 2012), interpreted by many as meaning military action. A mass-casualty CW attack in eastern Ghouta in August 2013 appeared to galvanise the US, UK and France to prepare a show of force against Assad. Moscow insisted that it was difficult to attribute responsibility and that the attack could have been a planned provocation to justify a military intervention (Putin 2013a; Lavrov 2013b). On 29 August the UK parliament voted against an armed attack, which the David Cameron government had sought under the doctrine of humanitarian intervention (Buys and Garwood 2019, 18). Still, on 31 August Obama stated that the US already had firepower ready for launch against Syrian military targets, while ruling out placing boots on the ground in Syria; he sought authorisation from Congress for military strikes, limited in scope and duration, that would not be rejected by a 'paralyzed' UN Security Council (The White House 2013; Bowen et al 2020, 821–822). Even though Obama had been advised that the evidence for the use of CW was not indisputable, some in his own administration expected him to respond to public pressure and initiate military action (Goldberg 2016; Phillips 2016, 180). Investigations by one respected journalist, based on US military intelligence sources, subsequently found that US agencies possessed evidence that the al-Nusra front had in fact developed the nerve agent sarin and might have been responsible for the Ghouta incident, but that 'the [Obama] administration cherry-picked intelligence to justify a strike against Assad' (Hersh 2013). The crisis was only averted when Russia and the US jointly proposed a plan, accepted by the Assad leadership, to carry out full chemical demilitarisation and place Syria's CW programme under international supervision, with Syria acceding to the Chemical Weapons Convention (CWC). The UN Security Council unanimously approved the plan by adopting resolution 2118 in September 2013.

As one expert suggests, 'to the extent that the Syrian civil war has been primarily a conventional weapons war, international consensus over the destruction of chemical weapons was only marginally consequential to the resolution of the crisis and the protection of Syrian civilians' (Tocci 2014, 5). Nevertheless, it was a considerable triumph for Russia, ultimately highlighting the reluctance of the Obama administration to launch a military intervention and Moscow's ability to seize the diplomatic initiative and present a positive picture of its own contribution to disarmament efforts. Two fundamental points underscored this notable shift in influence in MENA affairs. The first was that resolution 2118 did not mandate an immediate Chapter VII response; it was up to the OPCW – an impartial and respected global regime – acting together with the UN Secretary-General, under the terms of an OPCW-UN Joint Mission set up in October 2013, to review Syria's compliance at regular intervals and submit evidence of any further CW use to the Security Council, which would then decide on further steps, up to and including Chapter VII measures. This solution would, Lavrov asserted, thus prevent any 'politicised' approach by the Western powers who are 'blinded by their ideological mission of regime change' in Syria (Lavrov 2013b; see Notte 2020, 209–210). Second, Lavrov emphasised that cooperation between the US and Russia to resolve the CW crisis demonstrated the importance of collective decision-making underpinned by international law, concluding that 'we have all come down on the "right" side of history' – a clear response to Western critics who accused Russia of trying to hold back a tide of change sweeping through the Arab world (Lavrov 2013c; see also Averre and Davies 2015, 821, 824–825). Indeed, Lavrov pointed to John Kerry's public statement that the US and Russia are 'two of the world's most powerful nations' acting together (US Mission 2013; Lavrov 2013d; see Notte 2020, 214). But in the following years Assad would go on to flout its commitments under the CWC with diplomatic cover provided by Moscow, as discussed later in this chapter.

In January and February 2014 Brahimi, in close consultation with Russia and the US, convened two rounds of the Geneva II negotiations. These involved around forty states and delegates from the UN, EU, LAS and Organisation of Islamic Cooperation and brought together government and opposition groups for talks on political transition and the issue of humanitarian access. Differences again surfaced, with Moscow voicing fears that unrestricted humanitarian access might prove the first step towards some form of external military incursion into Syria (Lavrov 2014a; Tocci 2014, 5). Though the presence of a Syrian government delegation was hailed by Moscow as proof of its commitment to the political process, it offered no meaningful concessions (Phillips 2016, 190–193). The opposition was still divided; the Syrian National Council, unhappy that the National Coalition had accepted that Assad could leave power at a later stage of transition rather than immediately, refused to join the negotiations (Hinnebusch and Zartman 2016, 16; Akpinar 2016, 2295). The National Coalition had also insisted that Iran, Assad's principal regional backer, be excluded from the talks, to Russia's irritation. Nevertheless, on 22 February 2014, the UN

Security Council unanimously adopted resolution 2139 demanding that all parties, in particular the Syrian authorities, allow access for UN and other humanitarian agencies, protect civilians and lift the sieges of populated areas. Even though this resolution reaffirmed that those responsible for atrocities must be brought to justice, Moscow allowed it to pass since, according to Churkin, the wording took Russian considerations into account and did not open the door to the automatic imposition of sanctions compromising Syrian sovereignty (UNSC 2014a; see also Tocci 2014, 13). Resolution 2139 was later reinforced by resolution 2165 of 14 July 2014, when it became clear that UN human rights officials were being denied access to Syria and that the UN humanitarian aid effort was being obstructed. Another UNSC resolution, 2170, introduced Chapter VII sanctions against Islamic State and the al-Nusra front – designated as terrorist groups by the Security Council in May 2013 – for the 'gross, systematic and widespread abuse' of human rights.

Despite this flurry of activity at the UN, reciprocal recriminations between Russia and the Western powers continued. Brahimi acknowledged frankly that he was unable to exert sufficient diplomatic pressure to make progress in the conflict: his efforts were obstructed by hostility to Assad on the part of both the Western powers and some Arab states, Assad's own intransigence, factionalised rivalries fuelled by external actors, and militant extremism that threatened the integrity of the Syrian state (see Phillips 2016, 190–192; Akpinar 2016, 2295). Military power had become the driving factor. On one side it was dispersed among government forces and its supporting militias, including Hezbollah, and on the other among nationalists and various moderate and extremist Islamist groups, including foreign fighters. Resolutions 2139 and 2165 had little initial impact on the humanitarian situation, particularly for large numbers of people held under siege in several parts of the country, against the background of a mounting toll of deaths and internally displaced persons.

Following the failure of Geneva II, a French UNSC draft resolution of 22 May 2014, which decided to refer the Syria conflict to the Prosecutor of the International Criminal Court (ICC), was vetoed by Russia and China, even though Moscow had not vetoed the similar UNSC resolution 1970 in the Libya case (Martin 2022, 13–14). The French representative to the UN called this draft resolution – co-sponsored by sixty-five member states – 'an appeal to human conscience. It is not a political gesture; it is quite simply a moral act', while the US representative demanded justice for 'the victims of Al-Assad's industrial killing machine' and accused Russia and China of obstructing 'accountability for war crimes and crimes against humanity'; Churkin in response queried the authenticity of evidence of atrocities, remarking that P5 unity to advance a political settlement was being sacrificed and that referral to the ICC was yet another pretext for armed intervention in Syria (UNSC 2014b). In UN meetings Churkin routinely pointed to the lessons of the 2003 invasion of Iraq – which 'wiped out its State institutions and essentially abandoned the country's religious and ethnic communities to their own resources' – and of NATO's Libya intervention. According to him, Western political and economic pressure on the Assad Government was 'used as a battering ram to crush inconvenient regimes' and was only aiding the 'violence and genocide' of militant Islamists that threatened the entire region, while Russia's advocacy for national dialogue free of outside interference went unheeded (UNSC 2015a). Russia's position had hardly shifted, insisting on fulfilling the provisions of the 2012 Geneva Final Communiqué, namely the inclusion of elements of the present government in political transition negotiations and the fight against Islamic State as the primary threat.

Staffan de Mistura had taken over as Special Envoy in July 2014, following Brahimi's resignation in May of that year. In a briefing to the Security Council on 30 October, de Mistura introduced an action plan for an incremental, strategic de-escalation of violence between government and opposition forces in selected locations, starting with Aleppo, that would not replace a national political process but could impact at the national level (UNSC 2014c). He also initiated tentative talks towards a Geneva III conference. Lavrov still held regular and intensive talks with Kerry, as well as several meetings with regional states. Considerable diplomatic capital was invested in organising 'intra-Syrian consultative' meetings in Moscow (the 'Moscow platform') in January and April 2015, designed to establish a dialogue between the Assad government and opposition forces and pave the way for meaningful political progress. The talks were based on a list of principles close to those outlined in the Geneva Final Communiqué: preserving the sovereignty and territorial integrity of Syria, fighting international terrorism, using peaceful political methods of conflict resolution and determining the country's future based on the free and democratic will of the Syrian people. But Moscow continued to emphasise the inadmissibility of external interference in Syria's internal affairs or any foreign military activity on its territory without the agreement of the incumbent government, as well as the removal of sanctions – effectively what Russia had demanded from the outset (MFA 2015a, 2015b). Little progress was made on the fundamental differences separating the warring groups. The National Coalition refused to attend the Moscow meetings; the inflexibility of the Assad government and some opposition parties meant that no agreement was reached regarding clear modalities towards a resolution of the conflict or even confidence-building measures.

At the same time, the Assad government was coming under increasing military pressure on the ground, both from the intensifying jihadi threat and from Gulf-supported opposition factions. In August to September 2014, the US had initiated operations in Syria against Islamic State – criticised by Moscow as illegitimate since they did not take place with the assent of the Assad government – and in July 2015 Turkey also attacked Islamic State targets on Syrian territory. At this point large swathes of the country were under the control of militant Islamists, intensifying a political and human rights crisis which was spilling across borders. The conflict had escalated into unimaginable levels of violence, documented in stark detail in reports by the IICI and by Human Rights Watch, which put the death toll as of October 2015 at more than 250,000, including over 100,000 civilians; the number living under long-term siege at 640,000; and those internally displaced at an estimated 7.6 million, with 4.2 million refugees having fled to neighbouring countries (HRW 2016b, 547).

In the earlier stages of the increasingly bitter civil war Russia's policy was largely conceived within the framework of its broader foreign policy aims rather than constituting a clear strategy for its role in Syria. Those aims – to prevent regime change and the disintegration of the Syria state, while achieving a political resolution involving the broader opposition – proved irreconcilable. With Assad under threat and negotiations in stalemate, the Putin leadership began to implement military plans which were to prove a major turning point. On 30 September 2015, Lavrov addressed a UN Security Council meeting on peace and security in the MENA region, in which he sought to legitimise Russia's policy in Syria by arguing that the 'euphoria' of the Arab Spring had been replaced by horror at the interconfessional violence which gripped the region; yet again he claimed that instability was caused by external intervention and terrorism and appealed for political dialogue among the leading external and regional powers aimed at a negotiated settlement (Lavrov 2015b). That same day, Russia launched its military intervention, which was to change materially the course of the conflict.

Phase 2: Russia's military intervention in Syria

In a keynote interview at the height of the chemical weapons crisis, Putin had stated that 'we are definitely not going to and will not get involved in any conflicts' (Putin 2013a). Yet his decision to launch a military intervention – which over the course of a few months comprised thousands of air sorties carried out from the Khmeimim air base in Latakia, as well as the deployment of long-range bombers from Russia, combat helicopters, tanks and heavy munitions – effectively tipped the military balance in Assad's favour. In a newspaper interview, General Valerii Gerasimov, the head of Russia's General Staff, confirmed that the operation was decided on and planned well in advance (Baranets 2017). Following the signing in August 2015 of a bilateral Russia–Syria agreement on the deployment of a Russian aviation group in Syria (RIA Novosti 2016), aircraft and personnel were transferred to the Khmeimim air base (Phillips 2016, 217). A joint Russian-Iranian-Iraqi-Syrian intelligence coordination centre was set up in Baghdad, supposedly to prosecute the fight against Islamic State; Baghdad subsequently granted Russia conditional permission to use Iraqi air space to launch strikes in Syria (UNSC 2016c, 6). Shortly after Russia's intervention began, Iranian ground forces launched offensives near Aleppo using Russian air cover. It was reported that Iranian Quds Force commander Qassem Soleimani, who at that time had a leading role in directing Syria's military campaign, had visited Moscow to agree the parameters of joint intervention, though Russia officially denied this (Bassam and Perry 2015). Putin met Supreme Leader Ayatollah Khamenei in Tehran in November 2015, with reports suggesting that agreement between the two countries over the Syria conflict was accompanied by a resounding joint condemnation of US policy.

Russia's intervention marked a crucial shift that changed the reckoning of all actors involved in the Syrian civil war. One authoritative account has assessed its impact not only in military terms but in terms of 'the effect that Russia's assumption of irreversible authority *inside* Syria has had upon the international community's geopolitical calculation and upon individual governments' strategies for dealing with the crisis' (Lister 2017, 395; emphasis in original). Unforeseen incidents also conspired in Russia's favour. In response to the downing of a Russian aircraft by Turkish fighter jets in November 2015 – raising concerns over a possible escalation by Moscow against a NATO ally – the deployment by Russian aerospace forces of surface-to-air missiles around Latakia closed the western part of Syrian airspace to coalition aircraft: 'By doing so, Russia became the most important military factor in Syria' (Shumilin and Shumilina 2017, 120).

At the same time, de Mistura stepped up diplomatic efforts towards a political resolution of the conflict. Despite criticism from some quarters of his equivocation over the status of Assad in any transition process and not having a plan underwritten by international guarantees and endorsed by the UN Secretary-General (Akpinar 2016, 2295), his efforts culminated in multilateral negotiations, co-sponsored by the US and Russia, at the Vienna meetings on 30 October and 14 November 2015. This led to the establishment of the International Syria Support Group (ISSG), which consisted of major external and regional countries – including Iran – the Arab League, the EU and the UN. On 18 December, UNSC resolution 2254 was adopted, which supported a ceasefire between government and opposition (while excluding Islamic State, al-Nusra and other terrorist groups) and scheduled peace talks for January 2016, with a call for elections to be held under UN supervision (Blockmans 2016b). Backed up by resolutions 2258 and 2268, it also appealed to parties in the conflict to allow humanitarian access to besieged areas and cease attacks against the civilian population. A meeting in Istanbul in November brought forty-four non-state armed opposition groups together to form a military council to coordinate positions for negotiations under the Vienna process (UNSC 2015d).

The ISSG effectively created a framework for international talks on political transition and constitutional reform in Syria, based on the provisions in the June 2012 Geneva Final Communiqué and the Vienna Statements of November 2015 (IICI 2016, 3–4). It established a Ceasefire Task Force, with Russia and the US as co-chairs, and a Humanitarian Task Force chaired by the UN. The statesmanship of Lavrov and Kerry (who met eighteen times over the period of a year) was acknowledged by UN Secretary-General Ban Ki-moon; he also welcomed a meeting convened in Riyadh to bring opposition groups together and approved the decision to effect a transition to inclusive and non-sectarian governance within six months, as well as the drafting of a new constitution, cessation of hostilities and UN-supervised elections within eighteen months (UNSC 2015c). Following a further meeting in Vienna in May 2016, the ISSG declared that a transitional governing body with full executive powers was to ensure the continuity of government institutions in a 'Syrian-owned and Syrian-led' transition, as laid out in the Geneva Final Communiqué, with Russia–US cooperation leading international efforts; it also noted Russia's commitment to 'work with the Syrian authorities to minimize aviation operations over areas predominantly inhabited by civilians' (ISSG 2016). Russia also supported UNSC resolution 2258, which renewed the authorisation of cross-border passage of humanitarian aid into Syria, despite its concerns over the supply of arms to terrorist groups via that route.

This period of intensive diplomacy effectively gave Russia most of what it wanted. Lavrov's address to the UN Security Council, on the day resolution 2254 was adopted, was explicit. The UN's international legal weight henceforth underpinned collective efforts to prepare negotiations, confirming the international commitment to a political resolution based on the principles outlined in the 2012 Geneva Final Communiqué. In Lavrov's words, Russia's military support for the 'legitimate' Syrian government had made a substantive contribution to fighting terrorism: 'This approach has no alternative – if we really are putting above all else the interests of the Syrian people and the state of Syria above geopolitical ambitions' (Lavrov 2015c). Nevertheless, differences over Assad's future remained, with no formal change in the positions of the Western powers regarding his departure, amid reservations over whether he would agree to rein in military operations and enter into substantive negotiations. Moreover, the issue of transitional justice implied by resolution 2254 – 'a sine qua non of the future of Syria' (Akgün et al 2017, 22) – presented the formidable task of marshalling resources to deal with a divided society ridden with sectarian tensions and demanding accountability for the crimes committed.

Since de Mistura's appointment, some opinion-formers in the West – concerned about the increased terrorist threat, as well as the numbers of refugees fleeing to Europe – had begun to consider more extensive cooperation with Russia over political transition in Syria, albeit with reservations (Barnes-Dacey and Levy 2015, 2–3). Russia's intervention meant that a military defeat of Assad, whose forces were gradually making strategic gains, was now unlikely. Moscow's insistence on prioritising Islamist terrorism, rather than Assad, as the main threat lent some international credibility to its support for the Syrian government; de Mistura himself had conceded in February 2015 that Assad was '"a crucial part of the solution" when originally, he had been identified as a crucial part of the problem' (Gaub 2018a, 61), thereby losing the confidence of the armed opposition (Lister 2017, 331). Kerry stated the following month that Assad could be included in negotiations about a transition, even though direct talks with him were not in the offing (Gordon 2015). The Western powers were still publicly damning in their condemnation of Assad but, as the balance of power shifted, understood that a change in their approach was necessary, even if there was no clear idea what form that might take. The second Obama administration was still opposed to extensive military involvement in the MENA region and needed some kind of political resolution in Syria.

A different mood pervaded talks about an inclusive transition at the Vienna meeting on 14 November 2015, the day after the terrorist attacks in Paris that left 130 people dead. Several states appeared more willing to negotiate directly with the Syrian government about eliminating the threat of Islamic State and effecting a political transition (De Groof 2016, 43). French President François Hollande visited Moscow later that month for discussions on coordinating air strikes against Islamic State. Another possible factor was that the Western powers did not want to endanger the nuclear deal with Iran, a key Syria ally (Akpinar 2016, 2296). Moscow also appeared to change its approach, being more prepared to engage with opposition groups committed to a peaceful resolution, which would strengthen its role in mediation (Khodinskaya-Golenishcheva 2018, 23–24). The Russian foreign ministry asserted that it was prepared to include moderate Syrian opposition fighters in an anti-Islamic State coalition and coordinate the efforts of Syrian government forces and the Free Syrian Army, which it had earlier dismissed as composed of extremist groups (MFA 2015c).

The Geneva III talks opened formally on 1 February 2016, after a delay due to opposition demands for an end to Syrian and Russian air strikes and

Russian objections over who should represent the opposition. The Syrian government and opposition groups refused a face-to-face meeting, but a majority of the latter were present within the High Negotiations Committee (HNC), formed in 2015 to represent the opposition in the Geneva talks. Delegates from the Russian-backed wing of the opposition not party to the HNC were also invited, despite claims that their presence compromised the legitimacy of the process. Although the talks were suspended on 3 February in response to the Syrian army's offensive in Aleppo, an agreement on a 'nationwide cessation of hostilities' apart from operations in terrorist-held areas – intended to pave the way for a nationwide ceasefire and humanitarian access to siege areas – was reached in Munich in talks between Russia, the US and other ISSG members on 11–12 February (EEAS 2016; Phillips 2016, 227–228). Russia and the US began to coordinate efforts to ensure that the ceasefire would hold. A centre at Russia's Khmeimim airbase began operating as a venue for monitoring and facilitating reconciliation talks between opposition and government forces (Akpinar 2016, 2296–2297), with frequent video conferences held between Khmeimim and the US military stationed in Amman. Further rounds of negotiations were held in Geneva on 9 March and 14 March, as the reduction in violence and an improvement in humanitarian access held out the promise of political progress. However, the following month talks broke down, with Russia-supported government air strikes against opposition positions threatening the cessation of hostilities agreement as the Aleppo campaign gained momentum (Black 2016).

On 15 March Russian began the withdrawal of the main body of its forces from Syria, though Russian air force operations would be maintained. There are several possible explanations for this unexpected move. First, the withdrawal may have been down to the Russian leadership's awareness of its responsibilities in the peace process. Its intensive diplomacy over the previous months may be seen as more than an attempt simply to legitimise Russia's military support to Assad; Putin himself invested considerable political capital to ensure that the cessation of hostilities endured, even telephoning leaders of the major Middle Eastern states (Phillips 2016, 229). A second explanation is that the withdrawal was a renewed attempt by Russia to put pressure on the Syrian leadership to negotiate a transition. Churkin voiced Moscow's frustration over Assad's obduracy in an interview shortly before the withdrawal: 'If the Syrian authorities, despite their internal political arrangements … follow Russia's leadership in resolving this crisis they have a chance to make a fitting retreat from it. If they somehow stray from this path … a very difficult situation may arise, including for themselves' (Churkin 2016; ICG 2016b, 3–4). A third is that, with one eye on public opinion, the Putin leadership wanted to avoid becoming enmeshed in an intractable military conflict of uncertain duration.

All of these explanations conceivably played a part. Preventing Assad's overthrow and forestalling the breakdown of state order were central to Russia's approach to the Syria conflict and in the Middle East more widely; failure would have been a massive blow to Russia's credibility. Moscow was under intense international pressure to contribute to a breakthrough after five years of war and devastation and sought to leverage its political gains to achieve a resolution and claim a diplomatic success both at home and abroad. At the same time, the stark reality was that Russia's primary aim of helping Assad to consolidate his power had been achieved: a smaller military presence was sufficient to maintain its strategy. Indeed, Moscow's continuing support to Assad in prosecuting the siege of Aleppo, with its air strikes targeting the opposition rather than Islamic State, marked a return to large-scale fighting and overshadowed any optimism about the achievements of Geneva III. Western states censured the 'systematic destruction', 'collective punishment' and 'war crimes' perpetrated by the Assad government, while Churkin praised the political negotiations and again blamed opposition groups for being unwilling to compromise and joining forces with jihadis financed by external sponsors (UNSC 2016d).

On 28 July 2016, Russia announced the start of a large-scale evacuation of the civilian population of Aleppo through humanitarian corridors, working in coordination with the UN. Precious little appeared to change in the conduct of the conflict, however. The relationship between Lavrov and Kerry, which had promised sustained efforts to secure the cessation of hostilities and create a political basis for a ceasefire, was fraying, with repeated mutual accusations of armed support for opposing forces. Lavrov again excoriated the West's 'heinous practice of geopolitical engineering' to inflict forcible regime change, while Kerry accused Lavrov of living 'in a parallel universe' and ignoring the fact that international agreements were being 'shredded by independent actors and spoilers who do not want a ceasefire' in a conflict that 'has provided the greatest humanitarian catastrophe since the Second World War'; he added that 'everyone is entitled to their own opinion, but they are not entitled to their own facts ... If we are going to deal with this situation, I do not think that we can let anybody here have their own set of facts about Syria' – a more or less direct charge of blatant deceit on Moscow's part (UNSC 2016e). Other Western representatives deplored Russia's abuse of its responsibilities as a P5 power and compared Aleppo to Russia's military campaign in Grozny during the Chechen conflict, an acutely sensitive matter for Russia (UNSC 2016f). De Mistura himself lamented the imminent failure of resolution 2254 and came close to rejecting outright the Russian account of targeting only terrorists. In a long and irate response to the charge of Russia's connivance in abuses committed by Assad's forces, Churkin claimed that the Western powers not only sponsored the opposition but even provided heavy weaponry to jihadi groups (UNSC 2016g).

The Aleppo campaign – against a background of continuing fierce fighting in Idlib, Hama, Homs, Ghouta and parts of Damascus – marked a tipping-point in the ferocious war of words between Russia and the Western powers. Russian statements in the earlier stages of the Syria conflict were generally confined to defending its positions on international legal norms and regional security. Now, with its policies under sustained attack, the information campaign was stepped up by Russian government agencies and media outlets to discredit Western narratives and actions. Lavrov intensified his long-standing criticism of the amorality of Western policy by asserting that 'the decency and legitimacy of any member of the international community should be measured by their respect for the principles of sovereign equality of states and non-interference in the internal affairs of others' (Lavrov 2016b). Responding to the international condemnation of the Syrian government's prosecution of 'starve-and-surrender' sieges, Churkin accused opposition backers of doing nothing to stop armed Islamist groups from using force to derail the cessation of hostilities and prevent civilians from leaving eastern Aleppo through the humanitarian corridors set up under Russian initiatives (UNSC 2016h; IICI 2018, 9).

Western claims that Russian air strikes were indiscriminate and caused heavy civilian casualties were routinely dismissed by Moscow as fake information intended to manipulate international public opinion (MFA 2017a). Moscow also obscured the distinction between jihadis and recognised opposition groups; the civilian population of opposition-held areas were identified as combatants and therefore as legitimate military targets. Lavrov asserted that, whereas Russia was supporting the incumbent government in fighting international terrorism and contributing to regional stability, the US was tolerating Jabhat al-Nusra with a view to its eventual use as an instrument to overthrow Assad (Lavrov 2016c). The formidable foreign ministry spokesperson Maria Zakharova (MFA 2017b) accused the West of peddling 'lies and dirt, from minor fantasies to the global manipulation of public opinion' in attempting to discredit Assad, even claiming that 'the US is defending Islamic State – there is now no doubt about it' (MFA 2016b). Indeed, some commentators have suggested that Russian nationalist elites and the defence establishment, including Gerasimov himself, believe that Islamic State is a creation of Western intelligence services and that 'it is in the interest of the United States to create "manageable turmoil" by means of destabilizing the Middle East in a bid to redraw the geopolitical map' (Souleimanov and Petrylova 2015, 68–69; Gaub 2018a, 62).

The field of fire was broadened to include a litany of wrongs committed by the Western powers. A report detailing 'crimes' committed by the US-led coalition and the moderate Syrian opposition, some apparently exaggerated, was published and distributed among UN member states (Baikova and Asatryan 2016). Following a BRICS summit in October 2016, Putin attacked Western attempts to link Syria with the confrontation over Russia's annexation of Crimea, stating explicitly that Western policy in Ukraine was part of a long-term strategy to contain Russia (Putin 2016a). Official Russian sources even began to attack UN agencies and respected international organisations such as the OPCW when their reports, though objective and based on scrupulous analysis of available data, ran counter to Russian interests. Yet, this virulent information campaign was often accompanied by a sober analysis of events and praise for Western states and international agencies, reflecting a bizarre interplay of cooperation and confrontation.

A book-length study would scarcely suffice to convey the relentlessness of Moscow's media attacks and assess the veracity of its claims. Russia's assertion that its military support for Assad's forces in the Aleppo campaign was directed against Islamist terrorists was contradicted not only by Western government sources and think tanks (such as the Institute for the Study of War and the Atlantic Council) but also by evidence presented by the UN and human rights organisations from open-source analysis. This evidence suggests that the majority of Russian air strikes targeted the broader opposition, Free Syrian Army (FSA) militias and moderate or secular Islamist groups who were not directly linked with Islamic State and the al-Nusra Front, in areas of key strategic significance to Assad, with the aim of shoring up his administration and avoiding committing ground forces (see Gaub 2018a, 57–58; Souleimanov 2016, 108–109). In August 2016 UN officials gave a graphic depiction of the extent of the Aleppo catastrophe – an 'apex of horror' – and of the impact of Russian assistance to Syrian government offensives 'unparalleled in the over five years of bloodshed and carnage in the Syrian conflict [that] has long since moved from the cynical to the sinful'; they cited Physicians for Human Rights' documentation of 373 attacks on medical facilities since the adoption of UNSC resolution 2139, 336 of which 'were by Syrian Government and allied forces', and a Human Rights Watch report stating 'that the joint Syrian-Russian air campaign had violated international law by dropping incendiary munitions on civilian areas' (UNSC 2016h 3, 5–6). One IICI report referred to daily air strikes in Aleppo conducted by Syrian and Russian air forces using aerial bombs, air-to-surface rockets, cluster and incendiary bombs and improvised air-delivered munitions (UNGA 2017, 5). Human Rights Watch also reported that Russia had used cluster munitions. UN sources referred to reports by the Syrian Observatory for Human Rights that casualties from Russian air strikes far exceeded those from US-led coalition strikes. At the same time, there were numerous reports of atrocities committed by forces opposed to

Assad, allowing Moscow to maintain that jihadi groups represented the main threat to Syria and the wider region.

On 9 September 2016, after months of negotiations, Russia and the US reached an agreement to revive the cessation of hostilities – which required Syrian forces to discontinue air sorties against the non-jihadi opposition – as well as facilitate humanitarian access and improve military cooperation. It came into effect on 12 September and for several days reduced the violence. However, on 19 September, the Syrian government declared an end to the cessation, claiming it was responding to violations by armed opposition groups, and three days later announced a renewed offensive on eastern Aleppo. This marked the beginning of a decisive escalation. De Mistura reported to the UN that, following the agreement announced in Geneva by Russia and the US, Assad had announced his intention to 'liberate every inch of Syria' (cited in UNSC 2016g). Intensive deliberations within the ISSG and at the UN Security Council produced no concrete results. The breakdown of the 9 September agreement led to a US announcement on 3 October that it would suspend bilateral links with Moscow.

On 15 October, talks in Lausanne between Russia, the US, the UN and regional actors concentrated on ways to address the escalating humanitarian crisis in Aleppo, institute a nationwide truce and resume talks on a political settlement. In early November, the UN devised a four-point plan to provide the besieged areas of eastern Aleppo with humanitarian assistance, but it was not possible to persuade all parties to agree on its implementation. Russia vetoed draft resolutions of 8 October and 5 December 2016 which called for the reinstatement of the cessation of hostilities, including aerial bombardments, and called for a resumption of negotiations and facilitation of humanitarian access. But demands at the UN for the warring parties to halt indiscriminate attacks on civilians and lift sieges were little more than a plaintive appeal amidst the violence and humanitarian abuses. On 15 November, Moscow announced a large-scale offensive, resulting in a resumption of air strikes, which lasted several weeks and culminated in government forces recapturing the city. A mass evacuation of civilians from the eastern part of Aleppo eventually took place with Russia's assistance, the siege was ended and a ceasefire was announced on 30 December 2016. Recognition by the international community of the end of this phase of hostilities was sealed the next day by the adoption of UNSC resolution 2336, which backed Russia's and Turkey's efforts to end the violence and introduce a country-wide ceasefire.

These final stages of the Aleppo campaign may be considered the point where Moscow's support for Assad's forces far outweighed its efforts in peace negotiations: Russia effectively acted as a military ally in supporting a carefully planned operation against the opposition. Kerry's and de Mistura's statements cited earlier, alluding to Russia's duplicity, certainly support this assessment. But the triumphalist tone of Russian announcements also reinforces this impression. Defence minister Sergei Shoigu praised the Russian armed forces' role in furthering the political process and delivering humanitarian relief in Syria. But his central narrative was that Russia had halted the spread of international terrorism in the MENA region, with militant groups having been routed in Hama and Homs and forced to withdraw from Latakia, and the strategic cities of Aleppo and Al-Qaryatayn having been retaken. In Shoigu's words, the military operation had 'resolved a number of geopolitical problems', with Moscow and Damascus signing long-term agreements for Russia's use of the Khmeimim and Tartus facilities, thereby bolstering Russia's military presence in a strategically important part of the world: 'the disintegration of the Syrian state was prevented and the chain of colour revolutions that multiplied in the Middle East and Africa was cut short' (President of Russia 2016). Other comments by senior defence figures at the time reflected how Aleppo had underlined the importance of Russia's military might, not only in defending national interests but also in restoring its status as a world power (Sakwa 2017, 231).

In a nationwide broadcast on 23 December, Putin exceeded the bounds of credibility in declaring that the Aleppo campaign was

> achieved without military action ... We simply organised and carried out the evacuation of tens of thousands of people ... This is the biggest ... international humanitarian action in the modern world. It could not have been carried out without the active efforts of the Turkish leadership, the Turkish President, the President of Iran and all other Iranian leaders, and without our active participation. (Putin 2016b)

And indeed, cooperation between Moscow, Ankara and Tehran became a key factor in the next phase of the Syria conflict.

Phase 3: The Astana process and the later stages of the conflict

The tumultuous fifteen months between the launch of Russia's first air strikes and the ceasefire in Aleppo marked a decisive shift in regional affairs. Assad's forces and their proxies had made substantive gains across strategically important parts of the country, though with some outlying territories still in the hands of various externally supported opposition groups, while the US and Russian campaigns against Islamist extremists had diminished the latter's fighting capacities. In early 2017 a reduction in military activity across many parts of the country, in major centres such as Aleppo,

Deir ez-Zor, Homs, Idlib, Raqqah and Rif Dimashq, was primarily attributable to the 30 December ceasefire, though the latter did not include terrorist groups or Kurdish areas. The political process also underwent a notable shift. Following the adoption on 20 December 2016 of the Moscow Declaration, in which Russia, Turkey and Iran expressed their readiness to become guarantors of an agreement between the Syrian government and opposition to resume the political process (MFA 2016c), a meeting took place in Astana on 23 and 24 January 2017 between the Syrian government and thirteen opposition groups, convened by Russia, Turkey and Iran, with the US, Kazakhstan and the UN all present; a trilateral mechanism comprising Russia, Turkey and Iran was put in place to monitor compliance with the ceasefire mentioned in UNSC resolution 2254 (MFA 2017c). This was fleshed out in a concept paper agreed in Astana on 16 February. As well as implementing the ceasefire, the mechanism would pursue confidence-building measures, carry out an investigation of violations based on an exchange of information with the UN, arrange the release or exchange of detainees and facilitate humanitarian access to civilians (MFA 2017d).

This arrangement became known as the Astana format – the central forum through which Moscow henceforth tried to steer talks towards a resolution of the Syria conflict. The leading Western powers were concerned that the Astana talks would sideline the UN Geneva format and enable Russia to manipulate the peace process (Aksenyonok 2019, 14). Lavrov asserted that the Astana format should facilitate, rather than replace, the Geneva process; the ISSG had not met at ministerial level for some time but its sub-groups on ceasefire monitoring and humanitarian affairs had continued to function, and Lavrov looked forward to an improved partnership with the incoming Trump administration, which appeared to be more focused on combating terrorism (Lavrov 2017b). But it was clear that Russia, having reached an impasse in its bid to secure Assad's leadership through a partnership with the US, would now have a freer hand in managing the conflict along with Turkey and Iran, with the Geneva process giving a seal of international approval on any decisions reached.

The Astana meetings were in fact complemented by UN-facilitated intra-Syrian political negotiations in Geneva in February to March 2017, the first for ten months. A clear agenda emerged in Geneva and a process towards a new constitution, free and fair elections and security and confidence-building measures was initiated, with further rounds of intra-Syrian negotiations held in May to explore legal and constitutional issues in a political transition. Russian and US officials had been carrying out joint work on a draft constitution for some time; it provided for the separation of powers and a degree of decentralisation, with the establishment of autonomous regional entities, including a Kurdish one, with broad powers of self-government

(Frolov 2017b). Lavrov underlined that the goal was not to create conditions for the partition of Syria but to move towards a complete cessation of hostilities across Syrian territory, facilitating humanitarian access and creating conditions for the voluntary return of refugees and displaced persons. Further meetings also took place in Astana in February and March, where a decision was taken to expand the role of Iran, and in Tehran on 18 and 19 April, attended by a delegation of UN observers, to tackle the implementation of the ceasefire regime, as well as confidence-building measures. In addition, an international conference was held in Brussels on 4–5 April, with participants pledging substantial funding to support humanitarian, stabilisation and development activities. Following the fifth round of the Geneva talks a UN report stated that 'invitees demonstrated a new maturity and commitment to continuing the process notwithstanding all the political and military difficulties' (UNSC 2017b, 16).

This optimistic statement masked the fact that many of the fundamental problems of the civil war remained in place. Reports of significant numbers of civilian casualties from indiscriminate attacks showed that the ceasefire was under strain, and restrictions by the conflicting parties on aid delivery and humanitarian access for the UN and partner organisations continued. De Mistura held talks with the Syrian government and opposition in May and July 2017 but was unable to bridge the differences between them. Assad was now in a much stronger position to negotiate the political future of the state. Despite their role as Astana guarantor states, Russia and Iran had continuing military involvement in the conflict on the side of the government. Turkey's antagonism towards Assad in the early stages of the conflict moderated as Ankara stepped up its campaign against Islamic State in Jarabulus and continued to prioritise its suppression of the Kurdish Democratic Union Party (PYD) in northern Syria (see Hazbun 2018, 8–9). As one authoritative commentator argued at the time,

> it is now clear that a viable political process cannot be about a transition away from Assad, which has consistently been the point at which previous initiatives have unravelled … The political vision must now incorporate the reality on the ground, which is that the regime will remain the dominant actor for the foreseeable future. (Barnes-Dacey 2017, 2, 3)

At the same time – as Russian proposals for a draft constitution involving decentralisation made plain – power and authority across the country were divided, with opposition strongholds still backed by external actors.

With no sign of a political resolution in sight, military tensions had to be addressed. Eight Astana meetings held in 2017 aimed to tackle these issues by involving the non-extremist elements of the armed opposition, taking into account the interests of the major regional powers. Moscow had been talking directly to powerful opposition groups, including Islamists, for some time. On 4 May 2017, a memorandum was signed by Russia, Iran and Turkey creating four temporary de-escalation zones in the most conflict-prone areas, promising unhindered humanitarian access, with a cessation of hostilities and a joint working group to be established (MFA 2017e). Russia was to coordinate with Turkey over the largest zone in the north, covering Idlib and parts of Latakia, Aleppo and Hama, and with Jordan over the southern zone near the Syria–Jordan border. The signatories committed to separate the armed opposition from Jabhat al-Nusra and other jihadi groups. Moscow also directed its attention to parleying among the various regional and external actors, seeking agreements that might lead not only to de-escalation but also ultimately to a settlement of the conflict – something that the rather narrow Astana format could not achieve.

Alongside the Russia/Iran/Turkey-backed de-escalation zones, a meeting between Putin and Trump on 7 July at the G20 summit in Hamburg produced a separate ceasefire/de-escalation agreement in southwest Syria between Russia, the US and Jordan; the Amman process was created involving these three countries and Israel, and the following month an agreement was reached to set up a monitoring centre in Amman. This was negotiated outside of the Astana format, without the participation of Iran and Turkey, establishing a zone free of Iran-backed militias, a priority for Israel. Egypt hosted a separate platform for talks on de-escalation zones in Homs and eastern Ghouta (Isaev et al 2018, 24–26). Discussions were also held with the US about the establishment of a de-confliction line in the east of Syria. Russia pursued another separate dialogue with Saudi Arabia and Qatar, with the Saudis joining efforts to unite the fragmented opposition and encourage peace talks. The 'regionalization' of Russia's Syria policy – reflecting a broader trend in its emerging MENA strategy – thus began to take shape: Russia's aim was to move the conflict towards a political solution, avoid a protracted military campaign and 'diminish its direct engagement in and ownership of the Syria problem, while keeping and expanding its multiple regional partnerships in the broader Middle East' (Stepanova 2018b, 1–2; see also Isaev et al 2018, 22). It should be noted that cooperation with the US was an important contributing factor in these developments.

Despite a general reduction in fighting over the course of 2017, the various de-escalation processes were messy and contested, reflecting an uneasy balance of interests among the external actors against a background of alternating violence and negotiation. Russia faced several hurdles in implementing the accords. The first was to create viable guarantee mechanisms to ensure that conflict did not break out, as breaches of ceasefires inside the de-escalation zones continued. Local agreements between the Syrian government and non-state armed opposition groups in besieged areas were not subject to supervision by the UN, raising concerns about security guarantees. The second hurdle was that the zones did not cover other conflict-prone areas. Finally, the perennial problem of the intransigence of the Assad leadership – which could not dictate the terms of the agreements but sought to take advantage of the talks to pursue its strategic objectives – threatened progress. The external powers' continuing support for opposition groups raised expectations that the latter could shape the peace talks, whereas the situation on the ground was worsening and fighting among them continued. An attempt by Moscow to draw Assad into national negotiations through the Astana process was rejected by the opposition and those of its international backers who demanded his exclusion; without a national political settlement to underpin them, the regionalised agreements were 'divorced from the wider political track' (Barnes-Dacey 2017, 4).

Moscow was also faced with the quite different aims pursued by its Astana coalition partners. As discussed in Chapter 1, Turkey's primary aim is to cement a Sunni zone of influence in northern Syria and prevent the formation of a Kurdish stronghold there. In January 2018, Ankara launched Operation Olive Branch to clear out the PKK-affiliated YPG from the Kurdish-majority area around Afrin, eventually capturing the town, where Russian troops had been stationed to protect the YPG. The operation took place with Moscow's tacit acquiescence, apparently in return for Ankara's acceptance of Assad's offensive against Idlib and continuing cooperation in securing a settlement in Syria. During the various negotiations in 2017 and into 2018, the Russian air force continued to support Syrian government troops in intensive operations in Idlib, eastern Ghouta, Homs, Hama and elsewhere, ostensibly to clear out jihadi groups which were not part of the ceasefires, thereby increasing the chances that a resolution of the conflict would inevitably favour the incumbent authorities. Idlib and the surrounding area had become the last major stronghold of anti-Assad forces, as well as the destination of displaced refugees from other areas retaken by Syrian government troops. Moscow had also to take into consideration Iran's ambition to consolidate its positions in Syria to achieve strategic depth; Tehran was at times ignoring de-escalation agreements, prompting Israel to counter the spread of Iranian influence towards its borders (Boms 2017, 331).

Another major bone of contention between Moscow and the Western powers resurfaced at this time. Numerous further allegations of chemical weapons (CW) use were made against the Syrian authorities, despite Syria's accession to the CWC in 2013 and purported commitment to carry out chemical demilitarisation. The OPCW had established a fact-finding mission (FFM) in April 2014 to investigate these incidents, with Assad's reluctant agreement, and submitted regular detailed reports based on its findings to the UN. In February 2015, the FFM stated that it was able to confirm the systematic use of chlorine, but its mandate did not include attributing blame to the perpetrator. In several other cases, the FFM was unable to establish whether chemicals had been used as a weapon. Moscow had supported the adoption of UNSC resolution 2209 in March 2015, which reiterated the Security Council's authority to impose measures under Chapter VII of the UN Charter in the event of non-compliance with resolution 2118. At the same time, Churkin stressed the need for OPCW impartiality and the inadmissibility of Chapter VII sanctions without allegations being substantiated, arguing that, as in the August 2013 Ghouta incident, there was no proof of CW use; according to him, the FFM's findings were based on 'subjective facts provided by certain witnesses' (UNSC 2015b).

Still, Russia voted for the adoption in August 2015 of UNSC resolution 2235, authorising the establishment for one year of a non-judicial, independent OPCW-UN Joint Investigative Mechanism (JIM) – something there was no precedent for – which was to identify where possible perpetrators of attacks using CW. Extensive and meticulous procedures, mechanisms and planning were put in place by the OPCW, based on its considerable expertise, with proof of the use of CW only to be confirmed to the UN if there was no reasonable doubt. Twenty-nine out of 116 alleged incidents mentioned in FFM reports were investigated up to February 2016, including one in Darayya, a suburb of Damascus, in which exposure to the sarin or a sarin-like substance was deemed highly likely (UNSC 2016a). An OPCW report to the UN in August 2016, based on an exhaustive investigation, concluded that the Syrian armed forces had been involved in using toxic chemicals delivered as weapons in barrel bombs in three cases, in Talmenes, Qmenas and Sarmin, and that Islamic State had used artillery shells primed with sulphur mustard gas in Marea (UNSC 2016b). Later reports identified the Hama and Khmeimim airbases, both controlled by the Syrian government, as the likely location where the helicopters loaded with barrel bombs had flown from. The Russian foreign ministry responded by claiming that unconvincing evidence had been presented by the JIM to underpin an 'anti-Syrian decision' and complaining that the highly respected OPCW was 'being turned by a group of countries that are set on changing the Damascus government into an instrument of political and economic pressure and blackmail' (MFA 2016a).

The gravest subsequent incident took place on 4 April 2017 when an air strike hit Khan Sheikhun in southern Idlib, which drew a punitive missile attack by the US on the military airbase in Homs where the strike was alleged to have originated. Russia condemned the US attack as aggression against a sovereign state in contravention of international law. Zakharova accused the West of 'demonising' Damascus and staging provocations favouring 'bandits, criminals and media opportunists' hostile to Syria, and of 'planting' a draft resolution at the UN; harking back to the unjustified allegations of weapon of mass destruction (WMD) use in Iraq in 2003, she maintained that Russia presents 'facts' rather than the 'fake news' purveyed to the media by Western governments (MFA 2017a). In comments widely repeated by other Russian officials, Lavrov criticised 'an attempt to create a distorted reality', querying the impartiality of its investigative team, both sections of which were at the time headed by UK nationals (Lavrov 2017a). The FFM subsequently investigated the Khan Sheikhun incident and identified approximately 100 fatalities and at least 200 other casualties who had survived acute exposure, supporting the presumption of toxic chemical dispersal in the environment, although it was unable to establish for certain the means of its deployment (UNSC 2017a). An IICI report concluded that there were reasonable grounds to believe that Syrian forces used sarin, thereby committing a war crime as well as violating the Chemical Weapons Convention (IICI 2017, 15–16). In October 2017 the JIM submitted a report to the UN Secretary-General attributing direct responsibility to the Syrian government for the Khan Sheikhun sarin attack; in response, Russia vetoed the extension of the JIM mandate.

Further CW attacks took place, notably in Douma in April 2018, which again drew missile strikes by the US, UK and France on Syrian military targets, to Moscow's anger. While occasionally praising the OPCW for certain decisions favouring Moscow's interpretation of incidents, Zakharova again accused the Western countries of bias and of 'doing everything possible to turn [the OPCW] into a tool for achieving their own geopolitical goals'; in her words, the Czech chairperson of the OPCW had abandoned neutrality by defending Western interests: 'the unsubstantiated information campaign around Syria's "chemical dossier" and the staged "poisoning" of Russian nationals in Great Britain last year [a reference to the poisoning of Sergei Skripal] are links in a chain' (MFA 2019a). Russia's position received the backing of a number of non-Western states. Moscow's public information campaign included a news conference in July 2019 in The Hague, home of the OPCW, condemning further 'provocations' and unsubstantiated allegations by Western states of CW use by Syrian forces, querying procedures used in attributing responsibility and condemning 'politically biased falsification of reports' (MFA 2020c). Meanwhile, the Investigation and Identification Team (IIT), set up in June 2018 to investigate other instances in which the FFM had determined the likely use of CW and identify the perpetrators, found 'reasonable grounds' to believe that aerial bombs containing sarin had been used in Ltamenah in March 2017 and concluded that 'military operations of such a strategic nature … only occur pursuant to orders from the highest levels of the Syrian Arab Armed Forces' (OPCW

2020). A subsequent IIT report concluded that in February 2018 a Syrian military helicopter had dropped a cylinder on eastern Saraqib, releasing chlorine and injuring local inhabitants. With Russia's relations with the West increasingly under strain, Moscow thus effectively found itself defending the Assad government's commission of war crimes, prioritising Russia's immediate national interests over international legal commitments to protect the nonproliferation regime (Schmitt 2020, 939; Notte 2020, 216).

Following meetings in November 2017 between Putin and Assad, and subsequently between Putin, Erdoğan and Iranian President Hassan Rouhani, Russia made a new attempt to push negotiations towards a settlement by convoking the Congress of the Syrian National Dialogue in Sochi in January 2018, aimed at holding unofficial consultations among various Syrian groups and their sponsors on political issues. Despite de Mistura's presence, a substantial part of the opposition represented in the HNC and the PYD (both of which at the time still controlled large areas of Syria) and many states from outside the region refused to attend. The opposition feared that the congress would divert attention away from the UN-sponsored Geneva process and that no political change would result; indeed, the Assad government yet again proved reluctant to offer any meaningful concessions and was now directing its offensive against Idlib and other as yet unrecovered areas (ICG 2018b). Nevertheless, following an agreement reached by Putin and Trump at the Asia-Pacific Economic Cooperation summit in November 2017, the Sochi congress final statement recommitted the participants to create a constitutional committee, made up of delegates from the Assad government and selected opposition groups, to examine governance issues, confidence-building measures and an allocation of power which could provide the basis for draft constitutional reform proposals (MFA 2018c; see Stepanova 2018b, 3–4). This was to be coordinated with de Mistura working within the Geneva process, though little headway was being made there and Lavrov made it clear that much of the work was being done in the Astana format (Lavrov 2018b; ICG 2018b). Multilateral negotiations were also held between Russia and the Saudi-convened Riyadh group, as well as with the Gulf Cooperation Council.

On the ground, humanitarian access remained a major problem due to Syrian government restrictions on international aid and the depletion of local infrastructures, with opposition groups and civilian populations being compelled to move from place to place once government forces 'liberated' a city. This situation was only partly alleviated by a rare moment of unity when the Security Council adopted resolution 2401 in February 2018, demanding that the warring parties cease hostilities for at least thirty days to facilitate humanitarian aid deliveries and medical evacuations, to which the Russian authorities were contributing (UNSC 2018a; Bellamy 2018, 329).

The de-escalation agreements referred to earlier resulted in a partial reduction in fighting across Syria in the second half of 2018, though this was also due to government forces reasserting control over large parts of territory, particularly in the south, with reports suggesting that air bombardments continued during this period. Most of the agreements eventually petered out; no nationwide ceasefire that might have paved the way for sustainable post-conflict conditions endured for any length of time.

Consensus among the Security Council P5 members, and between Assad and the main opposition groups, over a legitimate pathway to peace based on agreement in the constitutional committee proved difficult to achieve, despite de Mistura's intensive consultations with Syrian and international parties. Progress in drawing up lists of opposition and civil society delegates to participate in it was slow, though by the end of 2018 some common ground was found. Even though de Mistura, working within the Geneva process, was supposed to decide on its composition and mandate, Assad still insisted that the constitutional process was a 'purely sovereign affair' and should proceed without external interference (Aksenyonok 2019, 15). The broad opposition complained that the majority of delegates were Assad government loyalists (Shaikh and Notte, 2018). The information war persisted; Russia criticised the Western powers for impeding the formation of the constitutional committee and railed against the US military deployment in eastern Syria, as well as condemning Washington's increasingly hard line on Iran. The seventy-third session of the UN General Assembly in September 2018 was marked by bitter disputes, with Russia condemning what it saw as the politicisation of human rights issues and announcing its intention to vote against the draft resolutions on human rights in Iran and Syria (UNSC 2018b). Nevertheless, a Russian deputy foreign minister spoke about a crucial shift within the wider international community: '[At the Assembly] I can say that nobody raised the matter of the Syrian president's departure. There is an understanding that this country, a member of the UN, has the right itself to determine where it is going. The people of this country must and will determine who rules them' (MFA 2018a). The insistence of the Western powers on Assad's departure had thus begun to shift towards the need for constitutional reform and free elections under UN supervision, as stipulated in UNSC resolution 2254 (Aksenyonok 2019, 15), raising the possibility of Assad retaining far-reaching decision-making authority. Even if Russia's assessment of a sea change in the political process was exaggerated, Syria fatigue was becoming a major factor, with no end to the civil war in sight.

Under constant diplomatic pressure, Lavrov defended Russia's humanitarian record and disparaged the efforts of the newly formed Small Group on Syria, consisting of France, the US, the UK, Germany, Saudi Arabia, Jordan and Egypt, which, he claimed, was 'seeking regime change at any cost' (Lavrov 2018c). At the same time, Putin met with Erdoğan, Macron and Angela Merkel in Istanbul in October 2018 for talks about constitutional reform, the situation in Idlib and humanitarian and refugee issues. Neither this meeting nor the eleventh round of Astana talks in November made any substantive progress on the constitutional committee, despite the presence in Astana of de Mistura, who resigned shortly afterwards. Heavy fighting between pro-government and militant opposition forces in a de-militarised buffer zone around the opposition-held northwestern Idlib enclave, set up by Russia and Turkey on 17 September, resumed and continued into the first half of 2019.

The Trump administration's erratic plans added a new element of uncertainty. Turkey's role in Syria had expanded after its intervention in the Afrin district; Trump's announcement in December 2018 of a US withdrawal from Syria, leaving the YPG and Kurdish-led Syrian Democratic Forces (SDF) without any support in the northeast, provided Turkey with a fresh opportunity to intervene there, while at the same time raising Damascus's hopes of recovering territory. Trump subsequently made a partial retreat and authorised a small US contingent to remain, reflecting the need to continue support for both the YPG and Turkey – still a key US regional ally – and his reluctance to allow Assad to make gains. Russia's own aims, to enable Damascus to restore sovereignty over Syrian territory while maintaining its partnership with Ankara, were compromised by the US's residual presence and its support for Kurdish forces. Erdoğan still refused high-level contact with Assad, while the latter accused Ankara of supporting terrorists among the opposition and occupying Syrian territory, demanding the pull-out of Turkish troops (ICG 2018c, 15–17, 22–23).

In early March 2019, Lavrov visited the Middle East in a bid to normalise relations between Damascus and the other principal Arab states. In spite of de Mistura having expressed serious misgivings over the lack of a safe and neutral environment (UNSC 2018c, 5–6), Zakharova claimed that over 190,000 people had returned to Syria since July 2018 and that more than a million internally displaced persons (IDPs) had returned to their permanent residences since Russia's intervention (a figure that had risen to 577,853 by April 2020). According to her, this was happening in spite of 'the "fairy-tales" we are being fed about Syrians being afraid and unwilling to come back to their native country' (MFA 2019e). Russia's information campaign redirected its fire, first against US actions that supposedly hindered UN humanitarian relief to the Rukban camp for IDPs – the Russian foreign ministry described the US's policy in these camps as 'a form of modern genocide' (MFA 2019d) – and second, US attempts to create governance structures, with the support of sympathetic Kurdish factions, to replace state authorities in a zone around its 'illegal' Al-Tanf military base, from which the Syrian authorities were barred and where Islamic State had taken root (MFA 2018b; see also Aksenyonok 2018). According to Lavrov, this amounted to a US attempt to destabilise Syria further by creating a 'prototype new state' east of the Euphrates (Lavrov 2018c). The Trump administration stepped up the pressure on the Assad leadership by introducing the Caesar Syria Civil Protection Act, which from June 2020 enforced a range of crippling sanctions on government bodies and businesses engaged in economic activities supporting Syria's war effort; the Act was subsequently extended to cover Russian, Iranian and Chinese entities. To date, there has been scant evidence of its efficacy in terms of changing Assad's behaviour and enforcing accountability for military excesses, despite the harm done to the Syrian people. The humanitarian situation continued to deteriorate.

Tensions over Syria's Idlib campaign also threatened to derail Russia's cooperation with Turkey. The partial ceasefire of September 2017 had been reinforced by an agreement between Turkey and Russia in September 2018 in Sochi, which halted the offensive by Assad's troops. However, the ceasefire committed the parties to isolate and neutralise jihadi groups and remove them from a demilitarised zone established around Idlib, which Turkey was unable or unwilling to do; as a result, the fighting escalated and continued throughout 2019 – in spite of a unilateral ceasefire announced by Russia in August – with the militant group Hay'at Tahrir al-Sham (formed from a merger between Jabhat al-Nusra and other jihadi groups) infiltrating the population, unrestrained by the various moderate opposition forces operating in Idlib. An offensive by Turkey and the Turkish-backed Syrian National Army along the northeastern Turkey–Syria border under Operation Peace Spring, after a pull-out of US troops, led to a mass exodus of civilians. Syrian government forces continued to rely on Russian air support to carry out renewed attacks in southern Idlib from December 2019.

Following the failure of a Russia–Turkey ceasefire in January 2020, bloody clashes between Turkish and Syrian government forces (reportedly supported by the Russian air force) flared in February 2020, with Ankara increasing its troop presence in the de-escalation zone to reinforce its positions against Syrian attempts to reconquer Idlib. At the same time, air and ground attacks, again supported by Russian aircraft, by Syrian government troops against moderate and Islamist militant opposition were repulsed by the Syrian Democratic Forces, supported by the US-led coalition. With the US under Biden reluctant to be drawn further into the hostilities, Moscow subsequently sought to persuade the SDF to accept a settlement with Assad, in return for Russia's protection from Turkish strikes (Phillips 2021). Another ceasefire was agreed by Putin and Erdoğan on 5 March, with joint patrols put in place in a security corridor, but it was repeatedly violated; the problem of separating jihadis from other opposition parties remained, highlighting the tensions between the Astana guarantors (Lavrov 2020c). Mutual recriminations among the main actors persisted, with Moscow continuing to accuse the US of sponsoring terrorists. Despite deconfliction measures taken together with the US, the danger of direct confrontation between Russia and Turkey in northern Syria remained. Hostilities between Iran and Israel are ongoing, with frequent Israeli air strikes on the Syrian government and Iranian targets being censured by Russia. Fighting between government and opposition forces persisted into 2021, with sporadic clashes taking place in localities across Syria. US support for the Kurds continued, bringing risks to the US–Russia deconfliction line. In June 2022 Erdoğan announced his intention to launch a new operation – apparently discussed with Putin, despite Russian reservations – to reinforce Turkey's control over the security zone along its border with Syria and clear out 'terrorists'; this was seen as yet another attempt to clamp down on the PKK and YPG and expel the SDF from the zone, as well as to repatriate Syrian refugees from Turkish soil (Aliboni 2022).

Regarding developments in the constitutional committee, an agreement was reached in September 2019 – coordinated by the Astana troika and the new UN Special Envoy, Geir Pedersen, and finally launched a few weeks later – between the Syrian government and opposition parties on procedural rules. This was only a small step forward against this background of ongoing hostilities, however. The slow and painful work of the constitutional committee in Geneva continued, with the successive rounds of the drafting commission in October 2021 producing little progress. In 2022, meetings of the drafting commission were suspended, partly because Geneva 'has lost the status of a truly neutral platform as a result of Switzerland supporting the anti-Russian and anti-Syrian sanctions' (UNSC 2022a).

At the same time, the security environment has changed substantially since the early period of the civil war. The battle lines have largely remained frozen. At the same time, shifting alliances have turned large-scale battles into a series of smaller conflicts fuelled by local rivalries and external involvement, with periodic escalations and atrocities by all sides against civilians – including the use of illegal weapons by Syrian government troops – still commonplace. The abatement of large-scale fighting has been overshadowed by the human costs of the external actors' failure to bridge their differences and, with some exceptions, to ensure access to humanitarian agencies and independent conflict monitors; there is little or no accountability for serious war crimes committed by parties to the conflicts. In Afrin and other Turkish-controlled regions in northern Syria, local administrations are subordinate to the Turkish authorities; large territories east of the Euphrates (Raqqa and Deir ez-Zor) are under the government of local councils representing Kurdish coalition forces from the Syrian Democratic

Forces, together with Arab tribes; a small corps of US troops is still periodically rotated and re-equipped to support the Kurds and police specific areas (Aksenenok 2020). Russian concerns persist over separatist movements in the east of the Euphrates. No substantive progress in the political process has taken place.

Russia's persistent arguments about restoring sovereignty under the 'legitimate' Assad government and winning the fight against terrorism thus mask a situation in which genuine sovereignty is severely compromised by territorial divisions, with some areas still prey to Islamic State, Hay'at Tahrir al-Sham and various militias. A potential resurgence of Islamic State in Syria is of particular concern; Russian and Syrian forces have been fighting it in the Badia region since 2015 but only initiated regular air strikes from late 2020, helping to contain its activity for now (ICG 2022, 3, 9, 12). Russia itself has limited military capacity to extend its influence in disputed areas. The economy and health provision in Syria remain in a critical state and human capital is unlikely to recover for generations. As a former Russian ambassador and Middle East expert has acknowledged, Moscow's calls for a return of refugees to their homes in Syria are questionable, given the dire situation on the ground and the threat of arbitrary detention or kidnapping; failure to change this situation means that 'the fruits of [Russia's] military success could be lost' (Aksenyonok 2019, 20, 23).

Any constructive Russian proposals, such as a political process for the Persian Gulf region, aimed at fostering military transparency and confidence-building measures and involving regional organisations, the UN P5 member states and the EU – something akin to the Conference on Security and Cooperation in Europe that enabled negotiations between Soviet and Western allies during the Cold War (Lavrov 2021; Vakil and Quilliam 2021, 30–31) – are accompanied by Moscow's continuing attempts to frustrate Western aims by invoking procedural detail and limiting the interference of external powers in conflict resolution talks. Moscow continues to rely on support from Iran and Turkey in the Astana format. While only a minority of respondents in one expert survey perceived Russia as a destabilising actor in the MENA region, they voiced scepticism over whether Moscow – lacking resources and credibility as a strategic player – has the capacity and will to broker a genuine multilateral framework for security in the region (Fusco 2021, 19–20). Russia continues to rely on an information campaign aimed at legitimising its actions that suggests obfuscation and manipulation. The sins of omission or commission of the Western powers – discussed in more detail in the concluding chapter – have in turn reinforced Russia's mistrust and vitiated cooperation; the vituperative tenor of their exchanges at the UN Security Council has hardly changed. An end to the Syrian civil war appears a remote prospect.

Russia and the Syria conflict: key questions

Russia's involvement in the Syrian civil war raises a number of vital questions. The first relates to the argument that has gained wide currency in Western commentary: that Moscow's overriding aim was to defend the Assad government at any cost and that the US and Europe 'were being cynically played for fools. Neither Russia, Iran nor the Assad regime had any intention of subjecting themselves to a political process that would have seen Assad eased from power' (Lister, 2017, 396). This conclusion ignores important aspects of Russia's approach. In the earlier stages of the conflict, Moscow undertook intensive diplomacy that was more than simply an attempt to deceive or placate the Western powers. Moscow's argument was reasonable; it believed that, by supporting the Assad leadership's putative commitment to reform, it could facilitate an inclusive transition to restore stable governance in the country and prevent state breakdown that might lead to wider regional destabilisation as in the Iraq or Libya model. Even in the later stages, Moscow made persistent efforts to engage external and wider regional support for a political settlement based on the Geneva Final Communiqué and UNSC resolution 2254; one authoritative source has catalogued dozens of contacts with external and regional actors initiated by Moscow, right up to foreign minister and even presidential levels, in the period between the Geneva II conference and Russia's military intervention (Charap et al 2019, 6–7). In a meeting with Assad shortly after Russia's intervention, Putin tried to obtain his assurances that he would engage in talks with the opposition with a view to stepping down after a transition period, thereby opening up the prospects of a political settlement which would guarantee Moscow's continuing access to Syrian state structures (Frolov 2015b). Even after initiating the Astana process, Moscow still tried to cultivate Syrian opposition groups and engage with regional actors.

The second question concerns the Western states' own equivocal approach to the political process. Armed intervention to accomplish regime change was never part of their planning, but their implacable antipathy to Assad – articulated forcefully and consistently after Gaddafi's demise (see Docherty et al 2020; Ralph et al 2017) – meant that 'the question of external direct military intervention hung over the conflict and in many ways shaped it ... Obama's unwillingness to dispel the myth that he might intervene served as a conflict escalator as rebels and regional allies pursued strategies that rested on eventual US military support' (Phillips 2016, 187). Western demands for Assad to step down came well before the conflict escalated into civil war. Russia's aversion to Western-promoted regime change is deeply ingrained in its foreign policy thinking; there were genuine fears that Assad's removal would unleash destructive forces that might have torn Syria apart.

Russia refused to withdraw its support, fearing a repeat of Gaddafi's fate. Moscow's mediation efforts were continually frustrated by the vexed question of whether Assad was to retain a measure of power, with the Western states committed to his removal and the Sunni Arab powers seeking increasingly to advance their own interests. The glaring contradiction between the West's rhetorical commitment to a political transition and its support for the opposition was a major factor, with the result that the Geneva process became deadlocked (Welsh 2021, 234).

The fatal flaw in Russia's own approach lay in supporting a well-resourced and hierarchical Alawite leadership, rooted in a Syrian political culture with minimal experience of pluralism and backed from the outset by powerful Syrian groups and Iran, that rejected demands for reform (see Phillips 2016, 57, 68). By early 2013, Moscow had realised that Assad would not relinquish power, but continued to invest hopes in the peace process (see Lavrov 2013g); yet Assad's determination to emerge victorious with marginal concessions, combined with the intransigence of opposition groups incapable of presenting a united front, obstructed Russia's policies at almost every turn. As the death toll mounted, Russia's support became increasingly difficult to justify. While the Syrian government was prosecuting a systematic and pitiless campaign that assailed the civilian population as well as the armed opposition, Moscow repeatedly used its Security Council veto – fifteen times as of June 2022 – and failed to put sufficient pressure on Assad to change his behaviour by making security guarantees conditional on progress in political negotiations. By the later stages of the Syrian military campaign in Aleppo and Idlib, Russia's appeal to the international legal norms of sovereignty and non-intervention – an appeal to which other non-Western powers were sympathetic – had raised the political costs of future liberal interventions by the West. This is discussed at greater length in Chapter 4.

Moscow compounded its failure with persistent attempts to legitimise its military support for Assad by discrediting Western claims through an extensive diplomatic and media campaign – 'a masterpiece in strategic disinformation' (Gaub 2018a, 57) – that at times bordered on the incredible. Even taking into account the atrocities carried out by anti-government forces, and the likelihood of exaggeration or falsification of excesses by both sides, Moscow's claim that Russia–Syria air offensives were precision strikes directed exclusively against jihadi forces has been flatly contradicted by evidence publicised by respected international organisations and in UN reports, notably those by the IICI. Moscow's attempts to refute evidence substantiating chemical weapons attacks by Assad's forces – a blatant violation of international law and a breach of Russia's commitment to the nonproliferation regime – is a glaring example of how the information campaign over Syria became linked together with other issues to provide 'proof' of Western conspiracies against Russia. The increasing antagonism between the Putin leadership and the West, not least over the annexation of Crimea in 2014, contributed materially to Moscow's siege mentality. A baleful irony is that, while Russia genuinely sought a UN-sponsored political transition process, its increasingly frantic attempts to justify its position meant that the Security Council became less a site for diplomatic negotiation than a forum for bitter reciprocal recriminations by the putative guarantors of the peace process. The information war has not only compromised the goal of bringing peace to a war-torn state but has also undermined trust and shared principles that lie at the basis of the UN Charter-based international legal order.

The third question touches on Russia's narrative about the 'fight against terrorism'. Were Moscow's warnings about the threat posed by Sunni jihadi groups infiltrating the protests invoked purely to justify its political and military support for Assad against the legitimate opposition? Brahimi himself acknowledged that some of Moscow's arguments were valid; studies by respected international organisations have highlighted the threat of jihadi movements, such as Hay'at Tahrir al-Sham, embedding themselves with moderate opposition groups desperate for support to fight off Assad's offensives (see Heller 2018). The widely shared concern over the rapid rise of Islamic State did result in some cooperation between Russia and the US, as it represented a direct threat to regional security and to Russia itself. Also, Russia was prepared to talk to moderate Islamist groups, and even to some radical elements opposed to transnational Salafist jihadism, about power-sharing solutions (Stepanova 2018a, 41–42; see also Adamsky 2018, 12). But official Russian statements delegitimised, or even 'criminalised', large swathes of the armed opposition, allowing Moscow both to cherry-pick opposition groups prepared to concede ground in talks with Assad and to influence US and European public opinion at a time when terrorist attacks were hitting EU countries (see Martini 2020, 731–732). By presenting the civil war as a binary choice between Assad and Islamist extremism, Russia was able to put the problem of identifying the legitimate opposition at the top of the agenda, vindicating its support for the Assad government as a legitimate party to negotiations over Syria's future (see Barnes-Dacey and Levy 2015, 6). This was 'a stratagem designed to change Western policy on Syria – and towards Russia itself' and deflect attention from the root causes of the Syrian uprising (Gaub 2018a, 59).

The final question, examined at greater length in Chapter 6, is whether Russia's approach to Syria signals the calculated return of a resurgent global power to the Middle East. Even Russian commentators who generally broadcast objective views have argued that Moscow's intention was to revive the 'bipolar format' of Russia–US relations, thereby guaranteeing predictability and mutual self-restraint in their approaches to the MENA region and cementing Russia's global status (cited in Frolov 2016a). Russia's self-perception as a global power is amply reflected in its foreign policy rhetoric. Lavrov himself has declared that a strategic success of Russia's foreign policy in the Middle East is that it is no longer defined by its relations with the West (Lavrov 2019b); he has spoken repeatedly about 'the entire world system being reformatted' and railed against the West's 'ideological persistence in containing our country [for] standing up for its legitimate interests' (Lavrov 2014c).

But the argument that Russia's policy had the primary goal of restoring global parity with the US must be seen in context. Moscow's intervention in Syria was facilitated by a commensurate decline in the Western powers' authority in the Middle East, but whether it can be translated into strategic power gains, or even durable influence as a security guarantor, is uncertain. As argued in Chapter 1, the constraints facing Russia in the unpredictable regional security environment preclude political-military supremacy achieved at the expense of the West. Despite Lavrov's and Shoigu's at times overblown rhetoric, Moscow was careful not to let diplomatic clashes with the US over the Aleppo campaign spill over into military confrontation. Russia's campaign in Syria was decisive, but its withdrawal of the major part of its forces, once Assad's war effort had been shored up, reflects its intention to avoid becoming mired in regional conflicts. In Putin's own candid assessment in an interview with the *Financial Times*, Russia's aims in intervening were modest: the elimination of the major part of the threat posed by militant Islamists; preserving Syrian statehood and thereby contributing to the stability of the region and securing Russia's own security; establishing 'business-like' relations with many regional countries; and enhancing the operational experience of the Russian armed forces (Putin 2019). Moscow needed political support from the external powers, and an equitable balance of forces among the regional powers, to secure its interests and limit its future direct engagement in the conflict (Stepanova 2018b, 6–7). Any increase in Russia's influence stems from its pursuit of partnerships with regional actors that do not add up to a geopolitical Cold War-type rivalry with the West.

Conclusions

Surprised by the unexpected and rapid development of the Arab Spring and the scale of the protests in Syria, Russia's initial support for Assad was largely a reaction to persistent Western calls for his departure from power following the overthrow of Gaddafi in Libya. But as the fighting in Syria escalated into a devastating civil war, Moscow manufactured an account of the conflict based on reductive narratives. The first was 'no regime change'. According to Moscow, any political settlement must be decided in a 'Syrian-led and Syrian-owned transition', which effectively meant a place for Assad in a future Syria; the external states must respect international agreements secured by UN Security Council resolutions. The second centred on the imperative of prosecuting the fight against terrorism: any armed opposition to the Assad government should be designated as terrorist and dealt with accordingly. The result was Moscow's decisive, if not wholly indiscriminate, support to a Syrian governing elite that interprets its legitimate entitlement to exercise a monopoly of violence only too literally. At the same time, Moscow aimed to channel international cooperation into a political settlement, albeit one that allowed it a large measure of control over the transition process, increasing its power to steer outcomes to its advantage. But the refusal of the Assad government and powerful externally backed opposition groups to agree on a vision of a post-Arab Spring Syria obstructed Russia's aims. This was compounded by the failure of both Russia and the Western powers to elaborate and agree on a clear definition of what the Geneva process should entail and what reforms implemented by the government would satisfy the antagonists (Samaha 2019, 25). The search for peace was thus eclipsed by military solutions.

After more than a decade of civil war, with the battle over Idlib still ongoing and with only glacial progress in the constitutional committee, the implications for Russia's Syria policy are yet to emerge clearly. The future stability of Syria and the preservation of its statehood – and indeed Russia's ability to secure its own economic and security interests – depend on national reconciliation, facilitated by a shared commitment to a political resolution among the major external and regional powers. As it stands, transitional justice to restore faith in state institutions is still inhibited by the problems of sectarian tensions in the region – which show few signs of abating – and insufficient resources to rebuild a ravaged country. The fight against terrorism has not eradicated Islamist militants, who are still able to cross lines of control and prolong the insurgency. Assad's domestic legitimacy remains contested, presenting massive challenges to recreating a public sphere and reconstituting the state; his attempts to rehabilitate Syria in the Middle East are proceeding slowly, though relations are improving with Egypt, the UAE and Jordan. Far from becoming an indispensable regional power, Russia is struggling to dictate the course of events and risks becoming mired in inter-state rivalries that undermine regional stability. Future coercive intervention by Moscow in the MENA region can not be ruled out, but sustaining an influential presence there would require committing resources and political capital that may well be beyond its capacity.

The legacy of Syria in Russia's wider foreign policy is open to interpretation. Western recognition of Russia as a responsible actor was severely compromised by its disregard for humanitarian norms in colluding with Assad's forces in committing atrocities, together with its neglect of legal obligations by allowing the indiscriminate use of weaponry against the population and disregarding the international norm prohibiting chemical weapons. Russia's invasion of Ukraine in February 2022 – breaching the sovereignty norm it has upheld in Syria and using tactics that appear to repeat some of the worst excesses there – is unquestionably a fundamental challenge both to Western interests and to the rules governing European security. At the same time, the notion that its Syria intervention represents a first step towards realising the Putin leadership's wider strategic aims requires careful consideration, discussed in more detail in the concluding chapter of this book. A definitive account of Russia's war in Ukraine is yet to be written, but it does appear to signal an even greater reliance on military power as an instrument of statecraft and a more prominent role for Russia's defence and security elites in its foreign policy decision-making. It is the domestic sources of Russia's policies in the Arab Spring that we turn to in the next chapter.

3

Russia's domestic politics and the Arab Spring

> One of the main strategic successes of Russian foreign policy in the Middle East ... is that it has become a value of its own and has ceased to be a derivative of Russia's relations with the West. (Lavrov 2019b)

Chapters 1 and 2 offered an empirical analysis of the causes and consequences of the Arab uprisings, Russia's understanding of the conflicts, its relations with the MENA countries and its intervention in Syria. One of the central points to emerge was Russia's disdain for Western attempts to intervene in the internal political arrangements of the states of the region and impose 'ready-made solutions' from outside. Over the course of the Syrian civil war, the diplomatic cover Moscow provided for what it depicted as the legitimate Assad government became even more pronounced. At the same time, the inception of the Arab Spring coincided with stricter controls over domestic governance in Russia and the more vigorous promotion of official narratives defending Russian sovereignty against external interference and rejecting liberal Western norms. This led one authoritative scholar to argue that the key underlying determinant of Russia's policy in the MENA region is the structure of political power in Russia and Putin's preoccupation with domestic state order; in the case of Syria, this explains Russia's alignment with an illiberal Syrian leadership (Allison 2013b, 796, 818).

In this chapter, we explore how Russia's domestic politics has influenced its approach to the Arab Spring. Several questions arise. How do the beliefs and perceptions of Russian elites impact its approach to the MENA region? To what extent does the dominance of a conservative and illiberal Russian leadership translate into support for authoritarian governments there? Can the Syria intervention be explained by the need to rally domestic support for the Putin government in opposition to Western policies, motivated by the 'imperative of regime survival' (see Götz 2017, 233–234)? How do we understand the link between Russia's domestic politics and its foreign policy practice in the MENA region? How is Russia's involvement there shaped by bureaucratic structures and vested interests and how do they influence decision-making? What part did public debates play in facilitating or constraining Russian policy?

The next section highlights the link between domestic and foreign policy and explores how Russia's national belief systems have been manifested in its approach to the Arab Spring – how conservative ideas, expressed both in political thinking and its cultural and civilisational identity, have increasingly permeated Russian foreign policy narratives in a quest for political legitimacy and state cohesion. We then go on to analyse how internal political developments in Russia affect its external relations, at a time when it is intent on playing a more assertive role in the MENA region, and examine political, economic and security actors and institutions in Russia in order to identify the key sources of decision-making. Finally, we consider the role of public debates and media commentary in shaping Russia's involvement in the Arab Spring, assessing the criticism levelled at the leadership by opposition groups and independent commentators.

National beliefs and foreign policy during the Arab Spring

The role of internal political arrangements in forming a country's foreign policy is well-established in the academic literature. Goldstein and Keohane argue that 'ideas influence policy when the principled or causal beliefs they embody provide road maps that increase actors' clarity about goals or ends-means relationships, when they affect outcomes of strategic situations in which there is no unique equilibrium, and when they become embedded in political institutions'; actors generally behave in a self-interested and rational manner, but ideas – the 'collective myths that affect conceptions of self-interest' – are also significant in terms of shaping agendas that frame outcomes and facilitate or constrain policy choices (Goldstein and Keohane 1993, 3, 5–6). The concept of the 'national interest', as interpreted by state actors, has considerable power in legitimising state action through shared meanings that help to make sense of the world (Weldes 1996, 276). Since foreign policy plays a central role in constituting the nation, both state and society are involved in a country's external relations and are 'engaged in a permanent process of learning and socialisation that modifies their identity and perceived interests' (Sakwa 2011, 964). Clunan points to how 'the intersubjective national identity shared among a country's elites and populace entails agreement about the country's rightful international status': the proper rights and obligations conferred on a country by its international partners have as much bearing on its foreign policy as material power (Clunan 2014, 290). The interests and strategies that flow from a state's interaction with its domestic and international social environment are thus shaped by 'a never-ending political process that generates publicly understood standards for action' (Katzenstein 1996, 21, 24).

Earlier in this book we highlighted how the ideas and perceptions underpinning Russian foreign policy reflect a constant preoccupation with structural shifts and the emergence of new threats and challenges in the contemporary strategic environment. A constant theme in official narratives has been the challenge, both to international security and to Russia's traditions of governance, stemming from attempts by Western states to impose external standards of legitimacy. Putin himself has repeatedly argued that the uncertainties caused by a fractured international security system are compounded by attempts by 'the so-called "victors" in the Cold War' to flout the checks and balances of international law, including in the Middle East:

> The measures taken against those who refuse to submit are well-known and have been tried and tested many times. They include use of force, economic and propaganda pressure, meddling in domestic affairs, and appeals to a kind of 'supra-legal' legitimacy when they need to justify illegal intervention in this or that conflict or toppling inconvenient regimes. (Putin 2014, 2012b)

The Putin leadership, frustrated by deteriorating relations with the Western powers, is concerned with defending the sovereignty and legitimacy of its domestic governance against the intrusion of progressive Western models.

Russia's governing elite has sought to consolidate a strong domestic state authority, manufacturing a 'thick' national and cultural identity through close elite-society interaction, in order to reassert Russian statehood and reinforce societal cohesion (Hedetoft and Blum 2008, 8). Putin's reforms have been aimed at strengthening central government in order to uphold the domestic and international foundations of statehood; the Russian leadership's understanding is that the state represents the source and embodiment of national power and sovereign independence (Blum 2008, 353–354; Gel'man 2015, 76–77). It is the state that defines national interests and embodies the collective will of the nation, while the role of civil society is to help strengthen state structures and mobilise support for government policy, rather than importing alien norms into the body politic (Richter 2008, 195–196). Putin himself, right at the start of his presidential tenure, declared that 'For Russians, a strong state is not an anomaly to fight against. Quite the contrary, it is the source and guarantor of order, the initiator and the main driving force of any change'; society and the individual are subordinate to the state and its interests (cited in Hill and Gaddy 2013, 36–37, 39). Authority and control are thus invested in the state in what Krasner terms domestic sovereignty: the belief systems that frame Russia's broader foreign policy allow a large measure of jurisdiction for the state in domestic affairs (Krasner 1999, 10). These processes have become embedded in its domestic order and are underpinned by what one influential Russian statesman calls 'real sovereignty' – 'the ability of a state to conduct independent domestic, foreign, and defense policies in practice (and not declaratively)' – defending its domestic political order from the imposition of external values and norms by all necessary means (Kokoshin 2014, 453; see Hill and Gaddy 2013, 42).

As well as structural and material power, a 'critically important component of real sovereignty is the cultural and civilizational identity of a nation state as an agent of world politics' (Kokoshin 2006, 456). Conservative ideas, rooted in cultural-civilisational distinctiveness, are promoted by state elites to unite Russian society behind a national idea and provide ideological support for the system of governance that Putin has created (Evans 2015, 409). Putin has emphasised the imperative of 'recreat[ing Russia's] original *cultural code* as the basis for a societal consensus', reinforcing its self-perception as a great power representing an inclusive inter-civilisational civic entity (Chebankova 2012, 328; emphasis in original). At the same time, Russia's cultural and civilisational identity, expressed in its preferred norms and values, is projected into international diplomacy. As one leading scholar has argued, in trying to shape the international order states

> seek to institutionalize preferred meanings and identities, engineer consent for these institutions, and limit the scope for innovation ... This involves the cultural narration of identity ... order-builders are not animated solely by strategic calculation, but are commonly informed by their own beliefs about what constitutes a legitimate cultural order. (Reus-Smit 2018, 13)

Recent iterations of the Russian Foreign Policy Concept – the foundational document outlining the basic principles, priorities, goals and objectives of its foreign policy – have stated that, with the West losing its monopoly over global processes, 'global competition is acquiring a civilizational dimension, which suggests competition between different value systems and development models ... the cultural and civilizational diversity of the modern world is increasingly in evidence' (Kremlin 2008; see MFA 2016d; Lomagin 2012, 509).

These ideas pre-date the inception of the Arab Spring but have impacted markedly upon Russian thinking over the past decade. Officials have increasingly asserted the primacy of national identity and traditions which stand apart from, and in some respects in opposition to, the West's promotion of human rights in a liberal international order. Lavrov has called for an international system 'which reflects the modern world's cultural and civilizational diversity, respects peoples' right to decide their own future, and will ultimately reinforce global and regional security by setting it on an enduring foundation of international law' (Lavrov 2016a). He has criticised 'supporters of ultraliberal approaches in some states' and argued that

> no country or group of countries has exclusive authority to create unilaterally any new 'norms of behaviour' which do not rest on this universal basis. Imposing one's own interpretation of human rights standards on others will only aggravate cultural and religious contradictions and risks provoking a conflict of civilizations and undermining efforts to establish a stable system of global development. (Lavrov 2014b)

Putin voiced an even more vigorous defence of traditional values with specific reference to MENA countries, where Western attempts to foster 'supposedly more progressive development models' have resulted in 'barbarity and extensive bloodshed' (Putin 2013c). In contrast, Russia's governing elite portrays itself as a unifying force in the region, supporting secular or moderate Islamic states which follow their own values and beliefs – widely recognised as legitimate by most of the international community – and claiming a global identity linked to historical relations with Christian, Islamic and Asian civilisations and resting on secure institutional foundations. As discussed further in Chapter 5, Russia believes itself to be 'uniquely placed to use its position in the UN in order to support a "multilateral dialogue of cultures, civilizations and states"' befitting a great power (Morozova 2015, 6). A former Russian deputy foreign minister has pointed to the contrast between Russia's respect for different religions and cultures in the Islamic world and the West's 'geopolitical "engineering"' aimed at relegating the MENA countries to a 'periphery and space for expansion (*Lebensraum*)' (Yakovenko 2019).

Russia's governing elite has thus translated cultural-civilisational value systems into foreign policy narratives in order to justify its activism in the Middle East, distancing itself from the West and reclaiming its historically diversified global role within international society (see Zvyagelskaya and Surkov 2019, 4). In Chapter 4 we examine how Russia strives to legitimise its international policy in legal terms by 'position[ing] itself as a staunch supporter of multilateralism within the framework of the UN and a guarantor of sovereignty, non-intervention and other principles of international law ... sovereignty became a repository of cultural and political uniqueness and a *sine qua non* of global diversity' (Morozova 2015, 7). Cultural diversity reflects differences not only in values across international society but also in political, social, economic and institutional orders, challenging the 'hidden hierarchy' of Western ideational and institutional power which allows the West to exercise cultural hegemony in international society (O'Hagan 2005, 224; see also Reus-Smit 2018). Cultural and civilisational concepts have increasingly become part of scholarship on international legal theory in Russia, underpinning its preferred normative system that privileges sovereignty and non-intervention (Mälksoo 2015, 143–144).

Domestic order and foreign policy in the MENA region

But how has the evolution of domestic politics in Russia influenced its policy *practice* in the MENA region? To what extent does the Russian leadership use arguments about cultural-civilisational diversity *instrumentally*, to shield illiberal and repressive states from Western interference in their internal arrangements, thereby strengthening claims for the legitimacy of its own domestic order? Prominent Western commentators have argued that Russia's foreign policy assertiveness in opposition to the West, particularly since the onset of Putin's third presidential term, has been manufactured by an increasingly authoritarian regime for which external sources of legitimacy compensate for its failure to meet domestic challenges (Stoner and McFaul 2015, 169, 178–179). This explanation is offered for Moscow's intervention in Syria, which 'has transformed the civil war there into a proxy U.S.-Russian conflict and has raised the stakes in the ongoing standoff between Moscow and Washington. It has also succeeded in diverting attention away from Russia's destabilization of Ukraine, making it impossible for the West to continue to isolate the Kremlin' (Stent 2016, 106). Dannreuther argues that domestic unrest during the Bolotnaya protests in 2011–2012 was critical in understanding why Putin saw a resolute response to the uprising in Syria as necessary to strengthen his domestic base of support; he also claims that Russia's annexation of Crimea and incursion into eastern Ukraine provided the context for Russia's military intervention in Syria on the side of the Assad government (Dannreuther 2019, 727–728; 2015, 79–80). Some Russian Middle East experts have advanced similar views, maintaining that the Putin leadership used the Arab Spring protests – likened to externally provoked 'colour revolutions' – to warn of the threats facing Russia, eventually authorising the intervention in Syria to create a 'rally round the flag' effect at a time when the mobilising effect of Crimea was waning (Issaev and Shishkina 2020, 99–100, 106; Zvyagel'skaya 2014, 74–83; see also Petrov and Gel'man 2019, 457). Defence minister Sergei Shoigu's claim that Russia's intervention in Syria had prevented the chain of 'colour revolutions' in the Middle East may well have been directed primarily at domestic audiences to underline the leadership's determination to counter external interference in Russia's internal affairs (President of Russia 2016).

Russia's approach to the Arab uprisings undoubtedly reflects persistent concerns about order, which predispose it to resist regime change and the overthrow of incumbent authorities. As Allison suggests, 'a key element of continuity is the strong reflection in Russia's conception of international order of the priority of preserving its domestic power structure'; Russian officials and commentators in fact suggested that the MENA uprisings were seen as a warning to the Putin leadership that it might suffer a similar fate (Allison 2017, 522–523; 2013b, 817–818). However, the arguments that 'Russian strategy towards Syria directly supported Putin's efforts to strengthen his domestic base of support' by sidelining liberalising elites and signalling externally a return to a great power foreign policy – and that the Bolotnaya protests were a 'catalyst' for Russia's reaction to Gaddafi's overthrow in Libya – are problematic (Dannreuther 2019, 732, 739–740). As discussed earlier in this book, Russia abstained from, rather than vetoing, UNSC resolution 1973 due to regional states' and organisations' antipathy to Gaddafi and Moscow's own concerns about his disruptive behaviour; the subsequent overthrow of Gaddafi prompted serious misgivings in the wider international community – not just in Russia – over the destabilising effects of regime change in the MENA region, the threat of state and societal breakdown and the rise of Islamist extremism (UNSG 2011g; Dunne and Teitt 2015, 382). These specific factors represent a powerful alternative explanation for Russia's policies.

Respondents interviewed for this book confirmed that the Russian leadership was concerned about 'colour revolutions' but only two (both generally critical of the leadership's MENA policy) affirmed a direct link between the Putin leadership's support for Assad and domestic consolidation against putative Western designs on Russia (interviews #2, #9). Survey data published by the respected non-governmental Yuri Levada Analytical Center show that Putin's approval ratings actually *fell* by several percentage points over the period between the start of the Arab uprisings and the end of 2013, suggesting that there was no 'rally round the flag' effect stemming from Moscow's response to events in Libya and Syria; only after the Crimea annexation in 2014 was there a marked surge in support for the leadership, prompted by official narratives about external threats to Russia's sovereignty and the need to mitigate security vulnerabilities on its periphery (Levada Center n/d). Domestic protests in Russia in 2011–2012 did prompt increasingly authoritarian measures in Putin's third presidential term to combat perceived challenges to internal order, but evidence that they constituted a significant causal factor in Moscow's approach to the Arab Spring is lacking.

While Moscow's campaign in Syria and related events, such as the downing of a Russian aircraft by the Turkish air force, did excite public interest due to the casualties suffered, its decision to intervene 'did not result primarily from Russia's domestic political dynamics ... none of the crises outside Russia's immediate vicinity in Eurasia have been "internalised" by Russian society, or even had any domestic resonance to speak of' (Stepanova 2018a, 9; interviews #2, #3, #5; see also Levada Center 2016b). The region does not constitute a key priority in Russian foreign policy; the absence of an immediate threat to the Putin leadership casts doubt on a direct link between domestic politics and a 'diversionary' foreign policy (Issaev and Shishkina 2020, 97; Götz 2017, 234–235; interview #5). Levada Center surveys appear to support this view. One in late October 2015, immediately after Russia's military intervention in Syria, found that 75 per cent of respondents did not follow events there closely or know anything about them; only 7 per cent of respondents believed that Russia had intervened to distract the population from domestic crises and poor governance (Levada Center 2015a). A study by prominent US experts based on interviews in Moscow concluded that, while Putin's image as the defender of the country against external threats does have wide currency, there was no overwhelming public support for Russia's military intervention in Syria (Charap et al 2019, 8–9). In another Levada survey, conducted in March 2016, almost 70 per cent of respondents stated that Russia–West relations had improved or remained the same as a result of Russia's military intervention (Levada Center 2016a), contradicting the argument that it was an important factor in Putin's mobilisation of domestic support against Western-inspired threats to his incumbency. A recent study shows that Levada Center data refute the notion that the Russian public accepts official anti-US narratives and the conception of Russia as a 'besieged fortress' (Frye 2021, 169–170).

Contrary to the notion that the domestic consequences of the Bolotnaya protests sparked a more assertive MENA policy, there was much more continuity than change in official Russian positions on the risks of Western-backed liberalisation and the destructive consequences of regime change. Russia's military intervention resulted in marginal domestic gains for the Putin leadership. Domestic political culture does influence foreign policy thinking, but we argue that internal political arrangements impacted upon policymaking in the MENA region in a more limited and exceptional way: drawing a causal link between illiberal domestic trends and an assertive, even confrontational foreign policy risks underestimating the longer-term determinants that frame the Russian leadership's perception of specific circumstances in Syria and other countries in the MENA region (see Gunitsky and Tsygankov 2018, 386; Lo 2015, 14–15).

The argument that Russia's strategy in Syria was material in supporting Putin's efforts to strengthen his domestic power base has been taken a step further by some prominent commentators. McFaul maintains that Putin's 'support for autocrats compelled him to intervene militarily [in Syria] ... What happened inside Syria mattered to Putin, as did what kind of leader and regime governed' (McFaul 2020, 132). Dannreuther claims that

> the essentially conservative and reactionary nature of the 'Russian idea' resonated with the spirit of the 'counter-revolution' to the Arab Spring. The autocratic and military leaders ... in the region found Russia to be an increasingly reliable supporter and as having a similar outlook on the need to re-assert an authoritarian political order. (Dannreuther 2019, 739–740)

This interpretation appears to be influenced by the argument that authoritarian trends in Russia's domestic politics, which strengthened in response to the 'colour revolutions' in the post-Soviet space, prompted the Putin leadership not only to undermine democratic movements in Russia but also to project domestic institutional arrangements into its foreign relations, thereby forming an 'authoritarian alignment in the international system' dedicated to ensuring regime survival and bolstering resistance to democratisation (Ambrosio 2009, 5, 19; see also Silitski 2010, 339–340). In this reading, Moscow promotes an 'ideology of conservatism' in opposition to Western liberalism, not only to encourage support for its domestic political order but also to engage in 'social competition' in the international arena: '[Putin] has become more willing to present his regime and its worldview as a model that others around the globe may approve and some states may imitate' (Evans 2015, 424). One stratagem is to establish a caucus of authoritarian states to uphold Russia's influence in international organisations and contest the liberal global governance order by resisting interventionist political norms (Newman and Zala 2018, 881; Ambrosio 2009, 22, 24; Cooley 2015, 52). Some Russian experts have argued bluntly that Moscow prioritises collaboration with 'entrenched regimes and brutal dictatorships' to ensure stability, exacerbating the causes of the Arab uprisings (Issaev and Shishkina 2020, 101).

A case can be made that similar techniques of political control are used by the Putin government and authoritarian leaderships in the MENA region. In Russia, Putin has strengthened the coercive capacity of the state, compelling elites to subordinate themselves to the governing faction by employing formal institutions and legal norms to enforce a consensus, using the security apparatus as a key tool in domestic and foreign policy and achieving a high level of mass support by elevating the strong state as a rhetorical reference point and guarantor of stability (see Gel'man 2015, 73, 81). Many of the MENA countries exhibit features of authoritarian state-building similar to Russia's: imposing from above a social bargain that delivers security and welfare in return for the political compliance of society, thereby undermining the potential for independent political mobilisation; promoting the state, personalised in the leader, as the sole legitimate defender of the national interest as defined by the governing elite; managing political parties and parliamentary elections; establishing a strong presidency at the apex, with the next level comprising the bureaucracy, senior military figures, intelligence agencies, business groups, a religious establishment, agents of ideological legitimation and a pliant judiciary; and co-opting opposition forces via 'pluralized' authoritarianism (see Kamrava 2018, 22–37). Many governing elites in MENA countries try to build a coalition in the security apparatus, bureaucracy and business community through repression or redistributive policies in order to dominate the social contract between state and society (Achy 2015, 315). They exhibit 'a capacity for authoritarian learning ... upgrad[ing] their capacities to deal with and repress street protests, uprisings, and insurgencies ... incumbents use state resources, unfair media access, electoral manipulation, and harassment' to their advantage (Kamrava 2018, 75–76). As shown later in this chapter, Russian state and private interest groups have taken advantage of Syria's dependence on Moscow to help restructure its military and security apparatus in ways favourable to Russia's interests.

But does the consolidation of authoritarian trends in Russia in response to perceived challenges to its constitutional order have a direct *causal* link with support for like-minded governments in the Arab uprisings? We argue that there are several weaknesses in the argument that, with regard to its policies in the Arab Spring, Russia has devised an unalloyed strategy of promoting and defending an authoritarian ideology or governance models across the MENA region. First, it is problematic to classify the MENA states into one ideal-type category given their diversity; the governing elite in each country faces quite specific political, institutional and social conditions and its policies are informed by differing political cultures. The normative bias of Western political science, which has fostered the notion of a linear transition to representative government resulting from the politics of resistance in the Arab uprisings, has 'discouraged taking seriously alternative regime types except in the search for their flaws and vulnerabilities'; the Arab Spring has produced varying legacies, with different forms of authoritarianism shaping governance in different ways, so that 'both the theory and practice of transition from authoritarianism are complex, contentious and still unresolved' (Anderson 2014, 42, 44; see also Ayoob 2014, 403).

Second, in many of the MENA states the preconditions already existed for policy decisions against liberalisation. Syria is a good example. Influenced by the legacy of his father Hafez, who was concerned that Syria might follow the USSR's example and disintegrate if political reform was pursued too far too fast – particularly given Syria's ethnic, religious and socio-economic problems – Bashar al-Assad was cautious about loosening the reins of power. Moreover, the US had identified Syria as a potential target for coercive regime change after the Iraq invasion and the inception of the Arab Spring only reinforced this sense of insecurity (see Leverett 2005, 70–71, 137–138). Assad's crackdown in 2011–2012 did not lead to immediate overwhelming support from Russia after the Bolotnaya protests; the Putin government was still formulating a coherent response to the Arab Spring and exploring prospects for a political transition that might stabilise Syria, and did not have a carefully planned strategy to help Assad reassert an authoritarian political order.

Third, while questioning the Western 'delusion' that the Arab states could embrace liberal democracy, Moscow has not tried to impose any alternative ideologically or culturally predisposed models there. Preserving regional stability and the functionality of state institutions while protecting Russian interests – rather than simply defending like-minded authoritarian leaderships against Western designs – were the key criteria underpinning Moscow's relations with Assad and other MENA leaderships. International observers have often missed Russia's pragmatic readiness to accept power-sharing and more representative and pluralist systems in MENA, negotiating between rival forces rather than just backing the region's 'strongmen', for example in Libya, Egypt (prior to al-Sisi's coup), Algeria and even up to a point in Syria (Stepanova 2018a, 39–40, 42). Fourth, whereas Russia is more able to shape relations in its immediate neighbourhood through engagement with authoritarian states in the Collective Security Treaty Organisation and Shanghai Cooperation Organisation, it has weakly institutionalised relations with regional MENA organisations and, with the partial exception of Syria and Egypt, limited bilateral institutional links with individual states. While in some respects they do share governance traits and practise similar techniques of political control, the structural and ideological preconditions for an alliance between Russia and illiberal MENA states are lacking.

The diverse nature of domestic orders and state–society relations across the MENA region means that the 'authoritarian alignment' argument – that regime type is a key determinant shaping Russia's policy – is inadequate to explain its approach to the Arab uprisings. Understanding the changing context of security in the MENA region and avoiding 'the temptation to view democracy as the measuring rod for politics' (Anderson 2014, 43) is crucial in assessing Russia's response to the problems and opportunities that have arisen there. The declining influence of the Western powers, structural socio-economic problems, weak governance and the limited involvement of societal actors in national politics in MENA countries provide opportunities for Russia to pursue its interests transactionally, which often means dealing with illiberal governments – something that the Western countries themselves are well-versed in. A Russian expert interviewed for this book, with a Western academic background and recent experience of working in Syria independently from official Russian structures, stated that the Putin leadership's central aim was to develop trade and economic links across the region rather than to promote specific political models or conservative ideology (interview #10; also interview #3).

Russia's elites and policymaking in the MENA region

The behaviour of Russian elite actors is guided by the broadly accepted foreign policy beliefs of the state leadership in a centralised and hierarchical state system, as discussed above. However, their particularistic interests may change in response to shifting circumstances, presenting problems in understanding how they deal with new policy challenges in specific situations and how decisions are made. Authoritative Russian political scientists have examined how the changing structure of Russia's elites has impacted their influence in foreign policy; while decision-making has become less pluralist over the past decade within 'a system with bureaucratic mechanisms of control and subordination', informal ties have become increasingly important (Petrov and Gel'man 2019, 450–451). What are the political and institutional opportunities and constraints shaping Russian elites' interests in the MENA region and which domestic groups have gained influence over specific areas of policy? Given the high degree of centralisation in Russia, our analysis is mainly confined to competing interest groups within government, but we also take into consideration the role of other actors – private businesses, non-governmental organisations, religious lobbies and opinion formers.

Evidence suggests that there has been a discernible evolution of Russian decision-making with regard to the MENA region. At the inception of the Arab Spring, it was fragmented between the presidential administration, the main government agencies and economic and non-governmental actors (Kozhanov 2016, 22). There was an unprecedented internal debate within the leadership over how to respond to the NATO-led campaign in Libya, leading to an apparent difference of opinion between then-President Dmitrii Medvedev – whose decision it appears to have been not to veto UNSC resolution 1973 authorising 'all necessary measures' to protect Libyan civilians – and Putin, who was prime minister at the time (see Martin 2022, 23–24, 35). However, between 2011 and Russia's military intervention in Syria in September 2015, there was a marked consolidation of national actors under Putin's leadership and foreign policy decision-making became extremely centralised: 'it was no longer the arena for major open discussions and stark disagreements among elites ... dissenting voices were truly marginal' (Petrov and Gel'man 2019, 451; see also Dannreuther 2015, 82–83; Sakwa 2017, 114–115). Dmitri Trenin, director of the Carnegie Moscow Center, has stated that 'going into Syria was President Putin's personal decision ... It was not discussed among the elite very much, and it was certainly not discussed publicly. It was very much the President's own decision, just like the decision with regard to Crimea' (Trenin 2017b). Vladimir Gel'man, a leading Russian political scientist, has stated that the war with Ukraine in 2022 has led to even greater centralisation of decision-making (Roth and Sauer 2022, 32).

Putin himself, heading a close inner circle in the presidential administration, now appears to be the ultimate arbiter of all key foreign policy, security and defence issues, to the extent that policymaking 'comes to a standstill when Vladimir Putin is absent' (Lund 2019, 42; Petrov and Gel'man 2019, 451). At the strategic planning level, policy is coordinated by the Russian Federation Security Council, composed of key ministers and state agency heads and with its own apparatus and staff, which Putin chairs. Decisions on all issues of national importance depend heavily on information received from the military and security agencies – headed by the permanent members of the Security Council with similar patriotic world views to Putin, who generally enjoy high approval ratings among the Russian population – who formulate proposals and execute policy decisions taken under direct presidential management (Trenin 2017a; Bacon 2019, 120–124; Monaghan 2018, 15; interviews #6, #8).

The opinions of experts, including Russian academics interviewed for this book, differ on the precise implementation of decision-making on MENA affairs. The foreign policy establishment, led by the formidably experienced Lavrov as a permanent member of the RF Security Council, provides considerable expertise on the MENA countries. Lavrov himself appears to have taken the initiative in persuading the US to accept the Syrian chemical weapons disarmament agreement in 2013 (Lo 2015, 11). At deputy foreign minister level, Mikhail Bogdanov, a fluent Arabic speaker, has acted as Putin's personal envoy to the region, responsible *inter alia* for the Syrian settlement; Sergei Ryabkov has been responsible for relations with the US, including the Iranian nuclear file; and a former head of the foreign ministry's Middle East desk, Sergei Vershinin, has had a key role in overseeing diplomacy on Syria (Lund 2019, 41). Another vastly experienced career diplomat in MENA issues, Vladimir Safronkov, was recalled from his post as deputy Permanent Representative to the UN to become special representative of the foreign minister on the Middle East peace process. Aleksandr Lavrent'ev has had a visible role as special presidential envoy to Syria. Aleksandr Kinshchak, Russia's ambassador to Syria from 2014 to 2018, is head of the foreign ministry's Middle East and North Africa department and was appointed in 2020 as special envoy for the Syrian settlement.

At the same time, several interview respondents concurred that, while the foreign ministry implements the broad parameters of policy in the diplomatic arena, the 'power agencies' – in other words, the military and security structures – play the leading role in driving decision-making on Syria (interviews #4, #7; see also Lund 2019, 42). One respondent stated that the military has a direct line, through the defence ministry, to the decision-making apex in the presidential administration (interview #10). Two respondents referred to disputes between the defence and foreign ministries over MENA policy, with the former sidelining the latter over the prosecution of the Aleppo campaign (interviews #2, #9). Others argued that differences were inevitable, given the military challenges of the Syria operation on the ground, and that relations between the two agencies have been generally cooperative rather than conflictual (interviews #3, #5).

In any case, evidence points to the heightened prominence of the military in foreign policy. It is worth noting that, when asked to comment on military operations in press briefings on Syria, Lavrov and foreign ministry spokesperson Maria Zakharova frequently referred the questioner to the defence ministry. John Kerry is reported as stating that Lavrov 'appeared out of the loop' when asked to explain Russian troop movements in Syria (Weiss and Ng 2019). When confronted by a direct question from an interviewer: 'Who is the main guardian of peace now, the military or the diplomats? What enables Russia to maintain parity: state-of-the-art armaments or the power of words?', Lavrov concluded a rather circumlocutory reply by saying 'it is highly regrettable that in today's world no one will talk to you, unless you have a strong army and modern weapons' (Lavrov 2019a). Responding to another's interviewer's remark: 'We say that "if you don't listen to Lavrov you will listen to [defence minister] Shoigu"', Lavrov commented wryly: 'I did see a shirt with that written on it' (Lavrov 2020f). This appears to reflect a wider trend. Influential elite groups surveyed by authoritative Russian political scientists have in recent years increasingly expressed the belief that military force is more important than economic strength in international affairs, leading to a degree of 'militarization' of policy preferences (Petrov and Gel'man 2019, 456–457).

Although the extent of the militarisation of state policy should not be overstated, the defence ministry has gained substantially in terms of strategic decision-making influence. Shoigu, a popular figure in Russia at the time, stated at the end of the Aleppo campaign that 'the role of the military in international relations has increased' (President of Russia 2016). With Russia's intervention in Syria, he became the most prominent figure within the core group of decision-makers among the Security Council permanent membership, drafting his own staff and operating under the direct command of the presidency (Petrov 2017, 121, 125–126). Gerasimov, another key figure as head of the Russian General Staff, is reported as saying in 2014 that he had been assigned additional powers to coordinate federal agencies in case the country needed to mobilise on a war footing (Monaghan 2016, 28). Reflecting a military revival that can be traced back to the pre-Putin era, Gerasimov referred specifically to the Arab uprisings in his analysis of how the rules and methods of war had changed: faced with a US monopoly on the use of force, he argued, Russia had to be ready to deal with armed conflict and foreign intervention on its periphery in order to avert threats arising from state collapse and civil conflict (Sakwa 2017, 103–104; Monaghan 2016, 14). Russian concerns over internal order and stability in the face of these challenges provide the justification for the increased centralisation of the domestic political process (see Renz 2019, 819).

The centralisation of power within Putin's inner circle has led to limited decision-making pluralism and raised doubts among many elites outside of the 'power agencies' about their ability to influence foreign policy (Petrov and Gel'man 2019, 452–453). At the same time, closer examination exposes a more complex picture of how Russian interest groups translate their preferences into influence over state policy in the MENA region. While prominent actors depend on the favour of the leadership and generally follow its line, there are different factions within the presidential administration, as well as functional divisions within the various government agencies, including those which have been involved in special operations in Syria (and more recently in the Ukraine war; see Roth and Sauer 2022, 34). State businesses – foremost among them the oil/gas and energy companies, the nuclear power industry, the defence complex, state-linked engineering concerns and some private groups – were specifically identified by interview respondents as influencing the development of Russia's MENA policy (interviews #3, #7, #9; see Chapter 6).

The overall picture is that of a division of labour, with key decisions taken at presidential level, some within the RF Security Council and some by groups of officials depending on the specific policy issue at hand (Lund 2019, 41; interview #5). Elites are loosely controlled by the state leadership but pursue their own informal – often competing and only partly transparent – interests and incentives, so that 'there is hidden yet stiff competition among various cliques for power, rents, and resources' (Petrov and Gel'man 2019, 451; interviews #8, #9). The formal role played by the governments of Russia's Muslim-populated republics and the Orthodox Church and the informal role of Jewish communities also come into consideration when dealing with various MENA countries (Gvosdev 2019, 5). The policies of Chechen President Ramzan Kadyrov, from personal diplomacy in forging relations with Gulf Arab elites to direct involvement in Russia's military support for the Assad government by sending Chechen troops to Syria (Lund 2019, 43), have prompted several interview respondents to emphasise his prominence in Russia's policymaking in the MENA region (interviews #4, #5, #7, #8, #9; see Chapter 5). One Russian expert concludes that rather than a rigid bureaucratic decision-making 'vertical', policy in the MENA countries is influenced by 'a variety of competing, overlapping, and contradictory policy impulses' (Gvosdev 2019, 8–9).

How has this impacted the cohesion and effectiveness of decision-making authority in Russia? Aleksandr Gol'ts, a veteran commentator on defence and security policy, argues that the RF Security Council in reality acts more like an advisory body. Putin transmits instructions to the heads of agencies represented in the Council, who then seek proposals from their staff and other bodies and send back those which they favour – sometimes with evidence contradicting the expectations of the leadership filtered out – to the presidential administration, which accepts or rejects their recommendations; since authority comes from Putin personally, this decision-making system is

> a source of crises. Any of the leader's ideas can be accepted and implemented without any serious expert assessment ... The annexation of Crimea came down to an emotional reaction by Putin, who was facing the overthrow of the pro-Russian regime in Ukraine and interpreted it as the result of a conspiracy by Western countries. The same holds true for the decision to launch the military operation in Syria, which embroiled Russia in a conflict for which it had no plan, let alone a strategy. (Golts 2018, 10–11; see also Herd 2019, 19–20)

Gol'ts adds that Putin acknowledged that he was out of his depth in dealing with MENA affairs, an opinion backed by one of our interview respondents (interview #9), which may explain why the military has had a freer hand in making crucial decisions over Syria. This has led to costly errors. The Russian defence ministry, without notifying its Iranian partners or (it appears) the Russian foreign ministry, announced that its aircraft had been authorised to fly combat missions from an Iranian air base – trumpeted by some Russian media outlets as 'another geopolitical victory for Russia, its triumphant return to the Middle East' – but was subsequently forced to withdraw them amid criticism from the Iranian defence minister, much to Lavrov's irritation (Frolov 2016b). The weakness of formal institutions and the personalisation of politics result in dysfunctional governance and the deprofessionalisation of the state bureaucracy, with the information contained in strategic planning documents not subject to critical assessment or too vaguely worded, causing delays in the planning process and problems in implementing policies (Petrov 2019, 116; see also Monaghan 2018, 15–17).

Policy reports by MENA experts, based on interviews in Syria, have analysed the impact of Russian actors and structures on its involvement in the conflict there. The civil war has compelled the Assad government to reconfigure its social base, restructuring its military and security apparatus and adapting its economic governance models (Kamrava 2018, 100; Mehchy et al 2020, 33). As a result, key Syrian government agencies, militia leaders and other informal actors compete for resources in what is effectively a war economy, depleting institutional capacity further and making the Assad leadership dependent on networks of domestic and external power-brokers. These include Russian security, intelligence, business and defence industry interest groups with the result that 'Russia is shaping Syrian state institutions according to its own interests … Both Russia and Iran have also made Syria into an arena for their own military and economic competition' (Khatib and Sinjab 2018, 2; see also Samaha 2019, 9–10; Aksenyonok 2020).

One sphere in which Russian interest groups compete for resources is the use of private military contractors (PMC). Around 4,000 regular soldiers, special forces and advisors have been deployed at all levels of the Syrian military to advise on combat operations, but Russia has also used an estimated 2,500 PMCs, sometimes engaged directly in combat, in the Syria conflict (Charap et al 2019, 11; see also Adamsky 2018, 29–30). A US air strike near Deir ez-Zor in February 2018 may have killed as many as 300 private contractors from the Wagner Group – controlled by Evgenii Prigozhin, who is reported to have links with the RF Main Intelligence Directorate (GRU) – prompting concern in Russian political circles, due both to a potential escalation of political-military confrontation with the US and to their unregulated deployment in secret operations without public oversight or proper coordination with Russian commanders on the ground. The Russian government tried to block information about the incident, but details spread on independent media and social media channels. The failure of the operation called into question the role of PMCs in competition for lucrative state-funded contracts and threatened to compromise the image of Russia as an influential actor in the region (Menkiszak et al 2018; Weiss and Ng 2019). At the same time, available evidence points to their unregulated deployment in Libya, Mali and other conflict-hit countries continues, and latterly in the war with Ukraine; deaths of PMCs are not counted in official casualty figures, allowing Moscow to portray its overseas operations as relatively uncostly in human terms.

The Russian leadership's decision-making in the MENA region reflects longer-term developments in its foreign policy. By the end of 2014, the quality of policymaking in Russia in terms of assessing priorities and engaging professional expertise had declined, partly as a consequence of domestic political and economic problems but also under the pressure of external events. Deficient information and the lack of effective feedback mechanisms have generated misperceptions and encumbered its ability to interpret rapidly unfolding events, increasing the risk of reactive rather than strategic decision-making and favouring force and information management rather than adaptation, as well as reinforcing the trend towards the militarisation of the policymaking process (Gel'man 2015, 101, 103, 128). One informed Russian commentator has warned that the long-term consequences of the Syria operation could lead to overstretching abroad and destabilisation at home, advocating '[the] need for an open discussion about the need for institutional limitations on the President's freedom of action in taking foreign policy and military decisions so that we don't suddenly wake up to war in some place like Sudan' (Frolov 2017a). Recent changes in decision-making procedures and bureaucratic organisation mean that 'the regime's rising personalism in major policy directions ... and the decline of auxiliary political institutions ... is likely to turn into a principal feature of the Russian regime' (Gel'man 2015, 127–128). The relevance of this factor to Russia's war with Ukraine is examined in the concluding section of this chapter.

Public debates and media representation of the Arab Spring

To what degree the presidential inner circle takes into account public views is an additional factor to consider. Survey data collected by Russian scholars indicate that representative bodies and public opinion have minimal direct influence on foreign policy decision-making (Petrov and Gel'man 2019, 455; see Romanova 2018, 87). At the same time, domestic opinion does play a role in legitimising foreign policy (see Wilhelmsen 2019, 1092). Public debates on MENA affairs, articulated by deputies in the Russian Federation Council and State Duma, have been sharply polarised along internal political fault lines, often regurgitating well-worn opinions designed to satisfy their constituencies but only superficially addressing the real issues. Vociferous criticism among communist and nationalist deputies in the State Duma over Moscow's abstention on UNSC resolution 1973 in the Libya crisis, seen as a failure to stand up for the norm of non-intervention and leave the way open for Western-inspired regime change elsewhere – dealing a blow to Russia's international credibility – may well have contributed to the leadership's decision to prevent a similar scenario in Syria (Zhekova 2018, 53, 57; interview #1). Communist and nationalist politicians and commentators have portrayed Russia's involvement there as a face-off with the US, arguing that Russia should ally itself with Washington's antagonists (Trenin 2013,

16). Gennadii Zyuganov, General Secretary of the RF Communist Party, spoke of a 'new type of colonial war' across the Middle East, in which Western intervention in Syria in pursuit of regime change – supported by local 'mercenaries' (the opposition in the form of the Free Syrian Army) – has been thwarted by Russia's and China's vetoes in the UN Security Council, prompting the West to pursue its aims by allying itself with terrorist groups (Pravda 2013). Vladimir Zhirinovsky, at the time head of the far-right Liberal Democratic Party of Russia, argued that US-inspired regime change in the region constitutes a direct threat to Russia and that, if Syria were to fall, the battle would be taken to countries nearer to Russia, such as Iran (see Zhekova 2018, 75–77). Aleksandr Prokhanov, the editor-in-chief of the extreme nationalist newspaper *Zavtra*, claimed that the US is trying to instigate 'chaos' in a huge area of instability between Russia and China, and thereby establish a 'new conception of world order' by fomenting conflict among regional states (Orlov 2012).

Nationalist constituencies are forthright in asserting Russia's role as a great power in the international arena; their views are often reflected in official statements, even if actual decision-making has been more pragmatic and less confrontational. They have far greater influence than liberal opinion formers, who have criticised the leadership's preparedness to sacrifice relations with the West and the major Arab economic powers in favour of playing a more assertive independent role in the MENA region. The leading liberal politician Grigorii Yavlinskii argued that Russia's 'short-sighted' policy is alienating the US, as well as potential allies among the Arab states, and risks overextending itself militarily in both Ukraine and Syria at the expense of domestic priorities: 'Further participation in the Syrian war on the side of brutal dictator Bashar al-Assad, who probably does not disdain of chemical weapons, as well as adventurism with bloody consequences in Ukraine, is morally unacceptable and represents an absolute political dead-end' (MEMRI 2017). Mikhail Zygar', the liberal founder and editor of the only Russian independent news TV channel, *Dozhd'*, during the early years of the Arab Spring, inferred that, by supporting Assad, Russia was renouncing its pretence of being a democracy and would end up 'as a normal Eastern tyranny, a normal rogue state' (Zygar' 2015). The opinions of respondents interviewed for this book were divided, between a majority who broadly support the state's interpretation of events and a minority who are more critical of Russia's response to regional trends and advocate a more cooperative approach to relations with its Western partners.

The media's role as an intervening factor between state decision-making and public opinion also deserves consideration. Russian media sources have, unsurprisingly, tended to reflect the political affiliation of the outlet concerned; given the level of state control over the media, they have mostly sought to legitimise the Putin government's approach to the Arab Spring, engaging in politically active agenda-building in opposition to what are portrayed as deficient Western policies (Judina and Platonov 2019, 158; see also Yablokov 2015). Important influence on public opinion is exerted by the state television channel *RT* (formerly *Russia Today*), which in 2007 launched its Arabic service covering the Middle East and Europe, attracting a lot of attention in Arab countries. Its promotion of 'soft power' in a network of MENA countries is supported by the *Rossotrudnichestvo* federal agency, responsible for propagating Russia's cultural and humanitarian presence abroad (Kozhanov 2018, 25). Analysis of a sample of social media comments in response to *RT* videos on YouTube revealed that they reflected closely Russian government narratives about the Syria conflict, called 'Russia's first live television war'. Coverage intensified from the day Russia's intervention was approved and went on to emphasise its brevity and proportionality, while magnifying the culpability of the Western powers; its framing of the conflict sought to provide legitimation for Russia as a guarantor of security, contributing to conflict resolution and acting in accordance with international law in coming to the aid of Syrians. *RT* viewers largely accepted its representations, with strong majority support for intervention; they mainly expressed anger towards the US and mistrust of international actors and institutions, alongside respect and gratitude towards Russia for its role in the conflict (Crilley and Chatterje-Doody 2020).

The extensive state-managed media campaign to promote Russia's foreign policy successes appears to have been largely accepted by the public, which perceives as positive the strengthening of Russia's international status and military capabilities (Petrov and Gel'man 2019, 451). Levada Center polling data suggest that a solid majority of survey respondents had an entirely or mostly positive attitude towards the strikes on Islamic State by the Russian air force, an opinion which remained consistent over three polls carried out in the months following Russia's intervention, in early October 2015, at the end of October 2015 and in March 2016 (see Levada Center 2015b, 2015a, 2016a). Respondents in the latter two surveys accepted that the government's main goals were to neutralise armed threats by Islamist extremists spilling over into Russia and defend the Assad leadership against US-provoked 'colour revolutions'; only a fifth of respondents accepted Western media claims that Russian air strikes were causing civilian casualties in Syria. A substantial majority in the March 2016 survey supported the withdrawal of the main part of Russian forces in Syria, judging that the military campaign had achieved its aims.

At the same time, some Levada Center opinions also reflect criticism of Russia, with a large minority of respondents concerned over possible longer-term involvement in Syria or the risk of casualties among Russian troops arising from military action or terrorist attacks (Levada Center 2015b). Only a small minority voiced support for direct military involvement in the form of boots on the ground (Levada Center 2015a). Dmitri Trenin reported that members of his staff approached him for private advice about whether their sons were likely to be drafted into the military and sent into Syria, indicating fears about an 'Afghanistan effect' (Trenin 2017b). Russian non-governmental and human rights organisations have co-authored a detailed report analysing human rights and international humanitarian law violations during the Syria conflict, with the aim of alerting Russian society to gaps in official reporting (Russian NGOs, 2021, 7). Public concern may thus have been a constraining, if not decisive, factor in the way that the Syria campaign was managed. It should be noted that some of the Levada findings differ from social media comments in response to *RT* videos cited above; how official narratives were promoted to the Russian public debates through the governing elite's information campaign in order to seek legitimation of its policies, and to what extent public perceptions were influenced by alternative arguments and concerns over the impact of military action, merit a more extensive programme of research in order to generate a more accurate assessment of the influence of public debate on Russian foreign policy in the Arab Spring.

Conclusions

The impact of Russia's domestic politics on foreign policymaking in the MENA region must be seen in the context of the challenges that the Arab Spring has presented to political authority at the national level. The response of Russia's elites to the overthrow of incumbent governments was motivated by the defence of Russia's legitimacy and sovereignty against the West's transformative agenda:

> Putin's external policy in the Syria crisis, the justifications he offers for the support of incumbent if illiberal regimes, his aversion to projecting external standards (democratic or otherwise) for the legitimacy of rulers and his insistence on the illegality of policies promoting regime change all reflect his preoccupation with central political control in Moscow. (Allison 2013b, 815)

In response, Russia's governing elite has sought increasingly to consolidate a strong state authority to preserve domestic power structures and insulate the country against externally promoted liberal ideas, advancing conservative beliefs rooted in a distinctive cultural and civilisational identity in order to unite state and society behind its system of governance. At the same time, it projects its preferred norms and values into its external relations in competition with the more progressive development models that the West claims to offer. These now appear to be longer-term trends in Russian foreign policy.

However, there is scant evidence to sustain the claims of some scholars that, first, the assertive policy of an illiberal Russian governing elite constitutes an attempt to distract attention from domestic weakness and rally support at home, and second, that it translates directly into support for incumbent leaderships in the Arab countries in a process of authoritarian diffusion. While the beliefs of the Putin leadership broadly determine foreign policy, decision-making on specific issues depends significantly on complex, multi-level transactions with other countries and the contingency of often unforeseen events. The actions of Russian elites are transactional rather than ideological. Liberal Western scholarship, privileging reductive explanations to do with ideology or regime type, has often mistaken or misrepresented causal factors to explain the influence of Russia's domestic order on its MENA policy: a more sophisticated appreciation of the interaction between Russia's foreign policy and its domestic context is needed. Underestimating contextual factors means that we risk losing sight of how Russia's self-understanding translates into a set of durable beliefs about its role in the international order that serve to legitimise the policies of its governing elite.

Russia's involvement in the MENA region, particularly in the Syrian civil war, has undeniably influenced the Putin leadership's policy practices and contributed to the reconfiguration of institutions and elite structures towards a greater centralisation of decision-making, with a more pronounced role in state policy for the military and security agencies. At the same time, informal ties between actors, operating within formal institutions or structures in a non-transparent 'vertical' of power, influence policy in specific areas, occasionally causing problems for Russia's external relations due to the closed and sometimes dysfunctional nature of a personalised political system. The concentration of power at the top generates flaws in policymaking; far from presiding over a smoothly functioning transmission belt of decision-making, the governing elite struggles to identify emerging problems and initiate policy shifts in response. This led to costly errors in Syria – more of which may yet become apparent – and could prove to be a crucial factor in the outcome of Russia's present war with Ukraine; as the eminent UK scholar Lawrence Freedman suggests, Putin's key defence and security advisors act as an 'echo chamber', suppressing open and critical feedback from experts that might have warned against a risky military operation against Kyiv (Beaumont 2022).

A final point relates to Russia's promotion of cultural narratives, rooted in its national belief systems, that shape its state identity and role in the international order. This may be seen as part of a global trend in which 'shifting power configurations are entwined with new or reemergent expressions of cultural difference' (Reus-Smit 2018, 222). As argued earlier, emphasis on cultural diversity not only reflects differences in values across international society but also challenges the hierarchy of ideational and institutional power in the international system. The study of a nation's cultural identity and of temporally contingent state interests as causal factors in foreign policy should remain conceptually and analytically distinct (see Darwich 2019, 32; Owen et al 2018, 289), but the interaction between ideational and material forces is manifest in Russian approaches to the Arab Spring. Russia's contemporary foreign policy is determined both by structural factors and by principles relating to state legitimacy and cultural diversity, reflected in the governing elites' interpretation of international legal norms. It is this that we turn to in Chapter 4.

4

Russia, the Arab uprisings and international norms

> The UN Charter, the fruit of the great Victory over Nazism, remains the keystone of the entire international system … Of course the UN is not ideal but, as Dag Hammarskjöld remarked, it was not created to take mankind to heaven, but to save humanity from hell. (Lavrov 2015d)

Right up to the end of the Soviet period, the Third World – as it was then known – was described as 'an arena where revisionist political aspirations could be promoted or opposed' by the superpowers to preserve their spheres of influence; in regions such as the Middle East and North Africa, they engaged in 'pre-emptive, preventive and reactive commitments' to client states, defending or subverting legitimate governments through the provision of political and where necessary military support, even if their interests there were marginal (Allison and Williams 1990, 2–3, 19; see also Allison 2013a, 24; Herrmann and Ned Lebow 2004, 2–3). In the political and security context of the Cold War, 'the balance of power and shared understandings of spheres of influence played a central role and in ways that were very hard to reconcile with legal norms seeking to regulate the use of armed force' (Hurrell 2005, 17). This raises a number of questions of direct relevance to this study. How have the approaches adopted by Russia and the Western powers in the MENA region changed in recent years? How do we understand Russia's interpretation of the legal norms that underpin international order in analysing its thinking and behaviour during the Arab Spring?

Recent Western commentary has largely portrayed Russian foreign policy as challenging the post-Cold War international order, driven by a revisionist impulse and antagonistic to liberal Western interpretations of key norms and the US's use of coercive power. As Roy Allison suggests, Russia's legal arguments, seen in their political context, can not be divorced from both structural and normative power factors (Allison 2013a, 170). Others argue bluntly that Russia's policy in the MENA region is aimed at asserting its great power status through 'destabilizing policies that challenge the existing order in Ukraine, Syria, and elsewhere'; while Russia projects itself as a constructive actor committed to resolving the Syria conflict, its policies 'will continue to be subordinate to its *larger geopolitical and security goals of revising the international order*' (Krickovic and Weber 2018b, 374, 380; emphasis added). A recent study of Russian diplomatic practice in international organisations, including the UN, has concluded that Moscow consistently defends policies that are motivated more by status considerations than cooperative efforts to manage security challenges (Schmitt 2020, 923). Richard Sakwa describes Russia as neo-revisionist rather than revisionist, practising 'voluntaristic' decision-making in both domestic and international politics (Sakwa 2015, 68–69; 2017, 128–131). According to leading Russian commentators, Moscow's strategic aim in MENA is to restore its global power status, strengthening its claims by presenting a simplified account of Western plots to undermine sovereign states in the Arab world (Frolov 2016a; Zvyagel'skaya 2014, 79). At the same time, Moscow defends the political legitimacy and moral rightness of its own policies in the MENA region; Lavrov has repeatedly denounced Western attempts to contain Russia for standing up for its own legitimate interests (Lavrov 2014c).

The contest over both power and norms has thus become a defining feature of Russia's current relations with the West. In this chapter we examine how Russia's distinctive perception of international legal norms shapes its response to the problems posed by the Arab Spring. The first section explores how Russia articulates its understanding of international norms in opposition to Western approaches, staking a claim to legitimacy and defending its conception of proper behaviour in international society. We then offer a closer analysis of Russia's interpretation of legal and constitutional norms governing the use of force, sovereignty and sovereign equality, before going on to examine its approach to the doctrine of Responsibility to Protect and humanitarian assistance in the case of the Syria conflict. We conclude by considering the implications of Russia's use of legal normative arguments to further its strategic aims in the MENA region and how this might shape its future role there.

Russia and the international legal order

Andrew Hurrell identified emerging problems of global governance in the post-Cold War era:

> In many cases the new security threats derive not from state strength, military power, and geopolitical ambition; but rather from state weakness and the absence of political legitimacy; from the failure of states to provide minimal conditions of public order within their borders; from the way in which domestic instability and internal violence can spill into the international arena; and

from the incapacity of weak states to form viable building blocks of a stable regional order. (Hurrell 2005, 26)

International responses to the challenges posed by conflict in weak states to ensure human security were brought into even sharper focus by the Arab Spring. The MENA region has witnessed the erosion of the exclusive power of states and the emergence of de-territorialised power relations across national borders; non- or quasi-state actors, with strong roots in social or religious identities, have taken on an increasing number of governance functions in pursuit of their interests (Marchetti and Al Zahrani 2017, 109–110). The privatisation of violence, with various groups mobilising armed forces in pursuit of self-protection or self-interest, complicates the problem of distinguishing between legitimate resistance and the activity of criminals and terrorists. In some countries, state and non-state actors interact within a framework of pluralist governance while at the same time engaging in political rivalries (Hazbun 2016, 1054; Naumkin 2017b, 27). In others, authoritarian governments have responded to threats to their survival by narrowing the space for reform and cracking down on political opposition, lacking not only the will but also the capacity to tackle acute social and economic crises and resolve the fundamental causes of intra-state conflicts.

Intense debates have raged in international relations scholarship about the legitimacy and legality of external intervention to manage or mitigate these internal conflicts and deal with threats to international security, about the effectiveness of the UN as the source of collective legitimation of norms for the use of force, and about the consequences of inaction in cases where populations are subjected to government-enforced repression. Russian arguments have in fact been reflected in longstanding debates in Western scholarship. Hurrell maintains that

> There are ... powerful legal and moral arguments for seeking to reinstate the centrality of procedural legitimacy and for rejecting the view that international legitimacy should be based around the effective implementation of a set of allegedly shared substantive moral values ... in an international society characterised by deep and fundamental value conflict and by the constant difficulty of managing unequal power, a viable and stable international legal order must be built around shared processes and procedures, accepted understandings of legal sources, and a commitment to diplomatic negotiation and dialogue. The alternative is both normatively unacceptable and politically unviable, namely to open the door to a situation in which it is the strength of a single state or group of states that decides what shall count as law. (Hurrell 2005, 29)

Lawrence Freedman has suggested that liberal interventions and occupations, inspired not by strategic imperatives but by protecting Western values, are inherently *illiberal* in terms of both the means used to prosecute them and the ensuing consequences (Freedman 2005, 103, 2021, 39). While good governance and human rights are projected by the liberal West as empowering the individual against unrepresentative, corrupt and repressive government, many of the non-Western powers believe in a privileged place for the state in the management of international order: in their view,

> justice can be attended to only in these circumstances of order, and normative change has to be resisted where it can be seen as an attack on this inter-state order. They are united in their suspicions that the most powerful Western states will flout Westphalian norms in pursuit of their special interests, and will use international law and organization as tools of those interests. (Foot 2003, 16–17; see also Hurrell 2003, 28)

External actors are faced with apparently irreconcilable political and moral dilemmas when interceding in conflicts and have struggled to agree on ways to promote human security against both state-sanctioned abuses and economic and social neglect.

Suspicions over liberal Western designs lie at the heart of Russia's response to challenges to the international legal normative order. As Lavrov has made clear, Russia's bid for legitimacy rests on respect for the core traditional principles of state sovereignty, sovereign equality, non-intervention and domestic jurisdiction over internal governance, as expressed in the UN Charter – in other words, the pluralist 'Westphalian' norms that underpin the legal basis of international order; only on this basis can Russia cooperate with the West (Lavrov 2015f; see also Allison 2013a, 16; Sakwa 2011, 971; Newman and Zala 2018, 878–879). Russia's defence of these norms is inseparable from power considerations. In a keynote speech, in which the Syrian civil war and the Crimea crisis were very much at the forefront, Putin himself voiced Russia's fundamental concerns about Western claims to 'the right of leadership, or *diktat*':

> International law has been forced to retreat over and over by the onslaught of legal nihilism. Objectivity and justice have been sacrificed on the altar of political expediency. Arbitrary interpretations and biased assessments have replaced legal norms ... We must clearly identify where unilateral actions end and we need to apply multilateral mechanisms, and as part of improving the effectiveness of international law, we must resolve the dilemma between the actions by international community to ensure security and human rights and the principle of national sovereignty and non-interference in the internal affairs of any state ... international relations must be based on international law, which itself should rest on moral principles such as justice, equality and truth. (Putin 2014)

Lavrov has repeated these themes in numerous uncompromising statements, referring to a 'battle of ideas' and defending Russia's positions against continuing attempts by the West to dominate international affairs (Lavrov 2015e). Quoting the former UN Secretary-General Dag Hammarskjöld (see the epigraph to this chapter), he went on to reaffirm the UN Charter principles and attack the West's attempt to foment 'regime change' by exerting pressure on sovereign states to accept liberal Western political, economic and ideological standards (Lavrov 2015d). At the UN General Assembly, he referred specifically to Western-inspired

> unilateral reckless solutions of very complex conflicts and crises which we see in the bleeding region of the Middle East and North Africa, resulting in the destruction of the foundations of global stability ... the decency and legitimacy of any member of the international community should be measured by their respect for the principles of sovereign equality of states and non-interference in internal affairs. (Lavrov 2016d)

He has claimed the support of leading states in Eurasian organisations and across the non-Western world in deploring

> the attack of militant revisionism on the contemporary international legal system. The basic principles of the Middle East settlement process ... and much more are under attack. Our Western colleagues seek to replace the rule of law in international affairs with some kind of 'rules-based order'. These rules are made up according to political expediency and conform to a pattern of double standards. Unfounded accusations of interference in the domestic affairs of particular countries are made while simultaneously engaging in an overt policy of undermining and overthrowing democratically elected governments. (Lavrov 2018d)

Russia thus represents itself as a status quo power, repudiating 'revisionist' Western notions of a 'rules-based' order in favour of preserving the traditional international legal norms that lie at the basis of the pluralist society of states in the modern era (Lavrov 2020d; see also Allison 2020; Averre and Davies 2015, 829). In Russian eyes, legitimacy resides in a common set of rules, defined and established by dialogue and consent over mutual obligations rather than the promotion of 'dubious "values"', and underpinned by the legally structured constitutional order based in the UN Charter system (Lavrov 2020d; see also Allison 2013a, 211–212; Clark 2005, 6). The West's interference in the internal affairs of what it designates as criminal or aggressor states in order to further its humanitarian agenda is tantamount to ideological hegemony and lacks legitimacy. The Western challenge to established sovereignist norms in favour of human rights standards revives historical memories of European great power dominance and cultural-civilisational clashes:

> Solidarist efforts to encourage and defend human rights must be implemented while strictly observing the commonly recognized norms and principles of international law ... no country or group of countries has exclusive authority to create unilaterally any new 'norms of behaviour' which do not rest on this universal basis. Imposing one's own interpretation of human rights standards on others will only aggravate cultural and religious contradictions and risks provoking a conflict of civilizations and undermining efforts to establish a stable system of global development. (Lavrov 2014b; see also Freedman 2005, 101)

Russia has asserted at the UN General Assembly that states bear primary responsibility for protecting and promoting human rights, with UN structures playing a supportive role; it opposes linking the work of the Human Rights Council with the Security Council and condemned the use of human rights as a pretext for interfering in the internal affairs of sovereign states in contravention of the fundamental principles of international law (MFA 2020a, paragraph 54).

These principles have become firmly established in Russian legal circles, which align closely with Russia's foreign policy doctrine and the views of state elites (Mälksoo 2015, 80; see also Allison 2017, 526), though alternative views have been expressed by some officials and experts (see Baranovsky and Mateiko 2016, 52). A leading figure in Russia's academic legal establishment has argued that customary law enshrined in the Universal Declaration of Human Rights embodies only the moral and political commitments of UN member states and has no priority over international legal norms, and in fact, often contravenes Russia's interests; he has criticised Western violations of international law in Libya and Syria (Khlestov 2003, 119; 2013, 20–21). As one expert concludes, in Russian eyes,

> individual violations of human rights, while deplorable, are not comparable to all the damage that abuse of Western-inspired human rights discourse could do to Russia as a country ... no references to the necessity to protect human rights may justify attempts to violate such principles as the sovereign equality of states, non-intervention of states in each other's internal affairs, use or threat of force in international relations. (Mälksoo 2015, 122–123, 124)

The Western emphasis on individual human rights in evolving liberal doctrines – discussed further with reference to the Responsibility to Protect later in this chapter – thus often appears at the forefront of the normative contest in which Russia is perceived in the West as an illiberal actor in international law.

How international norms justifying interventions in exceptional situations should be applied – which values should be privileged in particular cases and what can be accepted as a consensus on which to take action – was highlighted by Lavrov at the Munich international security conference, with direct reference to the MENA region:

> Who is a legitimate ruler and who isn't? When is it permissible to cooperate with authoritarian regimes ... and when is it allowed to support their overthrow by force? In which cases should we recognise forces who have come to power through democratic elections and in which cases should we refuse contact with them? What are the criteria and standards determining all of this? (Lavrov 2013h; see also Allison 2013b, 816)

At the UN, Russia has launched a fierce defence of its conception of a 'multipolar' international order underpinning a more democratic system of global governance, seeking to legitimise its policies in the Syria conflict and loosen the West's grip on decision-making authority (see Lavrov 2020b). Russia's resistance to the hegemonic designs of the US involves both defending the norm of sovereignty in legal and constitutional terms before international society and at the same time using it to reinforce its status as a great power in the international order (see Deyermond 2016, 971–972; Lo 2015, 73).

Legal, moral and constitutional norms are translated into legitimate principles through negotiation and diplomatic pressure in which both power and ideational differences matter (Clark 2007, 3–4; see also Allison 2013a, 11–12). Put simply, strong states – particularly the great powers – vie to influence international law through trade-offs among competing goals and interests (Hurd 2018, 273–274). Russia's claim to legitimacy is closely bound up with its P5 veto power in the UN Security Council, which allows it to shape rule-making and define the legal-normative agenda to meet its objectives. Its defence of the sovereignty norm and attempts to justify its own involvement in the Syria conflict – claiming that its support for Assad is motivated by averting regime change and that its military operations against the opposition were aimed at fighting Islamist terrorism – clearly illustrate the extent to which Moscow makes political use of legal arguments (Allison 2020, 977; see also Schmitt 2020, 939).

The use of force

As suggested above, the use of military force by Western states to intervene in internal conflicts, prompted by declarations of humanitarian concern, is one of the most contentious foreign policy issues of the post-Cold War era. Western interventions have challenged established norms in seeking to reconcile legitimate action to avert massive human rights violations with the legality of using force against sovereign states. The Russian leadership has constantly harked back to NATO's Operation Allied Force in 1999, a humanitarian intervention in response to Serbian attacks on Kosovar Albanians; it was widely perceived by Western experts as legitimate if not formally legal, as it did not have a clear UN mandate, but Russia presented it as an attempt to enforce the West's normative agenda and carve out a sphere of influence (see Averre 2009; Allison 2013a, chapter 3; Freedman 2005, 102–103). Russia has also repeatedly denounced the US-led coalition's invasion of Iraq in 2003, carried out again without UN Security Council authorisation, as a cynical manipulation of international legal rules (see Gray 2008, 352–358). In Russian eyes, both cases constituted an attack on the international society of sovereign states, with long-term adverse consequences for the international system.

Moscow was on firm ground in querying both the legality and legitimacy of the 2003 Iraq intervention – a pivotal moment in the recent history of the Middle East. The George W. Bush administration appealed to pre-emptive self-defence against an imminent attack using WMDs, widely recognised to be admissible under international law, but in fact inclined towards a more permissive and open-ended concept of preventive self-defence (Heinze 2011, 1073; see also Allison 2013a, 100–101). A secondary argument, largely for public consumption rather than a legal proposition, was that Iraq constituted a liberal humanitarian intervention to facilitate regime change and democratic reform. When no WMDs were found in Iraq after the invasion, the case for intervention came to depend on the humanitarian argument. However, experts concluded that 'there is little reason to afford this argument meaningful legal significance toward creating a customary law exception for humanitarian intervention' (Heinze 2011, 1075; see also Byers 2005, 60–63). Freedman reflected the common view that the US's argument could be challenged on three accounts: first, any gain for the Iraqi people in terms of human rights had to be weighed against the ensuing chaos and violence; second, the international community may be sympathetic to humanitarian claims but would be equally concerned that these claims could be used to justify less clear-cut interventions; third, the failure to obtain a second UN Security Council resolution to gain international support weakened the case for coercive military action (Freedman 2005, 93–94).

Despite its support at the time for the US 'war on terror', Russia reflected the majority view that there was no justification for military action bypassing the Security Council given the lack of proof that Iraq was supporting international terrorism or had WMDs, asserting that 'the desire to change the political regime in that country [is] in direct contradiction with international law' (cited in Gray 2008, 364). Moscow opposed moves by the US to view war as ultimately a discretionary instrument of foreign policy by claiming legitimacy in exceptional circumstances and setting aside strict legalistic interpretations contained in the UN Charter. As one leading authority concluded, 'there seemed insufficient grounds to validate the Iraq war because of its legality, and no persuasive reason to affirm its legitimacy' (Falk 2005, 35, 41). Indeed, the process subsequently mandated by the UN Secretary-General to examine action to address major contemporary threats, in preparation for the 2005 World Summit, concluded that no change in the UN Charter provisions was needed; the prohibition of the use of force in Article 2(4), the right to self-defence in Article 51 and Chapter VII on collective action were considered adequate to deal with new threats (Gray 2008, 3–4).

The tension between legal norms governing the use of force and the strategic foreign policy aims of powerful states re-emerged during the Arab Spring. As detailed earlier in this book, Moscow's belief – supported by available evidence (see Martin 2022, 162–163) – that NATO's intervention in Libya exceeded the mandate in UNSC resolution 1973 to protect civilians and was an elaborate cover for regime change – ultimately leading to regional destabilisation, as in the aftermath of the Iraq war – shaped its resolute opposition to any measures that might open the door to intervention in the Syria conflict. The threat of force by the US and its allies to punish the alleged use of chemical weapons by Assad's forces in August 2013 was also portrayed by Moscow – pointing to the spurious accusations by the US and UK of the imminent use of WMDs by Iraq in 2003 – as a prelude to regime change. Russia has also disputed US arguments in favour of pre-emptive or preventive action against Iran – graphically illustrated in the drone strike in 2020 that killed Qassem Soleimani, the powerful Iranian military commander – deriving from longstanding concerns in Washington over Tehran's sponsorship of terrorism, the challenge it poses to Middle East peace, the threat posed by its alleged nuclear weapons programme and its denial of the aspirations of its people for freedom. Moscow's defence of Tehran at the UN is not unconditional, as it is sensitive to the threat posed by Iran's nuclear enrichment programme to the nuclear nonproliferation regime, but its fears of the consequences of US attacks – likely to be even more destabilising than the Iraq intervention – compel it to oppose US coercive measures.

Russia justified its own armed intervention in Syria in international legal terms as support for the legitimate authorities in resisting outside subversion, responding to an invitation by the Assad government to deal with the internal threat posed by international terrorism and denying that it was intervening on the side of Assad in the civil war. In contrast, Moscow has roundly criticised the 'illegal' presence on Syrian soil of US troops fighting Islamic State alongside Kurdish forces. State practice has shown that the legality of intervention by invitation is permissible (see Gray 2008, 81–82, 84); the other external powers did not in fact express any legal reservations against the purposes of Russia's intervention and confined themselves to criticising its targeting of the civilian population. At the same time, widespread criticism – including by some non-Western states – of Russia's support for Assad's war effort, and its portrayal of the opposition as 'terrorists' in order to delegitimise them politically, showed that the international community is not ready to bestow automatic sanction on foreign interventions in civil wars under the cover of invitation by governments (see Bannelier-Christakis 2016, 761–764). Moreover, the majority vote at the UN General Assembly in 2016 in favour of preparing an investigation into war crimes and human rights breaches in Syria – in spite of Russia's objections – highlighted the extent to which the international community rejects the absolutist defence of state sovereignty in cases of violations of international humanitarian law and is prepared to accept norms obliging states to accept responsibility for human rights (Allison 2020, 990).

The application in practice of the principles legitimising the use of force in international law is neither clear nor uncontested. Legal reform within the UN to close the gap between legality and legitimacy is fraught with difficulties, due to the mistrust of some leading states of the humanitarian rationale for intervention and their opposition to a more expansive interpretation of permissible force, even when sanctioned by the UN (Falk 2005, 39). A prominent factor in the Russian position has been its resistance to the post-Cold War Western 'liberal triumphalism' that 'attributes to "liberal democracies" an inherent peacefulness in their relations with one another, a greater "moral reliability" than other states in their international relations, and an unmatched record of achievement in the protection of their citizens' civil and political rights' (Reus-Smit 2005a, 72, 75–76). Russia – apprehensive over the challenge posed by the liberal Western democracies' claim to be 'on the right side of history' – has raised fundamental procedural issues about coercive external interventions: when a democratic coalition can be said to exist, at what point it constitutes a legitimate decision-making forum and what forms of international support it should rest upon. While democratic governance and the privileging of human rights are widely seen as part of a new standard of international legitimacy, questions remain over whether democratic coalitions can claim sufficient legitimacy to justify the use of force, particularly when a UN Security Council mandate can not be obtained.

Hurrell has identified differences between 'liberal constitutionalists' – including Russia and many of the non-Western powers – and 'cosmopolitan moralists' – comprising the Western liberal democracies – in debates to justify and legitimise coercive action. For the former, legitimacy depends on the use of coercive power being constrained by constitutional procedures, especially as embodied in the UN Charter; for the latter, rules relating to the use of force

> should be interpreted in the light of the substantive moral values on which the legitimacy of international law and of international society must ultimately depend ... It has become very common to argue that a community of liberal democratic states should be the body that legitimises the use of force in cases of humanitarian intervention or expanded self-defence. But this community has either no institutional embodiment or deeply imperfect ones (as in the claim that NATO as a military alliance should play such a role). (Hurrell 2005, 21, 24; see also Falk 2005, 34)

The political contest between 'liberal constitutionalists' and 'cosmopolitan moralists' poses key dilemmas that have emerged with renewed urgency in the Arab Spring. The first dilemma is a crisis in the laws of war, in which the costs of non-compliance for states violating accepted humanitarian norms are being reduced by powerful actors seeking to justify their use of force. Moscow has consistently denied that its air campaign in Syria, supposedly against Islamic State, breaches these norms and maintains a diplomatic and information offensive to repudiate claims about the illegality of its actions, raising concerns that it is using the threat of terrorism as a pretext to downgrade the domestic protection of human rights (Clark et al 2018, 321, 335). At the same time the US, though now reluctant to undertake large-scale coercive interventions, alleges that illiberal regimes in Iran and Syria pose threats due to their sponsorship of terrorism and violation of non-proliferation regimes, and the selective use of lethal force by Washington and its allies cannot be ruled out.

The second dilemma is a crisis of multilateralism, stemming from actors' differing conceptions of contemporary international society and from the lack of capacity and will to supply consistent leadership within international institutions. The problem has surfaced not only between the non-Western powers and the Western liberal democracies but also within the Western alliance itself, given the Trump administration's variable commitment to multilateralism (Smith 2018). Effective multilateralism is being abandoned for more limited forms of negotiation, within narrower formats that incorporate a group of partner states adhering to a specific set of rules that they recognise as legitimate (see Lo 2015, 76–77). Russia claims the support of non-Western states in regional formats where it plays a leading role – the Collective Security Treaty Organisation, the Shanghai Cooperation Organisation and the BRICS group. Many of these states have aligned themselves with Russian sovereignist policy in the Middle East, even though their support for Moscow has not been unequivocal (Allison 2020, 988; Deyermond 2016, 980–981). In dismissing the Western-promoted 'rules-based order', Russia makes ample use of its own set of rules that rely on mutual obligations and interests among its partners, even though Lavrov has stated that the UN remains 'an indispensable venue for overcoming disagreements and coordinating the international community's actions' and that regional groupings should remain subordinate to it (Lavrov 2018d). The liberal order is thus being challenged by 'multiple, crosscutting international orders' (Acharya 2017, 272); the shifting distribution of power within the international system gives rise to increased pluralism in a number of sub-systems exhibiting distinct legal and normative characteristics – a 'normative regionalism' – and resisting the encroachment of liberal norms on a country's domestic order (Allison 2017, 530; 2013a, 6–7; see also Sakwa 2017, 44–46). This now appears to represent a longer-term trend in Russia's future use of its influence in the international system.

Sovereignty and sovereign equality

As highlighted earlier in this chapter, Russia explicitly privileges the core norm of sovereignty – the '*grundnorm* of international society' (Reus-Smit 2001, 519) – against the threat to the stability and integrity of the state posed by external intervention. Emerging human rights norms that challenge the traditional legal disposition of sovereignty and non-intervention have been fiercely disputed by Russia. Putin himself, shortly after becoming president in 2000, declared at an international meeting in Moscow dedicated to advancing the Middle East peace process that the basic legal principles of sovereignty and territorial integrity could not be overridden by the 'slogan' of humanitarian intervention, calling for the strengthening of the role of the UN and collective efforts to tackle global problems (Petrov 2000). Internal conflicts in the MENA countries during the Arab Spring have exposed the fundamental tension between sovereignty and the demands of justice expressed in evolving human rights norms, leading to political divisions among the leading powers.

Moscow has sustained a vigorous diplomatic offensive in support of its position. Lavrov has asserted that the international legal instruments of the UN Security Council are universal in their application and are adequate to solve the world's crises if they are not violated by the Western powers; he explicitly contrasted the success of the UN with the failure of the League of Nations which 'did not have a mechanism to take account of the interests of the leading states, on which the general state of security in the world depends' (Lavrov 2014d). Russia's approach in claiming to support collective approaches to resolving the Syria conflict through consensus and compromise in the Security Council, rather than by undermining Syria's sovereignty through coercive intervention – in Lavrov's words, 'more correct, more ethical, if you like' – derives from an understanding that it is the *moral* purpose of sovereign states to maintain peace and security in an international environment characterised by increasing interdependence and the proliferation of security challenges (Lavrov 2014e).

But a fundamental problem with Russian arguments lies in the weakness of postcolonial states in the MENA region. Despite the recognition by international society of their formal legal entitlement to sovereignty, several of these states struggle to provide political goods to their citizens and lack the institutional features of empirical statehood as defined by classical international law; deficient in political will and institutional authority, they fail to ensure effective legal or constitutional restraints aimed at protecting human rights against the abuse of power (see Jackson 1990, 21, 47; also Reus-Smit 2001, 524). Non- or sub-state actors – various rebel, militia and insurgent groups, either serving sectional interests or with strong roots in social or religious identities, operating in situations where rules are disputed or ignored – pose a fundamental challenge to state authority, creating a form of 'hybrid sovereignty' (Hazbun 2016, 1054), a situation complicated by the increasing permeability of state boundaries to transnational security challenges. In the case of Syria, governance structures are dispersed among networks of actors, either competing or cooperating to perform key state tasks; while Assad has been able to exploit the state's existing institutional and administrative capacities, huge differences exist between territories nominally under his control (Collombier et al 2019, 41–42). The conflict has not only left some areas outside of government control but has transformed Syria 'from a "shadow state" dominated by the security apparatus into a "transactional state" dominated by regime-aligned profiteers', thereby further eroding Syria's domestic sovereignty (Khatib and Sinjab 2018, 1–3; see also Gaub 2018b).

Syria's dependence on external actors is an additional factor. The Assad government is partnered with foreign states, particularly Russia and Iran, and with foreign non-state militias, while opposition forces are also supported by external governments and their proxies. Syria's domestic sovereignty is thus compromised in terms of the effectiveness, legitimacy and territorial reach of the state's authority (Del Sarto 2017, 771; see Kaldor 2013, 125). The country is effectively divided between Russian, Iranian, Turkish and US protectorates. Russia, together with Iran, has continued to deploy military forces in support of its efforts to force a political resolution to the civil war. Turkish forces occupy a swathe of territory along the border with Syria and administer the Idlib governorate, while US and French forces patrol the Kurdish autonomous administration in the northeast. This kind of fragmentation is mirrored in Libya and Yemen, and to an extent in Iraq. Although some experts emphasise that the MENA regional system of states and borders is likely to remain largely intact, the picture that emerges from the Arab Spring is radically different to the simplified image, promoted by Russia, of a strong public authority governing a sovereign state. As a leading MENA expert concludes, 'the Arab uprisings ... have led to a protracted process of contestation and at least the partial unravelling of the authoritarian contract on which prior sovereignty was based' (Fawcett 2017, 804).

Russia's official statements on the Arab Spring, reaffirmed in its foreign policy concept, also lay explicit emphasis on the norm of sovereign equality (MFA 2016d; Lavrov 2020b), which is firmly embedded in UN Charter-based international law and entitles states to equal rights in the international system and sovereign self-government 'regardless of material capabilities or internal social/political arrangements' (Welsh 2010, 427; see also Gray 2008, 67–68; Krasner 1999, 14). In order to protect these sovereign rights and ensure the maintenance of peace and stability in international society, coercive action internationally has been limited in important respects. As detailed earlier, states may only use force legitimately if they are acting either in self-defence or collectively to uphold international peace and security, and then only multilaterally through the UN Security Council (Lavrov 2011b; see also Reus-Smit 2005a, 71). Sovereign equality thus serves as legal protection against the encroachment of external norms on domestic arrangements; in Russian eyes, interventions to improve social and political governance in states where civil conflicts have varying deep-rooted causes threaten the consensus underpinning the pluralist nature of international society and provoke confrontation. The right of non-intervention has generally been upheld (albeit selectively) by other non-Western leaderships who reject the notion of a privileged position for Western states in drawing up the rules of conduct for others (Chebankova 2017, 222–223; Ayoob 2002, 47–48). Russia, using its weight as a P5 member of the UNSC, thus resists the liberal intrusion into the sovereign equality norm deriving from international humanitarian law; Lavrov has declared that the core precepts underpinning the governance of international society are at stake (see Averre and Davies 2015, 830).

The Responsibility to Protect

Following the end of the Cold War, liberal understandings of human rights began increasingly to shape the central norms of international society. A body of international law developed by the UN against grievous humanitarian offences affirmed the moral and legal justification for action to lessen human rights abuses by state authorities; the sovereign privileges of a state should depend on its willingness and ability to protect the core rights of its citizens, the violation of which may lead in extreme cases to the state's loss of immunity from armed intervention under Chapter VII of the UN Charter (Hurrell 2005, 20; Jackson 1990, 144–145; Morris 2005, 276). This notion of sovereignty as responsibility paved the way for the doctrine of Responsibility to Protect (R2P), a framework for which was laid out in the 2001 International Commission on Intervention and State Sovereignty (ICISS) report, which elaborated principles for intervention and appeared to call for a change in UN Security Council practice under the UN Charter (Falk 2005, 40). The ICISS findings were reinforced in the 2005 World Summit Outcome (WSO) document, which affirmed the responsibility to protect civilians against genocide, war crimes, ethnic cleansing and crimes against humanity. This was reaffirmed in UNSC resolution 1674 of 28 April 2006, which stated that the 'commission of systematic, flagrant and widespread violations of international humanitarian and human rights law in situations of armed conflict, may constitute a threat to international peace and security' that might lead the UN to adopt appropriate (albeit unspecified) steps. This was followed up in the 2009 UN report *Implementing the Responsibility to Protect*, which contained recommendations on authorising enforcement measures and at the same time designated the UN as the ultimate authority to approve action (see Averre and Davies 2015, 815).

The WSO document shifted the emphasis from coercive intervention to strengthening sovereignty, primarily through diplomatic and non-military measures, in order to prevent serious human rights abuses. The possibility of Chapter VII enforcement measures remained, but only if authorised by the UN Security Council to respond to threats to international peace and security. As a result, 'R2P does not add to the body of UN procedural laws or impart new competences to or change the powers of the Security Council, or create any legal obligations for states to act'; the onus remains on the P5 states to find consensus to approve enforcement measures (Averre and Davies 2015, 817; Hehir 2013, 152; see also Garwood-Gowers 2013). Crucially, a majority of UN member states rejected the ICISS's recommendation to include decision-making criteria about when to use force to intervene in the domestic affairs of states. Consensus thus depends on the political will of powerful states, often motivated by national interests, to agree on what can be achieved (Forsythe 2012, 12). Russia's initial response to the ICISS report appeared positive. It supported the purpose of R2P as expressed in UNSC resolution 1674 and has engaged with the first two 'pillars' of the concept, namely the state's responsibility to protect populations and the international community's duty to support states in meeting its responsibility (Averre and

Davies 2015, 822). At the same time, Moscow voiced reservations over incorporating the 'immature concept' of R2P into UN documents, which might lead to a broader and more arbitrary interpretation of its provisions (Baranovsky and Mateiko 2016, 50; Allison 2013a, 67–68).

Establishing a normative consensus in the P5 presented a significant problem in the case of Libya. As mentioned earlier in this book, Russia supported UNSC resolution 1970, invoked under Chapter VII, and condemned the violence used by Gaddafi's forces against the protesters, exhorting the Libyan authorities to observe the norms of international civil and human rights law. Moscow did not initially invoke the sovereignty principle, recognising that Gaddafi had lost legitimacy and that some enforcement measures were needed, once the League of Arab States, GCC and OIC had approved a no-fly zone in response to continuing violence by Libyan government forces and the perceived threat of a massacre in Benghazi. At the same time, Moscow called for a political settlement, accepting restrictive measures on those guilty of abuses against the civilian population but rejecting sanctions (UNSC 2011f; Garwood-Gowers 2013; Dunne and Teitt 2015, 380). Russia subsequently abstained from voting on UNSC resolution 1973, again influenced by the LAS's support for it.

However, Russia's position shifted following the use of air strikes by the NATO-led coalition and statements from Western leaders urging the forcible removal of Gaddafi, prompting widespread concern among non-Western states about the prospect of a 'Libya model' for the Alliance's future expeditionary operations (UNSC 2012e; Dietrich 2013, 341). Moscow's criticism of the intervention in Libya was targeted at the means of implementing responsible protection, rather than the purposes underlying R2P, and centred on three main issues (see Garwood-Gowers 2013, section IIIB). The first was the charge that, in the course of its military operation, NATO had exceeded the scope of the mandate in the UNSC resolutions by arming the rebels and attacking targets beyond those necessary for the protection of civilians. The problem was compounded by vague enforcement mandates that authorise states to use 'all necessary means' to protect people. The second issue related to the claim that civilian protection was used as a pretext by some Western powers to achieve the strategic aim of removing Gaddafi, leading to a clear accountability deficit (UNSC 2011g; Martin 2022, 62–63, 162). The third was that the spread of violence and instability across Libya's borders resulting from the intervention proved to be worse than the consequences of inaction.

Russia increasingly highlighted the threat to the norms of sovereignty and non-intervention represented by R2P's pillar III enforcement measures under Chapter VII. Lavrov queried the criteria for coercive action:

> If we want to debate seriously the Responsibility to Protect, then we should ask the question: is it a right or a duty ... if we say it is a duty, where are the criteria for interventions? How many victims among the civilian population constitute an acceptable level? A hundred, a thousand? (Lavrov 2013j)

China mounted a defence of non-intervention similar to Russia's, arguing that humanitarian intervention in principle violates UN Charter-based international law and in practice causes more harm than good, serving the interests of intervening states rather than the target state's population (Chen and Yin 2020, 788; Davis 2011, 273). Other leading non-Western powers also supported Russia's objection to the West's framing of the Libya conflict, taking the view that NATO's operation had shifted from enforcing a no-fly zone to facilitating regime change, exceeding the mandate of resolution 1973 (Dunne and Teitt 2015, 382; see also Negrón-Gonzales and Contarino 2014, 265–268; Tocci 2014, 15–16). While endorsing the principle that atrocities committed by state authorities are a legitimate concern to international society, they argued that R2P did not entail an automatic international response in cases of a failure to protect the population.

As highlighted in Chapter 2, Russia made it clear that its response to the hostilities in Syria could not be considered separately from the Libyan case (UNSC 2011b; see also Gifkins 2016, 158). R2P had become firmly linked in American political discourse with the idea of Assad's overthrow, despite the fact that there is no intrinsic link between the principles underlying R2P and regime change to protect the population from atrocity crimes (see Docherty et al 2020, 256–259), apparently justifying Russian warnings and prompting Moscow and Beijing to veto a series of Security Council resolutions targeting the Assad leadership. As the Syria conflict gathered pace, and a few days before Gaddafi's demise, Lavrov delivered a clear-cut summary of Moscow's position:

> A group of countries, primarily Western countries and some Arab regimes, think that the so-called 'concept of Responsibility to Protect' should be universally applied in all cases where peoples begin to express discontent [and] the authorities use forceful methods to restore order. We unambiguously oppose any violence against the civilian population and support international norms in the field of human rights and respect for democratic principles in state-building. But we proceed, first, from the view that there are no freedoms without limitations and that these limitations are clearly prescribed in all international legal acts concerning the protection of human rights and freedoms ... second ... the main aim of the international community when such situations arise is the need to sit the authorities and the opposition down at the negotiating table. (Lavrov 2011b)

In fact, none of the Western states had argued for a Libya-style military operation to protect Syrian civilians; even after the alleged use of chemical weapons by Assad's forces in Ghouta in August 2013, the US and its allies were mindful of the likely costs and consequences and argued that any coercive action ought to be proportionate, limited in time and scope to degrading Syria's CW capacity in order to avert humanitarian suffering (Glanville 2014, 46). Yet, as US military action over the Ghouta atrocity appeared imminent, Russian official sources repeatedly asserted that 'even if one adopts the position that [the R2P] concept is applicable to the events in Syria, armed intervention within its framework may be carried out only with UNSC sanction … attempts to revive the celebrated concept of "humanitarian intervention", which has not gained international recognition, evoke complete astonishment' (MFA 2013b). Lavrov's dismissal of Western approaches was categorical:

> We can not agree with the logic of those that attempt to justify the unilateral use of force by referring to the so-called 'responsibility to protect' concept. The 2005 World Summit outcome document … clearly confirmed that it has to be mandated by the UN Security Council in each specific case. This is international law. *All the rest is slyness. Unilateral interference will always be selective and inevitably aimed at promoting the political interests of countries behind it* … unilateral military actions lead to a dramatic rise in instability, both regionally and globally. (Lavrov 2013i, emphasis added)

Russia was increasingly intent on achieving its preferred normative consensus, raising the threshold for future interventions that challenge the sovereignty principle while still supporting R2P-linked peacekeeping and humanitarian protection missions in less sensitive cases (Chen and Yin 2020, 790–791). Even though Moscow consistently failed to mobilise the support of states other than China in opposing draft UNSC resolutions condemning atrocities by Syrian government forces, suggesting that its support for Assad lacked legitimacy in wider international society, the political imperative of keeping Assad in power was decisive (Dunne and Teitt 2015, 385, 387; Baranovsky and Mateiko 2016, 58). A recent Russian foreign ministry statement is unequivocal: 'We will continue to block attempts by certain countries to legitimize within the United Nations the concept of "responsibility to protect" (R2P), which no longer enjoys consensual support' (MFA 2020a, paragraph 53).

While some experts remain convinced that R2P provides a normative framework to respond to the challenge of dispensing global justice against mass atrocity crimes (see Thakur 2019), others conclude that 'Western compulsory power to affect the Syrian civil war diminished over time. Aware of their relative inability to bring about the desired outcome, realist prudence within the West militated against an R2P intervention' (Tocci 2014, 11). The hardening of Russia's position over R2P in response to the political and security dilemmas presented by the Libya and Syria conflicts may have longer-term implications for the international community's response to abuses against civilian populations. A leading R2P expert has pointed to a series of reports from UN bodies, human rights organisations and think tanks recording an increase in atrocity crimes and state oppression, which was 'exemplified by the steady deterioration of the crisis in Syria, where bitter divisions among the P5 have rendered them incapable of implementing a coordinated remedial strategy ... the Security Council had "too often failed to live up to its global responsibility"'; the provisions of the 2005 WSO document

> have been interpreted by a bloc of predominantly developing world states to reiterate the principles of sovereign inviolability and sovereign equality, and to enhance the primacy of the state in protecting its citizens and resolving intra-state crises ... at the expense of the external regulation of compliance with international human rights law. (Hehir 2017, 340, 342–343)

The complex local and regional dynamics associated with the Syrian civil war; the failure of NATO member states to deal with the instability in Libya after its military operation; the UN Security Council's largely passive approach to the atrocities taking place in Yemen since Saudi air strikes began in 2015, without Security Council authorisation; conflicting geopolitical interests among the major powers; and varying levels of enthusiasm for military intervention on the ground – all these factors have contributed to a growing unwillingness or inability to enforce responsible protection of civilians through UN decision-making (see Cater and Malone 2016, 290–291). Recent studies have highlighted the potential for the wider abuse of humanitarian rationales for intervention, such as in Russia's claims for its military incursions in Georgia in 2008 and Ukraine in 2014, as well as in the Saudi-led coalition's use of force in Yemen, supposedly for human rights protection even though its intervention is largely driven by strategic considerations of constraining the expansion of Iranian influence (Buys and Garwood-Gowers 2019, 28–30; Cater and Malone 2016, 290; see also Allison 2013a, 156–159).

Two further issues relevant to how the international community deals with intra-state conflicts are worth considering. The first concerns referrals of states carrying out atrocities by the UN Security Council to the International Criminal Court (ICC). In May 2014 Russia vetoed a draft UNSC resolution to refer the crisis in Syria to the ICC, even though it had supported a similar referral of the situation in Libya in UNSC resolution 1970 (see Martin 2022, 14). Signalling the ICC's declining credibility, it also withdrew its signature from the Rome Statute in 2016; along with China (a non-signatory) and the US (which has not ratified the Statute), it is able to veto UNSC resolutions that could expand the ICC's jurisdiction. The major powers are thus able to shield their allies from investigation by the court while referring other non-signatory states to its jurisdiction: the lack of support for a referral of Syria 'has confirmed … that states with powerful allies among the P-5 can act with relative impunity. This selective use of ICC referrals by the Council suggests that legal principles are viewed as subservient to political agendas' (Arbour 2014, 198–199). With the ICC undertaking an investigation into the Russian leadership's aggression in Ukraine in 2022, the legal and procedural problems of proving and punishing atrocity crimes have surfaced yet again.

The second is that, with the Security Council often deadlocked over questions of sovereignty and intervention, liberal peacebuilding approaches to address the underlying conditions of intra-state conflict are increasingly contested by Russia and other authoritarian governments willing to countenance the use of coercion by states to reinforce domestic power structures. This gives rise to the practice of 'authoritarian conflict management [which] promotes a hegemonic discourse that seeks to achieve the delegitimisation of armed opponents of the state as potential partners for negotiation', suppressing or contesting alternative sources of information about the facts on the ground (Lewis et al 2018, 493). An arrangement of domestic and external power-brokers has been institutionalised in the Astana format, where norms and practices are promoted that seek to manage conflict by re-establishing political order; this enables state coercion by excluding sections of the population and reinforcing authoritarian governance structures while imitating liberal practices of negotiation and mediation (Abboud 2021, 327–328). In the Syrian civil war, Russia has been complicit in fostering a delegitimising discourse aimed both at the opposition, indiscriminately branded as terrorist, and at local and international NGOs accused of fabricating information and criticising the Assad government. This approach can be traced back to the Chechnya war, in which Russia privileged 'a set of norms that valorized sovereignty and hierarchical authority over any claims to justice or human rights'; the Syria case further reflects potentially significant challenges by Russia, not only to liberal peacebuilding but increasingly to wider liberal norms and practices in the contemporary international system (Lewis, 2022, 653, 660; Abboud 2021, 342).

Russia and humanitarian aid

A salient aspect of Russia's MENA policy has been to frame its role as a constructive humanitarian actor, upholding standards of appropriate behaviour as part of its bid for political legitimacy (Morozova 2015, 3). A policy framework for Russian development assistance can be traced back to 2007, with humanitarian aid mainly targeted at the CIS states; with time, Russia has also channelled assistance to other countries, often through multilateral bodies including the UN and World Bank (Richmond and Tellidis 2014, 571). Following the Arab uprisings, humanitarian issues became an important element of international engagement with the MENA region, including in the Geneva negotiations on Syria. The Russian government has cooperated with UN agencies and international organisations such as the International Committee of the Red Cross, the Office of the UN High Commissioner for Refugees, the UN Development Program and the European Civil Protection and Humanitarian Aid Operations office (Russell 2016). Syria became the largest recipient of Russian aid over the five-year period to 2015, with Libya and Palestine also targeted. Moscow pledged to transfer $17 million to UN agencies to support humanitarian projects in Syria in 2020, together with food aid, a staple of Russian overseas development assistance.

At the same time, Russia's approach to humanitarian assistance aligns with its commitment to the norms of sovereignty and non-interference – recently enshrined in Russian law through a decree signed by Putin – with less emphasis on individual freedoms and human rights which underpin Western conceptions of humanitarian cooperation (Morozova 2018, 355, 359–361; President of the Russian Federation 2022, paragraphs 20–21). According to one study, Russia and some non-Western states have introduced a new political approach to aid and donor activity that differs from Western assistance because of its lack of conditionality, seeking both to enhance their status and safeguard the sovereignty of recipient countries; they do not adhere to OECD Development Assistance Committee principles,

> ma[king] traditional donor organizations speak of 'rogue aid' for the first time since the end of the Cold War ... the fragmentation of aid delivery, the violation of corporate and national governance standards, free riding on debt relief, unfair business competition, and a scramble for extraction rights of valuable resources [reflect] the weakness of global governance and liberal peacebuilding. (Richmond and Tellidis 2014, 567, 578; see Gray and Murphy 2013, 190–191)

Russia has criticised cross-border humanitarian aid deliveries by Western donors as external interference in Syria's internal affairs, aimed at destabilising the country and potentially leading to regime change. In contrast, Moscow's own efforts have relied on close cooperation with the Syrian authorities, targeting aid and reconstruction assistance mainly at locations where Assad's troops are fighting opposition forces or government-controlled areas (Sosnowski and Robinson 2020). Damascus has restricted the activities of international organisations on Syrian territory and has approved few local partners for international NGOs, apart from the Syrian Arab Red Crescent and the Syria Trust for Development (headed by Assad's wife Asma); this has prompted Western concerns about the authorities' control of aid delivery by denying direct access to populations in vulnerable situations – sometimes called 'surrender or starve' tactics – and thereby undermining the principles of humanity, neutrality, impartiality and independence (ICG 2019c, 20). Overseas and local humanitarian groups have struggled to overcome disagreements among warring parties and deliver sufficient aid to Syrians unable to leave the country.

Assistance from UN agencies and their partners has largely been confined to areas under Syrian government control or situated directly over the border from countries hosting refugees; UN Security Council resolutions on the provision of cross-border aid have had limited impact on the humanitarian situation in Syria (Grisgraber and Reynolds 2015, 3). Russia works partly outside of wider humanitarian frameworks such as the UN Office for the Coordination of Humanitarian Affairs (UNOCHA), often operating through non-state informal organisations that lack transparent reporting and monitoring, reinforcing concerns about the 'strategic' use of aid to undermine the Syrian opposition and further Moscow's political aims (Sosnowski and Hastings 2019; Dieckhoff 2020, 573), though it is worth noting that some sources have spoken of positive cooperation with Russia in delivering supplies into parts of Syria (French Embassy 2018). Russia's approach has thus contributed to a 'polarized aid environment', in which NGOs such as Médecins Sans Frontières have had to respect the sovereignty principle demanded by Damascus and Moscow and negotiate an 'informal space of aid delivery' outside of the traditional system dominated by UN organisations and state donors (Whittall 2014, 1, 4).

Most controversially, Russia has restricted humanitarian deliveries by voting along with China to oppose the renewal of a mechanism introduced by UNSC resolution 2165 (July 2014), which allowed the UN and its approved partners to ship food, medical and other cross-border aid from neighbouring countries – Turkey, Iraq and Jordan – into opposition-controlled areas of Syria without the Assad government's approval. In 2020 Russia and China blocked the UN from using all but one of the border crossings, Bab al-Hawa in northwest Syria, which serves parts of Idlib and Aleppo; it eventually supported resolution 2585 (2021), which extended its previous authorisation of the Bab al-Hawa crossing point for six months 'subject to the issuance of a substantive report by the Secretary-General on transparency in aid delivery operations and progress on cross-line access' (UNSC 2021), with successive six-month extensions into 2023 being agreed under subsequent UNSC resolutions. Blocking aid destined for civilians has been condemned by international human rights organisations as contravening international humanitarian law. In response, Russian officials have cited guidelines for delivering humanitarian aid under UN General Assembly resolution 46/182 (1991, annexe 3), stating that it should be based on the consent of the target country and respect for sovereignty, territorial integrity and national unity and criticising the 'politicisation' of human rights by Western countries in order to settle scores with political opponents (MFA 2019c, 2020b). Moscow has claimed that Western aid deliveries intended for civilians in opposition-held areas frequently find their way into the hands of Islamist militants and serve to legitimise the illegal presence of US-led coalition forces in Syria (Lavrov 2020e; Khlebnikov 2022a). Cross-border aid has thus become yet another negotiating tool in talks at the UN Security Council over the future political and security situation there, with Russia continuing to exert a dominant influence on external aid governance. Deteriorating relations with the West over the war with Ukraine have raised the prospect that humanitarian assistance to Syria may become a casualty of failure to reach a lasting agreement (ICG 2022b).

Moscow has supplied detailed descriptions of its apparently generous financial and material aid to civilian groups in Syria and to refugees fleeing the fighting, channelled mostly through the Russian defence ministry-linked Centre for Reconciliation of Opposing Sides and Refugee Migration Monitoring at the Khmeimim air base. However, according to Human Rights Watch, drawing on data from Oxfam International and UNOCHA, Russia's contribution to the relief of Syrian refugees has been negligible and Moscow – despite its involvement in the conflict – has declined to offer any resettlement places for asylum seekers or to assist displaced civilians. According to an independent Russian source, 2,631 Syrian citizens petitioned for refugee status in Russia, but only three were granted it; temporary asylum was given to 4,492 people but in many cases it was not extended and Russian migration services have curbed any further asylum claims (Russian NGOs 2021, 162, 165).

Russia's contribution to the humanitarian funding burden was only 1 per cent of its share, calculated based on gross national income, and 0.1 per cent of total contributions to UN appeals for the Syria crisis response as of 2016, the lowest among thirty-two donor countries surveyed; Moscow claims that it is contributing by supporting the Assad government in fighting terrorism and that the burden of assisting Syrian refugees should fall on countries whose policies exacerbated the civil war (Human Rights Watch 2016a). This is in line with a figure of around 0.1 per cent of total paid and pledged donations committed by Russia between 2018 and 2020 for UNOCHA and related programmes (UNOCHA 2020). A report for the

European Parliamentary Research Service noted that, while Syria was the largest recipient of Russian humanitarian aid – 19 per cent in 2011–2015 – Russia's overall contribution is modest in comparison to that of established donors, and some Russian aid 'appears to serve geopolitical rather than humanitarian objectives' (Russell 2016). At the same time, a network of at least thirteen Russian non-state organisations, including the Russian Humanitarian Mission and the Akhmat Kadyrov Public Foundation as well as Orthodox and Islamic charitable bodies, have become steadily more adept at targeting those in need, which boosts Russia's 'soft power' image in the region. These bodies have even discussed aid cooperation with renowned Western NGOs such as Oxfam and Médecins Sans Frontières, while still channelling assistance through the Syrian Arab Red Crescent, raising concerns that the Assad government may be using it for political purposes (Hille et al 2018; Sosnowski and Hastings 2019; see Lewis 2022, 663).

Russia is likely to remain marginal in terms of direct investment and development aid to tackle the post-conflict challenges posed by Syria's reconstruction and humanitarian needs. The EU, the likeliest major external donor, has to date confined its assistance to humanitarian aid and may withhold finance for reconstruction projects without a guarantee of meaningful political transition. This raises questions over how and whether Russia will engage with Europe, which perceives the status quo under Assad as contrary to its strategic interest in long-term stability, while the Syrian leadership shows no immediate sign of negotiating compromises with the West. Moscow wants recognition for its part in resolving the conflict and post-conflict normalisation so as not to bear the costs of reconstruction but, according to one authoritative source, may be content with the status quo if Europe and the Arab states refuse to accept the rehabilitation of Assad (ICG 2019c).

Conclusions

This chapter has investigated how Russia has dealt with the complex – and in many respects bitterly contested – issues concerning the use of force, sovereignty and intervention, responsible protection of populations and humanitarian assistance during the Arab Spring. It has addressed fundamental questions about how norms are negotiated to manage unequal power relations, consistent with Russian notions about the evolving multipolar world in which the Western powers and leading non-Western states vie to shape the rules of legitimate international conduct underpinning global security. Russia's normative concerns over Western interventions in the MENA region have been manifested in a sustained diplomatic offensive in support of the core principles of state sovereignty and sovereign equality, grounded firmly in the UN Charter-based legal framework that regulates the international system. Its approach is driven both by a normative preoccupation with shifting interpretations of the legality and legitimacy of the use of force and by a need to exert its political and diplomatic power to deal with perceived Western challenges and secure its standing in the international order. Russia claims in the case of Syria that its support of the traditional sovereignty norm does not amount to legal revisionism; in Russian eyes, it is the Western notion of a rules-based order that is a revision of, or an attempt to traduce, the traditional 'Westphalian' understanding of international legal norms (Allison 2020, 991; see also Chan 2021). Who makes the rules is Moscow's overriding concern.

In opposing the selective interpretation by Western states of international norms, Russia voices the deep-seated concerns of many non-Western states about the threat to the inter-state order and potential instability deriving from external coercive intervention in weak and divided MENA countries. As Lawrence Freedman argues, the liberal West 'has not performed well in the face of a series of challenges [from illiberal states] and is now in crisis' (Freedman 2021, 37). Russia's reversion to a narrow sovereignist interpretation of international law is bound up with a wider criticism of the West's hegemonic goals; Moscow is compelled to engage in a constant struggle to enlist international support for its actions and legitimise its authority (see Allison 2017, 536; Lewis 2022, 670). At the same time, even though Russian preference for a pluralist international order is widely reflected across the non-Western states, Moscow has not received those states' unequivocal support for its Syria policy. Each state in a pluralist international system has a distinctive position, rooted in cultural and historical experience, on issues of sovereignty, human rights and the use of force and seeks a legitimate voice in crucial debates over the evolution of broadly accepted, if often contested, international norms. As Tocci suggests,

> international responses to the Libyan and Syrian crises do not validate a broadbrush account of the systemic power shift. They do reveal how power is diffusing globally, and that global outcomes are already being determined by the complex interplay of various forms of power exercised by various actors ... This diffusion of power is and will continue to have consequential effects on broadly accepted global norms. (Tocci 2014, 23)

Debates over international norms during the Arab Spring have often focused on the human rights imperative of ending mass atrocities and promoting justice. Moscow's variable engagement over human rights norms in the early phase of the Libya and Syria conflicts was largely abandoned when the

Western powers were perceived as using force to impose a more liberal use of responsible protection norms that challenged sovereign rights. Russia's governing elite values stability as a fundamental public good and believes that maintaining order within conflict-prone societies should outweigh liberal Western preferences for human rights or self-determination (see Hurrell 2003, 31). But Moscow's approach to the vexed question of responsible protection has been seen simply as blocking effective diplomatic mediation to mitigate human rights abuses by obstructing UN Security Council resolutions with majority support authorising action on matters of grave humanitarian concern, compromising Russia's legitimacy as a constructive global actor (Averre and Davies 2015, 832; Baranovsky and Mateiko 2016, 58).

Moscow's legalistic insistence on respecting procedural matters in decision-making at the UN and refusal post-Libya to limit its veto power in the Security Council, allowing the Assad leadership to prosecute a civil war that has inflicted unimaginable suffering – destroying infrastructure, targeting civilians and manipulating humanitarian corridors during the sieges of Aleppo and Idlib, and even controlling the delivery of humanitarian assistance – appear to signal a decisive shift *away* from engagement with the liberal West over human rights in general. The danger is that the international system 'is being reshaped by the leading illiberal states, notably China and Russia. Brutal regimes act with impunity, and there is little appetite or capacity to stop them' (Freedman 2021, 38). Russia has offered no real answer to humanitarian challenges in a fragmented, corrupted and brutalised Syria, where domestic sovereignty and political order are in many respects deficient: as a result of Russian vetoes, the UN Security Council has failed, in Lavrov's own reference to Dag Hammarskjöld in the epigraph to this chapter, to 'save humanity from hell'. At the same time, interventions in internal conflicts by Western states are often perceived as driven by particularistic interests, reproducing unequal power relations and compromising their own legitimacy in the wider international community. In both cases, the costs to states of non-compliance with international norms on sovereignty and the use of force are being reduced, leading to a legitimacy deficit and presenting an ongoing challenge. Russia's practice of selective use of legal arguments, reproduced to reinforce its claims in its immediate neighbourhood (see Deyermond 2016, 957–958; Allison 2017, 519–520), has acquired a new dimension with the invasion of Ukraine, a flagrant breach of sovereignty that demonstrates Russia's readiness to resort to coercive interventions while playing fast and loose with international rules. This theme is considered in greater depth in the final chapter of this book.

5

Religion and terrorism: the challenge of the Arab Spring

Question: I hope Russian diplomacy will make a considerable contribution to blocking the spread of terrorism.

Sergey Lavrov: Diplomacy has several allies in this endeavour – Russia's Aerospace Forces, Army and Navy. (Lavrov 2016b)

The Arab Spring – or 'Arab Awakening', the term often used by leading Russian scholars to denote the magnitude of the political, social and religious trends of the last decade (Naumkin et al 2013, 62) – highlighted the growing influence of political Islam across much of the MENA region. The variable impact of Islamist movements on secular political processes and social relations in each country constitutes a complex puzzle that becomes even more challenging when taking account of inter-state rivalries and the role of external actors (see Quero and Sala 2019). As Russian experts have argued, 'the rise of political Islam in Arab and international politics continues to radically alter the alignment of forces in the region' (Naumkin et al 2013, 86). The surge in the military and ideological influence of Islamic State, together with the rise of other militant extremist groups, internationalised the Syria conflict and had a striking impact on the threat perceptions of the external and regional powers (Phillips 2016, 189; see also Lister 2017, 1–3, 69). This is particularly true of Russia, whose own experience of insurgency during its campaigns to quell militancy and separatism in the North Caucasus, particularly the wars with Chechnya in the 1990s and 2000s, has to a significant extent determined its approach to the Arab uprisings.

Several issues surrounding the core motivations of Russia's approach to political Islam during the Arab Spring are considered in this chapter. The next section examines how the reductive narrative of an 'uncompromising fight against terrorism' has permeated Russia's foreign policy statements (UNSC 2102d, 15), deliberately obscuring the complex phenomena associated with militant Islamism, in particular the participation of violent non-state actors in social and economic governance in war-torn MENA countries; it goes on to investigate how the Russian state's campaign against those designated as terrorists has been shaped by internal debates over the threat to state cohesion posed by the spread of extremist Islamism in Russia, and how that campaign has in turn affected its domestic policies. The second section analyses the influence of foreign Islamists on the North Caucasus insurgency and investigates the impact of Russian-speaking 'foreign fighters' returning from conflicts in Iraq and Syria. One commentator writes that, by mid-2012, 'more than any other non-Syrian nationality or race, "Chechens" had already stood out for their emerging role in Syria's conflict' (Lister 2017, 81). How has Moscow dealt with this challenge? The third and fourth sections consider how Russia, as a secular multiethnic and multi-confessional country, promotes the religious aspects of its national identity, both domestically and internationally. Russia's indigenous Muslim population has been officially portrayed as a fundamental part of the Russian state, living alongside other confessional groups in a spirit of mutual tolerance; Putin has even declared that Russia represents a significant part of the Islamic world (Dannreuther 2012, 548). At the same time, the recent period has witnessed the growing political influence of the Russian Orthodox Church in the external projection of the country's cultural and civilisational values in foreign policy narratives. How does this impact Russian society's approaches to Islam and its policies in the Arab world more generally? The final section analyses the prominent role of the Chechen leader Ramzan Kadyrov, both in Russia's policy towards domestic Islam and in its relations with the MENA region.

The complex and indeterminate coexistence of state and non-state actors in the MENA region complicates any clear-cut definitions (Gaub 2018b, 59). To avoid conceptual bias we confine the use of the term 'terrorism' – often used instrumentally to delegitimise violent acts, as discussed below – to quotations from published sources, employing less loaded terms such as violent non-state actors or insurgents to describe the militant opposition challenging the legitimacy of incumbent governments in MENA countries. This opposition includes transnational movements such as Islamic State, Al-Qaeda and their offshoots, with their aims of global jihad, and other groups adopting a variety of tactics and means with the aim of securing territory or political influence. We employ the broad term foreign fighter to denote Russian-speaking volunteers who have participated in armed conflict in the Middle East, while recognising the differences among them in terms of adherence to Islamic discourse, kinship/identity and motivation for mobilisation; transnational activist is used in connection with the larger multi-ethnic movement involving Russian-speaking militants spanning parts of Russia, Europe and Central Asia (see Moore 2015; Moore and Tumelty 2008). As in Chapter 1, we use the term Islamist to denote political Islam, without identifying specific political movements or ideologies, and extremist or militant Islamism when referring to violent political thought or action.

Russia's approach to domestic Islam: the challenge of extremism

The threat of fragmentation of the Russian state along ethnic and national lines in the 1990s revealed increasing differences within domestic Islam. Radical forms of Islamism, brought to Russia by teachers from the Middle East and South Asia and preached in newly established mosques, spread through religious training, while North Caucasian Muslims travelled to the Middle East for education, resulting in a vigorous exchange of ideas. Islamist thought began to play a more active social and economic role in Russian regions with Muslim populations, challenging the legitimacy of 'traditional' moderate Islamic organisations within indigenous communities. A small number of foreign fighters, including Arabs, fought on the side of Chechnya during its first war against Russia from December 1994 to August 1996 – ended by the Khasavyurt accords and the subsequent peace treaty which effectively gave Chechnya autonomy and led to the withdrawal of federal forces from the capital, Grozny – helping to spread radical ideas in the region (Moore and Tumelty 2008, 418). While ethno-nationalist separatism was the primary motivating force for the Chechen insurgency, Islamist radicalism began to be used as a form of political protest, posing a larger threat to Russia's security which the Yeltsin government struggled to control. The growth of the population of Russia's Muslim-populated regions – forecasted by one source to increase from 16.4 to 18.6 million over the twenty-year period to 2030 – was accompanied by increasing labour movement of Muslims from USSR successor states into other regions of Russia, raising concerns over illegal migration, transnational crime and the increased threat of terrorist acts on Russian territory (Münster 2014, 4).

A subsequent series of violent incidents, perpetrated by insurgent factions on Russian territory, ended talk of reconciliation between Moscow and the Chechen leadership and led to the resumption of hostilities in August 1999. A 'securitising narrative' condemning 'terrorism' – effectively meaning virtually all forms of non-traditional Islam – emerged towards the end of Yeltsin's second presidential term. Despite an alternative narrative rejecting the association of Chechens with terrorism – voiced by Evgenii Primakov, former Russian prime minister and a leading Arabist, among others – parties across Russia's political spectrum forged an overwhelming elite consensus on the threat to Russia of 'terrorists' and 'bandits' represented in the insurgent forces, if not on the methods to be employed against them. Increased authority was conferred on the security agencies to combat the threat (see Wilhelmsen 2017, 100–105). This resolute response was carried over into Putin's first term as president. The second Chechen war – marked by the use of extra-legal means to combat the domestic insurgency, while at the same time portraying terrorism as a criminal act requiring a legal response – was defined 'purely and simply as a counterterrorist operation. The military were given *carte blanche* to conduct the war in whatever way was necessary to bring decisive victory' (Dannreuther 2010a, 115). The hard-line approach maintained that 'terrorism, as a radical violation of all "rules of the game" should leave no room for compromise' (Makarychev 2008, 183). This narrative gained some legitimacy internationally as a result of the post-9/11 'war on terror', which prompted greater acceptance in the West of Russia's anti-insurgency policy, albeit mixed with unease at the indiscriminate coercive tactics employed by Moscow (Forsberg and Herd 2005, 468–469; see also Martini 2022, 19–20; Russell 2009).

The second Chechen campaign was accompanied by tighter control over foreign Islamic organisations operating in Russia. One scholar likened the Putin government's policy to that pursued by many Middle Eastern countries 'where policies of severe repression can be said to work in sustaining the existing political system against the Islamist challenge but where the underlying sources of conflict, primarily the problems of economic and political governance, are left essentially intact and unresolved' (Dannreuther 2010a, 118). This approach did not stem the insurgent violence, however. One reliable source estimated that, between 1999 and 2016, violent non-state actors carried out over seventy-five attacks, classified by official sources as major 'terror acts', against targets in Russian cities, as well as hundreds of assaults on state security service personnel and moderate religious and political leaders in the North Caucasus (ICG 2016a, 1). The mass casualty attack on the Dubrovka theatre in Moscow in 2002 and the Beslan school massacre in 2004 – a genuine national tragedy – were the most prominent manifestations of a threat that the Russian authorities struggled to contain.

At the same time, an alternative approach by the Russian authorities to dealing with domestic militant Islam was developed in the 2000s. It focused on paying more attention to socioeconomic development and good governance in the North Caucasus, using legal and where possible non-violent means to counter the insurgency, while re-centralising power in federal institutions to re-establish order. This 'desecuritising' policy allowed Russian Muslims to follow non-traditional Islamic teaching and rehabilitated them as long as they did not have blood on their hands (see Kazenin and Starodubrovskaya 2014), exploiting divisions between Salafist jihadists espousing violence and 'traditionalist' Islamist forces; it was dictated by the need to reach out to reformist and moderate Islamist movements, both at home and abroad, even countenancing selective contact with Middle Eastern radical Islamist groups opposed to Salafist jihadism (Stepanova 2018a, 41). The Putin government tried to improve Russia's relations with the Islamic world, emphasising the ethno-confessional plurality of the Russian Federation and providing financial support for Russia's moderate Muslim communities through the Fund for Islamic Culture and Education, which helped with building mosques, training imams, Islamic education and scholarship (Dannreuther 2010a, 120). A renewed attempt to deal with extremism was made during the latter years of Dmitrii Medvedev's presidency. Russian and local authorities trialled non-coercive methods to combat the Islamist insurgency, liberalising the approach towards non-violent Salafis by allowing them greater participation in public life and freer assembly, as well as initiating a dialogue between Sufi and Salafi groups aimed at mitigating sectarian disputes in Dagestan, by then the hotbed of extremist activism (ICG 2018d). A government-funded development programme for 2013–2025 was subsequently established for the North Caucasus region (Hedenskog 2020, 22–23).

A readiness to engage with Islamist movements abroad became an important factor in Russia's MENA policy during the Arab Spring. Moscow was ready to accept more inclusive and pluralist Islamist governments, such as the Muslim Brotherhood-supported Morsi administration in Egypt, or to undertake conflict mediation with leading Islamist forces which were crucial to power balances, such as the Government of National Accord and the Misrata militias in Libya (Stepanova 2018a, 47–48). Moscow has also engaged with Hamas and Hezbollah, seen by Russian Muslims as being sympathetic to their interests. Russia had already become an observer state at the Organisation of the Islamic Conference in 2005. The link between the domestic and international aspects of Islam was underlined by Putin in 2013, with an explicit endorsement of Russia's approach to tackling the threat of militancy:

> Islam's new 'socialisation' should be seen as developing traditional Muslim lifestyles, thinking and views in accordance with current social realities, as opposed to the ideology of radicals ... I also believe that the voice of Russian Muslim leaders should resonate louder in the international arena, among the global Islamic community ... today Russia's presence is in increased demand in the Middle East and the Islamic world as a whole. (Putin 2013b)

Nevertheless, it proved difficult to reconcile the hard-line approach adopted against extremist Islam with the cultivation of non-violent Islamic groups in Russia. Internal disputes continued over exactly what defined 'traditional' Russian Islam. The attraction of militant Salafism in the North Caucasus could not be entirely suppressed; ongoing disturbances from early 2013 resulted in a shift towards the repression of non-traditional Islam, largely initiated by the federal law enforcement agencies, who not only cracked down on insurgents but also targeted non-violent Salafi believers and suppressed their mosques (Kazenin and Starodubrovskaya 2014; ICG 2018d). The 'desecuritising' frame that permitted non-traditional Islamic teaching thus clashed with a cultural and normative context that privileges state security and sovereignty in the Russian governing elite's political thinking, ultimately leading to a shift away from addressing the causes underlying the 'terrorist' threat towards its 'resecuritisation'; poor coordination between civil and military approaches undermined the legitimacy and credibility of state policy and obstructed a solution to the regional insurgency (Campana 2013, 468).

A dual approach to Islamism has thus emerged over the last two decades or so. On the one hand, Moscow has continued to emphasise cultural and civilisational unity between Russia and the Islamic world, promoting both more active political cooperation with Muslim countries and greater social, economic and cultural engagement with Islam (Yakovenko 2019). The widespread view among Russian elites was that the Arab Spring represented a conflict between moderate political Islamism, represented by movements such as the Muslim Brotherhood, and the violent extremist Islamism represented by Islamic State and Al-Qaeda, with the secular Arab nationalist model increasingly under threat (Dannreuther 2015, 81). Primakov argued that extremist Islamism was essentially hostile to Russian interests but that fundamentalist elements, while opposed to secular Russian values, might be cultivated if their actions were not harmful to national security (Dannreuther 2010b, 15). Other leading Russian experts reasoned that Russia is well placed to draw lessons from how religious and secular forces interact in the MENA region in order to devise approaches that correspond more closely to international and domestic realities and foster better understanding (Naumkin et al 2013, 104–106).

On the other hand, the Russian leadership's response to the challenge to state order arising from insurgencies across the MENA region must be understood in the context of its restoration of state control over the North Caucasus through the consolidation of executive power and suppression of externally-sponsored militant Sunni Islamism. Reflecting its approach to its domestic insurgency, Moscow portrayed the Syrian civil war as central to the 'fight against terrorism' – an existential threat to national and international security with which there can be no collusion – shifting responsibility for the violence onto foreign fighters intent on establishing an international extremist Islamist front and allied with radicalised domestic groups, thereby delegitimising the opposition and justifying the use of military force there.

Russia's narrative has acquired an additional dimension, highlighted earlier in this book. It is interwoven with criticism of the West's attempts to promote in the MENA countries liberal ideas which, in Russian eyes, are 'alien and incomprehensible' to a substantial part of the local population and which contribute to the overthrow of incumbent governments, intensifying inter-confessional and ethnic contradictions and facilitating the rise of militant opposition forces (Naumkin et al 2013, 102). Putin's December 2015 presidential address to the Federal Assembly acknowledged the sacrifice of Russian servicemen fighting terrorism 'in the name of freedom, truth and justice' and lamented the fact that 'recently stable and rather well-doing countries in the Middle East and North Africa – Iraq, Libya and Syria – have now plunged into chaos and anarchy that pose a threat to the whole world … Our military personnel are fighting in Syria for Russia, for the security of Russian citizens' (Putin 2015b). Putin thus positioned Russia as defending itself against extremist forces and making common cause with Arab countries in the 'fight against terrorism', while warning that 'tensions between the West and the Islamic world are on the rise. Some people try to play with this issue and throw fuel on the fire. I want to tell you straight away: we are not interested in this' (Putin 2013b).

The Western notion that illegitimate, repressive governments such as Assad's neglect social problems and create breeding grounds for discontent that terrorists can exploit, and that international efforts should therefore confer legitimacy on authorities dedicated to improving governance, clashes with Russia's preoccupation with stability and order (see Martini 2022, 23–24, 30–31). This was reflected in Russia's response to UN Secretary-General Ban Ki-moon's Plan of Action for Preventing Violent Extremism, a US-inspired initiative that highlighted the threat posed by foreign fighters and put forward recommendations to UN member states to develop comprehensive and systematic national plans to counter it. The validity of the plan was questioned both by Muslim-majority countries and by Russia, unsettled by its conferring a more prominent role on civil society and human rights relative to the state (Ucko 2018, 251, 260, 267). Russia's conviction that states should manage counterterrorism issues without external interference in their internal affairs, avoiding debates about human rights issues and sidelining civil society, is firmly established in official pronouncements (MFA 2020a, section 30). At Russia's insistence, the UN Office of Counter-Terrorism, established in 2017 under the Secretary-General of the UNGA, appointed a Russian diplomat, Vladimir Voronkov, as Under-Secretary-General together with a number of other Russian officials in key UN counterterrorist positions (Hedenskog 2020, 30). Voronkov's position, coordinating UN counterterrorism policies, may allow Russia greater scope to shape the Plan of Action (Ucko 2018, 269).

The mobilisation of Russian 'foreign fighters' in Syria and Iraq

The spread of Islamist extremism across the MENA region during the Arab Spring brought with it the prospect of thousands of Russian-speaking foreign fighters hostile to the Russian federal government returning to the restive North Caucasus and fuelling the violence there, posing a considerable security challenge. Scholars carrying out extensive research on the topic have argued that

> Foreign activists played an important role in the North Caucasus insurgency, impacting its trajectory, ideology and perceived legitimacy ... [they] formed part of a broader social movement and played an important role in Chechen Republic of Ichkeria (ChRI) state building. They had a lasting impact on the tactics and ideology on the insurgency that continues to resonate today. (Moore and Youngman 2017, 20)

While North Caucasus militants had avoided foreign jihad in Afghanistan and pre-Arab Spring Iraq due to cultural and linguistic differences and their preoccupation with the domestic insurgency, the war in Syria offered them a viable alternative to fighting Russia at home (Ratelle 2016, 223). Numerous insurgents from other Russian regions and neighbouring countries – exiled diasporas and Turkic, Georgian and Central Asian networks hostile to Russia, some of which have roots in Afghanistan and Pakistan – were also involved. Official Russian estimates put the total number of volunteers active in the Syria and Iraq conflicts at around 4,000 Russian citizens, together with an additional 5,000 from the CIS, with other credible sources putting the figure at between 2,900 and 5,000 Russian speakers out of 30,000 or more foreign fighters in total in Syria (Moore and Youngman 2017, 2, 42–44; Lister 2017, 1; ICG 2016a, 4). As well as fighters active in the Middle East, numerous natives of the North Caucasus visit the region for education and Islamic religious instruction, increasing the influence of returnees (Moore and Tumelty 2008, 425).

North Caucasus activists developed self-sustaining networks that were difficult for outsiders to penetrate and helped to facilitate their departure to fight in Syria. Following an initial exodus, a second wave of Russian-speaking fighters (as many as 85 per cent of the total) left for Syria at the end of 2013; the movement accelerated with Islamic State's military success in Iraq in 2014 and mainly involved ideologically motivated Salafists from Dagestan and Chechnya, for whom the battle against Assad's forces 'was often seen as a religious duty similar to the Hajj' prior to their return to the North Caucasus (Ratelle 2016, 224, 226). The international nature of the challenge is underlined by the fact that some Russian foreign fighters, fleeing persecution at home, work or study in Turkey or pass through there on their way to Syria and Iraq. The Turkish authorities often refused to extradite Russian nationals linked with North Caucasus Salafist groups, which are mostly supporters of Erdoğan and the AKP, suspecting Russia's security agencies of organising the assassination of Chechen activists on their territory (Bechev 2018, 98–99). Before Islamic State attacks against Turkey were stepped up in 2015, the Erdoğan government was reluctant to detain these Salafist groups and other anti-Assad Sunni extremists and even financed their transit to the conflict zones (ICG 2016a, 9–11).

Tracing the movements of Russian-speaking foreign fighters in the Iraq and Syria conflicts, and assessing the dynamics, capacities and motivations of the groups concerned, is a matter of considerable complexity. Small armed groups allied with bigger ones across conflict fronts, periodically fragmenting and merging, with individual fighters transferring from one commander to another (ICG 2016a, 12). Divisions between and within the main militant Islamist movements Al-Qaeda and Islamic State, both encompassing numerous affiliated groups, clouded a constantly evolving insurgency picture in the MENA region even more (see Lounnas 2018a, 2–4). Many Russian-speaking volunteers originally formed a North Caucasus-led group which split towards the end of 2013, with one faction attaching itself to the Al-Qaeda affiliate Jabhat al-Nusra (later renamed Hayat Tahrir al-Sham) and another joining Islamic State ranks; after further splits, its fighters were joined by non-North Caucasians and later established the *Imarat Kavkaz* (Caucasus Emirate) in Syria group: 'The boundaries between non-IS groups appear to be relatively fluid and based as much on personal loyalties as ideological distinctions' (Moore and Youngman 2017, 9). What appears certain is that the strong connections between North Caucasus insurgents were reinforced by the incorporation of some of them into Islamic State, potentially posing a continuing problem for Russia as they became involved in Islamist activism in their native republics. The attractiveness of Islamic State to Russian insurgents was considerable for several reasons: first, the appeal of religious fundamentalism and the prospect of living in an Islamic state, linked with a sense of resentment at the humiliation of Muslims around the world; second, the promise of just and effective Islamic governance; third, welfare and justice linked to social equality and economic well-being, in contrast to the authoritarianism and predatory government practices found in the North Caucasus; and fourth, the effectiveness of Islamic State propaganda in resisting attempts to counter its ideology (see ICG 2016a, 24–29).

The prospect of a fragmented Caucasus security map pitted with ungoverned spaces and prey to Islamist State extremists – a picture not unlike parts of the MENA region – was one that the Russian authorities wanted to avoid at all costs. Moscow's response to the increased threat posed by the movement of North Caucasus insurgents to the Middle East and the subsequent return of surviving foreign fighters to Russia was therefore harsh. As discussed earlier, official Russian narratives began relentlessly to frame the insurgency as political violence devoid of legitimacy; this framing was reinforced to justify Moscow's intervention in the Syria conflict by inscribing it in the global 'war on terror', shaping understandings about the legitimate use of extreme political violence to quell insurgency (see Martini 2020, 726–727). Article 208 of the RF Criminal Code was amended in 2013 to criminalise the participation of individuals in armed formations deemed contrary to Russian interests, including those operating on the territory of other states, and prison terms for breaking this law were increased (see President of Russia 2013). Putin stated in a national broadcast that it was better to destroy militants on Syrian territory than to confront them in Russia (Putin 2018). Insurgents trying to return to Russia were arrested at the borders or killed, criminal cases were opened – including against non-violent Salafists, reversing the Medvedev-era policy – and there were reports of mistreatment of suspects in preliminary detention (ICG 2016a, 5–6). Individuals recruiting or financing transnational activists were also targeted.

Islamic State repeatedly threatened federal and regional authorities in the North Caucasus and promised a $5 million reward for the assassination of Ramzan Kadyrov; Russia's air campaign in support of the Assad government prompted Islamic State's press secretary to declare *jihad* against Russia. Islamic State also claimed responsibility for the downing of a civilian aircraft that crashed on a flight from Egypt in October 2015, killing 224 passengers, mainly Russians. The Russian National Anti-Terrorism Committee reported at the beginning of 2016 that Islamic State-affiliated groups had infiltrated Russia to the extent that most North Caucasus insurgents had switched allegiance to the movement, with only a few small groups in Dagestan and Kabardino-Balkaria remaining part of the weakened Caucasus Emirate: 'The export of the North Caucasus jihad to the Middle East has made Russia new enemies and transformed the problem from national to global … Even though jihadist activity fell in Russia in 2015, the security challenge remains serious' (ICG 2016a, i). Although overall armed attacks in the North Caucasus have abated in recent years, partly due to the outflow of insurgents to Iraq and Syria, there is still agreement among militants about the legitimacy of continuing to fight the Russian security services. Attacks carried out in Russia between September 2015 and April 2018 by transnational activists claiming allegiance to Islamic State numbered twenty-six, with several subsequent incidents recorded (Wilhelmsen and Youngman 2020, 2). One local source reported a growth of younger militants joining the ranks of the Chechen underground (Kavkazskii uzel 2019).

Official statements indicated that, by November 2015, 650 criminal cases had been opened against a thousand Russian citizens for joining 'illegal armed formations' abroad, with an additional 770 insurgents and their accomplices arrested and 156 fighters killed in the North Caucasus, and over 150 returnees from Syria and Iraq sentenced to prison; at the same time, the outflow of Islamist activists to fight the Assad government continued, apparently facilitated by the security services opening the border for them to leave before the Sochi Olympics in an attempt to export the immediate problem, though this policy was later reversed (ICG 2016a, 16–17). Russia has sought to legitimise its policies in diplomatic fora, contributing substantially to the abovementioned UN Office of Counter-Terrorism, as well as to the regional Eurasian Group on Combating Money-Laundering and the Financing of Terrorism, the Commonwealth of Independent States Anti-Terrorism Centre and the Shanghai Cooperation Organisation Regional Anti-Terrorism Structure. In 2018 Lavrov announced that Russia's Federal Security Service had set up a database of foreign terrorist fighters, sharing information with forty-two security services from thirty-five countries, including G20 member states (Lavrov 2018e).

At the same time, the challenge appears to have been largely brought under control in the recent period. Not all proponents of radical Islamist ideologies within the indigenous Muslim population and migrant communities fought in Iraq and Syria; although Islamic State replaced the Caucasus Emirate as the primary insurgent group in the North Caucasus, ideological differences between them undermined trust (Youngman 2016, 210–211). Experts have concluded that 'the regional insurgency has been in long-term decline and IS has failed to transfer its appeal to local groups' (Moore and Youngman 2017, 14). Islamic State has been severely depleted by defections and 'special operations' carried out by the authorities in the North Caucasus; a Russian security agency source is reported as saying 'If [Russian-speaking foreign fighters] want to return now, we are waiting for them at the borders. Everyone's happy: they are dying on the path of Allah, and we have no terrorist acts here and are now bombing them in Latakia and Idlib. State policy has to be pragmatic; this was very effective' (ICG 2016a, 16). Put briefly, a large part of the insurgency's leadership has been physically eliminated and tight control at Russia's borders has stemmed the return of foreign fighters.

Moreover, the North Caucasus region comprises a demographically mixed population and presents few difficulties for strengthened federal and local authorities in terms of forestalling large-scale terror attacks. Support for insurgent groups has largely been confined to Dagestan and parts of the north-east Caucasus, while the 'Russified' areas of the north-west have been more resistant to the appeal of the jihadis (Wilhelmsen and Youngman 2020, 6; Souleimanov 2014, 160–161). Recent armed attacks on Russian territory claimed by Islamic State have been limited in terms of operational capacity and scope; not all are linked to militants returning from Syria and Iraq, undermining official Russian claims that domestic insurgent activity is exclusively linked with threats emanating from the Middle East. While official and media sources have grouped all militants under the Islamic State banner, serving Russia's broader justification both of its military involvement in Syria and its policies in the North Caucasus, 'there is to date little open source evidence to suggest that returnees are likely to radically alter the trajectory of the North Caucasus insurgency ... the threat arguably remains domestic rather than foreign in nature' (Moore and Youngman 2017, 17).

Islam and Russian society

How has Russia – as a secular state containing a variety of confessional groups, including its substantial and growing minority of Muslims – dealt with the religious aspects of its national identity in the context of its involvement in regional MENA affairs during the Arab Spring? The leading Russian scholar Vitalii Naumkin has pointed out that the majority of Russian Muslims belong to the Sunni Hanafi tradition and argued that, despite cultural differences, historically there has been no mutual hostility between Christianity and Islam in Russia, since Russian Orthodoxy is close to Islam in terms of values systems (Naumkin et al 2013, 101). While Russia's support for Assad's largely Shia forces was a factor in radicalising Sunni youth in Russia, Moscow insists that its policy in Syria has no sectarian agenda and has been aimed at restoring unity among Muslims (Wilhelmsen and Youngman 2020, 7; see also Notte 2015). Respondents interviewed for this book were broadly in agreement that the overall impact of the Arab Spring is unlikely to be profound; there has been no fundamental shift in state-Islam relations in Russia as a consequence of its role in the conflict in Syria (Interviews #4, #5, #7, #8, #9).

At the same time, several respondents also pointed out that the Russian authorities are forced to adapt their strategy to the constantly shifting challenges to domestic stability posed by extremist Islamist influence stemming from the MENA region. The Russian authorities need to develop a coherent policy on the country's Muslim communities, both by promoting moderate Islam and discouraging radicalism imported through Islamic teaching (Interviews #1, #7, #9) and by paying more attention to socioeconomic conditions (Interview #4, #5). Russian experts have offered a frank assessment of the extent of the problem:

> In a number of Russia's Muslim regions, this socio-cultural rift is very pronounced and characterized by clan-based politics, archaic elements, a lack of

social justice, biased law enforcement, utterly unfair wealth accumulation, unemployment, and systemic corruption. Faced with the discrepancy between proclaimed, constitutionally guaranteed principles and the actual situation on the ground, people turn to radicals who offer clear and simple solutions. (Naumkin et al 2013, 102)

Moreover, no authoritative spiritual leader of Russia's indigenous Muslims has emerged to balance the influence of Middle Eastern clerics. While North Caucasian Salafi insurgents point to religious affinity with their Sunni Muslim brothers and sisters (the mobilisation of women was a feature of transnational activism) as a key motivation in joining the conflict in Syria, other underlying factors – unaccountable and non-transparent governance, a poor socio-economic environment and a profound feeling of injustice and disenfranchisement – drive radicalisation and contribute to the insurgents' embrace of jihad (ICG 2016a, ii). Indeed, it is suggested that, rather than the 'radicalization of Islam', the North Caucasus has witnessed the 'Islamization of radicalism' as Islam is primarily a channel for protest against political and social conditions rather than a source of violence in itself; only some social movements become violent (Wilhelmsen and Youngman 2020, 6).

The argument that poor governance drives the sense of alienation, rather than tensions between Russian and Islamic identities, is supported by the findings of field work carried out in the North Caucasus by prominent Russian scholars. The complexity and variability of geographical and social conditions, ethnic diversity and conflicts of interest among various groups mean that demographic, sociocultural, technological and institutional modernisation differs from that in other Russian regions. The moral principles seen by North Caucasian Muslims as fundamental to social order – honesty, justice and the observance of law in social relations, social responsibility, transparency and good business practice – often clash with local corruption and erratic law enforcement. Finally, the lack of scope for independent decision-making and opportunities for self-realisation, which has persisted throughout the post-Soviet era, has not been properly addressed by the federal authorities; the implementation of regional development programmes, highlighted earlier in this chapter, has had limited impact, as the level of socioeconomic development remains the lowest in Russia (Kolosov et al 2019).

The wider historical and sociocultural context of the evolution of Islam in the North Caucasus is thus influenced both by recent global trends in Islamist movements and by state-society relations in Russia. Islam

> is seen as fulfilling a variety of various functions in the region, such as being an ethnic, cultural or national marker; a force for resistance against perceived injustice committed by secular or religious authorities; a force for social conservatism; and a tool for strengthening a country's international image ...

some 20 years after the re-Islamisation of the region started, there is no common 'idea' about what it should mean to be a Caucasus Muslim. (Bedford and Souleimanov 2016, 1575)

Disillusionment with the secular state in Russia among the followers of political Islam to an extent mirrors developments in the Arab states, albeit with a lesser impact in terms of undermining state cohesion. The consolidation of religious identity, the failures of secular institutions and the lack of an attractive national idea prompts the younger Muslim generation to involve itself in theological debates, seek an Islamic education or even join the conflicts in the Middle East, impacting external perceptions of Russia as an actor in the Islamic world (see Markedonov 2017). The long-term influence of this trend on Russia's national identity poses an ongoing challenge to state and society.

Islam and the Russian Orthodox Church

The Russian state's relationship with Islam is also influenced by the growing authority of the Russian Orthodox Church (ROC). The traditional role of the ROC as a defender of Orthodox religion, community and nation extends beyond domestic politics and security to project traditional values in its international dealings; it acts as an instrument of cultural attraction and contributes to Russian foreign policy, aimed at reasserting statehood and sovereignty, building closer relations with traditionalist religious forces abroad – including in the global South – and 'promoting philosophical conservatism, including the Russian religious philosophical tradition' (Stoeckl 2016, 144; see also Lomagin 2012). The ROC builds alliances in conservative political circles and distances itself from liberal trends both in Russian society and abroad, underlining the dichotomy between 'a secular–liberal–individualistic ideology and a religious–communitarian and traditionalist world view', promoting values-based narratives that challenge Western liberalism (Stoeckl 2012, 216; Malashenko 2020, 101). Both Orthodoxy and moderate Islam in Russia adhere to a concept of national and religious identity that alludes to the West's moral degradation and rejects its values-based cultural expansion, though their motivations for rejecting Western values differ (Zvyagelskaya 2016, 75). The ROC's involvement in broader inter-confessional public diplomacy extends both to establishing harmonious relations with domestic Muslim groups and to playing a wider role among the international Muslim community.

The Russian government's approach to Islam thus contains a religious-cultural as well as a political dimension: it supports moderate Muslim representation through a carefully regulated and hierarchical structure alongside the ROC, thereby extending the Russian nation's religious identity to include 'traditional Islam' (see Dannreuther 2015, 90). Russia's Muslim leaders contribute to building international partnerships with MENA countries. The Council of Muftis of Russia elaborated in 2001 'Basic Guidelines of the Social Program of Russian Muslims'. This document states that domestic matters have priority over foreign ones but recognises that contacts with Muslim states overseas, and with institutions such as the Organisation of Islamic Cooperation (formerly Organisation of the Islamic Conference) and the League of Arab States, are important in strengthening Russia's partnership with MENA countries and supporting its role as a mediator in the Islamic world; at the same time, it aims to develop joint positions on combatting terrorism and isolating extremists in the Northern Caucasus from the global *ummah* (Curanović 2012, 15, 19; see OIC 2020). These efforts are supported by the Russia-Islamic World 'Strategic Vision Group', a state-led initiative established in 2006 – headed initially by Evgenii Primakov and the first president of Tatarstan, Mintimer Shaimiev – and coordinated by the foreign ministries of Russia and partner countries. Its explicit remit is to develop new principles for a partnership of civilisations and cultures between Russia and the Islamic world in order to avoid religious conflicts. Its development was interrupted by the Arab Spring, but a renewed agenda after 2014, boosted by Russian foreign ministry representation at deputy minister level, has included jointly combatting international terrorism and improving economic interaction between Russia and Muslim countries, as well as inter-civilisational dialogue (Gimatdinov and Nasyrov 2019, 183–184). Its website effectively functions as an extension of the foreign ministry's information campaign targeted at Middle Eastern countries and other parts of the Islamic world.

The ROC, while supporting Russia's involvement in the Syria conflict, has parleyed with political and religious leaders in the Middle East in order to secure the protection of Orthodox and other Christian minority groups, a cause approved by the Putin leadership to gain both external and domestic legitimacy. The ROC has also appealed in defence of Christians across the MENA region at the UN Human Rights Council and the OSCE, a pressing issue given the deteriorating security situation following the Arab uprisings and emergence of militant Islamism (Adamsky 2019, 50–52; see also Curanović 2019, 261). An estimated 10,000 to 40,000 Russian nationals, some married to Syrians and living in Syria, may seek protection from Russia if their security is compromised, together with others of various Orthodox denominations and Circassians from the North Caucasus (IISS 2012, 3). Representatives of the ROC, which has an organisational presence within the Main Political Directorate of the Russian General Staff, are embedded with Russian soldiers in Syria to instil in them 'a sense of purpose and mission' (Adamsky 2020, 433). Local Orthodox religious leaders have also tackled humanitarian problems faced by the Syrian population, including undertaking mediation in hostage situations. Lavrov has described how the Imperial Orthodox Palestine Society, which has historical links with the MENA region and contributes to amicable relations between Christians and Muslims, has involved itself in humanitarian and educational activities to build relationships between faiths against a background of persecution of Orthodox believers in the Middle East (Lavrov 2016e). He has also welcomed the efforts of the Roman Catholic Church alongside the ROC in supporting the political resolution of conflicts there (Lavrov 2019b).

Russia's political and religious leaders, while projecting a favourable image of the country's historical mission of fulfilling its obligations to all Christians in the Arab world, are also explicit in their criticism of Western involvement there. Putin is reported as stating that two million Orthodox believers in Syria and Lebanon, out of five million Christians across the MENA region, must be saved from the chaos caused by US interventions (Isaev and Yur'ev 2017, 29). The West is criticised by Russia's religious leaders as it 'continues to play the same role it did a hundred years ago – as a two-faced power indifferent to the fate of Christians', further legitimising Russia's role as a 'peace-provider [and] promoter of human rights' both by saving traditional Christian communities and by stabilising the Middle East (cited in Curanović 2019, 261–262). The challenges that Russia faces both at home and globally thus coalesce in the MENA region, where it claims to be simultaneously battling extremist Islamism and opposing the damage caused by the Western countries' self-interested promotion of liberal ideas.

In spite of the narrative of Russia's civilisational mission in the Middle East, there is a strong undercurrent of antipathy to non-Orthodox confessions in parts of Russia's religious establishment and society that engenders a growing distrust between Muslim communities and the Russian state, exacerbated by the latter's harsh policies towards Islamist activism (Münster 2014, 12–13). Naumkin has underscored the civilisational exceptionalism promoted in Russia during the Putin presidency, based on an attachment to traditional norms and values, arguing that the struggle among adherents of various conceptions and models of Russia's 'civilisational identity' has not been resolved; supporters of traditionalist values who are at odds with Western liberalism are at the same time often prejudiced against Muslims (Naumkin 2014, 42–43). Moreover, there is no agreement among Christian leaders in the Middle East about Russia's role in Syria, with some defending its military intervention and others opposing air strikes that have resulted in civilian fatalities (Issaev and Shishkina 2020, 110). As highlighted earlier, Russian experts interviewed for this book asserted that the MENA conflicts have not had a significant impact on state–Islam relations. At the same time, to what extent the events of the Arab Spring have exacerbated public mistrust in Russia of Islam – not just of militant Islamism – is an ongoing issue meriting further research.

The Kadyrov factor

A distinctive perspective on Russia's domestic religious governance and relations with the Islamic world is found in the policies of Ramzan Kadyrov, head of the Chechen Republic. Kadyrov – who professes an amalgam of Chechen Sufism, popular Islam, canonical Sunni Islam and Christian practice (Radio Free Europe 2012) – promotes himself as a fighter against religious extremism and terrorism. He has carried out repressive policies against Salafi advocates of an Islamic theocracy in the North Caucasus, suppressing Salafi mosques in Chechnya and calling on all Muslim countries to fight Islamic State, which he has called the 'State of Satan'; he has proposed that Russian-speaking militants fighting in Syria should lose their citizenship and be barred from returning to Russia (ICG 2016a, 22–23). Kadyrov likens Chechen Islamic morality and traditions to Russian Orthodoxy, emphasising their differences from 'Western decadence, ungodliness, and hostility to tradition and the family', and supports extreme conservative Russian state actors in their challenge to Western liberalism (cited in Halbach 2018, 17). At the same time, he habitually uses cultural and religious Islamic symbols and rhetoric to foster a return to Chechen tradition rooted in Sufism, with pro-Moscow Chechen elites portraying themselves as committed Islamic fighters against 'alien', 'Wahhabi' heretics; while fighting the Islamist insurgency and championing 'Chechen Islam' as an antithesis to Salafism, he has spoken out against secular governance in Chechnya, even declaring the aim of establishing *sharia* law there (see Bedford and Souleimanov 2016, 1571–1573).

The reduction in violence in Chechnya during Kadyrov's incumbency, at the price of widespread human rights violations there and the personalisation of his rule, has been tolerated by the Russian authorities, as Kadyrov works with Moscow to advance the state's aims. The antagonism of large parts of the Chechen population to the Russian state appears to have subsided. 'Kadyrovism' is seen as bringing together various groups previously hostile to each other and reconciling varying interpretations of Chechen identity:

> traditionalists who want to revive the norms of the common law (*adat*) that has been valid for centuries within a tribal society; Islamic purists who only

recognise sharia as a legal system; nationalists who insist on Chechnya's sovereignty, basing themselves on the tradition of anti-colonial resistance; and autonomists who prefer a self-determined Chechnya within great-power Russia. (Halbach 2018, 17)

However, potential problems are re-emerging as a result of authoritarian governance under Kadyrov and of Chechen youth's receptiveness to Islamic education and even to radical Islamist propaganda, suggesting that – contrary to official claims – the republic may become once again a pocket of resistance to Russian rule.

The challenge relates to foreign as well as domestic policy. Kadyrov presents himself not only as the national and religious head in Chechnya but also as the representative of Russian Muslims abroad, effectively the key intermediary between Russia and the rest of the Islamic world. He has sent Chechen troops to support the Russian campaign in Syria – reported to be part of four military police battalions from the North Caucasus – in a deployment lasting several months. Indeed, Kadyrov appointed his own ambassador to the MENA region, charged with repatriating Russian and CIS nationals from conflict zones reconquered by Assad's forces. Several reciprocal visits have been made by official religious delegations from Syria and Chechnya. Kadyrov has also contributed to humanitarian efforts in Syria. The Akhmat Kadyrov Foundation has financed the restoration of Aleppo's main mosque and other mosques in Homs, and Kadyrov has also offered to host international humanitarian aid conferences (Hauer 2017; Halbach 2018, 26–28).

Kadyrov's informal diplomacy has caused problems for Moscow. In 2016 he hosted a theological conference for traditionalist Sunnis in Grozny, attended by senior state-appointed clerics from Syria, Egypt and Jordan as well as Sufi figures with links to Arab governments, and offended Arab delegations as well as Russia's official Muslim representatives by controversially including Wahhabism and Salafism among religious extremist movements that should be denounced. Kadyrov also defied Moscow's policy by allowing demonstrations in Grozny – repeated elsewhere in Russia – against Moscow's support of the Myanmar government, accused of committing atrocities against Rohingya Muslims, and by organising humanitarian aid for Rohingya refugees (Lund 2019, 43; Halbach 2018, 27). Kadyrov is reported to have lobbied Putin for the repatriation of Russian-speaking fighters from Islamic State in Syria to Chechnya, together with their women, so that he could monitor their activities, a move opposed by the Russian security agencies (Roth 2019, 41).

Nevertheless, he repaired relations with Arab leaders and is welcomed as a visiting dignitary and invited to talk about bilateral political and economic relations with Russia (Lund 2019, 42–43). Following the visit of the Saudi king to Russia in 2017, the Chechen mufti claimed that Chechnya was 'a reliable bridge between the Islamic world and Russia', highlighting how the Kadyrov leadership seeks to bolster Russia's legitimacy in Muslim countries (cited in Halbach 2018, 28–29). Lev Den'gov, a businessman and Kadyrov adviser, chairs the Russian contact group on intra-Libyan settlement; reports suggest that his activities in Libya are coordinated not only with the Russian foreign ministry and State Duma but also with the Chechen leadership (Hurska 2018). Russian experts underline the emergence of Kadyrov as a prominent foreign policy actor in the Islamic world: 'Under Kadyrov, the republic has been granted not just the autonomy to make its own local policy decisions but the freedom to make ideological and now even foreign policy choices as well' (Markedonov 2017). Kadyrov is thus awkwardly positioned between being an agent of the Russian state and a largely autonomous actor, exercising a *de facto* monopoly of power within a distinct normative space, with his rule potentially acquiring antagonistic features and challenging Russia's system of governance and the integrity of Russian statehood (Wilhelmsen 2018, 920, 932; Markedonov 2017).

The fine line Kadyrov treads in his peculiar patronal relationship with Putin, demonstrating loyalty to the federal state government while contesting Moscow's authority in the North Caucasus and challenging Moscow's policies in parts of the Islamic world, has become increasingly blurred (see Wilhelmsen 2018, 931–932). Kadyrov's role in some respects mirrors the shift in power relations within some countries in the MENA region. The lack of accountability of the state and its inability to guarantee security and welfare, together with deteriorating socio-economic circumstances of the local population, inspire local actors to challenge the state-centred hierarchical order and take on governance functions, thereby enhancing alternative subnational identities and potentially impacting on regional and even transnational security (Kausch 2018, 67–68; Kamel 2017, 87–88).

Experts whose field work has examined the problem in detail have emphasised the need for a long-term, sustained shift in Russia's policy by improving development and governance in the North Caucasus. Efforts should be aimed at mitigating sectarian tensions between traditional and fundamentalist Muslims by sponsoring Sufi–Salafi dialogue and proscribing discriminatory practices, ameliorating the work of law-enforcement agencies and rehabilitating transnational activists while working with their international counterparts on deradicalisation; the alternative may be that jihadi Islamist groups will 'exploit legitimate grievances in the North Caucasus and instrumentalis[e] the sense of disenfranchisement, humiliation and persecution prevalent among mostly non-violent fundamentalist Muslim believers' (ICG 2016a, iii–iv, 30). The Russian state and Kadyrov may have successfully cooperated to check the return of North Caucasus foreign fighters from the Middle East and further their respective relations with Islamic countries there, but the relationship – in the context both of ongoing conflict in the MENA region and unresolved grievances and divisions in parts of the North Caucasus, potentially driving radicalisation and militant extremism – adds another layer to the complex and unpredictable nature of Russia's engagement with the Muslim world.

Conclusions

In the Chechen ethno-nationalist insurgency of the 1990s, the challenge of Islam in Russia appeared to be confined primarily to its expression as a form of political protest. With time, the influence of more radical forms of Islamism, exacerbated by extra-legal repressive measures and neglect of social and economic grievances by state authorities and fuelled by the ideology of foreign militants, spread across parts of the North Caucasus. The political, religious and socio-cultural forces at work, linking domestic and international challenges, could no longer be ignored. The Russian authorities sought to co-opt 'traditional' moderate Islamic movements in a bid to ameliorate relations while maintaining a coercive response to deal with both militant Islamists and, in some cases, non-traditional Salafi groups. At the same time, with the 'Arab Awakening', political Islam had become both 'a dominant ideological trend and a prominent socio-political actor' in the MENA countries; in its more extreme forms, it began to shape power struggles and pose a serious threat to regional stability (Meddeb et al 2019, 49–50). Ethno-confessional tensions fed the forces of transnational jihadi Islamism. One expert has concluded that

> there is ... little that was apologetic or defensive in the Russian approach to the Arab Spring. From Moscow's perspective, the Russian experience, forged through a long association and engagement with the Muslim world, is that social stability and multi-ethnic and multi-confessional toleration in Muslim societies are fragile social commodities which can rapidly be broken apart in periods of radical social change. (Dannreuther 2015, 91–92)

The more pluralist religious landscape, marked by divisions and subject both to external political as well as internal social and economic governance challenges, has impacted fundamentally on debates in Russia about the threat to state cohesion of political Islam, the religious aspects of national identity and the relationship between religion and politics. Russia's response rested heavily on the restoration of state control. The 'securitising' narrative purveyed by the authorities in the Chechen wars was extended to the Arab uprisings, overshadowing the underlying causes of the political, social and religious upheaval there in the fanfare surrounding the 'fight against terrorism'. An added dimension to this narrative has emerged: Russia's governing elite wastes no opportunity to deplore the instability engendered by Western intervention in the MENA countries which, it claims, is a primary factor exacerbating internal conflicts. The Russian Orthodox Church has lent its firm support through a 'geopolitical-messianic narrative' that corresponds with the Putin government's own portrayal of Russia's exceptional civilisational role as a force for stability in contrast to the liberal West (Adamsky 2020, 439; see also Curanović 2019, 263). Inter-civilisational dialogue, playing on contradictions between Islamic and Western models of social organisation, has thus become closely integrated into Russian foreign policy (see Naumkin et al 2013, 93).

The new international and domestic reality following the 'Arab Awakening', which laid bare conflicting religious and political interests across the Arab world, poses problems for Moscow. First, Russian and Syrian forces may well face a longer-term struggle to defeat, or at least contain, Islamic State operations in Syria (ICG 2022a, 3). Second, in defending its policies in Syria and the other Arab countries, Moscow is forced to explain its aims and ideas, including in dealing with the plight of Orthodox and other Christian religious minorities in the Middle East, to avoid being perceived as hostile to the interests of Islamist governments and political forces and being drawn into the confrontation between Shia and Sunni powers (Naumkin et al 2013, 105–106). Third, the Russian government's state-led approach, prioritising stability and opposing more radical forms of Islamism, may be inadequate to deal with the constantly evolving challenge of Islam; the experience gained from closer engagement with Arab countries risks becoming hostage to fixed notions of state–society relations and Russian antagonism to liberal Western norms. Managing tensions between 'traditional' moderate Islam and 'non-traditional' extremist Islamism in Russia's Muslim-majority regions has become a matter of both external and domestic policy.

The return of Russian-speaking foreign fighters to the North Caucasus and their links with Islamist activists abroad – albeit to date managed by Moscow to prevent another large-scale insurgency – has raised the spectre of renewed political destabilisation, placing pressure on state-Islam relations in Russia. Moscow struggles to conceive and implement new ideas and policies to tackle underlying problems, develop a deradicalisation programme, prioritise legal instruments to respond to social, economic and political grievances and address human rights violations (see ICG 2016a, ii–iii). The problem of maintaining stability and preserving state authority in the North Caucasus while contending with the political and religious influence – in both domestic and foreign affairs – of Ramzan Kadyrov presents an additional, unresolved layer of complexity. Kadyrov's bellicose stance on the war with Ukraine – criticising the Russian defence ministry for its failings in prosecuting the campaign and committing his own troops to fight there – appears only to have raised his profile; the longer-term implications for his role in Russian domestic politics remains to be seen, a topic considered in the final chapter of this book.

6

A Russian strategy for the MENA region?

> [P]olitical realism considers a rational foreign policy to be good foreign policy; for only a rational foreign policy minimizes risks and maximizes benefits and, hence, complies both with the moral precept of prudence and the political requirement of success. (Hans Morgenthau, *Politics Among Nations: The Struggle for Power and Peace*)

Russia's policies in the MENA region over the last decade have done much to foster the notion of a 'resurgent' Russia. As shown earlier in this book, Western commentary has represented Putin's use of coercive force in Syria as the latest step in Russia's recovery from its post-Soviet era weakness to play a more assertive and even confrontational role in international affairs; it challenges a Western-led security system that 'exists at the expense of Russia's security, and threatens Russia's future as a great, strategically competitive power' (Covington 2015, 2). Dmitri Trenin refers to Russia's 'return to the global geopolitical chessboard as a great power ... turning Syria into a geopolitical stronghold and a military base for Russia in the region' in an ongoing 'politico-military adventure' (Trenin 2018a, 21–22). These commentaries echo accounts of superpower competition in the Third World during the Soviet period, in which interaction among the major powers amounted to little more than short-term transactions in a pervasive 'geopolitical' competition for unilateral advantage (Allison and Williams 1990, 1–2). Indeed, one account argues that relations between the external and regional powers in the MENA region today 'looks increasingly like a replay of Cold War dynamics [involving] great power animosity, competition, jockeying for pre-eminence, a frantic quest for clients and protégés, and rising competition in the economic, political, security, military and ideological spheres' (Gaub and Popescu 2018, 13).

Russia's military intervention to change the balance of forces in the Syria conflict, together with its more active engagement with other MENA states, may yet prove a significant juncture in the politics and security of the region. But to what extent do they add up to a regional strategy which, as in the Soviet era, is 'ruthlessly opportunist and based upon the desire to seek maximum unilateral advantage wherever this could be done with impunity' (Allison and Williams 1990, 12)? If Russia has a MENA strategy, how is it encompassed within its broader foreign policy thinking and practice and how does the Putin leadership marshal its resources to implement its objectives? Does Moscow conceive of this strategy purely in terms of relative gains with respect to the US and Western powers, undermining their positions while maximising its own strategic advantages? Is the MENA region seen by the Russian leadership as a foreign policy priority in which defending its positions is vital to its security and trade interests? Or does it offer only peripheral benefits, with Russia's involvement more a demonstration of its ability to project military and economic power to support claims to regained global status?

In previous chapters we examined the broader context of Russia's MENA policies, the domestic sources of its foreign policy and its approach to international norms. Here we focus on the military and economic factors underpinning Russian statecraft and assess the incentives impacting its decision-making in the MENA region. In the next section, we evaluate Russia's military presence and consider whether it has the means to sustain a role as an indispensable security provider there, including expeditionary forces for the purposes of power projection. We then go on to examine the economic imperatives driving Russian policy and consider the opportunities and constraints it faces in securing its interests. Finally, we ask whether there are discernible elements of a strategic vision for its longer-term role in the region; we assess how the Syria campaign has impacted Russia's prosecution of the war with Ukraine and to what extent the latter might in turn prompt a shift in its policies in the MENA region. We argue that, rather than an unrestrained Cold War-type contest for power, the unpredictable security environment and Russia's limited resource availability mean that its deployment of military forces has been measured; substantive external and domestic factors limit its ability to achieve strategic pre-eminence in Middle Eastern affairs, not least the potentially ruinous consequences of the war with Ukraine. While a more influential Russian role in the MENA region can not be ruled out, it is not clear at present that there are sufficient incentives or opportunities to expect a more assertive regional power projection.

Russia's military presence in the MENA region

Russia's military performance in the Syria conflict represented a significant improvement on its deployment of coercive power in the 2008 war with

Georgia. Estimates suggest that the Russian contingent in Syria consists of 4,000–5,000 well-drilled and -resourced troops – it was around 10,000 at the peak of the military operation in 2015–2016 – complemented by advisors assisting with the Syrian army's offensives and supported by thirty to fifty tactical fighter aircraft, sixteen to forty helicopters and military transport and reconnaissance aircraft. Russian losses in the fighting were relatively low, with media sources reporting fifty-two combat-related deaths of service personnel out of ninety-one in total as of 2018, and the destruction of only seven aircraft and twelve helicopters during the intervention (Kofman 2019, 24; Lavrov 2018, 50–51; Zvyagelskaya and Surkov 2019, 9; Pukhov 2017). Most of the ground fighting was done by Syrian and Iranian troops and militias, with Russia supplying mainly air support – crucial in terms of shoring up Assad's campaign – and private military contractors (PMCs) in intensive combat situations (Adamsky 2018, 11, 29). The figures cited above do not include PMCs attached to Syrian units, of which there may have been as many as 2,500, with several hundred fatalities suffered over the course of the conflict (Menkiszak et al 2018). Russia's deployment of regular combat personnel to Syria was manageable in terms of overall defence resources and does not appear to have substantially impacted the availability of forces elsewhere (Kjellén and Dahlqvist 2019, 25).

While impressive enough in operational terms, the longer-term significance of Russia's Syria intervention lies in the fact that it provided 'a crucible for the evolution of Russian operational concepts, tactics, and new capabilities', allowing Russia's military to review its force structure, address its weaknesses and improve the means of fighting future wars while minimising combat losses (Kofman 2019, 23; Adamsky 2018, 13–16). Experts agree that it has had a substantial impact on how the armed forces will evolve in terms of training and tactics and how the state armament programme will be resourced in the future. Its exercises in Syria displayed improved command and control capabilities, with upgraded information means, better inter-service coordination in joint operations and enhanced sea-/air-lift capabilities; the armed forces gained valuable learning experience in developing air tactics for pilots and using advanced technologies such as precision-guided munitions fired in long-range sorties from the Caspian and Mediterranean seas (Thomas 2020, 4–5, 17–20; Kjellén and Dahlqvist 2019, 44; see also Barrie and Gethin 2018, 4–8). Moreover, the exercises were a proving ground for a generation of senior military district, combined arms and divisional commanders, who have returned to Russia to disseminate lessons learned in Syria in terms of applying operational theory and concepts in practice across the armed forces (IISS 2019, 168; Pukhov 2017; Kofman 2019, 26). This includes new ways of deploying special forces and PMCs, as well as using urban warfare tactics and drones, and employing new information and communications technologies (Thomas 2020, 2–3; Adamsky 2018, 19–20).

The Syria campaign prompted a predictable – and in some respects exaggerated – outcry from Western officials and commentators, who portrayed Russia's application of coercive power as further proof of its readiness to undermine US interests in the Middle East by means of a proxy conflict, part of a concerted drive for strategic advantage (Covington 2015, 1; see also Renz 2018, 7–8; Mead 2014, 76–77). Western military analysts pointed to a

> strategic recoupling of the military to Russia's core geo-strategic interests and Putin's core political aims [which] represents a remilitarization of Russia's overall security policy ... Putin's worldview has set a new purpose and identity for the Russian military, one built on the emotion of humiliation from the end of the Soviet Union and Soviet Army and the perception of subsequent exploitation by the West to Russia's great disadvantage. (Covington 2016, 39–40)

Russian commentators have in fact suggested that firing cruise missiles into Syria from the Caspian Sea served political as well as military purposes, demonstrating Russia's resolve both to the West and to domestic audiences and highlighting its ability to dictate its will to the Middle East (Sychov 2015; Thornton 2019, 13–14). Subsequent developments in military affairs heightened Western concerns. Putin's state-of-the-nation address to the Federal Assembly in March 2018 attracted considerable attention due to its extravagant, even belligerent, tone in presenting new weapons technologies to signal the leadership's advances in defence capacity, even though they are intended primarily for deterrence against the key threats presented by US ballistic missile defence and rapid global strike force capabilities and are as yet unproven (see Cooper 2018a; Connolly 2021, 23, 32).

At the same time, the broader context of Moscow's decision-making over Syria must be considered. The recent drive to modernise and provide better resources to the Russian armed forces stems from the military reform programme initiated in 2008 – well before the Arab uprisings, and at a time of relatively benign relations with the West – which was designed to redress years of neglect and underfunding. It came amid intensive discussion about the challenges posed to Russia by trends in international security. Putin pointed to regional wars and local conflicts, including near Russia's borders, in an environment of 'instability and deliberately managed chaos' in which the erosion of international law impacted Russia's security; in his words, Russia could not rely solely on diplomatic and economic methods to resolve conflicts but had to develop military sufficiency as 'an indispensable condition for Russia to feel secure and for our partners to listen to our country's arguments' (Putin 2012a). The Russian leadership's abiding preoccupation with achieving an adequate capacity to guarantee the defence of its sovereignty and territory against external threats and protect its legitimate trade interests, as well as reaffirming its status as a power with a historical legacy of playing an independent role in regional and global affairs – rather than an untrammelled bid to dictate its will – provides the basis for a more meaningful assessment of Russia's security goals in the MENA region (see Naumkin et al 2016, 28).

For Russia's defence establishment, the mobilisation of the economy, armed forces and state institutions to deal with an increasingly hostile international environment became more urgent in the context of the increasing turbulence of the Arab Spring (see Monaghan 2016, 28). A US analyst reports that just prior to the Arab uprisings, Russia's strategic operations staff – tasked with evaluating opponents' operational as well as tactical capabilities – had already briefed the US military about their assessment of the challenges posed by the southwestern strategic direction, encompassing Russia's North Caucasus region, the Black Sea area, Syria and the broader Middle East (Covington 2016, 19–20, 49 fn 14). In early 2013 Moscow announced plans for a permanent operational naval deployment to the Mediterranean, subsequently reaffirmed in its 2015 Maritime Doctrine (Thornton 2019, 9). The 2022 version of the Maritime Doctrine emphasised the importance of the Tartus naval base in Syria to securing Russia's long-term presence in the Mediterranean. The head of the Armed Forces General Staff, Valerii Gerasimov, stated that, before moving into Syria, the military had conducted snap inspections to test readiness to transfer personnel and matériel over long distances, allowing for logistics and air support to the Khmeimim air base; large-scale exercises carried out earlier in 2015 served as a rehearsal for the Syria operation, including the *Kalibr* missile strikes from the Caspian Sea (Thomas 2020, 4; Covington 2016, 19). Russian military thinking had evidently begun to incorporate plans, extending back over several years, for a strategic presence in the MENA region.

This shift in approach was confirmed in a new version of the RF Military Doctrine in 2014, which called for the protection of Russian national interests abroad using military means where necessary; an updated Foreign Policy Concept in 2016 also made clear Russia's ambition to play a bigger role in the MENA region to deal with instability and terrorism at source before it reaches Russian borders, presented as essentially a defensive and reactive response to external interference threatening international stability and security (Lavrov 2019b; MFA 2016d; see Barmin 2018b, 1–2). Gerasimov asserted that Russia 'must be ready to defend state interests in a military conflict on any scale involving widespread use by our opponent of both traditional and hybrid methods of engagement' (Gerasimov 2019). Moscow's criticism of coercive interventions by the Western powers prompted the Russian leadership to plan for a return of 'full-spectrum conventional, unconventional and nuclear capabilities' to underpin Russia's military objectives; with the Syria operation, Russia showed 'that it now has the capabilities to challenge what it saw as the US monopoly on the use of force on a global level and to claim a say in the course of events relevant to its national interests' (Renz 2019, 819, 828).

The conflict in Syria undoubtedly had an impact on Russia's military forecasting and planning. Amendments were made to the original draft of the State Armament Programme to 2027 (SAP 2027) based on up-to-date assessments of the high-intensity combat experience gained by Russia's forces there; the emphasis was on smaller, well-armed surface combat vessels and upgraded modern battlefield systems including hypersonic weapons, cruise missiles capable of launch from multiple delivery platforms, precision-guided munitions and electronic warfare and radio-electronic intelligence systems. The deployment of medium-range bombers and combat helicopters also underscored the need for improved integration and coordination of air and ground operations, together with the use of submarines and surface vessels in integrated naval platforms (Connolly and Boulègue 2018, 19, 27–28). While the foremost priority in defence procurement remains to upgrade the strategic nuclear deterrent, SAP 2027 would also focus on optimising C_4ISR systems, streamlining key technological developments aimed at strengthening command-and-control systems in the ground forces and creating capabilities to ensure territorial defence and carry out expeditionary operations to defend national interests in strategically important theatres (Adamsky 2018, 21–22; Kjellén and Dahlqvist 2019, 43–44). The navy was set to receive less funding, mainly directed at the continuing renewal of the fleet of strategic nuclear submarines and the acquisition of smaller surface vessels, allowing for improved force mobility and deployability. The aerospace forces would receive upgraded transport aircraft to improve airlift capabilities, with enhanced air defence systems and anti-access capabilities to boost deterrence remaining a priority (Connolly and Boulègue 2018, 2; Cooper 2018b).

Building on lessons learned in Syria, these recent developments thus provided a template for Russia to expand its military capabilities and adapt its deterrent posture to carry out further interventions where necessary. Gerasimov stated that a Russian military 'adviser apparatus' is attached to every battalion, brigade, regiment and division in the Syrian armed forces (cited in Thomas 2020, 4); Russia's ongoing military role in advising and rebuilding Assad's disorganised military thus becomes of functional as well as symbolic significance, apparently heralding a longer-term presence in Syria (see Lukyanov and Mamedov 2017). Putin's approval in 2017 of agreements with the Syrian government to lease its Tartus naval base and

Khmeimim air base to Russia for forty-nine years – with Tartus potentially able to host up to fifteen warships as well as submarines and carry out vessel repairs, and Khmeimim hosting strategic bombers – suggests a significant step towards the establishment of a more ambitious military presence in the wider MENA region. Moscow also aims to secure ports in Egypt and Libya and improve political-military relations with countries across North Africa, extending its links to Sudan in order to establish a naval base on the Red Sea, thereby helping to extend its foothold across the Mediterranean (Borshchevskaya 2019, 19; Barmin 2018b, 4–5; see also Mukhin 2020; Ramani 2019a; Adamsky 2018, 31–32).

A longer-term plan to achieve air and naval supremacy in the Black Sea and the Eastern Mediterranean areas through the development of an anti-access area denial (A2AD) strategy, bolstered by the deployment of S-400 air defence systems to Syria and Crimea, would give Russia the ability in future to challenge adversaries' operational freedom and control logistical and trade flows across large parts of the Middle East (Barmin 2018b, 3–4; Ausseur and Razoux 2021, 25; Covington 2016, 33–34; Kofman 2019, 18). A permanent naval presence across the eastern Mediterranean – supported by the Black Sea fleet and with reconnaissance aircraft and bombers, electronic warfare technology, anti-ship missiles and long-range ground-to-air missiles stationed at bases in the region – would be capable of deterring other naval forces without requiring the maintenance of a large blue-water fleet (Connolly 2017, 1, 11; Berger and Salloum 2021, 25; Thornton 2019, 21–22). Regarding Russia's vestigial blue-water capabilities, its only aircraft carrier, *Admiral Kuznetsov* – sent to the eastern Mediterranean in 2016, though more as a symbol of Russia's naval power rather than for combat purposes, and withdrawn in January 2017 – is being refitted; the *Admiral Gorshkov*, the first new blue-water surface vessel in a couple of decades, has been commissioned, with several other frigates reported to be near completion. Small-scale platforms and submarines armed with long-range cruise and anti-vessel *Kalibr* missiles and an amphibious landing ship, the *Ivan Gren*, have already been deployed to support the Syria operation and act as a potential deterrent to Western naval forces (IISS 2019, 173–175; Ülgen and Kasapoğlu 2021, 5–6; Thornton 2019, 18).

A thoroughgoing assessment of Russia's power projection capabilities and military strategy, which might provide a clear pointer to the potential for sustained large-scale expeditionary operations in the MENA region, is beyond the scope of this book. The above analysis suggests that Russia's military capabilities overall have improved substantially in recent years, allowing it to project power into the region. However, its ambition to sustain a strategic presence there faces considerable constraints. Perennial systemic problems in its defence industry – due to the lag in military-technical modernisation and lack of efficiency and quality control – may not allow it to fulfil the SAP 2027 programme. The defence complex is badly in need of an upgrade in research and development capabilities, a situation exacerbated by international sanctions on Russia's military-industrial sector, which is hindering the manufacture of systems requiring high-tech components not produced in Russia (Connolly and Boulègue 2018, 29–30). Many new Russian military technologies are at the development stage, some with their origins in the Soviet period, with limited utility for sustained regional power projection. Despite progress in modernising the fleet and improving naval infrastructures, low serviceability and delays in commissioning vessels have often restricted their availability (Kjellén and Dahlqvist, 2019, 30). The long-term problems faced by Russia's navy, which prior to the Syria conflict had suffered three decades of underinvestment, include an ongoing shortfall in military transport aviation and heavy sea-lift capacities (Kofman 2019, 23–24; IISS 2012, 2; Ülgen and Kasapoğlu 2021, 7). Despite the deployment of an aircraft carrier task force in the Syria campaign, there is uncertainty about the production of a new aircraft carrier, which may not come into service before 2030, reducing the strategic value of the Tartus naval base (Cooper 2018b, 9; Barrie and Gethin, 2018, 2).

Constraints on the state defence order, exacerbated by lagging economic growth rates and the falling value of the rouble, may well partly undermine or delay plans for further military modernisation (Cooper 2018b, 15; Malmlöf and Engvall 2019, 127). No increased spending on procurement in the period to 2027 is foreseen, so national security is likely to be guaranteed using low-cost 'asymmetrical' responses to threats (Cooper 2018a, 10). Military expenditure was on a downward trend in 2020–2021, with expert assessments putting it in the range of 3.7–3.9 per cent of GDP (though the Stockholm International Peace Research Institute calculated a slightly higher figure of 4.1 per cent in 2021, helped by higher oil and gas prices), with spending on national defence at 2.7 per cent (Oxenstierna 2019, 106, 110–111; Cooper 2019; Lopes da Silva et al 2022). Economic forecasts suggest a slight decline in the period to 2027. This shortfall is likely only to worsen as a result of losses sustained in the war with Ukraine and the need to restructure and re-tool parts of defence output, necessitating some hard choices. Despite Russia's ability to mobilise resources, it may well be able to make only incremental improvements in power projection over the coming period, ruling out significant capacity for joint sea/air/ground deployments that would require much larger bases and platforms overseas. One in-depth assessment concludes that, despite international concerns over what Putin's 'sabre-rattling' in flaunting new weapons technologies portends, 'defence-industrial production on a scale commensurate with heightened global ambition is simply out of the question' (Connolly and Boulègue 2018, 38).

Russia's putative engagement in strategic competition, involving the extensive use of armed force to protect its interests abroad, must thus be seen in the context of the constraints it faces (Oxenstierna and Westerlund 2019, 20). Russia is able to launch pre-emptive precision strikes and deploy special forces or PMC operations within a coordinated command and control infrastructure, supported by air defences, to enable an A2AD posture and influence the course of intra-state MENA conflicts. With its current resources, it is capable of disrupting Western influence in support of specific security and economic goals. However, its capabilities across the Mediterranean area and ability to make large-scale conventional deployments are inferior to those of the US and NATO. Without a sustained longer-term military expansion – not currently on the horizon – there is scant evidence to suggest that Syria heralds a more assertive interventionist course in Russian foreign policy aimed at achieving strategic predominance or even superiority in the MENA region. Gerasimov himself has written that the Syria operation involved selective strikes on military targets proportionate to the situation – a 'strategy of limited action' or '"active defense" … for the preemptive neutralization of threats to the state's security', including terrorist threats (Gerasimov 2019; Thomas 2020, 2, 5).

Despite the more influential role played by the military as a result of the relatively successful Syria deployment, political calculations of risks and costs still drive decision-making. In the case of a perceived threat to Russia's vital national security interests, a rapid expansion of defence spending and procurement may be expected. However, it is not clear that the MENA region constitutes a priority for Russia; also, it is far from certain that Moscow would be able to extend its alliances beyond Syria, in an unpredictable security environment (see Facon 2017, 21). The Syria intervention was essentially an expeditionary operation against 'hybrid' irregular forces, relying on relatively limited military assets to reverse the course of the civil war and neutralise opposition groups (Pukhov 2017; Adamsky 2018, 10). Authoritative military analysts have emphasised that, while capable of undertaking limited offensive actions, using operational-strategic scale A2AD capabilities to deny viable options to opponents and dictate terms to prevent a crisis from escalating into war, Russia has been forced to work together with the US in carrying out air and special operations in Syria (Covington 2016, 34–35; Thomas 2020, 2). Economic and diplomatic instruments, backed up by limited military deployments, have predominated in Russia's role in the MENA region hitherto. Putin's extravagant claims about Russia's military achievements overshadow the fact that its defence modernisation programme was not an ill-considered reversion to strategic confrontation with the West, but corresponds to longer-term assessments of the contemporary strategic environment and the leadership's political priorities and aims (see Covington 2016, 5).

Russia's economic interests in the MENA region

The previous section analysed the defence-related measures being taken to address the perceived political-military challenges to Russia's interests stemming from instability across the wider MENA region. What of Russia's strategic trade interests there? In a 2012 newspaper article, Putin voiced concerns about Russian companies losing contracts as a result of the upheaval caused by the Arab Spring, claiming that this was linked with Western states' interventions in a bid to gain a foothold on local markets (Neyaskin 2012). Securing influence and gaining access to resources in regions such as the Middle East and Africa are a matter of intensifying global competition. To what extent does the MENA region, itself suffering structural economic problems, constitute a priority for Moscow? What are the main trends in terms of trade and financial flows between Russia and the region?

Over the last decade, the weaker performance of the Russian economy across most indicators, compounded by lower energy prices on global markets and Western sanctions following the Crimea annexation, has prompted the Putin government to seek to diversify its overseas markets (Connolly 2022, 102; Hartwell 2019, 91–92). However, the share of the MENA countries in Russia's recent trade turnover remains modest, with little in the way of diversification beyond a few specific product groups. In 2020, the region accounted for 7.3 per cent of Russia's total global trade, of which 5.6 per cent was with Middle Eastern countries and 1.7 per cent with North Africa; Turkey accounted for around half of Russia's trade with MENA and 3.67 per cent of its global trade, with Egypt (0.8 per cent), the UAE (0.6), Algeria (0.5) and Israel (0.4) following behind, and Iran, Saudi Arabia and Morocco registering between 0.2 and 0.3 per cent (Russian Foreign Trade 2020; Trading Economics 2020). In addition, Russia's share of total merchandise trade with MENA in 2019 – 1.72 per cent for imports from Russia and 0.25 per cent for exports to Russia – was lower than for all of the world's other major economies (World Bank 2021a). At the same time, the trade balance with all of the MENA countries is overwhelmingly in Russia's favour, with the latter's main exports consisting of arms and military equipment, machinery, petrochemical, metallurgical and agricultural products, particularly grain (Connolly 2022, 116). The share of oil and gas exports from Russia to the region is relatively small, with the exception of the Turkstream project transporting gas from Russia into Turkey and southeastern Europe, though there are consumer markets for natural gas. Russia is a leading exporter of nuclear power technology and there is potential for high-tech cooperation in the space sector, for example for the GLONASS satellite navigation system.

As regards financial flows, Moscow has recently been exploring prospects for foreign direct investment by the richer Middle Eastern countries, particularly the Gulf States, into Russia and into overseas projects managed by Russian companies. There has been some success; the Russian Direct Investment Fund – the country's sovereign wealth fund – has signed agreements on cooperation and joint investments with a number of MENA countries, including within the framework of the Russia-Arab Business Council, with Saudi Arabia investing $10 billion of which $2.5 billion has already been disbursed, the UAE $2.3 billion, Kuwait $1 billion, Qatar $2 billion, Turkey $0.5 billion, and Egypt and Bahrain also signing agreements (Russian Direct Investment Fund 2021; see also Kozhanov 2018, 14–16). However, the joint funds are yet to realise their potential, due to an unpromising investment climate and poor corporate governance in Russia. Overall levels of MENA countries' investment remain low, accounting for 3.67 per cent of total foreign direct investment into Russia in 2019 (World Bank 2021b). Russia's own investment in the MENA region accounted for only 1.23 per cent of total Russian foreign direct investment overseas in 2020 (World Bank 2021c).

An important part of Moscow's economic and political strategy is to strengthen Russia's presence in global energy trade – vital to its national economy – by exploiting new markets across Asia and the global South, attracting investment and stabilising oil prices. The MENA region is a highly competitive environment for energy. The major hydrocarbon producers, particularly Saudi Arabia for oil and Qatar for gas, challenge Russia's positions on global markets, even though competition is balanced with recognition of mutual interest in cooperation. As a consequence, Russia has aimed to develop closer relations with the Organization of the Petroleum Exporting Countries (OPEC) and the Gas Exporting Countries Forum (GECF), a move made more pressing due to the sharp fall in the oil price in 2014. In December 2016 OPEC announced a coordinated cut in oil production, with a group of non-OPEC countries including Russia participating, in order to nudge the oil price higher on international markets and ease the pressure on state finances. This wider group became known as OPEC+ and the agreement was subsequently extended; in June 2018, Russia was admitted as an observer member of OPEC in a bid to formalise relations. According to one source, Russian mediation between Saudi Arabia and Iran is reported to have ensured the success of the move (Nakhle 2018, 32; see also Kozhanov 2018, 21–23). The OPEC+ arrangement broke down in March 2020 over production quotas, as the heads of leading Russian energy companies were unhappy with the arrangement; it was then renegotiated, with the result that Russian output levels were cut. In 2022, the Gulf states and Russia made common cause in reducing oil output to maintain higher global market prices, favouring Moscow's need for export earnings to compensate for losses sustained as a result of Western sanctions and Europe's reduced imports of Russian hydrocarbons. Still, in a volatile oil market and uncertain global economic climate – exacerbated by the war in Ukraine – Russia–Gulf states relations at best represent a partnership of convenience, with Russia the junior partner (see Allan 2021, 153–157).

At the same time, Russia's energy majors now have substantial experience in international markets and are pushing hard to form consortia with foreign firms to develop the extraction, supply and transportation of MENA oil and gas, including important liquefied natural gas resources (LNG). This includes the potentially lucrative Eastern Mediterranean oil and gas fields, which are of increasing interest to the US and Europe as an alternative to Russian supplies and central to Turkey's and Egypt's energy policies. The Russia-Saudi Economic Council was established in 2019 and Saudi Arabia is participating in developing Russian LNG production capacities and in joint ventures on oil and gas equipment, with projects reportedly worth around $3 billion (Mammadov 2018). Moscow has obtained exclusive rights for hydrocarbon extraction in Syria as part of an energy cooperation package to assist Damascus in rebuilding and upgrading extraction, refinery and transit infrastructure (Kortunov et al 2019, 17). In November 2017, Russia launched an 'oil-for-goods' programme whereby Iranian oil was traded for Russian machinery, helping Tehran to compensate for its lack of financial reserves; other potential large-scale contracts between Russian energy companies and Iran have been held back by international sanctions, including a deal involving a reputed $30 billion investment by the state oil company Rosneft. Rosneft has also acquired a 30 per cent stake in Egypt's huge Zohr natural gas field and signed an investment and oil purchasing agreement with Libya's National Oil Corporation in 2017; Qatar has bought a 19.5 per cent shareholding, reportedly worth over $11 billion, in Rosneft. The gas giant Gazprom has signed a memorandum of understanding with the Iranian national oil company to involve large-scale Russian investment in Iran's oil sector and, along with Rosneft, Lukoil and other Russian oil firms, is investing in several exploration and infrastructure projects in Iraq (including Iraqi Kurdistan). Other projects have been explored, though with few returns to date, in Algeria, Lebanon, Bahrain, Kuwait, the UAE and Oman (see Nakhle 2018, 33; Krutikhin 2021; Mammadov 2018; Hartwell 2019, 96; Kozhanov 2018, 16–19; Barmin 2017).

Overall, however, Russia has lesser involvement in the energy sector in MENA countries compared with other major global economies. The reasons for this are the relatively low levels of Russia's capital assets and inadequate investment in its high-tech sectors; its dependence on imports of advanced technologies; international sanctions in place against Russian state-linked companies; the persistence of regional tensions; and risks associated with doing business in Russia due to non-transparent corporate practice and excessive political interference in strategic economic decision-making – all factors that may well endure in the foreseeable future in the absence of substantive domestic reforms and regional stabilisation (Krutikhin 2021, 176). Disputes over energy extraction and transportation may represent a potential source of political friction in the Eastern Mediterranean area, as well as in Libya where Russia is competing for energy contracts agreed under Gaddafi (see Kandil 2020, 45–48).

Nuclear power is an important item in Russia's high-tech goods and services export portfolio. The state energy concern Rosatom is one of the few companies capable of the full-cycle building and servicing of nuclear power plants and aims to consolidate its global status in the coming years, while diversifying its export activity to include other advanced industrial technologies such as nuclear medicine, robotics, 3-D printing, nanotech, supercomputing and wind turbines (Connolly 2022, 104, 109). As of 2017 Russia had more than twenty reactors confirmed or planned for export, with foreign orders totalling $133 billion (World Nuclear Association 2021); Rosatom claims that 35 nuclear reactor projects are now under construction abroad (Rosatom 2021). Russia's plans for an expanded role for nuclear energy, including the development of new fast neutron reactor technology, are crucial to its national energy strategy.

The potential across the MENA region for cooperation on nuclear energy is considerable. Russia's contract with Iran for the Bushehr-1 plant, which dates back to the mid-1990s, was completed in 2011; construction of the Bushehr-2 complex, comprising two new reactors together with fuel and equipment for use throughout the life cycle of the plant, started in 2019 and agreements have been signed for the construction of up to six more reactors (Allan 2021, 147). In February 2015 Rosatom signed a contract for the construction of Egypt's El Dabaa nuclear power plant which will supply nuclear fuel over its entire life cycle, with three other reactors planned. Russia began construction of Turkey's first nuclear power plant in 2018, consisting of four units in total. Talks with Saudi Arabia to build a number of reactors are ongoing. Algeria, Kuwait and the UAE – which uses Russian enriched uranium for its first nuclear power plant – are also considering cooperation with Russia's nuclear industry (World Nuclear Association 2021; see also Barmin 2017, 133–134; Nakhle 2018, 34; Kozhanov 2018, 14, 25). In March 2015 Russia and Jordan agreed a $10 billion deal for Rosatom to build and operate two nuclear reactors, but the contract was cancelled in 2018 due to the costs involved.

Crucial to Russia's ties with the MENA region is the sale of major weapons systems and other types of military-technical cooperation, helping both to fund research and development in its defence complex and to further political-military relations with purchasing countries. Russia is seen as a reliable provider of affordable armaments systems and there is usually no political conditionality placed on its business, such as when the US reduced its arms supply to Egypt in 2013 in response to al-Sisi's military coup, allowing Russia to improve its position by supplying defence-related goods there. Five of the top ten global purchasers of major weapons systems in the 2016–2020 period – Saudi Arabia, Egypt, Algeria, Qatar and the UAE – are in the MENA region, where arms imports have been increasing sharply in recent years. Russia is the world's second-biggest supplier of weapons, with Asia (principally India and China) and Oceania together currently accounting for the major share of its total sales. At the same time, Russia increased its exports to the MENA region by 64 per cent in 2016–2020 compared with the previous five-year period; in that period, the Middle East accounted for 21 per cent of total Russian sales. Contracts with twenty-three countries in the MENA region, valued at $8 billion, were agreed in 2017, the main buyers being Algeria, Iraq and Egypt, with some of the Gulf states – whose arms purchases are at present overwhelmingly from the US and European defence manufacturers – also showing interest (Borisov 2018, 39). Russia emerged as the third biggest supplier to the MENA region in 2015–2019, with 11 per cent of the market, though the US remains the predominant supplier with a 53 per cent share, with major European countries also prominent (Wezeman et al 2020; Wezeman et al 2021; Statista 2021). Aleksandr Mikheev, head of the Russian arms export agency Rosoboronexport, has spoken of increasing overseas interest in weapons systems tested by Russia in Syria, principally air defence systems, cruise missiles and combat aircraft (Kuimova 2019, 9). Russia appears well placed to establish a regional presence in the MENA arms market (see Connolly and Sendstad 2017, 17–18).

Energy and military-technical trade with the MENA countries represent sources of capital and technology markets that promise durable benefits to the Russian economy, especially given the longer-term trend of diversifying its markets away from Europe. However, oil and gas markets are volatile, and Western sanctions restricting the supply of Western technology and finance into the energy sector are likely to have a detrimental, if as yet uncertain, impact on Russia's business. As for military-technical cooperation, Algeria and Egypt, and potentially Iraq, Iran and Syria, may eventually depend for a considerable part of their defence capabilities on Russian weapons, which may favour longer-term political partnerships (see Zvyagelskaya and Surkov 2019, 13). At the same time, there is stiff competition from other suppliers of defence-related goods, including from non-Western countries, with China in particular driving growth in arms exports to Asia; Russia's global share of major armaments deliveries declined from

26 per cent in the 2011–2015 period to 20 per cent in 2016–2020. Russia's inability to keep pace with innovation and the technological demands of network-centric warfare systems – exacerbated by Western sanctions on Russia's defence industry, US attempts to dissuade countries from buying armaments from Moscow and lower levels of state funding allocated to arms procurement in Russia – constitute structural factors that hinder its performance as a supplier of modern weapons (see Connolly and Sendstad 2017, 24–25). Supply chain disruption resulting from the Ukraine war is also impacting Russia's exports.

Beyond these sectors, Russia's foreign economic activity in the MENA region is currently negligible in terms of overall value compared to its trade with Europe and Asia, with low-added-value products – metals, basic chemicals and agricultural produce – predominating. Moreover, political instability and the lack of economic diversification in many of the MENA countries, together with low levels of infrastructure and regulatory barriers, inhibit development and complicate long-term trade and investment. As mentioned above, plans to attract finance from the wealthy Gulf states are very much at an early stage; the fall in the value of the rouble and international sanctions, first over Crimea and now over its invasion of Ukraine, are limiting Russia's ability to finance major investment projects overseas. The short- to medium-term prospects for its economic links with the region are unpromising. Turkey is a notable exception, but even there bilateral trade is potentially hostage to shifts in Moscow–Ankara political relations. Diplomatic alignment with Iran over Syria has not translated into substantive investments and in fact bilateral trade has been decreasing, due partly to US sanctions on Iran, though the above-mentioned Gazprom deal may signal a change. Any improvement in trade with Syria, Iraq and Libya requires political stability and economic reconstruction in those countries.

Russia faces competition not only from the developed Western economies but also from the growing economic involvement of China, India and other Asian states in the MENA region. China's and India's trade turnover with the region is several times that of Russia. Middle Eastern countries supply almost half of China's total foreign oil imports; China is an important trading partner for Saudi Arabia (oil) and Iran (gas) and is becoming a key source of finance for some countries in the region (House of Lords 2017, 41). Non-oil trade between the Gulf Cooperation Council states and Asia, as well as Gulf sovereign wealth fund investments into Asian countries, are also increasing. As detailed in Chapter 1 of this book, there is ample evidence of China's increasing strategic involvement there, and India too is seeking to increase its economic and security engagement. Beijing's Middle East strategy, reflected in its Arab Policy Paper, is based on aims similar to Moscow's – pragmatic relations free of interference in internal affairs – but its broad range of investment, trade, energy and infrastructure interests in the MENA countries may well provide comparative advantage in the future, with less direct political involvement compared to Russia's due to the latter's geographical proximity and cultural ties with the region.

A Russian strategy?

Earlier in this chapter we highlighted the argument of some commentators that Russia marshals its resources to extend its global reach and challenge the West's political and economic dominance in the MENA region: 'The bottom line for the Russians is, "We're back as a major force. We cannot be ignored"' (Trenin 2017b). It is clear that the Putin leadership is intent on restoring a more extensive political-military and trade presence there. This trend accords with what Moscow perceives as objective processes of change. Lavrov has pointed to structural shifts in the global economy in which the share of developing markets in terms of purchasing power parity is increasing relative to that of the G7 developed economies, with the result that the G20 is becoming 'the most representative and respected mechanism of collective leadership of leading states that meets the 21st century realities'; the prudent response to these shifts is to diversify Russia's trade relations with non-Western states in the global East and South (Lavrov 2019c).

Moscow has undoubtedly taken advantage of the turmoil across the MENA region to recover a measure of influence there. Russia maintains its partnership with Iran and has rebuilt its economic positions in Egypt, Turkey and Iraq. A more active regional policy has even brought Moscow a higher profile in the Arab Gulf states, and it seeks a more prominent role in Libya and elsewhere in North Africa. The transactional nature of its approach, coupling diplomatic campaigns with economic and – where prudent – military cooperation, means that Russia has improved its standing as a reliable partner, seen as decisive and at the same time responsive to political practice in the region (Khouri 2018, 9–10; Borisov 2018, 41; House of Lords 2017, 38). But to what extent does Russia have a coherent and consistent vision for a strategic role, commensurate with increased investment of political and material resources? Might its enhanced standing portend strategic competition with Western countries, exploiting perceived weaknesses in their approaches to the region, with further military power projection to maximise potential advantage?

We argue that the limited structural power at Russia's disposal is out of proportion to the long-term political-military and economic commitments that a commanding strategic presence in the region would demand. As noted earlier in this chapter, Russia's lagging economic and financial performance is compounded by technological shortcomings in the defence sector. Trade turnover with MENA countries is modest, with little in the way of technology exchange beyond the energy and military-technical sectors. Russia has no real alliances apart from Syria, an economically depleted state which has lost its leadership role in the region and where Russia's political influence will only produce big economic dividends if finance is made available for reconstruction; Europe and the Gulf states, the most likely donors, will only lift sanctions if political concessions are made by Moscow and Damascus (see Kortunov et al 2019, 21). A report based on field research in regime-held areas of Syria, including interviews with government officials and businessmen, has concluded that in spite of Moscow's support for the Assad leadership, 'Russia has not turned Syria into a client state nor established a position from which it can dictate internal reforms' (Samaha 2019, 10). Russia has weakly institutionalised relations in the MENA region; its business links with regional elites are largely controlled by a small but powerful group of state-linked business majors who promote their own sectional interests, reflecting overall trends in Russia's political economy and making it vulnerable to political shifts in relations and to economic downturns in countries afflicted by instability. The opportunities to carve out a longer-term strategic economic presence in the MENA region, generating more pronounced political influence, must thus be seen in the wider context of the constraints Russia faces.

While intervention in Syria and attempts to gain a political-military foothold in other MENA states have demonstrated Russia's resolve, there is limited evidence to support the proposition that it prefigures the projection of massive force to supplant Western influence and alter radically the balance of power in the region. Stepanova points to a 'critical paradox' whereby Russia's upgraded role in Syria

> was neither a goal in itself, nor part of any region-wide 'grand strategy' for the Middle East ... any successful achievements in regional security in the Middle East, with implications beyond the region, have come about only through *active* and *sustained multilateral efforts* and involved major diplomatic input and engagement by external powers and international organizations. (Stepanova 2016, 10, 12; emphasis in original)

This policy reflects continuity, rather than a radical departure from its approach prior to the inception of the Arab Spring: Russia essentially defends a fairly limited set of aims, pursuing national security interests and competitive economic advantage while minimising risks and maximising benefits – a course of action that would have gained the approval of the classical realists (see the epigraph to this chapter). As one military expert has put it, Russia is 'opportunistic on a strategic scale, and tactically deliberate inside this strategic framework' (Covington 2015, 4).

Further constraints, as yet unquantifiable, will be imposed by the consequences of the war with Ukraine. Restricted availability of data makes it very difficult to form a reliable picture, but one authoritative assessment suggests that the Russian state budget is already under considerable strain; with reduced levels of oil/gas income, a Ministry of Economic Development assessment forecasted a decline in GDP of 7.8 per cent and a fall in investment of almost 20 per cent in 2022. At the same time, allocations to national defence and economy, particularly to the armed forces, appear to have increased substantially, reflecting Putin's commitment to the Ukraine campaign (see Cooper 2022). To what extent this prefigures a longer-term 'remilitarisation' of Russian security policy is hard to predict; whether Russia can increase its defence spending and reallocate sufficient resources to Ukraine while sustaining its military activity further afield, including in the MENA region, is uncertain. The Syria intervention may have been important in terms of embedding new concepts, tactics and capabilities in military operations, but Russia is now fighting a war which places different demands on the leadership; its air force, successful in its campaign against a disorganised and poorly equipped Syrian opposition, is struggling to overcome Ukraine's air defence assets and the number of contract troops is insufficient to enlarge the areas controlled by Russia, leading to a potentially protracted stalemate or further costly clashes between the warring sides. For all that the Syria campaign brought with it improved command and control capabilities, the Russian armed forces have suffered notable reverses in Ukraine. As for Russia's foreign economic activity, reorienting trade towards Asia and the global South, including the MENA region, in response to the sharp downturn in trade with the developed Western economies could well have a deleterious effect on its overall economic development. A long-term strategy to mitigate the effects of the Ukraine war is yet to emerge.

Conclusions

Two main conclusions can be drawn from the analysis in this chapter. The first is that Russia's projection of power into the MENA region is likely to remain limited. Russia's variable political-military and economic gains from its relations with the MENA countries have to be balanced against the risks involved, demanding a pragmatic approach that avoids military escalation. Russia's policy has been to avoid undue exposure to the risk of escalation over Syria, and to other potentially more costly disputes elsewhere, and safeguard its interests by maintaining selective cooperation with the other external powers to manage regional tensions. Lavrov has argued that averting an intensification of crises in the MENA region demands a military response from all the major external powers, but only prior to negotiations aimed at establishing a durable regional security framework (Lavrov 2020b; see Stepanova 2018a, 47–48). As leading Russian experts have concluded, 'Russia's post-Soviet leadership does not aim to secure and expand its influence in the Middle East by binding "client" states to it through military-technical cooperation or economic aid. In other words, Moscow is not out to create a "sphere of influence" in the region' (Shumilin and Shumilina 2017, 116).

Interpretations of Moscow's MENA policy exclusively in terms of balance-of-power rivalry – with Russia bidding to regain its Soviet-era position as a counterweight to the US in an ambitious pursuit of influence in the Middle East to compensate for its decline elsewhere (Baev 2016, 60), and the corollary that the West needs to 'push back' against Russia – are flawed. Western policies, riddled with inconsistencies and vitiated by an absence of strategic clarity about the regional security environment, have led to a tendency to blame 'their own shortsightedness and inflexibility on a politically convenient external scapegoat (Russia) and on the familiar Russia-West binaries brought out of the mothballs of the Cold War' (Stepanova 2018a, 54). A more compelling argument is that Moscow's pragmatic approach to MENA crises has so far *inhibited* a strategic approach; a coherent region-wide strategy is yet to emerge (see Trenin 2018a, 27). Lavrov's response to an interviewer's question – 'What is Russia's exit strategy in Syria?' 'We don't have an exit strategy' (Lavrov 2017c) – should be understood in context: this was in an interview in which he praised Russia's intensive diplomacy with the US, free of ideological biases and aimed at incremental measures to de-escalate tensions in Syria.

The Putin leadership has proved tactically adept at juggling its political and economic policies in order to increase its diplomatic heft with most of the key players in the region, defend its legitimate interests and ensure its ability to act independently. For the defence and security establishment, these aims warrant a bigger naval presence in the eastern Mediterranean, anchored in a number of bases in MENA states. At the same time, the deployment in Syria of a fairly substantial expeditionary force backed up with heavy weaponry – impressive enough given the problems faced by the military over the last three decades – was limited to six months; a smaller contingent remains, supported by air power and consisting mainly of special forces together with an unknown number of private military contractors undertaking specific tasks. Any future expansion of Russia's presence in the MENA region would depend on policy decisions to prioritise it as pivotal to Russia's national interests and seek regional alliances in pursuit of long-term strategic competition with its adversaries.

The second conclusion concerns how the Russian leadership deals with the constraints imposed by the regional and global economic environment. As things stand, structural weaknesses in its resource-based economy are likely to restrict its ability to sustain a systematic expansion of its political-military presence overseas, let alone achieve any kind of all-embracing regional supremacy. Global financial crises, fluctuations in the oil price, regional conflicts and disruption of trade and investment flows stemming from the war with Ukraine – any combination of these factors may cause economic shocks that test Russia's resilience. The issue of whether Syria heralds further military interventions by Russia, and how the West might counteract them, distracts attention from more fundamental problems. Russia's real challenge lies in developing a longer-term broader strategic outlook for its role in the MENA region, one that takes account of both domestic developments and a changing international and regional environment. A credible and sustained attempt by Russia at more dynamic and competitive engagement with other external and regional actors is needed to exercise leadership across complex political, military, economic and humanitarian agendas, while moderating the propensity to define itself in opposition to the West. The countries of the MENA region need economic as well as security assistance to overcome their domestic problems; compared with the other developed economies, Russia's contribution is likely to be confined to specific trade and financial sectors.

Such a strategic policy approach appears highly unlikely for some time to come. Russia's ongoing war in Ukraine, in the region of its most critical strategic interest, presents formidable challenges to the Putin leadership. Its diplomatic isolation from the West, economic losses from sanctions, the depletion or redeployment of force structures, the potential revision of the state armament programme to meet the needs of the Ukraine campaign and the possible reorientation of its foreign trade towards Asia and the countries of the global South as a result of the war – and how all of these factors will reshape its global strategy – are yet to become clear. But the most likely outcome is that the MENA region will be relegated in terms of Russia's priorities, forcing Moscow to defend its security and economic gains more by diplomatic than military means; the longer-term prospect of Russia projecting power in the Eastern Mediterranean may even be in doubt. These questions are taken up in the concluding chapter of this book.

Conclusions

> Words carry us forward towards ideological confrontations from which there is no retreat. This is the root of the tragedy of politics. Slogans, clichés, rhetorical abstractions, false antitheses come to possess the mind ... language encloses politicians in the blindness of certainty or the illusion of justice.
> (George Steiner, *The Death of Tragedy*; cited in Hurrell 2005, 25)

This book has raised important questions that have far-reaching implications both for Russia's future role in the MENA region and for its wider external relations. The first question features prominently in Western academic and policy analysis, which generally focuses on Moscow's strategic aims in the MENA countries. As the Libya and Syria conflicts evolved from popular protest to armed conflict and civil war, was the decisive shift from (conditional) cooperation to (partial) confrontation with the Western powers caused primarily by the pursuit of strategic incentives? The second question relates to how Russia has managed the disruptive effects of political and social mobilisation across the Arab world, in terms both of the popular challenge to incumbent governments and the rise of political Islam. What part was played by the beliefs of Russia's elites, deriving from its self-perception as a global power and ideas about its legitimate role in a statist international legal order in opposition to liberal humanitarian intervention? The third question concerns the influence of Russia's internal politics on foreign policy. How has Russia's decision-making in the MENA region been influenced by the leadership's approach to domestic political order? The fourth question centres on the political methods and personal world view of Vladimir Putin. How did Putin deal with institutional constraints and exploit political opportunities at home to gain support for a more assertive foreign policy in MENA affairs?

In this book we have tried to identify fundamental trends in Russia's approach in terms of the rationale underpinning its foreign policy thinking, the configuration of domestic institutions and actors in policymaking, the ordering of relations with external and regional states and the commitment of resources to further its regional strategy. A key conclusion is that

Russia's foreign policy now firmly embraces a new framework of reference, the culmination of a long-term development stretching back before the Arab Spring, to the inauguration of the first Putin presidency and even earlier. The Putin leadership's belief that the West's predominance is a thing of the past is signalled in Lavrov's assertion that 'The world is objectively becoming "post-Western" ... we need to get used to the multipolarity of the world and the fact that the leading players must understand and put into practice their collective responsibility for peace and stability' (Lavrov 2017d). For 'post-Western' read 'post-liberal': Russia claims to lead a growing resistance among non-Western states to the liberal 'rules-based' order, perceiving it as an attempt to maintain the US's global political, economic and military dominance (see Mearsheimer 2019, 34). In Russian eyes, a conflictual international system, caused by structural shifts in the international order, is driven by an increasing reliance on military power amid the emergence of new threats and the weakening of international security mechanisms; these views have become deeply ingrained in Russia's belief systems. Russia's international relations are thus predicated on the active defence of its security interests, reinforcing its global role through a calibrated deployment of political-diplomatic and where necessary military capabilities, justifying its more assertive involvement in regional MENA affairs and consolidating a strong sovereign state to defend its domestic order.

At the same time, Russia has often sought to cooperate with the Western powers and engage in diplomacy to mediate conflicts in pursuit of stability, recognising that the MENA states are redefining their national security interests in response both to regional and domestic trends and to external interference in their domestic affairs. The complexity of post-Arab Spring MENA affairs at a time of rapid political, economic and social change compels Moscow to navigate a path between its own strategic priorities, the security interests of powerful regional actors and its relations with the external powers in a volatile region where contingency also plays a major role. Interpreting Russia's foreign policymaking as driven purely by authoritarian or revisionist tendencies in opposition to liberal Western thinking and practice, or as a propensity to act as a 'spoiler' in pursuit of transitory relative gains, is fraught with the risk of misunderstanding the contextual factors determining its actions.

In the introductory chapter, we proposed a framework encompassing four explanatory factors for the development of Russia's response to the Arab Spring: material factors and structural power; the ideas underpinning Russian elites' conceptions of international society and international norms; domestic politics as a determinant of its foreign policy; and the agency of Vladimir Putin. Each explanation – considered separately – allows for only a partial understanding of continuity and change in Russia's approach to the MENA region. Brought together, they allow for a wide-ranging and comprehensive critical analysis that explores the specific factors underlying Russian thinking and decision-making. We argue that certain conventional assumptions present in Western academic and policy commentary require reconsideration.

Structural power

A common argument is that Russia's actions in the MENA region are consciously designed to undermine Western positions as part of a strategic foreign policy shift, motivated by a drive for increased influence as a global power. In this interpretation, a resurgent Russia is bidding to recover its Soviet-era positions through unrestrained zero-sum rivalry, powered by militarisation and the use of regional proxies, acting as a spoiler to thwart Western intentions and supplant the US as the main external actor in the region. Parallels are drawn with the Cold War period, when the great powers attempted to influence regional affairs in order to alter foreign policy alignments and secure strategic advantage. One authoritative Russian commentator has argued that Moscow's primary aim is to promote 'a means of transition from a unipolar world to a new world order without the ideological confrontation of the Cold War' (Frolov 2016).

There is certainly evidence that Russia has identified opportunities to enhance its strategic presence in the wider MENA region, both to secure forward defensive positions against potential instability that may threaten national security and to protect its trade interests there. But we argue that the notion of a return to Cold War-like competition fails to account for the constraints imposed by the changing regional environment, where the leading MENA states exercise greater agency, limiting the external powers' influence and hindering the uninhibited pursuit of relative gains. While the major external states can still affect power balances through trade pacts and military support, their interventions are no longer able to suppress the indigenous regional security dynamic. They struggle to devise strategies to deal with intractable security and governance challenges, forcing them to work within a framework of non-binding, issue-specific agreements involving regional and local power-brokers. They have mostly failed to secure the resolution of regional conflicts and deal with the rise of non-state actors, ethno-confessional divisions and sectarian violence practised by local clients. The challenges faced by the external powers stem less from a contest over spheres of influence and more from the risk of involvement in military escalation due to the weakening of rules and norms regulating inter-state behaviour, in a constantly shifting balance of regional power.

There is scant evidence to support the argument that Russia's Syria intervention prefigures the pervasive use of military force to alter radically the balance of power in the region in its favour. As detailed in Chapter 2, Russia's policies have been directed towards a negotiated settlement in Syria – albeit one that preserves its interests – through the Geneva process underwritten by the UN, together with the Astana format and other initiatives aimed at de-confliction and de-escalation. These measures have been frustrated, first, by the intractability of the warring parties, clashing interests among the MENA powers and the lack of strong regional leadership that might have sponsored conflict resolution, and second, by general mistrust between Russia and Western governments, stemming partly from disputes over other policy issues and rooted in differing understandings of the causes of regional civil conflicts. This has inhibited any effective multilateral approach. Russia has consequently sought to maintain an uneasy balance between cooperating with the other external powers to limit regional destabilisation and the assertive pursuit of its immediate economic and security interests in the wider MENA region. Any comparative increase in influence has come from diversifying its links with the leading states there. Far from achieving any kind of regional predominance, Russia's 'agile diplomacy' has to date brought with it variable political and material gains.

As highlighted in Chapter 6, the resources available to the Putin leadership for power projection are limited. Until the invasion of Ukraine at least, there was no excessive militarisation of the defence budget; military reform has only partially redressed the underinvestment and lack of modernisation in the first two post-Soviet decades, placing constraints on further large-scale Russian military operations in the MENA region. Russia is now reordering its security priorities to deal with its campaign in Ukraine and may well be incapable in the foreseeable future of committing resources commensurate with a powerful strategic presence in the MENA region, or even sustaining a role as an important provider of security, trade, finance and technology. Indeed, its political-military assets are likely to be much less sought-after in rebuilding the region, inhibiting the consolidation of a longer-term strategic presence.

Ideas and norms

The contest between Russia and the Western liberal democracies over the norms that underpin the states system has been manifest in their approaches to the Arab Spring, exposing glaring differences in their conceptions of international society. As highlighted in Chapter 4, Western criticism of Russia's revisionist approach to the international order is met with Russian condemnation of Western attempts to challenge the sovereign legitimacy of incumbent state leaderships in the MENA region in the name of democracy and human rights, thereby exacerbating complex conflicts and aggravating cultural and religious tensions to the detriment of regional and global stability. Lavrov has consistently railed against Western attempts to promote a 'rules-based order' that seeks to undermine 'undesirable' states; he presents Russia's position as upholding the foundations of international law, in opposition to

> the actions of the real revisionists that are aimed at the unilateral revision of the norms of interstate relations as established in the UN Charter and the basic instruments of international law, which they would like to replace with their own rules … The overwhelming majority of states share Russia's approaches to interstate relations. They consider Russia a reliable guarantor of global stability and a balance in the world order that is now taking shape. (Lavrov 2018f)

The Russian leadership perceives the West's coercive attempts to promote 'progressive' models and norms purely as an expedient to maintain its supremacy in the MENA region, encroaching on Russian interests. It maintains that the UN alone, as the international institution embodying the understanding among social actors of legitimate statehood, confers legitimacy on the exercise of power; a stable international order should rest on shared understandings of legal authority among states, averting the risk that norms will be used instrumentally to serve the interests of the more powerful countries (see Reus-Smit 2005b, 88–89). Arguments by Western leaders, framing Moscow as shamefully calculating and driven by a narrow view of the national interest to advance its strategic interests in the MENA region – and Putin himself as 'hard-nosed [and] unsentimental' and guilty of 'monstrous hypocrisy' (cited in Ralph et al 2017, 888) – overlook the fact that Russia's response reflects its self-understanding as a legitimate actor abiding by traditional international law.

Some Western scholarship of global governance has in fact suggested compelling reasons for upholding the existing institutions of a pluralist international society, designed to manage power relations and preserve stability within a sovereignty-based international legal order; they argue that, in a global society of states with diverse political and cultural identities, arguments over values should give way to negotiation over interests in seeking a shared understanding of legitimate foreign policy conduct, rights and duties based on equal legal status:

> maintaining a strong focus on the emerging world comes from the need to break free from the dichotomizing all-or-nothing debate surrounding the Western-led global liberal order and to reframe that debate in terms of a new pluralism that might be able to stabilize existing power struggles and provide a basis for the accommodation of divergent values. (Hurrell 2018, 98–99)

Research on rising powers and international institutions has identified 'a more robust, differentiated pattern of order, less hegemonic and perhaps more enduring because it does not depend on US leadership ... generating new, more decentralized patterns of world order that could result in a more pluralistic system' (Larson 2018, 248–249). Russia's framing of its resistance to Western intrusion into the sovereign rights of MENA countries is an attempt to address structural inequalities in the international system and push back against the perceived Western monopoly on rule-making, consistent with wider global trends supported by other leading non-Western powers; its appeal to respect cultural and civilisational autonomy and diversity of governance models reinforces its demand for systemic pluralism.

Russia's appeal to the norms of sovereignty and non-intervention has been critically challenged by the Arab uprisings and subsequent events, however. Moscow's initial support for the widespread condemnation of Gaddafi, joining international demands for the protection of the Libyan people, was replaced by its refusal to countenance 'regime change' in Syria, using the 'fight against terrorism' narrative to justify its assistance to an uncompromising Assad government that prioritised force over political solutions. Russia's argument – that state authorities have a privileged place in the management of order and that justice can only be dispensed in conditions of order (see Foot 2003, 17) – appears hollow when legitimate social and political demands are met with massive violence by authoritarian leaderships. Russia's governing elite pays little attention to evolving norms that call on state authorities to respect good governance and human rights as fundamental requirements for rightful membership in contemporary international society. Russia's approach – even if its criticism of the Western powers' instrumental appeal to moral principles is justified – must be called into question. Its invasion of Ukraine has undermined its claim to respect the sovereign legitimacy of an internationally recognised state, threatening regional and, potentially, global security. We return to these issues later in this chapter.

Domestic determinants

In Chapter 3 we examined the question of how domestic factors have influenced Russia's approach to the Arab Spring. As authoritative scholars have argued, Moscow considers progressive Western norms and values not only as contrary to the interests of MENA states but also 'as potentially threatening Russian sovereignty and (increasingly authoritarian) domestic state order as well as a gauntlet thrown down to those committed to a pluralist global order' (Allison 2013a, 110). In this interpretation, Russia's foreign policy priorities are determined by the nature and structure of political power in Russia, developed during Putin's incumbency and supported by the majority of the country's elite (see Allison 2013b, 818). The leadership gains domestic legitimacy by providing internal order and stability, promoting a distinctive national identity against the intrusion of Western 'mentorship' and projecting these norms into its external relations; in Lavrov's words, a 'strategic success' of its foreign policy in the MENA region is that 'it has turned into a value of its own and ceased to be a derivative of Russia's relations with the West' (Lavrov 2019b). This translates, first, into Moscow's support for incumbent governments as custodians of national moral values and ethical norms, and second, into shifting resources to reinforce domestic political structures in order to combat the perceived threat of externally promoted liberal norms.

Evidence certainly suggests a deliberate trend under Putin towards consolidating a strong state authority by changing domestic coalitions and political institutions, minimising the influence of liberal constituencies preferring a more open and accountable system. However, some Western commentators have gone further, berating an authoritarian Russian leadership that provides sustained support for MENA autocracies; they draw an 'unavoidable parallel' between the Arab uprisings and demonstrations across Russia during the Bolotnaya protests in 2011–2012, suggesting that Putin's resolute response to protests in Syria was motivated by the need to rally a domestic base of support (Dannreuther 2019, 739–740; Stoner and McFaul 2015, 178–179). Others have claimed that, by preventing challenges to incumbent authoritarian governments, the governing elite contributes to creating a model or process of authoritarian alignment in the international system (Evans 2015, 424). In other words, they draw a direct causal link between domestic regime type and Russia's foreign policy preferences in the MENA region.

We challenge these arguments on several points in Chapter 3. First, the absence of an immediate threat to Russia's governing elite or to vital national interests casts doubt on whether intervention in Syria constituted a 'diversionary' foreign policy; evidence suggests that there was no decisive public support for military action there. Second, Moscow has not tried to promote any authoritarian political or ideological model in the Arab countries. The Russian leadership's concerns over instability and the vacuum of governance resulting from the overthrow of autocratic leaders are not directly motivated by support for illiberal regimes but reflect a fundamentally different perception of the nature of contemporary challenges, namely the threat to political order and societal cohesion posed by extremism following the Arab uprisings. Third, diverse national ideas and cultures shape specific political and institutional conditions in each MENA country; Moscow has been prepared to countenance more representative and pluralistic systems there rather than simply lining up with regional 'strongmen'. Russia does court authoritarian or illiberal MENA leaderships – a practice refined over the years by the Western liberal democracies – but this is context-dependent and transactional rather than ideological, aimed at maximising opportunities to project influence abroad while working towards a stable regional balance of power and interests. Fourth, while Russian state and private entities have lent support to security structures in Syria, Egypt and elsewhere, the preconditions in many MENA states – in terms of the security cultures and practices embedded in their political systems – already existed for policy preferences militating against liberalisation.

Western scholarship has generally overlooked essential aspects of how Russia's self-understanding, translated into a set of precepts about its role in the international order, has influenced its policies during the Arab Spring. Russia is unquestionably intent on defending the legitimacy of its domestic order in the face of intrusive Western liberalism, but the tendency to exaggerate the extent to which regime type influences foreign policy risks underestimating longer-term determinants that shape Russia's decision-making (see Lynch 2016, 110). The contending impulses influencing foreign policy result from a singular interplay between its domestic politics, national beliefs and interaction with the social and political environment in the countries of the MENA region.

Agency

For some, Putin's agency constitutes the primary causal factor driving decision-making in response to the Arab uprisings; it was his 'unique operational code' deriving from his own political credo and methods, rather than national interests or structural factors, that prompted Russia's intervention in Syria (McFaul 2020, 124–125). As detailed in Chapter 3, there is ample evidence of the increasing consolidation and personalisation of foreign policy decision-making under Putin, who stands at the apex of an institutionalised power vertical and manipulates the instruments of statecraft through an 'administrative regime' that blocks the emergence of independent political actors (Sakwa 2015, 67). The most important foreign policy decisions, including the Syria intervention, have been taken with his personal sanction, based on the authority invested in the presidency. Putin's resolve – especially when compared with recent US foreign policy – appears all the more imposing and effective; the restoration of Russia's international status, underpinned by its replenished military capabilities, has impressed both international and domestic public opinion.

At the same time, we argue that Putin acts within the framework of a coalition of actors, embedded in both formal structures and informal networks; his decision-making is calculated to win the political and institutional support of key domestic constituencies. He relies heavily on the defence ministry, security agencies and state-linked business majors, which have gained prominence over the last decade and pursue their own interests in the MENA region, competing for influence and state budget allocations (see Petrov and Gel'man 2019, 451, 457). These entities provide resources for Putin, but the notion of his personal agency as the pre-eminent factor in decision-making has also to take into account the influence of domestic political structures and the preferences of elite interest groups to explain policy choices, as well as material factors and longer-term determinants specific to the international and regional MENA environment.

The decision-making system, ostensibly a pillar of support for Putin's leadership as well as a source of societal cohesion, now poses increasing problems for both state and society. The weakness of formal institutions, the deprofessionalisation of the bureaucracy and the deficient information channelled up to the presidential decision-making apex – all of these factors impede its ability to react to rapid change and constrain the effective implementation of a foreign policy strategy based on a clear set of core national interests (Gel'man 2015, 101, 127–128). The increased influence of the military, reflected in defence minister Shoigu's triumphalist claims about Russia's success in opposing Western-inspired 'colour revolutions' in the MENA region, may in fact have been a factor – if not a causal trigger – in Putin's momentous decision to launch a potentially ruinous war with Ukraine. Returning to the epigraph to this chapter, Putin – caught in a vicious circle enclosing structure and agency – appears to suffer 'the blindness of certainty [and] illusion of justice': his beliefs are reinforced by information provided by key security and defence officials that corresponds to their own sectional interests and, in the absence of political and institutional checks and balances, are fraught with the risk of reckless involvement in conflicts abroad.

The failures of the external powers in the Arab Spring

The changes across the MENA region emerging from the Arab uprisings – described by one leading scholar as a 'psychological and epistemological rupture ... A revolutionary moment of political emancipation and self-determination' – have been profound (Gerges 2014, 1). The impact has been mainly felt at the domestic level, where the authority of the state has been undermined by the collective action of political and social movements, sparking multiple conflicts and facilitating the spread of Islamist ideas across national borders (see Kamrava 2018, 110–111), and at the regional level, where the rules of state–state interaction have been distorted by adversarial power politics, compounded by failures in entrenching regional institutions. But the widespread disorder and instability in the region have also exposed a deeper malaise at the international level. The explanations we put forward above of Russia's response to the Arab Spring therefore compel us to offer a critical analysis of the outcomes for the region that directly or indirectly resulted from its policies and those of the external powers.

The Syrian civil war has been the most dismal manifestation of this malaise. A lower-end estimate of fatalities over the ten years of conflict to December 2020, provided by the Violations Documentation Center and relying on information from a network of local activists, puts the total of battle-related deaths at 226,374 including 135,634 civilians, with government forces accounting for 156,329 and Russian forces 7,290 (BBC 2021). The Office of the United Nations High Commissioner for Human Rights reports that, in the ten-year period to March 2021, 350,209 deaths were recorded, including 143,350 civilians, with many more non-lethal casualties (IICI 2022a, 2–3). Out of a population of 22.1 million, 15.3 million people will require humanitarian assistance in 2023 as a result of conflict, as well as economic and public health crises; international aid continues to be held back by insufficient funding and operational difficulties, some of them caused by political disputes (UNSC 2022b). Syria has experienced a massive loss of human capital stock, with the displacement of more than half of the country's population and almost 6.8 million Syrian refugees still living in Turkey, Lebanon, Jordan, Iraq and North Africa as of July 2022 (UNHRC 2022). GDP has fallen by about two-thirds since 2011; basic infrastructure, including housing, health and educational facilities, is severely depleted and the cost of reconstruction is estimated at about twelve times the present annual GDP. By 2019 there had been a 50 per cent reduction in economic activity compared with 2010 (World Bank 2021d). Ninety per cent of Syrians live below the poverty line (IICI 2022b, 1). Political and economic life, rife with corruption and smuggling and with little or no prospect of governance reform under the present leadership, continues to be dominated by privileged patrons, officials and power-wielding security services and militias (Aksenenok 2020; ICG 2019c, 3–5). Routine violence by state forces, government-allied militias and Islamist militants, including against women and children, is endemic across large parts of the country.

Russia's policies have contributed to outcomes that could hardly have been worse, apart perhaps from a sweeping victory for jihadi forces. Moscow's continued insistence on 'intra-Syrian consultations' in which the

Syrian people themselves would decide the future of the country – aimed at averting external interference, with its own intervention justified by the invitation of the legitimate government – appears hollow when set against the scale of the fighting. In addition to battle-related deaths caused by Russian air assaults, Physicians for Human Rights (2021) corroborated 600 attacks to June 2021 on medical facilities, of which 298 were carried out by Syrian government forces and 243 by either Russian or Syrian forces. Russian military officials' attempts to intercede and prevent abuses committed by Syrian government-backed forces, as Assad regained most of his lost territory, did little to alleviate fears of further violence (ICG 2019b, I, 12–13, 19–20). Local agreements between Syrian forces and armed opposition groups, negotiated with Russian involvement, did not prevent violations of international humanitarian law by both sides and mass displacements of populations from besieged areas, flouting UNSC resolutions 2139 and 2165 (Amnesty International 2017, 6–7, 10, 25). Syria remains fragmented, with fighting continuing in several areas; in the strategic province of Deir-ez Zor, Russian private military contractors rub shoulders with Syrian army forces, Shia militias from Iraq, Iran and Lebanon and Sunni tribesmen. Damascus continues to prioritise coercive means to achieve a settlement, buttressed by Russian military and economic assistance and diplomatic cover at the UN Security Council. In the words of a former Russian ambassador to Syria, the false promise of 'national reconciliation' sets an abysmal precedent that reflects badly on Russian attempts to secure an agreement, despite its negotiations with other external powers (Aksenenok 2020).

A paper drawn up by the respected International Crisis Group has proposed a set of principles and standards for appraising effective policy responses to armed conflicts, against which Russia's involvement in the Arab Spring may be judged objectively (ICG 2017c, 41–43). On the positive side of the ledger, in the early stages of the Syrian civil war Russia tried to identify areas of common ground among the external actors as a basis of cooperation, particularly through the UN route, in order to mitigate hostilities and persuade regional actors to de-escalate as well. In the later stages, Russia encouraged deconfliction mechanisms to try to defuse tensions and reduce the risk of accidental clashes that might escalate into direct armed confrontation. Efforts were also made to promote confidence-building steps towards ceasefires and political talks. In Libya, Russia has operated largely outside of the Western-led contact group but has tried to mediate between rival factions to promote national dialogue to stabilise the country. Drawing on its diplomatic influence in other conflict-prone MENA countries, Moscow has voiced its readiness to sponsor a regional conference to explore the possibility of establishing a shared, inclusive vision among key actors aimed at effective political-military arrangements for the region (Lavrov 2021).

The scorecard on Russia's commitment to international principles and standards to control violence and enable the mobilisation of alternative political constituencies is much less encouraging. Rather than doing no (further) harm in civil conflicts, Russia has supported incumbent leaderships or powerful regional actors pursuing their own factional or divisive agendas, including providing arms and military support, thereby encouraging a militarised response to perceived threats, fuelling further radicalisation and undermining attempts to combat jihadist movements. There is limited evidence that pressure has been applied by Moscow on the warring sides in Syria as part of a clear political strategy to mitigate the complex challenges underlying internal and regional governance. Experts surveyed have acknowledged Russia's attempts to mediate in regional conflicts but are sceptical about Moscow's ambitious proposals to underwrite region-wide security arrangements; Russia is seen as opportunistic, lacking resources and credibility with Western powers to sponsor any regional settlement (Fusco 2021, 19–20; Vakil and Quilliam 2021, 63; Greenstock 2017, 426–427).

We have argued in this book that, contrary to common assumptions, Russia has not acted purely as a spoiler intent on exploiting opportunities in pursuit of untrammelled power in the MENA region. Moscow has prioritised regional dialogue and power-sharing solutions that have potentially been constructive. At the same time, it has played a central part in the *collective* failure to address the challenges of effective governance and human security, even if the preconditions for upheaval and violence in Libya, Syria and Yemen were already in place. In response to urgent and complex problems across the wider MENA region, it has contributed to authoritarian conflict management and done little to create the kind of environment in which the rule of law, good governance and reform might flourish. Russian notions of the sovereignty of states in a pluralist world order must be set against the abysmal situation in countries torn by conflicts or where the state practises repression as a matter of course.

But many of these failures can equally be ascribed to the other leading external states. The Arab Spring has exposed deep fissures between the principles underpinning the integrity of the international system and the actions of the external powers. The chairperson of the International Independent Commission of Inquiry (IICI) on Syria, Paulo Sérgio Pinheiro, has pointed to a collective global failure there arising from the 'selective intervention and woeful negligence of the international community' (The Observer 2021). Former UN special envoys to Syria and Libya Geir Pedersen and Ghassan Salamé have spoken of the deep mistrust among the international powers, and of the 'disintegration of the idea of collective security', disregard for the laws of war and 'deregulation' of the use of force as they pursue their own interests; UN Secretary-General António Guterres himself has bemoaned the lack of leadership in the UN Security Council and the general powerlessness of multilateral institutions (Wintour 2020).

The outlook across the wider MENA region appears bleak. Serious structural and systemic problems, exacerbated by failures of leadership, have produced a confusing plurality of state, non-state and transnational actors pursuing shifting goals and competing for power and resources in a bewildering and often harrowing *jeux sans frontières* (see Falk 2016, 2328; Sakwa 2017, 173). Progress in resolving the devastating internationalised civil wars in Syria, Libya and Yemen is slow and halting. Elsewhere, internal state–society tensions engendering mass protests – such as the recent disturbances in Algeria, Lebanon, Jordan, Iran and Iraq – leave countries subject to repressive, often corrupt authoritarian rule or pitted by civil conflicts (Boserup et al 2017, 13; Hilterman 2021; Lounnas 2020, 34–35). The sharp increase in exposure to conflict between 2010 and 2020, causing large-scale economic problems and displacement spillovers into neighbouring countries, has far-reaching welfare implications (Corral and Krishnan 2020). Over half of survey respondents in some countries (Tunisia, Algeria, Iraq and Egypt) claim that they do not regret the protests, but only a small minority across the region think that their lives are better than before the Arab Spring, with even fewer in most countries believing in a better future, prompting fears of another 'lost decade' (Safi 2020; see also Hiltermann 2021). The external powers have been more concerned with threats from Islamist militants across the region than with repression by illiberal governments or social and economic depletion (Khouri 2018, 12).

Shifts in the political priorities of the US have been a major factor in the regional turmoil. John Mearsheimer has argued that 'far from incorporating the Greater Middle East into the liberal international order, the United States and its allies inadvertently have played a central role in spreading illiberal disorder in that region' (Mearsheimer 2019, 28; see also Lynch 2021). Faced with multiple conflicts and shifting local alliances that it has neither the resources nor the will to resolve, the reduced ability of the US – for decades the pre-eminent external power – to control its traditional allies has combined with its retreat from global democracy promotion and diminished security commitment to the region (see Mueller et al 2017, 5–6; Fusco 2021, 15). Washington's role in encouraging regime change in Libya, with little in the way of a strategy or understanding of the conflict and still fewer plans for post-Gaddafi stabilisation – difficult though that might have been – was compounded by a lack of accountability in its interpretation of UN Security Council resolution 1973 (see Martin 2022, 85, 162–164). In the same way, US support was provided to a fragmented Syrian opposition without a clear strategy to manage the conflict. The IICI has identified 'systemic failures' by the US-led coalition to investigate hundreds of reports of civilian casualties caused by its air strikes in Syria (IICI 2022b, 5). These errors of commission or omission exacerbated civil conflicts and facilitated the growth of Islamist extremism, leading to flows of refugees and displaced persons across and even beyond the region. Washington has also supported Saudi Arabia in its Yemen intervention against the Iranian-backed Houthis; though the Biden administration has scaled down its support amid a downturn in US–Saudi relations, the ruinous civil war goes on (see Malley and Pomper 2021).

With regime change in Syria now unlikely, US policy appears directed at maintaining the Caesar Act sanctions and ensuring Assad's isolation, hindering international investment for reconstruction and inflicting a heavy toll on the population. Washington has turned a blind eye to growing illiberal trends in Turkey, its NATO ally, and to Israel's refusal, driven by right-wing political forces, to abide by international agreements on a Palestinian state; it reacted ambivalently to the changes in government in Egypt. In the face of public opinion against foreign interventions – and assurances in the 2022 US National Security Strategy that the Biden administration will avoid coercive regime change and prioritise practical diplomacy focusing on economic and security assistance – uncertainty persists over the future extent of a US military presence in Iraq and Syria, particularly given the diminished (for now) threat from Islamic militants. US vacillation over its response to Iran's nuclear programme has jeopardised the normalisation of Tehran's political and economic relations with its neighbours and antagonised the harder-line Ebrahim Raisi government; the potential for Iran's confrontation with the Gulf Arab states and Israel, as it bids to entrench its influence in the Middle East, remains alarming (see Posch 2019).

Europe's potential to play a major transformative role in mitigating the underlying problems in the MENA region by promoting economic and social development – through trade, investment, humanitarian assistance (with the EU being the main donor of aid and coordinator of international funding) and support for civil society, human rights, democracy and rule of law – remains unrealised. Immediate security challenges, in the form of conflict spillover into terrorist attacks and migration/refugee flows, impel European countries to insulate themselves from the instability resulting from regional upheavals rather than prioritising internal challenges in MENA states. As for the most interventionist Europeans, an incoherent UK strategy in Libya engendered a drift towards regime change with no clear post-uprising planning, with the David Cameron government subsequently losing a parliamentary vote on intervention in Syria; Nicolas Sarkozy's plans were driven primarily by France's and his own self-interest, namely increasing French political-military and economic influence in North Africa and enhancing his own political prospects at home (House of Commons 2016, 3, 10–11, 18; Martin 2022, 43, 59, 101). One authoritative report, based on numerous fact-finding missions and field research, has concluded that, with individual MENA countries exercising greater agency and being more influenced by the other global powers, the EU is perceived as a 'fractured or cacophonic actor', with its member states often pursuing varying or even opposing strategies (Colombo et al 2019, 5–6; see Youngs 2022). Some experts have concluded that 'the persuasive capacity of the EU as a normative actor is in doubt in a transitional international order in which liberal internationalism is in retreat' (see Newman and Stefan 2020, 485–486).

The EU's imposition of punitive sanctions on Syria has only led Assad to resist European involvement in the constitutional process and consolidate his grip on the instruments of power and patronage. Interviews in government-held areas with Syrian officials, businessmen and civilians concluded that

> Western countries have changed their main aim in Syria from 'regime change' to a 'change of behaviour'. But they do not clearly define the shift in behaviour they demand. For example, many European diplomats emphasise the importance of the Geneva process and the implementation of UN Resolution 2254 but, when pushed, none of them can provide a clear definition of what a political process means, what measures or reforms implemented by the government would satisfy the West, or even what constitutes the regime. (Samaha 2019, 25)

European states are split between seeking a partial accommodation with the Assad government, as Syria gradually resumes contacts with its regional neighbours – which would entail engaging with Moscow and Iran, Assad's key backers, over key issues – or leaving the country mired in destitution and internal conflict. The flood of refugees, some of them finding their way into Europe, continues. While constructive, EU involvement in negotiations over the Iranian nuclear programme depends heavily on US decision-making and is yet to produce a lasting agreement. As one authoritative commentator suggests, 'many elements of the EU's external action have been on [a] trajectory toward downgraded ambition and truncated commitment', with a lack of political will married to strategic calculation limiting its involvement in risky international initiatives (Youngs 2022).

Despite the West's lack of resolve over the MENA crises, one well-worn notion persists, namely that it must be wary of a geopolitical 'win' for Moscow – even when the need for Russian engagement in multilateral cooperation is recognised (Vakil and Quilliam 2021, 2; Chulov 2020). Russia continues to be seen as bidding to re-establish a strategic presence as a counterweight to US power and as a political and economic competitor with the EU (Colombo et al 2019, 5; Lynch 2021, 117), exploiting tensions between the Western powers' strategic and normative goals as part of a decisive foreign policy turn. Moscow has criticised the West for conspiring to marginalise Russian interests and manipulate decision-making in international institutions, such as the UN Human Rights Council and the Organisation for the Prohibition of Chemical Weapons. As mentioned earlier, Moscow rejects the 'rules-based' order called for by the Western states, fearing a renewed bid to influence regional affairs to their own advantage. But Russia itself has largely pursued transactional policies, interpreting agreements to suit its purposes and manipulating regional affiliations. Though it has tried to mediate in MENA crises, mindful of the hostilities and divisions that frustrate regional settlements, Moscow's own appeal to diplomacy and shared understandings of international law has been vitiated by its unwillingness to address, other than rhetorically, repressive state policies by incumbent leaderships. Moscow's core narrative in approaching conflict situations – that it is up to the people of the countries concerned to decide on political solutions – has proved inadequate in terms of shaping outcomes leading to effective governance.

At the same time, the notion of great power competition-by-proxy does not adequately explain the external powers' collective failure, first, to help resolve the tensions underlying regional rivalries, and second, to look beyond the blunt instruments of military interventions and economic statecraft in reacting to potential threats. They have struggled to encourage inclusive political transitions to embrace all population groups through interim governing mechanisms, based on power-sharing among key local actors. Providing humanitarian assistance that is 'politically colour-blind' has also been a problem. Creating mechanisms to ensure transitional justice, dispensing sufficient resources for post-conflict peacebuilding and allocating reconstruction aid are all contingent on ending armed conflict; however, establishing a formal crisis-prevention regime to stabilise the regional order, mooted by Russia in an attempt to broker a kind of regional détente, will fail without far greater political and economic investment by, and agreement among, the major external powers. An expert survey of European, US, Russian, Chinese and regional MENA experts and practitioners on the prospects for a new security architecture for the region concluded that, while positives could be found, the immediate outlook was pessimistic given inter-state rivalries (particularly that between Saudi Arabia and Iran), socio-economic and demographic challenges (exacerbated by the coronavirus pandemic), weak governance and interventions by external state or non-state actors: any positive shift 'would require fundamental political, ideological or societal breakthroughs of a completely different level of ambition' (Fusco 2021, 36; Vakil and Quilliam 2021, 19).

The dearth of collective action to deal with state-inflicted violence and ensure responsible protection of peoples is arguably the most baleful legacy of the Arab Spring. The rising tide of democracy across the Arab world – acknowledged even by the Russian leadership in its early stages – appeared to justify external intervention in the cases of atrocity crimes. But despite widespread support for the 2005 World Summit Outcome proposals on the doctrine of Responsibility to Protect and subsequent attempts to mainstream it into international practice, the will and capacity to apply it have been erratic, even among the liberal democracies. Russia and China have not been prepared to commit to voluntary self-restraint when vetoing draft UNSC resolutions, even when the use of coercive force against Assad was not on the table (Hehir 2016, 177–178). For these two P5 powers and some other countries, R2P means that the sovereign state still bears the primary responsibility to protect its citizens. They reject Western intervention, including the use of force to protect human rights and liberal values in states where they are under threat, practised selectively and sometimes tarnished by the illegitimate use of illiberal means and a lack of commitment to post-conflict peacekeeping (see Martin 2022, 163–164; Freedman 2021). Amid bitter great-power debates within the UN Security Council, the pursuit of justice for peoples subject to massive atrocities faces a 'gaping black hole, as multilateralism comes apart at the seams' (Welsh 2021, 244). The challenge has been complicated by the difficulty of reconciling the demands of responsible protection and counterterrorism strategies in complex conflicts, where state security forces, protesters and Islamist militants wage war over territory and resources and where decision-making sovereignty over the entirety of a state's territory is non-existent.

As the non-Western powers expand their influence in international society, will it be possible to find normative consensus and sustain the moral imperative towards the protection of peoples, inspired by domestic standards of governance advocated by the Western democracies? Or will states practise minimal cooperation in order to avoid potential challenges to their authority and disruption to international stability? The lessons of the Arab Spring are that the core institutions of sovereignty and great power management in the contemporary pluralist international system appear to be resilient against the promotion of democracy and human rights in states' internal affairs (see Murray 2017, 72, 77–79). Preserving the precarious normative momentum in favour of responsible protection, and persuading Moscow and Beijing that it is in their own interest to deter state authorities from committing atrocities, is likely to be an invidious task.

The Arab Spring and the war in Ukraine: implications for Russia's future foreign policy

In this book, we have tried to convey a sense of the dynamic processes of regional and global change that have formed the context for Russia's relations with the Middle East and North Africa since the inception of the Arab Spring. Recent developments suggest further shifts in regional patterns of amity and enmity that create new opportunities and risks. Turkey and some Arab states, particularly the UAE and Bahrain, are for various reasons tentatively seeking to restore relations with Syria; Libya's and Yemen's rival factions appear to be edging towards agreements but continue to be prey to the interests of external actors; an emboldened Iran may capitalise on its alignment with Moscow to provoke further regional destabilisation in pursuit of its strategic aims; détente in Israel's relations with leading Gulf Arab states may reduce Arab–Israeli tensions but equally may inflame hostilities with Iran and its proxies. Mutual antipathy and failures in communication between Russia and the Western powers continue to impact the region, creating the impression that the most intractable disputes there are impervious to political resolution. Domestic unrest in many of the MENA states persists. The regional picture is beset by too many uncertainties to allow for a definitive assessment of Russia's future policy there.

The picture is further complicated by Russia's invasion of Ukraine in February 2022, a momentous event causing an era-defining rupture in its relations with the West that is reverberating on a global scale. How might it affect Russia's foreign policy in the MENA region? With a few exceptions, notably Tehran and Damascus siding firmly with Moscow, the immediate response of the MENA countries to the invasion appeared equivocal. Almost all of them approved the UN General Assembly resolutions on 2 March and 24 March – the first deploring Russia's breach of Ukraine's sovereignty and demanding Russia's military withdrawal from Ukrainian territory, and the second demanding civilian protection and humanitarian access – with only Iran and Algeria abstaining and Morocco absent. However, it soon became apparent that they were generally responding to Western pressure, rather than voluntarily agreeing to isolate Russia; most MENA countries abstained in the 7 April vote suspending Russia from the Human Rights Council, with Algeria and Iran voting against and Libya under the Dbeibeh government, Israel and Turkey approving it. Many of them, including the Gulf Cooperation Council countries and Israel, have declined to impose sanctions on Russia, and the Arab League has pointedly avoided an anti-Russian position.

The transactional nature of MENA politics means that states are prioritising their own strategic trade and security interests in decision-making over Ukraine, in most cases seeking to avoid a firm alignment with either Russia or the Western powers. While aware that Russia has very few real allies, Putin has tried to use these divided loyalties to his advantage, appealing to the Arab League states, in a letter timed to coincide with its summit in November 2022, to support the establishment of a multipolar world order (Middle East Monitor 2022). The Western powers' narrative, that the invasion of Ukraine in contravention of the sovereignty norm has undermined Russia's international legitimacy, has so far failed to persuade the non-Western countries to sign up to its campaign to marginalise Russia. Their ambivalence may well reflect disapproval of the West's equivocation and inconsistency in its approaches to the Libya, Syria and Yemen conflicts and other regional disputes. One commentator concludes that, with most Arab states sceptical over Western intentions in trying to isolate Russia, 'The nonaligned movement of the Cold War years will reemerge in a new incarnation' in a '21st-century version of the Cold War', with the non-Western states avoiding an unequivocal commitment to either the US or Russia (Stent 2022). Russia's rejection of the Western-led order is increasingly bound up with its claim to support the non-Western countries' sovereignty and independence against US hegemony and Western neo-colonialism.

Russia's part in the events of the Arab Spring now appears to prefigure its war with Ukraine. A repeat of its tactics in Syria – bombing civilian targets in major population centres, besieging towns, using private military contractors in intensive combat situations without proper regulation, manipulating the use of humanitarian corridors and causing the enforced displacement of civilians resulting in refugee flows – has been met with a denial of responsibility that has been reinforced by a legally imposed crackdown on Russian media and an exorbitant information offensive that seeks simultaneously to delegitimise the authorities in Kyiv and to cover up the extent of military and civilian casualties in Ukraine (Chulov 2022). Iran's supply of drones and missiles to Russia, the reported recruitment by Moscow of Syrian mercenaries and its tacit acceptance of Ramzan Kadyrov's deployment of Chechen fighters loyal to Moscow in Ukraine, without official oversight – all of these tactics resemble a distorted mirror image of Russian actions in Libya and Syria and appear to align Russia with what many in the West consider to be rogue states and unregulated militias. Moscow's claims to be recovering historical territories, protecting the Russian population from Ukrainian state repression and preventing one more link in a chain of 'colour revolutions' – an existential appeal to domestic audiences to support Russia's right to exist, free from external threats – are underpinned by the increased clout of the Russian defence and security agencies and tighter controls over civil society.

The Western response in the form of sanctions, including possible secondary sanctions on entities trading with Russia, embargoes on military and dual-use technologies, and Russia's shift towards a greater reliance on domestic resources and closer engagement with non-Western countries for markets, technology and capital – a process that pre-dates the invasion (see Connolly 2018) – are disturbingly reminiscent of the Cold War. The European Parliament resolution in November 2022 declaring Russia a state sponsor of terrorism and perpetrator of war crimes effectively brackets it with the likes of Syria, while a draft resolution aimed at holding the Putin leadership accountable for crimes of aggression has been circulated at the UN (Wintour 2022). Lavrov has vigorously defended Russia's invasion against attacks by Western states and berated the latter for trying to 'privatise' the United Nations and marginalise Russia (Lavrov 2022b). Moscow's intensifying information campaign – aimed, with qualified success, at influencing opinion among the non-Western powers – seems more than ever to be deployed as a coercive instrument in a *strategic* confrontation with the West (see Pynnöniemi 2019, 216).

Despite the similarities between aspects of Russia's MENA policies and its actions in Ukraine, the notion of its Syria intervention as one link in a causal chain leading to its invasion of Ukraine is simplistic. A more sober assessment requires a comprehensive examination of the complex contextual factors shaping Russia's behaviour in both cases. While they are linked in terms of Russia's assertion of great power status and rejection of the Western-led order, the part played by Ukraine in Russia's historical self-understanding as state and nation transcends the latter's relations with the MENA states. Discerning the longer-term impact of Ukraine on its wider foreign policy – whether Moscow will be able to build upon its positions in the MENA region or will be forced to limit its engagement – precludes simple explanations. Glib historical parallels with the Soviet period should also be avoided. As detailed earlier in this book, the greater agency of the leading MENA powers as they bid to restructure the regional order to suit their own interests, the structural and systemic problems faced by their elites and unresolved regional rivalries all stem from a dynamic evolution of politics and security specific to the region. Notions of a reconfigured 'nonaligned movement' defined by a clash of interests between Russia and the West, or a Cold War-type ideological contest between liberalism and authoritarianism, driven by Russia's sense of mission and shaping conflicts across the globe, are inadequate to explain the current trend towards more differentiated and decentralised patterns of global and regional order in a more pluralistic system incorporating a widening range of state and non-state actors and issues (see Larson 2018, 248–249; Acharya 2014; Acharya 2017).

The most immediate implications of the Ukraine war for the MENA countries lie in the fact that it threatens to heighten instability and exacerbate existing challenges – refugee and migrant flows, Islamist insurgencies, social unrest among youth and marginalised communities, demographic factors – that now combine with financial shortfalls, health emergencies and food and energy security crises to pose new political, social and economic problems, including for many regional elites. Rising commodities and food prices are a serious concern for the major non-Western industrialised states. Fundamental issues relating to sovereignty, the use of force and the laws of war and post-conflict accountability and justice – examined in this book in the context of the Arab Spring – will also be revisited as the war with Ukraine unfolds, necessitating a comprehensive reconsideration of regional and global governance. The external powers are faced with rethinking their MENA strategies to take account of not only the rebalancing of regional power relations but also social and economic issues that are integral to both security and development. The prospects for a fundamental breakthrough are unpromising. Russia's call for a MENA-wide conference, bringing together external and regional states to work out principles for inter-state relations, security-building measures and humanitarian cooperation, comes at a time when the Organization for Security and Co-operation in Europe lies in tatters; restoring trust and confidence between the transatlantic powers and Russia that might impact positively in the MENA region represents a massive challenge.

The invasion of Ukraine has raised issues that affect many of the MENA states materially and will undoubtedly play into their relations with Russia and its Western antagonists. Attempts by Turkey, Saudi Arabia, the UAE and other MENA powers, as well as the Arab League, to mediate between Russia and Ukraine to settle the dispute over restrictions on grain exports and to facilitate prisoner-of-war exchanges attest to their growing international influence (see Khlebnikov 2022b). That Russia now has a more prominent role in the region makes it even more urgent for Moscow to devise a genuine regional strategy that also takes account of the foreign policy aims and security concerns of the Arab states, Iran and Turkey (see Lynch 2022). Russia's vital economic and security interests may well be at stake; it may be able to exist without the West, but reconfiguring the domestic economy to support defence procurement and reorienting external trade require mutually beneficial relations with the leading MENA countries to mitigate the effect of Western sanctions on its economic development. Moscow's transactional approach to the MENA region hitherto, cloaked in broad precepts about Russia's opposition to the liberal international order while negotiating opportunities and constraints tactically, may well prove wanting. A clearer understanding of its national interests and the ability to anticipate and react to shifts in regional affairs require more efficient government that is based on objective information and is not hostage to fixed notions of international politics. The Ukraine war may well translate into a fundamental shift towards Russia's political and economic alignment with countries of Asia and the global South, but whether it has the structural power and moral purpose to build on its influence in a new regional MENA security order remains to be seen.

Bibliography

Abboud, S. (2021). Making peace to sustain war: The Astana Process and Syria's illiberal peace. *Peacebuilding*, 9(3), 326–343

Acharya, A. (2014). Global international relations (IR) and regional worlds: A new agenda for international studies. *International Studies Quarterly*, 58(4), 647–659

Acharya, A. (2017). After liberal hegemony: The advent of a multiplex world order. *Ethics & International Affairs*, 31(3), 271–285

Achy, L. (2015). Breakdown of the authoritarian 'social contract' and emergence of new social actors: An ongoing process? In Sadiki, L. (ed.), *Routledge Handbook of the Arab Spring: Rethinking Democratization*. Abingdon and New York: Routledge, 303–318

Adamsky, D. (2018). *Moscow's Syria Campaign: Russian Lessons for the Art of Strategy*. Russie.Nei.Visions 109, Institut Français des Relations Internationales, July. At www.ifri.org/sites/default/files/atoms/files/rnv_109_adamsky_moscow _syria_campaign_2018.pdf (accessed 7 November 2021)

Adamsky, D. (2019). Christ-loving diplomats: Russian ecclesiastical diplomacy in Syria. *Survival*, 61(6), 49–68

Adamsky, D. (2020). Christ-loving warriors: Ecclesiastical dimension of the Russian military campaign in Syria. *Problems of Post-Communism*, 67(6), 433–445

Ahmadian, H. and Mohseni, P. (2019). Iran's Syria strategy: The evolution of deterrence. *International Affairs*, 95(2), 341–364

Akbarzadeh, S. and Barry, J. (2017). Iran and Turkey: Not quite enemies but less than friends. *Third World Quarterly*, 38(4), 980–995

Akgün, M. and Tiryaki, S. (eds) (2017). *Future of Syria*. Euromesco Joint Policy Study 7, European Institute of the Mediterranean (IEMed), April, at https://www .cidob.org/en/publications/publication_series/project_papers/euromesco/future _of_syria (accessed 18 August 2023)

Akgün, M., Tiryaki, S, Sheira, O., Ammash, M., Asiedu, M., Ersoy, N. and Kekeç, S. (2017). State-building: Political, structural and legal issues. In Akgün, M. and Tiryaki, S. (eds), *Future of Syria*. Euromesco Joint Policy Study 7, European Institute of the Mediterranean (IEMed), 9–37. At https://www.cidob.org/en /publications/publication_series/project_papers/euromesco/future_of_syria (accessed 18 August 2023)

Akpınar, P. (2016). The limits of mediation in the Arab Spring: The case of Syria. *Third World Quarterly*, 37(12), 2288–2303

Aksenyonok, A. (2018). *Steep Turns in the Middle East Policy: The US Can Become Hostage of Regional Powers Interests.* Valdai Discussion Club, 16 May. At http://valdaiclub.com/a/highlights/steep-turns-of-the-middle-east-policy-the-us/ (accessed 11 October 2018)

Aksenyonok, A. (2019). *The Syrian Crisis: A Thorny Path from War to Peace.* Valdai papers No. 104, Valdai Discussion Club, June. At https://valdaiclub.com/files/25348/ (accessed 4 May 2020)

Aksenyonok, A. (2020). *War, the Economy and Politics in Syria: Broken Links.* Russian International Affairs Council, 17 April. At https://russiancouncil.ru/en/analytics-and-comments/comments/war-the-economy-and-politics-in-syria-broken-links-/ (accessed 5 May 2020)

Aksenenok, A. (2022). *A U.S. Policy Case for Middle East under New Conditions.* Russian International Affairs Council, 12 August. At https://russiancouncil.ru/en/analytics-and-comments/analytics/u-s-policy-case-for-middle-east-under-new-conditions (accessed 10 November 2022)

Alaaldin, R. (2019). *Shaping the Political Order of the Middle East: Crisis and Opportunity.* Istituto Affari Internazionali paper 19/09, April. At www.iai.it/en/pubblicazioni/shaping-political-order-middle-east-crisis-and-opportunity (accessed 13 May 2019)

Alcaro, R. and Dessì, A. (2019). *A Last Line of Defence: A Strategy for Europe to Preserve the Iran Nuclear Deal.* Istituto Affari Internazionali paper 19/14, June, at www.iai.it/sites/default/files/iaip1914.pdf (accessed 30 June 2019)

Aliboni, R. (2022). *Will Turkey and Syria Reconcile?* Istituto Affari Internazionali commentary, 24 October. At www.iai.it/en/pubblicazioni/will-turkey-and-syria-reconcile (accessed 15 December 2022)

Allan, D. (2021). Trade, investment and politics: Prospects for Russian economic cooperation with the Gulf. In Kozhanov, N. (ed.), *Russia's Relations with the GCC and Iran.* Singapore: Palgrave Macmillan/Springer Nature, 132–158

Allison, R. (2013a). *Russia, the West, and Military Intervention.* Oxford: Oxford University Press

Allison, R. (2013b). Russia and Syria: Explaining alignment with a regime in crisis. *International Affairs* 89(4), 795–823

Allison, R. (2014). Russian 'deniable' intervention in Ukraine: How and why Russia broke the rules. *International Affairs*, 90(6), 1255–1297

Allison, R. (2017). Russia and the post-2014 international legal order: Revisionism and *realpolitik*. *International Affairs*, 93(3), 519–543

Allison, R. (2020). Russian revisionism, legal discourse and the 'rules-based' international order. *Europe-Asia Studies*, 72(6), 976–995

Allison, R. and Williams, P. (1990). Superpower competition and crisis prevention in the Third World. In Allison, R. and Williams, P. (eds), *Superpower Competition and Crisis Prevention in the Third World.* Cambridge: Cambridge University Press

Ambrosio, T. (2009). *Authoritarian Backlash: Russian Resistance to Democratization in the Former Soviet Union.* Farnham and Burlington, VT: Ashgate

Amirahmadian B. (ed.) (2016). *Russia-Iran Partnership: An Overview and Prospects for the Future.* Report 29, Moscow: Russian International Affairs Council. At https://russiancouncil.ru/common/upload/RIAC-IRAS-Russia-Iran-Report29-en.pdf (accessed 20 November 2019)

Amnesty International (2017). *'We Leave or We Die': Forced Displacement under Syria's 'Reconciliation' Agreements*. 13 November. At www.amnesty.org/en/documents/mde24/7309/2017/en/ (accessed 25 April 2020)

Anderson, L. (2014). Authoritarian legacies and regime change: Towards understanding political transition in the Arab world. In Gerges, F.A. (ed.), *The New Middle East: Protest and Revolution in the Arab World*. New York: Cambridge University Press, 41–59

Antipov, K. (2014). O nekotorykh aspektakh evolyutsii blizhnevostochnoi politiki Kitaya (Certain aspects of the evolution of China's Middle East policy). *Problemy Dal'nego Vostoka*, 2, 27–37 (in Russian)

Antonyan, T.M. (2017). Russia and Iran in the Syrian crisis: Similar aspirations, different approaches. *Israel Journal of Foreign Affairs*, 11(3), 337–348

Aras, B. and Falk, R. (2015). Authoritarian 'geopolitics' of survival in the Arab Spring. *Third World Quarterly*, 36(2), 322–336

Aras, B. and Falk, R. (2016). Five years after the Arab Spring: A critical evaluation. *Third World Quarterly*, 37(12), 2252–2258

Aras, B. and Yorulmazlar, E. (2016). State, region and order: Geopolitics of the Arab Spring. *Third World Quarterly*, 37(12), 2259–2273

Arbour, L. (2014). The relationship between the ICC and the UN Security Council. *Global Governance: A Review of Multilateralism and International Organizations*, 20(2), 195–201

Armstrong, D. and Farrell, T. (2005). Force and legitimacy in world politics: Introduction. *Review of International Studies*, 31(S1), 3–13

ASI-REM (2017). Israel's discourses and practices in the Mediterranean. In Ehteshami, A., Huber, D. and Paciello, M.C. (eds), *The Mediterranean Reset: Geopolitics in a New Age*. Global Policy, at www.globalpolicyjournal.com/projects/gp-e-books/mediterranean-reset-geopolitics-new-age (accessed 17 February 2018)

Ausseur, P. and Razoux, P. (2021). Russia in NATO's south: Expansionist strategy or defensive posture? In Berger, C. and Salloum, C. (eds), *NATO Defense College Research Paper* 16, January, 19–27

Averre, D. (2008). Russian foreign policy and the global political environment. *Problems of Post-Communism*, 55(5), 28–39

Averre, D. (2009). From Pristina to Tskhinvali: The legacy of Operation Allied Force in Russia's relations with the West. *International Affairs*, 85(3), 575–591

Averre, D. (2019). Russia, the Middle East and the conflict in Syria. In Kanet, R. (ed.), *Routledge Handbook of Russian Security*. Abingdon and New York: Routledge, 399–409

Averre, D. and Davies, L. (2015). Russia, humanitarian intervention and the Responsibility to Protect: The case of Syria. *International Affairs*, 91(4), 813–834

Ayoob, M. (2002). Inequality and theorizing in international relations: The case for subaltern realism. *International Studies Review*, 4(3), 27–48

Ayoob, M. (2014). Turkey and Iran in the era of the Arab uprisings. In Gerges, F.A. (ed.), *The New Middle East: Protest and Revolution in the Arab World*. New York: Cambridge University Press, 402–417

Babayan, N. (2017). Bearing truthiness: Russia's cyclical legitimation of its actions. *Europe-Asia Studies*, 69(7), 1090–1105

Bacon, E. (2019). The Security Council and security decision-making. In Kanet, R. (ed.), *Routledge Handbook of Russian Security*. Abingdon and New York: Routledge, 199–130

Baev, P.K. (2015). Russia as opportunist or spoiler in the Middle East? *The International Spectator*, 50(2), 8–21

Baev, P. (2016). Future approaches to the Greater Middle East. In Haukkala, H. and Popescu, N. (eds), *Russian Futures: Horizon 2025*. Paris: EU Institute for Security Studies, 55–60, at www.iss.europa.eu/sites/default/files/EUISSFiles/Report_26.pdf (accessed 26 March 2019)

Baikova, T. and Asatryan, G. (2016). Rossiya rasprostranila 'Beluyu knigu' po Sirii v OON (Russia has distributed the 'White Book' on Syria at the UN). *Izvestiya*, 1 November. At https://iz.ru/news/641948 (accessed 4 May 2020, in Russian)

Bannelier-Christakis, K. (2016). Military interventions against ISIL in Iraq, Syria and Libya, and the legal basis of consent. *Leiden Journal of International Law*, 29(3), 743–775

Baranets, V. (2017). My perelomili khrebet udarnym silam terrorisma (We have broken the back of the terrorist strike force). *Komsomol'skaya Pravda*, 27 December. At www.kp.ru/daily/26775/3808693/ (accessed 26 January 2021, in Russian)

Baranovsky, V. and Mateiko, A. (2016). Responsibility to Protect: Russia's approaches. *The International Spectator*, 51(2), 49–69

Baranovsky, V. and Naumkin, V. (2018). Blizhnii Vostok v menyayushchemsya global'nom kontekste: Klyuchevye trendy stoletnego razvitiya (The Middle East in a changing global context: Key trends in a century of development), *Mirovaya ekonomika i mezhdunarodnye otnosheniya*, 62(3), 5–19 (in Russian)

Barmin, Y. (2017). Russian energy policy in the Middle East. *Insight Turkey*, 19(4), 125–136

Barmin, Y. (2018a). *Russia and Israel: The Middle Eastern Vector of Relations*. Moscow: Russian International Affairs Council Working paper 42

Barmin, Y. (2018b). *Russia in the Middle East Until 2024: From Hard Power to Sustainable Influence*. The Jamestown Foundation, 8 March, at https://jamestown.org/wp-content/uploads/2018/03/Yuri-Barmin-WS3-Predictions-to-2024.pdf?x75907 (accessed 13 May 2019)

Barnes-Dacey, J. (2017). *To End a War: Europe's Role in Bringing Peace to Syria*. European Council on Foreign Relations, 12 September, at www.ecfr.eu/page/-/ECFR229_EUROPES_ROLE_IN_BRINGING_PEACE_TO_SYRIA.pdf (accessed 4 May 2018)

Barnes-Dacey, J., Geranmayeh, E. and Lovatt, H. (2018). *The Middle East's New Battle Lines*. European Council on Foreign Relations, 17 May, at www.ecfr.eu/mena/battle_lines/ (accessed 10 September 2018)

Barnes-Dacey, J. and Levy, D. (2013). *Syria: The Imperative of De-Escalation*. European Council on Foreign Relations policy brief 80, 24 May. At www.ecfr.eu/page/-/ECFR80_SYRIA_BRIEF_AW.pdf (accessed 20 November 2019)

Bibliography

Barnes-Dacey, J. and Levy, D. (2015). *Syrian Diplomacy Renewed: From Vienna to Raqqa*. European Council on Foreign Relations policy brief 151, 27 November, at www.ecfr.eu/publications/summary/syrian_diplomacy_renewed_from_vienna_to_raqqa5034 (accessed 23 September 2016)

Barrie, D and Gethin, H. (2018). *Russian Weapons in the Syrian Conflict*. Rome: NATO Defense College report 02/18, May, at www.ndc.nato.int/download/downloads.php?icode=549 (accessed 4 May 2019)

Barzegar, K. and Divsallar, A. (2017). Political Rationality in Iranian Foreign Policy. *The Washington Quarterly*, 40(1), 39–53

Bassam, L. and Perry, T. (2015). How Iranian general plotted out Syrian assault in Moscow. *Reuters World News*, 6 October. At www.reuters.com/article/us-mideast-crisis-syria-soleimani-insigh/how-iranian-general-plotted-out-syrian-assault-in-moscow-idUSKCN0S02BV20151006 (accessed 27 November 2019)

BBC (2021). Why has the Syrian war lasted 10 years? 12 March. At www.bbc.co.uk/news/world-middle-east-35806229 (accessed 9 July 2021)

Beach, D. and Brun Pedersen, R. (2020). *Analyzing Foreign Policy*. 2nd edition. London: Macmillan/Red Globe Press

Beaumont, P. (2022). Autocracies tend to make catastrophic decisions. That's the case with Putin. *The Observer*, 21 August

Bechev, D. (2018). Russia and Turkey: The promise and the limits of partnership. In Popescu, N. and Secrieru, S. (eds), *Russia's Return to the Middle East: Building Sandcastles*. Chaillot Paper 146, July, 95–102

Bedford, S. and Souleimanov, E.A. (2016). Under construction and highly contested: Islam in the post-Soviet Caucasus. *Third World Quarterly*, 37(9), 1559–1580

Bellamy, A.J. (2018). Ending atrocity crimes: The false promise of fatalism. *Ethics & International Affairs*, 32(3), 329–337

Bērziņš, J. (2018). The Russian way of warfare. In Deni, J. (ed.), *Current Russian Military Affairs: Assessing and Countering Russian Strategy, Operational Planning, and Modernization*. U.S. Army War College Strategic Studies Institute, July, 18–20

Black, I. (2016). Syria peace talks founder after dispute over transitional government. *The Guardian*, 19 April

Blair, E. (2012). Envoy Annan warns against more force in Syria. *Reuters Emerging Markets*, 8 March. At www.reuters.com/article/us-syria-annan-militarisation/envoy-annan-warns-against-more-force-in-syria-idUSBRE8270J520120308 (accessed 26 January 2021)

Blockmans, S. (2016a). Turkey's Putsch and Purge: Why and how the EU should re-engage with Ankara. *CEPS Commentary* 2 September 2016, at www.ceps.eu/publications/turkey's-putsch-and-purge-why-and-how-eu-should-re-engage-ankara (accessed 10 November 2016)

Blockmans, S. (2016b). Bleak prospects for peace in Syria. *European Neighbourhood Watch*, 127, June. At www.ceps.eu/system/files/NWatch127.pdf (accessed 23 September 2016)

Blum, D.W. (2008). Conclusion: Links between globalization, security and identity in Russia. In Blum, D.W. (ed.), *Russia and Globalization: Identity, Security and*

Society in an Era of Change. Washington, DC: Woodrow Wilson Center Press and Baltimore: The Johns Hopkins University Press, 329–364

Bøås, M. and Rieker, P. (2019). *EUNPACK Executive Summary of the Final Report & Policy Recommendations.* Brussels: Centre for European Policy Studies, March, at www.eunpack.eu/sites/default/files/publications/EUNPACK%20policy%20recommendations.pdf (accessed 13 May 2019)

Bogdanov, M. (2011). The Middle East and North Africa. *Mezhdunarodnaya zhizn'*, 12, 10–21 (text of interview with A. Oganesyan, in Russian)

Bokeriya, S. (2020). Key aspects of combined thinking of the BRICS countries on the Responsibility to Protect. *Global Responsibility to Protect*, 12, 336–354

Boms, N. (2017). Israel's policy on the Syrian civil war: Risks and opportunities. *Israel Journal of Foreign Affairs*, 11(3), 323–336

Borisov, T. (2018). Russian arms exports in the Middle East. In Popescu, N. and Secrieru, S. (eds), *Russia's Return to the Middle East: Building Sandcastles?* Chaillot paper No. 146, July. Paris: EU Institute for Security Studies, 37–43

Borshchevskaya, A. (2016). *Russia in the Middle East: Motives, Consequences, Prospects.* Washington: The Washington Institute for Near East Policy, February. At www.washingtoninstitute.org/policy-analysis/view/russia-in-the-middle-east (accessed 14 June 2019)

Borshchevskaya, A. (2019). *Russia in the Middle East: Is There an Endgame?* Washington: The Washington Institute for Near East Policy, January. At www.washingtoninstitute.org/policy-analysis/view/russia-in-the-middle-east-is-there-an-endgame (accessed 29 January 2020)

Boserup, R.A. and Colombo, S. (2019). Hybridization of domestic order-making in the contemporary MENA region. In Quero, J. and Sala, C. (eds), *The MENARA Booklet for Academia.* Barcelona: CIDOB

Boserup, R.A., Hazbun, W., Makdisi, K and Malmvig, H. (2017). Introduction: Regional politics and interventions in the wake of the Arab uprisings. In Boserup, R.A., Hazbun, W., Makdisi, K. and Malmvig, H. (eds), *New Conflict Dynamics: Between Regional Autonomy and Intervention in the Middle East and North Africa.* Copenhagen: Danish Institute for International Studies, 7–16

Bowen, W., Knopf, J.W. and Moran, M. (2020). The Obama administration and Syrian chemical weapons: Deterrence, compellence, and the limits of the 'resolve plus bombs' formula. *Security Studies*, 29(5), 797–831

Buckley, C.A. (2012). Learning from Libya, acting in Syria. *Journal of Strategic Security*, 5(2), 81–104

Buys, E. and Garwood-Gowers, A. (2019). The (ir)relevance of human suffering: Humanitarian intervention and Saudi Arabia's Operation Decisive Storm in Yemen. *Journal of Conflict & Security Law*, 24(1), 1–33

Byers, M. (2005). Not yet havoc: Geopolitical change and the international rules on military force. *Review of International Studies*, 31(S1), 51–70

Cadier, D. (2018). Continuity and change in France's policies towards Russia: A milieu goals explanation. *International Affairs*, 94(6), 1349–1369

Cadier, D. and Light, M. (2016). Conclusion: Foreign policy as the continuation of domestic policy by other means. In Cadier, D. and Light, M. (eds), *Russia's*

Foreign Policy. Ideas, Domestic Politics and External Relations. Basingstoke and New York: Palgrave Macmillan, 205–216

Çakmak, C. and Özçelik, A.O. (eds) (2019). *The World Community and the Arab Spring.* Cham: Palgrave Macmillan.

Calculli, M. (2015). Sub-regions and security in the Arab Middle East: 'Hierarchical interdependence' in Gulf-Levant relations. In Monier, E. (ed.), *Regional Insecurity After the Arab Uprisings: Narratives of Security and Threat.* New York and Basingstoke: Palgrave Macmillan, 58–81

Campana, A. (2013). Beyond norms: The incomplete de-securitisation of the Russian counterterrorism frame. *Critical Studies on Terrorism*, 6(3), 457–472

Carter, A. (2016). A strong and balanced approach to Russia. *Survival*, 58(6), 51–62

Carter, A. (2017). The logic of American strategy in the Middle East. *Survival*, 59(2), 13–24

Casula, P. and Katz, M. (2018). The Middle East. In Tsygankov, A.P. (ed.), *Routledge Handbook of Russian Foreign Policy.* Abingdon and New York: Routledge, 295–310

Cater, C. and Malone, D.M. (2016). The origins and evolution of Responsibility to Protect at the UN. *International Relations*, 30(3), 278–297

Chan, S. (2021). Challenging the liberal order: The US hegemon as a revisionist power. *International Affairs*, 97(5), 1335–1352

Charap, S., Treyger, E. and Geist, E. (2019). *Understanding Russia's Intervention in Syria.* Rand Corporation. At www.rand.org/pubs/research_reports/RR3180.html (accessed 23 July 2021)

Charbonneau, L. (2011). Russia, China resist U.N. Syria sanctions push: Envoys. *Reuters*, 26 August. At www.reuters.com/article/us-syria-un/russia-china-resist-u-n-syria-sanctions-push-envoys-idUSTRE77P4X920110826 (accessed 22 November 2019)

Chebankova, E. (2012). Contemporary Russian multiculturalism. *Post-Soviet Affairs*, 28(3), 319–345

Chebankova, E. (2017). Russia's idea of the multipolar world order: Origins and main dimensions. *Post-Soviet Affairs*, 33(3), 217–234

Chen, X. (2018). China in the post-hegemonic Middle East: A wary dragon? In Stivachtis, Y. (ed.), *Conflict and Diplomacy in the Middle East: External Actors and Regional Rivalries.* Bristol: E-International Relations, at www.e-ir.info/wp-content/uploads/2018/11/Conflict-and-Diplomacy-in-the-Middle-East-E-IR.pdf (accessed 23 September 2018)

Chen, Z. and Yin, H. (2020). China and Russia in R2P debates at the UN Security Council. *International Affairs*, 96(3), 787–805

Chinese Government (2016). *China's Arab Policy Paper.* Xinhua, 14 January, at www.china.org.cn/world/2016-01/14/content_37573547.htm (accessed 21 June 2019)

Chulov, M. (2020). US 'Caesar Act' sanctions could devastate Syria's flatlining economy. *The Guardian*, 12 June

Chulov, M. (2021). War still rages in Syria border town at heart of Iran's regional ambition. *The Observer*, 10 October

Chulov, M. (2022). Bombardment, brutality and biological warfare slurs: How Moscow honed tactics in Syria. *The Guardian*, 10 March

Churkin, V.I. (2016). Interview of Russia's Permanent Representative to the UN V.I. Churkin to the 'Kommersant' newspaper, published on 19 February 2016. At www.mid.ru/ru/foreign_policy/news/-/asset_publisher/cKNonkJE02Bw/content/id/2104524 (accessed 30 October 2019, in Russian)

Clark, I. (2001). *The Post-Cold War Order: The Spoils of Peace*. Oxford: Oxford University Press

Clark, I. (2005). *Legitimacy in International Society*. Oxford: Oxford University Press

Clark, I., Kaempf, S., Reus-Smit, C. and Tannock, E. (2018). Crisis in the laws of war? Beyond compliance and effectiveness. *European Journal of International Relations*, 24(2), 319–343

Clunan, A.L. (2014). Why status matters in world politics. In Paul, T.V., Larson, D.W. and Wohlforth, W.C. (eds), *Status in World Politics*. Cambridge: Cambridge University Press, 273–296

Clunan, A. L. (2018). Russia and the liberal world order. *Ethics & International Affairs*, 32(1), 45–59

Coe, B. (2015). Sovereignty regimes and the norm of noninterference in the global south: Regional and temporal variation. *Global Governance*, 21(2), 275–298

Collombier, V., Clausen, M.-L., Hassan, H., Malmvig, H. and Khorto, J.P. (2019). Armed conflicts and the erosion of the state: The cases of Iraq, Libya, Yemen and Syria. In Quero, J. and Sala, C. (eds), *The MENARA Booklet for Academia*. Barcelona: CIDOB, 38–48

Colombo, S. and Huber, D. (2016). *The EU and Conflict Resolution in the Mediterranean Neighbourhood: Tackling New Realities through Old Means?* EuroMesco series paper 27, European Institute of the Mediterranean, March

Colombo, S., Otte, M., Soler i Lecha, E. and Tocci, N. (2019). The art of the (im)possible: Sowing the seeds for the EU's constructive engagement in the Middle East and North Africa. MENARA Final Reports no 4, CIDOB, April. At www.cidob.org/en/publications/publication_series/project_papers/menara_papers/final_report/the_art_of_the_im_possible_sowing_the_seeds_for_the_eu_s_constructive_engagement_in_the_middle_east_and_north_africa (accessed 14 May 2019)

Connolly, R. (2017). *Towards a Dual Fleet? The Maritime Doctrine of the Russian Federation and the Modernisation of Russian Naval Capabilities*. Rome: NATO Defense College paper 02/17, June, at www.ndc.nato.int/news/news.php?icode=1061 (accessed 13 June 2019)

Connolly, R. (2018). *Russia's Response to Sanctions: How Western Economic Statecraft is Reshaping Political Economy in Russia*. Cambridge: Cambridge University Press

Connolly, R. (2021). Putin's 'super-weapons'. In Bendett, S., Boulègue, M., Connolly, R., Konaev, M., Podvig, P. and Zysk, K. (eds), *Advanced Military Technology in Russia: Capabilities and Implications*. Chatham House Russia and Eurasia Programme, September, 23–32

Connolly, R. (2022). Looking to the global economy: Russia's role as a supplier of strategically important goods. In Monaghan, A. (ed.), *Russian Grand Strategy in an Era of Global Power Competition*. Manchester: Manchester University Press, 98–127

Connolly, R. and Boulègue, M. (2018). *Russia's New State Armament Programme: Implications for the Russian Armed Forces and Military Capabilities to 2027*. London: Chatham House research paper, May, at www.chathamhouse.org/sites/default/files/publications/research/2018-05-10-russia-state-armament-programme-connolly-boulegue-final.pdf (accessed 10 September 2018)

Connolly, R. and Sendstad, C. (2017). *Russia's Role as an Arms Exporter: The Strategic and Economic Importance of Arms Exports for Russia*. London: Chatham House research paper, March, at www.chathamhouse.org/publication/russias-role-arms-exporter-strategic-and-economic-importance-arms-exports-russia (accessed 10 September 2018)

Cooley, A. (2015). Authoritarianism goes global: Countering democratic norms. *Journal of Democracy*, 26(3), 49–63

Cooper, J. (2018a). *Russia's Invincible Weapons: Today, Tomorrow, Sometime, Never?* Oxford: Pembroke College Oxford paper, May, at https://static1.squarespace.com/static/55faab67e4b0914105347194/t/5b0eb1b203ce644a398267ef/1527689654381/Russia%27s+Invincible+Weapons.pdf (accessed 19 August 2019)

Cooper, J. (2018b). *The Russian State Armament Programme 2018–2027*. Rome: NATO Defense College paper 01/18, May, at www.ndc.nato.int/news/news.php?icode=1167 (accessed 19 August 2019)

Cooper, J. (2019). Russian military expenditure in 2017 and 2018, arms procurement and prospects for 2019 and beyond. Research note, 25 January (personal communication to author)

Cooper, J. (2022). *Implementation of the Russian Federal Budget during January–July 2022 and Spending on the Military*. Stockholm International Peace Research Institute Background Paper, October

Corral, P. and Krishnan, N. (2020). One in five people in the Middle East and North Africa now live in close proximity to conflict. World Bank blogs, 23 March. At https://blogs.worldbank.org/opendata/one-five-people-middle-east-and-north-africa-now-live-close-proximity-conflict (accessed 16 April 2020)

Coşkun, B.B. (2015). Neighbourhood narratives from 'zero problems with neighbours' to 'precious loneliness': Turkey's resecuritized Middle East policy after the Arab Spring. In Monier, E. (ed.), *Regional Insecurity After the Arab Uprisings: Narratives of Security and Threat*. New York and Basingstoke: Palgrave Macmillan, 187–203

Council of Europe (2015). Opinion of the Commissioner for human rights legislation and practice in the Russian Federation on non-commercial organisations in light of Council of Europe standards: An update. CommDH(2015)17, Strasbourg, 9 July

Council of the European Union (2015). *Joint Communication to the European Parliament and the Council – The EU's comprehensive approach to external*

conflicts and crises. JOIN(2013) 30 final, 18 December (accessed 19 November 2019)
Council of the European Union (2017). Council adopts EU strategy on Syria. Press release, 3 April. At www.consilium.europa.eu/en/press/press-releases/2017/04/03/fac-conclusion/ (accessed 5 April 2020)
Covington, S.R. (2015). *The Meaning of Russia's Campaign in Syria.* Belfer Center for Science and International Affairs, December. At www.belfercenter.org/publication/meaning-russias-campaign-syria (accessed 17 February 2021)
Covington, S.R. (2016). *The Culture of Strategic Thought Behind Russia's Modern Approaches to Warfare.* Harvard Kennedy School, Belfer Center for Science and International Affairs, October. At www.belfercenter.org/sites/default/files/legacy/files/Culture%20of%20Strategic%20Thought%203.pdf (accessed 17 February 2021)
Crilley, R. and Chatterje-Doody, P. (2020). Emotions and war on YouTube: Affective investments in RT's visual narratives of the conflict in Syria. *Cambridge Review of International Affairs,* 33(5), 713–733
Crone, M. (2017). Filling a void? French interventionism in the post-American MENA region. In Boserup, R.A., Hazbun, W., Makdisi, K. and Malmvig, H. *New Conflict Dynamics: Between Regional Autonomy and Intervention in the Middle East and North Africa.* Copenhagen: Danish Institute for International Studies, 55–64
Curanović, A. (2012). *The Religious Diplomacy of the Russian Federation.* Paris: IFRI, June, at www.ifri.org/sites/default/files/atoms/files/ifrirnr12curanovicreligiousdiplomacyjune2012.pdf (accessed 16 August 2019)
Curanović, A. (2019). Russia's Mission in the World. *Problems of Post-Communism,* 66(4), 253–267
Dalacoura, K. (2021). Turkish foreign policy in the Middle East: Power projection and post-ideological politics. *International Affairs,* 97(4), 1125–1142
Dannreuther, R. (2010a). Islamic radicalization in Russia: An assessment. *International Affairs,* 86(1), 109–126
Dannreuther, R. (2010b). Russian discourses and approaches to Islam and Islamism. In Dannreuther, R. and March, L. (eds), *Russia and Islam: State, Society and Radicalism.* Abingdon and New York: Routledge, 9–25
Dannreuther, R. (2012). Russia and the Middle East: A cold war paradigm? *Europe-Asia Studies,* 64(3), 543–560
Dannreuther, R. (2015). Russia and the Arab Spring: Supporting the counter-revolution. *Journal of European Integration,* 37(1), 77–94
Dannreuther, R. (2019). Understanding Russia's return to the Middle East. *International Politics,* 56(6), 726–742
Dark, G. (2018). *EU Seen from the Outside: Local Elite Perceptions on the Role and Effectiveness of the EU in the Mediterranean Region.* MEDRESET Policy Paper 5, November, at www.iai.it/sites/default/files/medreset_pp_5.pdf (accessed 29 November 2018)
Darwich, M. (2019). *Threats and Alliances in the Middle East: Saudi and Syrian Policies in a Turbulent Region.* Cambridge: Cambridge University Press

Darwich, M. and Fakhoury, T. (2016). Casting the Other as an existential threat: The securitisation of sectarianism in the international relations of the Syria crisis. *Global Discourse*, 6(4), 712–732

Davis, J.E. (2011). From ideology to pragmatism: China's position in humanitarian intervention in the post-Cold War era. *Vanderbilt Journal of Transnational Law*, 44(2), 217–283

Debuysere, L. (2019). *Bouteflexit: Leave Means Leave in the EU's Southern Neighbourhood*. Brussels: Centre for European Policy Studies, commentary, 23 April, at http://aei.pitt.edu/97062/1/LD_Bouteflexit.pdf (accessed 13 May 2019)

De Groof, E. (2016). First things first: R2P starts with direct negotiations. *The International Spectator*, 51(2), 30–48.

Dejevsky, M. (2018). *Two Views of the Syria Conflict that Seem Never to Meet*. Valdai Discussion Club expert opinion, 1 March, at http://valdaiclub.com/a/highlights/two-views-of-the-syria-conflict/ (accessed 7 October 2019)

Del Sarto, R.A. (2017). Contentious borders in the Middle East and North Africa: Context and concepts. *International Affairs*, 93(4), 767–787

Deni, J. (ed.) (2018). *Current Russian Military Affairs: Assessing and Countering Russian Strategy, Operational Planning, and Modernization*. U.S. Army War College Strategic Studies Institute, July

Deyermond, R. (2016). The uses of sovereignty in twenty-first century Russian foreign policy. *Europe-Asia Studies*, 68(6), 957–984

Dias, V.A. and Freire, M.R. (2019). Russia and the Arab Spring: A counter-revolutionary power in the MENA Region. In Çakmak, C. and Özçelik, A.O. (eds), *The World Community and the Arab Spring*. Cham: Palgrave Macmillan, 161–183

Dieckhoff, M. (2020). Reconsidering the humanitarian space: Complex interdependence between humanitarian and peace negotiations in Syria. *Contemporary Security Policy*, 41(4), 564–586

Dietrich, J.W. (2013). R2P and intervention after Libya. *Journal of Alternative Perspectives in the Social Sciences*, 5(2), 323–352

Dixon, M. and Lawson, G. (2022). From revolution and terrorism to revolutionary terrorism: The case of militant Salafism. *International Affairs*, 98(6), 2119–2139

Docherty, B., Mathieu, X. and Ralph, J. (2020). R2P and the Arab Spring: Norm localisation and the US response to the early Syria crisis. *Global Responsibility to Protect*, 12, 246–270

Droz-Vincent, P. (2014). The military amidst uprisings and transitions in the Arab world. In Gerges, F.A. (ed.), *The New Middle East: Protest and Revolution in the Arab World*. New York: Cambridge University Press, 180–208

Dunne, T. and Teitt, S. (2015). Contested intervention: China, India, and the Responsibility to Protect. *Global Governance: A Review of Multilateralism and International Organizations*, 21(3), 371–391

Ehteshami, A., Huber, D. and Paciello, M.C. (2017). Introduction. In Ehteshami, A., Huber, D. and Paciello, M.C. (eds), *The Mediterranean Reset: Geopolitics in a New Age*. Global Policy, at www.globalpolicyjournal.com/projects/gp-e-books/mediterranean-reset-geopolitics-new-age (accessed 17 February 2018)

Ehteshami, A. and Mohammadi, A. (2017a). Saudi Arabia's and Qatar's discourses and practices in the Mediterranean. In Ehteshami, A., Huber, D. and Paciello, M.C. (eds), *The Mediterranean Reset: Geopolitics in a New Age*. Global Policy, at www.globalpolicyjournal.com/projects/gp-e-books/mediterranean-reset-geopolitics-new-age (accessed 17 February 2018)

Ehteshami, A. and Mohammadi, A. (2017b). Iran's discourses and practices in the Mediterranean since 2001. In Ehteshami, A., Huber, D. and Paciello, M.C. (eds), *The Mediterranean Reset: Geopolitics in a New Age*. Global Policy, at www.globalpolicyjournal.com/projects/gp-e-books/mediterranean-reset-geopolitics-new-age (accessed 17 February 2018)

Elitok, S.P. (2018). *Turkey's Migration Policy Revisited: (Dis)Continuities and Peculiarities*. Istituto Affari Internazionali paper 18/16, October, at www.iai.it/en/pubblicazioni/turkeys-migration-policy-revisited-discontinuities-and-peculiarities (accessed 24 November 2018)

European Commission/HR CFSP (2013). *Towards a Comprehensive EU Approach to the Syrian Crisis*. JOIN(2013) 22 final, Brussels, 24 June

EEAS (European Union External Action Service) (2016). Statement of the International Syria Support Group, 12 February. At https://eeas.europa.eu/headquarters/headquarters-homepage/5264/statement-international-syria-support-group_en (accessed 28 November 2019)

European Union (2011). Declaration by the High Representative, Catherine Ashton, on behalf of the European Union on EU action following the escalation of violent repression in Syria. 13488/1/11 REV 1, Brussels, 18 August

Evans, A. (2015). Ideological change under Vladimir Putin in the perspective of social identity. *Demokratizatsiya*, 23(4), 401–426

Facon, I. (2017). Russia's quest for influence in North Africa and the Middle East. Fondation pour la Recherche Stratégique, July, at www.frstrategie.org/web/documents/programmes/observatoire-du-monde-arabo-musulman-et-du-sahel/publications/en/8.pdf (accessed 4 May 2019)

Falk, R. (2005). Legality and legitimacy: The quest for principled flexibility and restraint. *Review of International Studies*, 31(S1), 33–50

Falk, R. (2016). Rethinking the Arab Spring: Uprisings, counterrevolution, chaos and global reverberations. *Third World Quarterly*, 37(12), 2322–2334

Fares, O. (2015). The Arab Spring comes to Syria: Internal mobilization for democratic change, militarization and internationalization. In Sadiki, L. (ed.), *Routledge Handbook of the Arab Spring: Rethinking Democratization*. Abingdon and New York: Routledge, 145–159

Fawcett, L. (2015a). Regionalizing security in the Middle East: Connecting the regional and the global. In Monier, E. (ed.), *Regional Insecurity After the Arab Uprisings: Narratives of Security and Threat*. New York and Basingstoke: Palgrave Macmillan, 40–57

Fawcett, L. (2015b). Rising powers and regional organization in the Middle East. In Gaskarth, J. (ed.), *Rising Powers, Global Governance and Global Ethics*. Abingdon and New York: Routledge, 133–151

Fawcett, L. (2017). States and sovereignty in the Middle East: Myths and realities. *International Affairs*, 93(4), 789–807

Feklyunina, V. (2018). International norms and identity. In Tsygankov, A.P. (ed.), *Routledge Handbook of Russian Foreign Policy*. Abingdon and New York: Routledge, 5–21

Fishman, B. (2022). Ten years after Benghazi: Getting past Groundhog Day. *Survival*, 64(5), 113–126

Foot, R. (2003). Introduction. In Foot, R., Gaddis, J. and Hurrell, A. (eds), *Order and Justice in International Relations*. Oxford and New York: Oxford University Press, 1–23

Forsberg, T. and Herd, G.P. (2005). The EU, human rights, and the Russo-Chechen conflict. *Political Science Quarterly*, 120(3), 455–478

Forsythe, D.P. (2012). *The UN Security Council and Human Rights: State Sovereignty and Human Dignity*. Berlin: Friedrich Ebert Stiftung International Policy Analysis, May

Freedman, L. (2005). The age of liberal wars. *Review of International Studies*, 31(S1), 93–107

Freedman, L. (2021). The crisis of liberalism and the Western alliance. *Survival*, 63(6), 37–44

Freedman, R.O. (2006). *Russia, Iran and the Nuclear Question: The Putin Record*. Carlisle Barracks PA: Army War College Strategic Studies Institute, November

Freedman, R.O. (1990). The superpowers and the Middle East. In Allison, R. and Williams, P. (eds), *Superpower Competition and Crisis Prevention in the Third World*. Cambridge: Cambridge University Press, 121–43

French Embassy in London (2018). France and Russia transport aid for Syrian civilians. French Ministry for Europe and Foreign Affairs, 23/27 July 2018. At https://uk.ambafrance.org/France-and-Russia-transport-aid-for-Syrian-civilians (accessed 13 April 2020)

French Republic Presidency (2017). *Defence and National Security Strategic Review*, 15 October. At https://espas.secure.europarl.europa.eu/orbis/document/defence-and-national-security-strategic-review-2017 (accessed 29 November 2020)

Frolov, V. (2015a). Chuzhaya voina: Chem Vladimir Putin riskuet v Sirii (Someone else's war: what Vladimir Putin is risking in Syria). *Republic.ru*, 21 September, at https://republic.ru/posts/56788 (accessed 4 May 2021, in Russian)

Frolov, V. (2015b). Kto ne skachet, tot IGIL. Kak Kreml' vidit politicheskoe uregulirovanie v Sirii (If he doesn't jump over to our side, he's ISIS. How the Kremlin sees a political settlement in Syria), *Slon.ru*, 25 October. At https://republic.ru/posts/58542 (accessed 4 May 2021)

Frolov, V. (2016a). Pochemu Rossiia vyvodit voiska iz Sirii imenno seichas (Why Russia is now withdrawing its troops from Syria). *Republic (Slon)*, 15 March (retrieved from EastView database, in Russian)

Frolov, V. (2016b). Propagandistskii kurazh. Kak rasskazy o podvigakh v Sirii possoril Rossiyu s Iranom (Propagandistic swagger: how stories about Russia's heroic exploits in Syria led to a row with Iran). At https://republic.ru/posts/72439 (accessed 14 July 2021, in Russian)

Frolov, V. (2017a). Kak rastsenivat' poezdku Putina v Siriyu? (How do we assess Putin's trip to Syria?) *Republic (Slon)*, 15 March (retrieved from EastView database, in Russian)

Frolov, V. (2017b). Konstitutsiya na eksport: Kak Rossiya prodvigaet demokratiyu na Blizhnem Vostoke (A constitution for export: How is Russia promoting democracy in the Middle East)? *Republic.ru*, 27 January. At https://republic.ru/posts/79006 (accessed 4 May 2021, in Russian)

Frye, T. (2021). *Weak Strongman: The Limits of Power in Putin's Russia*. Princeton, NJ: Princeton University Press

Fusco, F. (2021). *Countering Zero-Sum Relations in the Middle East: Insights from the Expert Survey*. Istituto Affari Internazionali paper 21/02, January. At www.iai.it/sites/default/files/iai2102.pdf (accessed 4 May 2021)

G8 (G8 Leaders' Communiqué) (2013). Lough Erne, 18 June. At https://assets.publishing.service.gov.uk/government/uploads/system/uploads/attachment_data/file/207771/Lough_Erne_2013_G8_Leaders_Communique.pdf (accessed 5 January 2016)

Garwood-Gowers, A. (2013). The responsibility to protect and the Arab Spring: Libya as the exception, Syria as the norm. *University of New South Wales Law Journal*, 36(2), 594–618

Gaskarth, J. (2017). Rising powers, responsibility, and international society. *Ethics & International Affairs*, 31(3), 287–311

Gaub, F. (2018a). Russia's non-war on Daesh. In Popescu, N. and Secrieru, S. (eds), *Russia's Return to the Middle East: Building Sandcastles?* Chaillot paper No. 146, July. Paris: EU Institute for Security Studies, 57–64

Gaub, F. (2018b). State vacuums and non-state actors in the Middle East and North Africa. In Kamel, L. (ed.), *The Frailty of Authority: Borders, Non-State Actors and Power Vacuums in a Changing Middle East*. Istituto Affari Internazionali. Rome: Edizioni Nuova Cultura, 51–66

Gaub, F. and Popescu N. (2018). The Soviet Union in the Middle East: An overview. In Popescu, N. and Secrieru, S. (eds), *Russia's Return to the Middle East: Building Sandcastles?* Chaillot paper No. 146, July. Paris: EU Institute for Security Studies, 13–20

Gause, G. III, F. (2019). Should we stay or should we go? The United States and the Middle East. *Survival*, 61(5), 7–24.

Gel'man, V. (2015). *Authoritarian Russia: Analyzing Post-Soviet Regime Changes*. Pittsburgh, PA: University of Pittsburgh Press

Geranmayeh, E. and Liik, K. (2016). *The New Power Couple: Russia and Iran in the Middle East*. European Council on Foreign Relations policy brief, September. At www.ecfr.eu/page/-/ECFR_186_-_THE_NEW_POWER_COUPLE_RUSSIA_AND_IRAN_IN_THE_MIDDLE_EAST_PDF.pdf (accessed 20 November 2019)

Gerasimov, V. (2019). Po opytu Sirii (The experience of Syria). *Voenno-promyshlennyi kur'er*, 7 March, at https://vpk-news.ru/articles/29579 (accessed 20 June 2019, in Russian)

Gerges, F.A. (2014). Introduction: A rupture. In Gerges, F.A. (ed.), *The New Middle East: Protest and Revolution in the Arab World*. New York: Cambridge University Press

Ghanem-Yazbeck, D. and Kuznetsov, V. (2018). The 'comrades' in North Africa. In Popescu, N. and Secrieru, S. (eds), *Russia's Return to the Middle East: Building*

Sandcastles? Chaillot paper No. 146, July. Paris: EU Institute for Security Studies, 73–82

Gifkins, J. (2016). R2P in the UN Security Council: Darfur, Libya and beyond. *Cooperation and Conflict*, 51(2), 148–165

Giles, K. (2017). *Assessing Russia's Reorganized and Rearmed Military*. Carnegie Endowment for International Peace Task Force White Paper, 3 May. At https://carnegieendowment.org/2017/05/03/assessing-russia-s-reorganized-and-rearmed-military-pub-69853 (accessed 10 November 2019)

Gimatdinov, R.R. and Nasyrov, I.R. (2019). Gruppa Strategicheskogo Videniya 'Rossiya-Islamskii Mir kak Instrument 'Myagkoi Sily' vo Vneshnei Politike Rossiiskoi Federatsii (Russia-Islamic World 'Strategic Vision Group' as a 'soft power' instrument in the Russian Federation's foreign policy), *Vostok (Oriens)*, 1 (in Russian)

Glanville, L. (2014). Syria teaches us little about questions of military intervention. In Murray, R.W. and McKay, A. (eds), *Into the Eleventh Hour: R2P, Syria and Humanitarianism in Crisis*. Bristol: E-International Relations, January, 44–48

Goldberg, J. (2016). The Obama Doctrine. *The Atlantic*. April, 317(3), 70–90

Goldstein, J. and Keohane, R.O. (1993). Ideas and foreign policy: An analytical framework. In Goldstein, J. and Keohane, R.O. (eds), *Ideas and Foreign Policy: Beliefs, Institutions, and Political Change*. Ithaca, NY and London: Cornell University Press

Golts, A. (2018). Determinants of Russian foreign policy: Realpolitik, militarism and the vertical of power. In Meister, S. (ed.), *Between Old and New World Order: Russia's Foreign and Security Policy Rationale*. Berlin: German Council on Foreign Relations, DGAPkompakt 19, September, at https://dgap.org/en/think-tank/publications/dgapanalyse-compact/between-old-and-new-world-order (accessed 3 June 2019)

Gordon, M.R. (2015). Kerry suggests there is a place for Assad in Syria talks. *The New York Times*, 15 March

Görgülü, A. and Dark, G. (2017). Turkey, the EU and the Mediterranean: Perceptions, policies and prospects. In Ehteshami, A., Huber, D. and Paciello, M.C. (eds), *The Mediterranean Reset: Geopolitics in a New Age*. Global Policy, 124–138, at www.globalpolicyjournal.com/projects/gp-e-books/mediterranean-reset-geopolitics-new-age (accessed 17 February 2018)

Götz, E. (2017). Putin, the state, and war: The causes of Russia's near abroad assertion revisited. *International Studies Review*, 19(2), 228–253

Gowan, R. and Brantner, F. (2008). *A Global Force for Human Rights? An Audit of European Power at the UN*. London: European Council on Foreign Relations Policy Paper, at www.ecfr.eu/page/-/ECFR-08_A_GLOBAL_FORCE_FOR_HUMAN_RIGHTS-_AN_AUDIT_OF_EUROPEAN_POWER_AT_THE_UN.pdf (accessed 5 July 2017)

Graham, T. and Moran, M. (2016). *Fear and Opportunity: Russia's Foreign Policy*. Carnegie Corporation of New York, 19 October, at www.carnegie.org/media/filer_public/c9/28/c928c339-8ddd-4362-97f3-d3ba4e834321/thomas_graham.pdf (accessed 11 June 2019)

Gray, C. (2008). *International Law and the Use of Force*. 3rd edition. Oxford and New York: Oxford University Press

Gray, K. and Murphy, C.N. (2013). Introduction: Rising powers and the future of global governance. *Third World Quarterly*, 34(2), 183–193

Greene, T. and Rynhold, J. (2018). Europe and Israel: Between conflict and cooperation. *Survival*, 60(4), 91–112

Greenstock, J. (2017). Is this Russia's moment in the Middle East? *Asian Affairs*, 48(3), 419–427

Grisgraber, D. and Reynolds, S. (2015). *Aid Inside Syria: A Step in the Right Direction?* Refugees International Field Report, 12 May. At www.refugeesint ernational.org/reports/2015/6/13/aid-inside-syria-a-step-in-the-right-direction (accessed 7 January 2020)

Gunitsky, S. and Tsygankov, A.P. (2018). The Wilsonian bias in the study of Russian foreign policy. *Problems of Post-Communism*, 65(6), 385–393

Gvosdev, N.K. (2019). Russian strategic goals in the Middle East. In Central Asia Program, *Russia's Policy in the Middle East: Determination, Delight, and Disappointment*. CAP paper No. 212, Institute for European, Russian and Eurasian Studies, George Washington University, January, 4–7

Halbach, U. (2018). *Chechnya's Status within the Russian Federation: Ramzan Kadyrov's Private State and Vladimir Putin's Federal 'Power Vertical'*. Stiftung Wissenschaft und Politik research paper 2, May, at www.swp-berlin.org/fileadmin/contents/products/research_papers/2018RP02_hlb.pdf (accessed 14 August 2019)

Hanania, R. (2020). Worse than nothing: Why US intervention made government atrocities more likely in Syria. *Survival*, 62(5), 173–192

Hartwell, C.A. (2019). Russian economic policy in the MENA region: A means to political ends. In Talbot, V. and Lovotti, C. (eds), *The Role of Russia in the Middle East and North Africa Region: Strategy or Opportunism?* Euromesco Joint Policy Study 12, April, 90–114. At www.euromesco.net/publication/the-role-of-russia-in-the-middle-east-and-north-africa-region-strategy-or-opportunism-4/ (accessed 15 April 2021)

Hauer, N. (2017). A war within a war: Chechnya's expanding role in Syria. *News Deeply*, 30 November. At www.newsdeeply.com/syria/articles/2017/11/30/a-war-within-a-war-chechnyas-expanding-role-in-syria (accessed 23 January 2020)

Hayward, T. (2019). Three duties of epistemic diligence. *Journal of Social Philosophy*, 50(4), 536–561

Hazbun, W. (2016). Assembling security in a 'weak state': The contentious politics of plural governance in Lebanon since 2005. *Third World Quarterly*, 37(6), 1053–1070

Hazbun, W. (2017). Beyond the American era in the Middle East: An evolving landscape of turbulence. In Boserup, R.A., Hazbun, W., Makdisi, K. and Malmvig, H. (eds), *New Conflict Dynamics: Between Regional Autonomy and Intervention in the Middle East and North Africa*. Copenhagen: Danish Institute for International Studies

Hazbun, W. (2018). *Regional Powers and the Production of Insecurity in the Middle East*. MENARA working paper 11, September, www.cidob.org/en/publications

/publication_series/menara_papers/working_papers/regional_powers_and_the _production_of_insecurity_in_the_middle_east (accessed 23 November 2018)

Hedenskog, J. (2020). *Russia and International Cooperation on Counter-Terrorism: From the Chechen Wars to the Syria Campaign*, Swedish Defense Research Agency (FOI), FOI-R--4916--SE, March

Hedenskog, J., Persson, G. and Vendil Pallin, C. (2016). Russian security policy. In Persson, G. (ed.), *Russian Military Capability in a Ten-Year Perspective – 2016*, Swedish Defense Research Agency (FOI), FOI-R--4326--SE, December

Hedetoft, U. and Blum, D.W. (2008). Introduction: Russia and globalization: A historical and conceptual framework. In Blum, D.W. (ed.), *Russia and Globalization: Identity, Security and Society in an Era of Change*. Washington, DC: Woodrow Wilson Center Press and Baltimore, MD: The Johns Hopkins University Press, 1–34

Hehir, A. (2013). The permanence of inconsistency: Libya, the Security Council, and the Responsibility to Protect. *International Security*, 38(1), 137–159

Hehir, A. (2016). Assessing the influence of the Responsibility to Protect on the UN Security Council during the Arab Spring. *Cooperation and Conflict*, 51(2), 166–183

Hehir, A. (2017). 'Utopian in the right sense': The Responsibility to Protect and the logical necessity of reform. *Ethics & International Affairs*, 31(3), 335–355

Heinze, E. A. (2011). The evolution of international law in light of the 'global War on Terror'. *Review of International Studies*, 37(3), 1069–1094

Heller, S. (2018). 'Frogs' and 'geckos': Syria's jihadists speak the language of rebellion. International Crisis Group op-ed, 22 October. At www.crisisgroup.org /middle-east-north-africa/eastern-mediterranean/syria/frogs-and-geckos-syrias -jihadists-speak-language-rebellion (accessed 28 May 2020)

Herd, G. (2019). Putin's operational code and strategic decision-making in Russia. In Kanet, R. (ed.), *Routledge Handbook of Russian Security*. Abingdon and New York: Routledge, 17–29

Herrmann, R.K. (2004). Learning from the end of the Cold War. In Herrmann, R.K. and Ned Lebow, R. (eds), *Ending the Cold War: Interpretations, Causation and the Study of International Relations*. New York and Basingstoke: Palgrave Macmillan, 219–238

Herrmann, R.K. and Ned Lebow, R. (2004). What was the Cold War? When and why did it end? In Herrmann, R.K. and Ned Lebow, R. (eds), *Ending the Cold War: Interpretations, Causation and the Study of International Relations*. New York and Basingstoke: Palgrave Macmillan, 1–27

Hersh, S.M. (2013). Whose sarin? *London Review of Books*, 35(24), 9–12

Hill, F. and Gaddy, C.G. (2013). *Mr. Putin: Operative in the Kremlin*. Washington, DC: Brookings Institution Press

Hille, K., England, A. and Khattab, A. (2018). Russia tries to win hearts and minds with aid in Syria. *Financial Times*, 12 August. At www.ft.com/content/e034bdde -96f0-11e8-b747-fb1e803ee64e (accessed 13 April 2020)

Hiltermann, J. (2021). The Arab uprisings in retro and prospect. International Crisis Group op-ed, 20 February. At www.crisisgroup.org/middle-east-north-africa/ arab-uprisings-retro-and-prospect (accessed 4 May 2021)

Hinnebusch, R. (2012). Syria: From 'authoritarian upgrading' to revolution? *International Affairs*, 88(1), 95–113

Hinnebusch, R. (2015). Back to enmity: Turkey-Syria relations since the Syrian Uprising. *Orient: Journal of German Orient Institute*, 56(1), 14–22

Hinnebusch, R. (2016). The sectarian revolution in the Middle East. *Revolutions: Global Trends and Regional Issues*, 4(1), 120–152

Hinnebusch, R. and Zartman, I.W. (2016). *UN Mediation in the Syrian Crisis: From Kofi Annan to Lakhdar Brahimi*. New York: International Peace Institute

Hopf, T. (ed.) (2002). *The Social Construction of International Politics: Identities and Foreign Policies, Moscow, 1955 and 1999*. Ithaca, NY: Cornell University Press

Hopf, T. (2005). Identity, legitimacy, and the use of military force: Russia's great power identities and military intervention in Abkhazia. *Review of International Studies*, 31(S1): 225–243

House of Commons (2016). *Libya: Examination of Intervention and Collapse and the UK's Future Policy Options*. House of Commons Foreign Affairs Committee, Third Report of Session 2017–19, HC119, 14 September

House of Commons (2018a). *The Responsibility to Protect and Humanitarian Intervention*. Foreign Affairs Committee Global Britain, Twelfth Report of Session 2017–19, 10 September

House of Commons (2018b). *Global Britain*. House of Commons Foreign Affairs Committee, Sixth Report of Session 2017–19, HC780, 12 March

House of Lords (2017). *The Middle East: Time for New Realism*. Select Committee on International Relations, 2nd Report of Session 2016–17, HL Paper 159

HRW (Human Rights Watch) (2016a). *Russia: Failing to do Fair Share to Help Syrian Refugees*, press release 14 September. At www.hrw.org/news/2016/09/14/russia-failing-do-fair-share-help-syrian-refugees (accessed 7 January 2020)

HRW (Human Rights Watch) (2016b). *World Report. Events of 2015*. At www.hrw.org/sites/default/files/world_report_download/wr2016_web.pdf (accessed 28 May 2020)

HRW (Human Rights Watch) (2017). *Syria: Events of 2016*. At www.hrw.org/world-report/2017/country-chapters/syria (accessed 7 January 2020)

Hurd, I. (2018). The empire of international legalism. *Ethics & International Affairs*, 32(3), 265–278

Hurrell, A. (2003). Order and justice in international relations: What is at stake? In Foot, R., Gaddis, J. and Hurrell, A. (eds), *Order and Justice in International Relations*. Oxford and New York: Oxford University Press, 24–48

Hurrell, A. (2005). Legitimacy and the use of force: Can the circle be squared? *Review of International Studies*, 31(S1), 15–32

Hurrell, A. (2018). Beyond the BRICS: Power, pluralism, and the future of global order. *Ethics & International Affairs*, 32(1), 89–101

Hurska, A. (2018). Lev Dengov: Ramzan Kadyrov's middleman in Libya. *Eurasia Daily Monitor* 15(153), 29 October. At https://jamestown.org/program/lev-dengov-ramzan-kadyrovs-middleman-in-libya/ (accessed 25 June 2020)

Ikenberry, G.J. (2017). The plot against American foreign Policy: Can the liberal order survive. *Foreign Affairs*, 96(2), 2–9

Ikenberry, G.J. (2018). The end of liberal international order? *International Affairs*, 94(1), 7–23

ICG (International Crisis Group) (2016a). *The North Caucasus Insurgency and Syria: An Exported Jihad?* Europe Report No. 238, Brussels, 16 March. At www.crisisgroup.org/europe-central-asia/caucasus/north-caucasus/north-caucasus-insurgency-and-syria-exported-jihad (accessed 11 August 2019)

ICG (International Crisis Group) (2016b). *Russia's Choice in Syria*. Crisis Group Middle East Briefing no 47, Istanbul/New York/Brussels, 29 March. At www.crisisgroup.org/middle-east-north-africa/eastern-mediterranean/syria/russia-s-choice-syria (accessed 25 April 2020)

ICG (International Crisis Group) (2017a). *The PKK's Fateful Choice in Northern Syria*. Report No. 176, 4 May. At www.crisisgroup.org/middle-east-north-africa/eastern-mediterranean/syria/176-pkk-s-fateful-choice-northern-syria (accessed 22 June 2017)

ICG (International Crisis Group) (2017b). *Syria: The Promise of Worse to Come and How to Avoid It*. Middle East and North Africa commentary, 22 February. At www.crisisgroup.org/middle-east-north-africa/eastern-mediterranean/syria/syria-promise-worse-come-and-how-avoid-it (accessed 22 June 2017)

ICG (International Crisis Group) (2017c). *Tackling the MENA Region's Intersecting Conflicts*. 22 December. At https://d2071andvip0wj.cloudfront.net/tackling-the-mena-region%20(1).pdf (accessed 25 April 2020)

ICG (International Crisis Group) (2018a). *Iran's Priorities in a Turbulent Middle East*. Middle East Report No. 184, 13 April, at www.crisisgroup.org/middle-east-north-africa/gulf-and-arabian-peninsula/iran/184-irans-priorities-turbulent-middle-east (accessed 25 April 2020)

ICG (International Crisis Group) (2018b). *Syria: from Vienna to Sochi*. Middle East and North Africa, 30 January. At www.crisisgroup.org/middle-east-north-africa/eastern-mediterranean/syria/syria-vienna-sochi (accessed 25 April 2020)

ICG (International Crisis Group) (2018c). *Prospects for a Deal to Stabilise Syria's North East*. Middle East report No. 190, 5 September. At www.crisisgroup.org/middle-east-north-africa/eastern-mediterranean/syria/190-prospects-deal-stabilise-syrias-north-east (accessed 24 April 2020)

ICG (International Crisis Group) (2018d). *Dagestan's Abandoned Counter-Insurgency Experiment*. Europe and Central Asia Commentary, 5 July. At www.crisisgroup.org/europe-central-asia/caucasus/russianorth-caucasus/counter-insurgency-north-caucasus-i-dagestans-abandoned-experiment (accessed 28 May 2020)

ICG (International Crisis Group) (2019a). *Iraq: Evading the Gathering Storm*. Middle East and North Africa briefing no 70, 29 August. At www.crisisgroup.org/middle-east-north-africa/gulf-and-arabian-peninsula/iraq/070-iraq-evading-gathering-storm (accessed 22 April 2020)

ICG (International Crisis Group) (2019b). *Lessons from the Syrian State's Return to the South*. Middle East report No. 196, 25 February. At www.crisisgroup.org/middle-east-north-africa/eastern-mediterranean/syria/196-lessons-syrian-states-return-south (accessed 5 May 2020)

ICG (International Crisis Group) (2019c). *Ways out of Europe's Syria Reconstruction Conundrum*. Middle East Report No. 209, 25 November. At www.crisisgroup.org/middle-east-north-africa/eastern-mediterranean/syria/209-ways-out-europes-syria-reconstruction-conundrum (accessed 5 May 2020)

ICG (International Crisis Group) (2020a). *Turkey Wades into Libya's Troubled Waters*. Europe and Central Asia report No. 257, 30 April. At www.crisisgroup.org/europe-central-asia/western-europemediterranean/turkey/257-turkey-wades-libyas-troubled-waters (accessed 18 May 2021)

ICG (International Crisis Group) (2020b). *What Prospects for a Ceasefire in Libya?* Middle East and North Africa, 18 January. At www.crisisgroup.org/middle-east-north-africa/north-africa/libya/what-prospects-ceasefire-libya (accessed 25 April 2020)

ICG (International Crisis Group) (2020c). *Rethinking Peace in Yemen*. Middle East and North Africa report No. 2016, 2 July. At www.crisisgroup.org/middle-east-north-africa/gulf-and-arabian-peninsula/yemen/216-rethinking-peace-yemen (accessed 18 May 2021)

ICG (International Crisis Group) (2020d). *Fleshing out the Libya Ceasefire Agreement*. Middle East and North Africa briefing no 80, 4 November. At www.crisisgroup.org/middle-east-north-africa/north-africa/libya/b80-fleshing-out-libya-ceasefire-agreement (accessed 18 May 2021)

ICG (International Crisis Group) (2022a). *Containing a Resilient ISIS in Central and North-Eastern Syria*. Middle East Report No. 236, 18 July. At www.crisisgroup.org/middle-east-north-africa/east-mediterranean-mena/syria/containing-resilient-isis-central-and-north#:~:text=ISIS%20is%20waging%20a%20resilient,often%20work%20at%20cross-purposes (accessed 15 October 2022)

ICG (International Crisis Group) (2022b). *A Vital Humanitarian Mandate for Syria's North West*. Middle East & North Africa, 5 July. At www.crisisgroup.org/middle-east-north-africa/east-mediterranean-mena/syria/vital-humanitarian-mandate-syrias-north-west (accessed 15 October 2022)

IICI (International Commission of Inquiry) (2016). *Report of the Independent International Commission of Inquiry on the Syrian Arab Republic*. UN Human Rights Council A/HRC/31/68, 11 February

IICI (International Commission of Inquiry) (2017). *Report of the Independent International Commission of Inquiry on the Syrian Arab Republic*. UN Human Rights Council A/HRC/36/55, 8 August

IICI (International Commission of Inquiry) (2018). *The Siege and Recapture of Eastern Ghouta*. UN Human Rights Council A/HRC/38/CRP.3, 20 June

IICI (International Commission of Inquiry) (2021). *Report of the Independent International Commission of Inquiry on the Syrian Arab Republic*. UN Human Rights Council A/HRC/46/55, 11 March

IICI (International Commission of Inquiry) (2022a). *Report of the Independent International Commission of Inquiry on the Syrian Arab Republic*. UN Human Rights Council A/HRC/51/45, 17 August

IICI (International Commission of Inquiry) (2022b). *Report of the Independent International Commission of Inquiry on the Syrian Arab Republic*. UN Human Rights Council A/HRC/49/77, 8 February

IISS (International Institute for Strategic Studies) (2012). Russia's Syrian stance: Principled self-interest. *Strategic Comments*, 18(7), 1–3
IISS (International Institute for Strategic Studies) (2019). *The Military Balance*. IISS
Isaac, S.K. (2015). A resurgence in Aran regional institutions? The cases of the Arab League and the Gulf Cooperation Council post-2011. In Monier, E. (ed.), *Regional Insecurity After the Arab Uprisings: Narratives of Security and Threat*. New York and Basingstoke: Palgrave Macmillan, 151–167
Isaac, S.K. and Kares, H.E. (2017). American discourses and practices in the Mediterranean since 2001: A comparative analysis with the EU. In Ehteshami, A., Huber, D. and Paciello, M.C. (eds), *The Mediterranean Reset: Geopolitics in a New Age*. Global Policy, at www.globalpolicyjournal.com/projects/gp-e-books/mediterranean-reset-geopolitics-new-age (accessed 17 February 2018)
Isaev, L., Korotaev, A. and Mardasov, A. (2018). Metamorphoses in the intra-Syrian negotiating process. *Mirovaya ekonomika i mezhdunarodnye otnosheniya*, 62(3), 20–28 (in Russian)
Isaev, L. and Yur'ev, S. (2017). Rossiiskaya politika v otnoshenii khristian Blizhnego Vostoka (Russian policy towards Christians in the Middle East). *Aziya i Afrika Segodnya*, 12, 25–30 (in Russian)
Issaev, L. and Shishkina, A.R. (2020). Russia in the Middle East: In Search of its place. In Mühlberger, W. and Alaranta, T. (eds), *Political Narratives in the Middle East and North Africa. Conceptions of Order and Perceptions of Instability*. Springer, 95–114
ISSG (International Syria Support Group) (2016). *Statement of the International Syria Support Group*, 17 May. At www.un.org/sg/en/content/sg/note-correspondents/2016-05-17/note-correspondents-statement-international-syria-support (accessed 22 June 2017)
Ivanov, I. (2016). Tri korziny dlya Blizhnego Vostoka (Three baskets for the Middle East). *Nezavisimaya gazeta*, 1 February, 9. At www.ng.ru/dipkurer/2016-02-01/9_korziny.html (accessed 4 May 2021, in Russian
Jackson, R. (1990). *Quasi-States: Sovereignty, International Relations and the Third World*. Cambridge and New York: Cambridge University Press
Jacoby, T.A. (2015). The season's pendulum: Arab Spring politics and Israeli security. In Monier, E. (ed.), *Regional Insecurity After the Arab Uprisings: Narratives of Security and Threat*. New York and Basingstoke: Palgrave Macmillan, 168–186
Judina, D. and Platonov, K. (2019). Newsworthiness and the public's response in Russian social media: A comparison of state and private news organizations. *Media and Communication*, 7(3), 157–166
Kalaitzidis, A. (2017). Elite choices, path dependency and the Arab Spring. In Boserup, R.A., Hazbun, W., Makdisi, K. and Malmvig, H. (eds), *New Conflict Dynamics: Between Regional Autonomy and Intervention in the Middle East and North Africa*. Copenhagen: Danish Institute for International Studies
Kaldor, M. (2013). *New and Old Wars: Organised Violence in a Global Era*. Cambridge: Polity Press
Kalehsar, O.S. and Telli, A. (2017). The future of Iran-Russia energy relations post-sanctions. *Middle East Policy*, 24(3), 163–170

Kamel, L. Ed. (2017). *The Frailty of Authority: Borders, Non-State Actors and Power Vacuums in a Changing Middle East*. Istituto Affari Internazionali. Rome: Edizioni Nuova Cultura

Kamrava, M. (2018). *Inside the Arab State*. Oxford and New York: Oxford University Press

Kandil, A. (2020). Geopolitics of gas in the Eastern Mediterranean region: Is there light at the end of the tunnel? In Colombo, S. and Soler I Lecha, E. (eds), *Infrastructures and Power in the Middle East and North Africa*. Euromesco Joint Policy Study 17, September, 34–59.

Katz, M.N. (2018). Russia and Israel: An improbable friendship. In Popescu, N. and Secrieru, S. (eds), *Russia's Return to the Middle East: Building Sandcastles*. Chaillot Paper 146, July, 103–108

Katzenstein, P.J. (1996). Introduction: Alternative perspectives on national security. In Katzenstein, P.J. (ed.), *The Culture of National Security: Norms and Identity in World Politics*. New York/Chichester: Columbia University Press, 1–32

Kausch, K. (2018). Proxy Agents: State and Non-State Alliances in the Middle East. In Kamel, L. (ed.), *The Frailty of Authority: Borders, Non-State Actors and Power Vacuums in a Changing Middle East*. Istituto Affari Internazionali. Rome: Edizioni Nuova Cultura, 67–84

Kavkazskii uzel (2019). Young people fill the ranks of Chechen underground. 20 September. At www.eng.kavkaz-uzel.eu/articles/48527/ (accessed 29 November 2021)

Kazenin, K. and Starodubrovskaya, I. (2014). *Severnyi Kavkaz: Quo vadis?* (The North Caucasus: Quo Vadis?). Polit.ru report, at http://polit.ru/article/2014/01/14/caucasus/#ultr006 (accessed 13 August 2019, in Russian)

Kenkel, K.M. and Stefan, C.G. (2016). Brazil and the responsibility while protecting initiative: Norms and the timing of diplomatic support. *Global Governance*, 22, 41–58

Khatib, L. and Sinjab, L. (2018). *Syria's Transactional State: How the Conflict Changed the Syrian State's Exercise of Power*. London: Chatham House, research paper, October, at www.chathamhouse.org/sites/default/files/publications/research/2018-10-10-syrias-transactional-state-khatib-sinjab.pdf (accessed 10 November 2018)

Khlebnikov, A. (2022a). *Russia's Approach to Cross-Border Aid Delivery to Syria*. Russian International Affairs Council, 15 July. At https://russiancouncil.ru/en/analytics-and-comments/analytics/russia-s-approach-to-cross-border-aid-delivery-to-syria/?sphrase_id=95413157 (accessed 15 October 2022)

Khlebnikov, A. (2022b). *Changing Roles; Why Countries of Middle East May Be Future's Best-Suited Mediators?* Russian International Affairs Council, 17 October. At https://russiancouncil.ru/en/analytics-and-comments/analytics/changing-roles-why-countries-of-middle-east-may-be-future-s-best-suited-mediators/?sphrase_id=94021957 (accessed 29 November 2022)

Khlestov, O.N. (2003). The rule of international law in international and domestic state relations: The Russian doctrine of international law. *Mezhdunarodnaya zhizn'*, 12 (in Russian)

Khlestov, O.N. (2013), Rossiiskaya doktrina mezhdunarodnoga prava (The Russian doctrine of international law). *Evraziiskii juridicheskii zhurnal*, 58, 19–22 (in Russian)

Khodinskaya-Golenishcheva, M. (2018). Siriiskii krizis v transformiruyushchemsya miroporyadke: Rol' emigrantskikh oppozitsionnykh struktur (The Syrian crisis in a transforming world order: The role of émigré opposition structures). *Aziya I Afrika segodnya*, 1 (in Russian)

Khouri, R.G. (2018). *The Implications of the Syrian War for New Regional Orders in the Middle East*. MENARA working paper 12, September, at www.iai.it/sites/default/files/menara_wp_12.pdf (accessed 23 November 2018)

Kjellén, J. and Dahlqvist, N. (2019). Russia's Armed Forces in 2019. In Westerlund, F. and Oxenstierna, S. (eds), *Russian Military Capability in a Ten-Year Perspective–2019*. Swedish Defence Research Agency, FOI-R--4758--SE, December, 23–58. At www.researchgate.net/publication/337948965_Russian_Military_Capability_in_a_Ten-Year_Perspective_-_2019 (accessed 17 February 2021)

Koch, B. and Stivachtis, Y.A. (eds) (2019). *Regional Security in the Middle East: Sectors, Variables and Issues*. Bristol: E-International Relations Publishing

Kofman, M. (2019). Russian combat operations in Syria and their impact on the force. In *Russia's Policy in the Middle East: Determination, Delight, and Disappointment*. Central Asia Program CAP paper No. 212, Institute for European, Russian and Eurasian Studies, George Washington University, January, 23–27

Kokoshin, A. (2014). Providing Russia with real sovereignty in the contemporary world. *Vestnik Rossiiskoi Akademii Nauk*, 84(12), 449–455

Kolosov, V.A., Vendina, O.I., Gritsenko, A.A., Zotova, M.V. Glezer, O.B., Panin, A.A., Sebentsov, A.B. and Streletskii, V.N. (2019). Transformation policies and local modernisation initiatives in the North Caucasus. In Oskanian, K. and Averre, D. (eds), *Security, Society and the State in the Caucasus*. Abingdon and New York: Routledge, 78–101

Kortunov, A.V. (2016). The inevitable, weird world. *Russia in Global Affairs*, 25 September. At https://eng.globalaffairs.ru/number/The-Inevitable-Weird-World-18385 (accessed 27 October 2019)

Kortunov, A. (2018). Politics as continuation of war by other means? *Modern Diplomacy*, 28 October. At https://moderndiplomacy.eu/2018/10/28/politics-as-continuation-of-war-by-other-means/ (accessed 22 November 2019)

Kortunov, A.V., Hiltermann, J., Mamedov, R.Sh. and Shmeleva T.A. (2019). *Squaring the Circle: Russian and European Views on Syrian Reconstruction*. Russian International Affairs Council report 48/2019, 5 June. At https://russiancouncil.ru/en/activity/publications/squaring-the-circle-russian-and-european-views-on-syrian-reconstruction/ (accessed 24 April 2020)

Kozhanov, N. (2016). *Russia and the Syrian Conflict: Moscow's Domestic, Regional and Strategic Interests*. Berlin: Gerlach Press

Kozhanov, N. (2018). *Russian Policy Across the Middle East: Motivations and Methods*. London: Chatham House, 21 February, at www.chathamhouse

.org/publication/russian-policy-across-middle-east-motivations-and-methods (accessed 10 November 2018)

Krasner, S.D. (1999). *Sovereignty: Organized Hypocrisy*. Princeton, NJ: Princeton University Press

Kremlin (2008). The Foreign Policy Concept of the Russian Federation. 12 January. At http://en.kremlin.ru/supplement/4116 (accessed 24 June 2008)

Krickovic, A. and Weber, Y. (2018a). What can Russia teach us about change? Status-seeking as a catalyst for transformation in international politics. *International Studies Review*, 20(2), 292–300

Krickovic, A. and Weber, Y. (2018b). Commitment issues: The Syrian and Ukraine crises as bargaining failures of the post–Cold War international order. *Problems of Post-Communism*, 65(6), 373–384

Krutikhin, M. (2021). Going beyond politics: Russian energy interests in the Gulf Region. In Kozhanov, N. (ed.), *Russia's Relations with the GCC and Iran*. Singapore: Palgrave Macmillan/Springer Nature, 159–176

Kuhrt N. (2015). Russia, the Responsibility to Protect and intervention. In Fiott D. and Koops J. (eds), *The Responsibility to Protect and the Third Pillar*. London: Palgrave Macmillan, 97–114

Kuimova, A. (2019). *Russia's Arms Exports to the MENA Region: Trends and Drivers*. EuroMesco policy brief 95, 1 April, at www.euromesco.net/wp-content/uploads/2019/03/Brief95-Russia-Arms-transfer-to-the-MENA-region.pdf (accessed 30 June 2019)

Kuznetsov, V. (2015). Kto voyuet v Sirii i kogda eto zakonchitsya (Who is fighting in Syria and when it will end). *RBK Daily* 181, 5 October 2015, 3 (in Russian)

Kuznetsov, V.A. (2019). Western Asia and North Africa in the neo-modernity context. *Russia in Global Affairs*, 1, at https://eng.globalaffairs.ru/number/Western-Asia-and-North-Africa-in-the-Neo-Modernity-Context--19992 (accessed 23 June 2019)

Kuznetsov, V, Naumkin, V. and Zvyagelskaya, I. (2018). *Russia in the Middle East: The Harmony of Polyphony*. Valdai Discussion Club, May, at http://valdaiclub.com/files/18375/ (accessed 31 May 2018)

Lake, D.A. (2012). Great power hierarchies and strategies in twenty-first-century world politics. In Carlsnaes, W., Risse, T. and Simmons, B.A. (eds), *Handbook of International Relations*. 2nd edition. Los Angeles, CA: Sage, 555–577

Larin, V. (2018). *The Big Game: Beijing's Interests in the Middle East*. Valdai Club Paper, 23 February, at http://valdaiclub.com/a/highlights/the-big-game-beijing-interests-in-middle-east/ (accessed 4 May 2018)

Larson, D.W. (2018). New perspectives on rising powers and global governance: Status and clubs. *International Studies Review*, 20(2), 247–254

Lavrov, A. (2018). Russia in Syria: A military analysis. In Popescu, N. and Secrieru, S. (eds), *Russia's Return to the Middle East: Building Sandcastles?* Chaillot paper No. 146, July. Paris: EU Institute for Security Studies, 47–56

Lavrov, S.V. (2010). Russian foreign policy: Contributing to strengthening international security and stability. Article by Russian foreign minister S.V. Lavrov in the 'Diplomatic Yearbook' for 2010, 28 December. At www.mid.ru/ru/foreign_policy/news/-/asset_publisher/cKNonkJE02Bw/content/id/223322 (accessed 19 November 2019, in Russian)

Lavrov, S.V. (2011a). Interview with Rossiiskaya gazeta, 21 September. At www.mid.ru/ru/foreign_policy/news/-/asset_publisher/cKNonkJE02Bw/content/id/194822 (accessed 19 November 2019, in Russian)

Lavrov, S.V. (2011b). Interview with 'Profil' magazine, 10 October. At www.mid.ru/ru/foreign_policy/news/-/asset_publisher/cKNonkJE02Bw/content/id/191354 (accessed 6 January 2020, in Russian)

Lavrov, S.V. (2011c). Interview with Bloomberg information agency, 1 June. At www.mid.ru/ru/foreign_policy/news/-/asset_publisher/cKNonkJE02Bw/content/id/204866 (accessed 6 January 2020, in Russian)

Lavrov, S.V. (2013a). Speech and answers to the media during a press-conference on the topic of chemical weapons in Syria and the situation in the SAR. Moscow, 26 August. At www.mid.ru/ru/foreign_policy/news/-/asset_publisher/cKNonkJE02Bw/content/id/98738 (accessed 30 October 2019, in Russian)

Lavrov, S.V. (2013b). Interview with Channel 1's 'Voskresnoe vremya' programme, Moscow, 22 September. At www.mid.ru/ru/foreign_policy/news/-/asset_publisher/cKNonkJE02Bw/content/id/95878 (accessed 30 October 2019, in Russian)

Lavrov, S.V. (2013c). Interview with 'Kommersant' newspaper, Moscow, 30 September. At www.mid.ru/ru/foreign_policy/news/-/asset_publisher/cKNonkJE02Bw/content/id/94330 (accessed 30 October 2019, in Russian)

Lavrov, S.V. (2013d). Interview with News on Saturday with Sergei Bril'ev programme. 14 September. At www.mid.ru/ru/foreign_policy/news/-/asset_publisher/cKNonkJE02Bw/content/id/96638 (accessed 30 October 2013, in Russian)

Lavrov, S.V. (2013e). Speech and answers to media questions at joint press-conference with Egyptian foreign minister N. Fahmy. Moscow, 16 September. At www.mid.ru/ru/foreign_policy/news/-/asset_publisher/cKNonkJE02Bw/content/id/96590 (accessed 30 October 2019, in Russian)

Lavrov, S.V. (2013f). Interview with TV company 'Russia Today'. Bali, 8 October. At www.mid.ru/ru/foreign_policy/news/-/asset_publisher/cKNonkJE02Bw/content/id/93218 (accessed 19 November 2019, in Russian)

Lavrov, S.V. (2013g). Interview for the documentary film on Syria by Hubert Seipel for the German channel ARD (aired on 13 February, in English), 15 February. At www.mid.ru/en/foreign_policy/news/-/asset_publisher/cKNonkJE02Bw/content/id/122730 (accessed 19 November 2019)

Lavrov, S.V. (2013h). Speech at the 49th Munich conference on international security, Munich, 2 February. At www.mid.ru/ru/foreign_policy/news/-/asset_publisher/cKNonkJE02Bw/content/id/124658 (accessed 18 December 2019, in Russian)

Lavrov, S.V. (2013i). Speech at the Egmont Royal Institute of International Relations on the theme 'The role of Europe in an era of change', Brussels, 15 October. At www.mid.ru/ru/foreign_policy/news/-/asset_publisher/cKNonkJE02Bw/content/id/92354 (accessed 6 January 2020, in Russian)

Lavrov, S.V. (2013j). Interview with 'Rossiiskaya gazeta', Moscow, 19 November. At www.mid.ru/ru/foreign_policy/news/-/asset_publisher/cKNonkJE02Bw/content/id/87526 (accessed 6 January 2020, in Russian)

Lavrov, S.V. (2014a). Speech and answers to questions during a joint press-conference on the results of talks with Norwegian foreign minister B. Brende,

Moscow, 20 January. At www.mid.ru/ru/foreign_policy/news/-/asset_publisher/cKNonkJE02Bw/content/id/80074 (accessed 27 November 2019, in Russian)

Lavrov, S.V. (2014b). Speech during a high-level segment of the 25th session of the UN Human Rights Council, Geneva, 3 March. At www.mid.ru/ru/foreign_policy/news/-/asset_publisher/cKNonkJE02Bw/content/id/72642 (accessed 22 August 2014, in Russian)

Lavrov, S.V. (2014c). Interview in a special edition of 'Sunday evening with Vladimir Solov'ev' on the Russia-1 channel, Moscow, 11 April. At www.mid.ru/ru/foreign_policy/news/-/asset_publisher/cKNonkJE02Bw/content/id/66102 (accessed 22 August 2014, in Russian)

Lavrov, S.V. (2014d). Interview on programme 'The Main Thing' on Channel 5, Moscow, 28 September. At www.mid.ru/ru/foreign_policy/news/-/asset_publisher/cKNonkJE02Bw/content/id/668820 (accessed 4 January 2020, in Russian)

Lavrov, S.V. (2014e). Interview on the 'Russia Today' TV channel and 'News of the Week' programme on the 'Rossiya' channel, New York, 27 September. At www.mid.ru/ru/foreign_policy/news/-/asset_publisher/cKNonkJE02Bw/content/id/668812 (accessed 4 January 2020, in Russian)

Lavrov, S.V. (2014f). Speech and answers to participants' questions at the 50th Munich Security Policy Conference. Munich, 1 February. At www.mid.ru/ru/foreign_policy/news/-/asset_publisher/cKNonkJE02Bw/content/id/78502 (accessed 22 August 2014, in Russian)

Lavrov, S.V. (2015a). Interview with NTV Channel's 'Pozdnyakov' programme, Moscow, 13 October. At www.mid.ru/ru/foreign_policy/news/-/asset_publisher/cKNonkJE02Bw/content/id/1846271 (accessed 30 October 2019, in Russian)

Lavrov, S.V. (2015b). Speech at a meeting of the UN Security Council on the topic 'Supporting international peace and security: resolving conflicts in the Middle East and North Africa and the battle with the terrorist threat in the region', New York, 30 September. At www.mid.ru/ru/foreign_policy/news/-/asset_publisher/cKNonkJE02Bw/content/id/1819214 (accessed 30 October 2019, in Russian)

Lavrov, S.V. (2015c). Speech at a meeting of the UN Security Council after the adoption of a resolution in support of the 'Vienna process'. New York, 18 December. At www.mid.ru/ru/foreign_policy/news/-/asset_publisher/cKNonkJE02Bw/content/id/1990596 (accessed 30 October 2019, in Russian)

Lavrov, S.V. (2015d). Speech at an open meeting of the UN Security Council on the question 'Supporting international peace and security: lessons from history, affirming adherence to the principles and aims of the UN Charter'. New York, 23 February. At www.mid.ru/ru/foreign_policy/news/-/asset_publisher/cKNonkJE02Bw/content/id/959527 (accessed 18 December 2019, in Russian)

Lavrov, S.V. (2015e). Speech at the Terra Scientia Forum on the Klyaz'ma River. Vladimir region, 24 August. At www.mid.ru/ru/foreign_policy/news/-/asset_publisher/cKNonkJE02Bw/content/id/1680936 (accessed 18 December 2019, in Russian)

Lavrov, S.V. (2015f). Interview with Channel's 'Russia 24' programme 'International Review', Moscow, 29 May. At www.mid.ru/ru/foreign_policy/news/-/asset_publisher/cKNonkJE02Bw/content/id/1339440 (accessed 18 December 2019, in Russian)

Lavrov, S. (2016a). Remarks and answers to questions at a meeting with students and faculty at MGIMO University. Moscow, 1 September. At www.mid.ru/ru/foreign_policy/news/-/asset_publisher/cKNonkJE02Bw/content/id/2417731 (accessed 10 September 2018, in Russian)

Lavrov, S.V. (2016b). Interview with Channel One's Vremya programme, Moscow, 9 October. At www.mid.ru/ru/foreign_policy/news/-/asset_publisher/cKNonkJE02Bw/content/id/2494612 (accessed 31 May 2018, in Russian)

Lavrov, S. (2016c). Remarks and answers to questions at a meeting of the 'Valdai' International Discussion Club, St. Petersburg, 16 June. At www.mid.ru/ru/foreign_policy/news/-/asset_publisher/cKNonkJE02Bw/content/id/2321176 (accessed 28 November 2019, in Russian)

Lavrov, S. (2016d). Speech at the 71st Session of the UN General Assembly. New York, 23 September. At www.mid.ru/ru/foreign_policy/news/-/asset_publisher/cKNonkJE02Bw/content/id/2468262 (accessed 18 December 2019, in Russian)

Lavrov, S.V. (2016e). Interview for internet site of the Imperial Orthodox Palestine Society, Moscow, 25 July. At www.mid.ru/ru/foreign_policy/news/-/asset_publisher/cKNonkJE02Bw/content/id/2367193 (accessed 27 January 2020, in Russian)

Lavrov, S. (2017a). Remarks and answers to media questions at a joint news conference following talks with High Representative of the EU for Foreign Affairs and Security Policy Federica Mogherini, Moscow, 24 April. At www.mid.ru/en/foreign_policy/news/-/asset_publisher/cKNonkJE02Bw/content/id/2736003 (accessed 25 November 2019)

Lavrov, S. (2017b). Remarks and answers to media questions at a joint news conference on the results of talks with Afghan foreign minister S. Rabbani, Moscow, 7 February. At www.mid.ru/ru/foreign_policy/news/-/asset_publisher/cKNonkJE02Bw/content/id/2630440 (accessed 29 November 2019, in Russian)

Lavrov, S. (2017c). Remarks and answers to media questions on the results of negotiations with US Secretary of State Rex Tillerson, Washington, 10 May. At www.mid.ru/ru/foreign_policy/news/-/asset_publisher/cKNonkJE02Bw/content/id/2751328 (accessed 3 February 2020, in Russian)

Lavrov, S. (2017d). Remarks and answers to questions at a joint press-conference on the results of a meeting with Vice-Chancellor and German Federal Minister of Foreign Affairs S. Gabriel. Moscow, 9 March. At www.mid.ru/ru/foreign_policy/news/-/asset_publisher/cKNonkJE02Bw/content/id/2669210 (accessed 29 November 2019, in Russian)

Lavrov, S. (2018a). Answers to media questions on the sidelines of the 73rd Session of the UN General Assembly. New York, 28 September. At www.mid.ru/ru/foreign_policy/news/-/asset_publisher/cKNonkJE02Bw/content/id/3362656 (accessed 9 September 2019, in Russian)

Lavrov, S. (2018b). Speech and answers to media questions during a joint press-conference on the results of a meeting with Slovak Minister of Foreign and European Affairs M. Lajčák, 9 October. At www.mid.ru/ru/foreign_policy/news/-/asset_publisher/cKNonkJE02Bw/content/id/3369807 (accessed 29 November 2019, in Russian)

Lavrov, S. (2018c). Interview with RT France, Paris Match and Figaro, 18 October. At www.mid.ru/ru/foreign_policy/news/-/asset_publisher/cKNonkJE02Bw/content/id/3377331 (accessed 29 November 2019, in Russian)

Lavrov, S. (2018d). Speech at the 73rd Session of the UN General Assembly. New York, 28 September. At www.mid.ru/ru/foreign_policy/news/-/asset_publisher/cKNonkJE02Bw/content/id/3359296 (accessed 12 December 2019, in Russian)

Lavrov, S. (2018e). Interview and answers to questions for the programme 'Moscow. Kremlin. Putin' on the sidelines of the G20 summit. Buenos Aires, 2 December. At www.mid.ru/ru/foreign_policy/news/-/asset_publisher/cKNonkJE02Bw/content/id/3425025 (accessed 22 January 2020, in Russian)

Lavrov, S. (2018f). Speech at the general meeting of the Russian International Affairs Council, Moscow, 20 November. At www.mid.ru/ru/foreign_policy/news/-/asset_publisher/cKNonkJE02Bw/content/id/3413324 (accessed 12 February 2020, in Russian)

Lavrov, S. (2019a). Interview with programme on Zvezda TV channel 'The Main Thing with Ol'ga Belova'. Moscow, 21 April. At www.mid.ru/ru/foreign_policy/news/-/asset_publisher/cKNonkJE02Bw/content/id/3622162 (accessed 12 December 2019, in Russian)

Lavrov, S. (2019b). Speech and answers to questions during the 'Valdai' International Discussion Club's panel on Russia's policy in the Middle East. Sochi, 2 October. At www.mid.ru/ru/foreign_policy/news/-/asset_publisher/UdAzvXr89FbD/content/id/3826083 (accessed 4 May 2020, in Russian)

Lavrov, S. (2019c). Interview with the Asharq Al-Awsat pan-Arab daily, 3 October. At www.mid.ru/ru/foreign_policy/news/-/asset_publisher/cKNonkJE02Bw/content/id/3829601 (accessed 4 May 2020, in Russian)

Lavrov, S. (2019d). Remarks and answers to media questions during a joint news conference following talks with Turkish Foreign Minister Mevlüt Çavuşoğlu at the Joint Strategic Planning Group meeting, Antalya, 29 March. At www.mid.ru/ru/foreign_policy/news/-/asset_publisher/cKNonkJE02Bw/content/id/3593631 (accessed 2 October 2019, in Russian)

Lavrov, S. (2019e). Remarks and answers to questions during a joint news conference following talks with Secretary General of the Organisation of Islamic Cooperation Yousef Al-Othaimeen, Moscow, 3 July. At www.mid.ru/ru/foreign_policy/news/-/asset_publisher/cKNonkJE02Bw/content/id/3709117 (accessed 2 October 2019, in Russian)

Lavrov, S. (2019f). Briefing by official representative of the Russian MFA M.V. Zakharova, Moscow, 11 April. At www.mid.ru/ru/foreign_policy/news/-/asset_publisher/cKNonkJE02Bw/content/id/3612738#12 (accessed 19 November 2019, in Russian)

Lavrov, S. (2020a). Speech at the Conference on Disarmament in the high-level segment. Geneva, 25 February. At www.mid.ru/ru/foreign_policy/news/-/asset_publisher/cKNonkJE02Bw/content/id/4058832 (accessed 4 May 2020, in Russian)

Lavrov, S. (2020b). Remarks and answers to questions at a plenary session of the Raisina Dialogue international conference. New Delhi, 15 January. At www.mid.ru/ru/foreign_policy/news/-/asset_publisher/cKNonkJE02Bw/content/id/3994885 (accessed 4 May 2020, in Russian)

Lavrov, S. (2020c). Speech and answers to media questions during a joint news conference following talks with Minister of Foreign Affairs and Expatriates of the Hashemite Kingdom of Jordan Ayman Safadi. Moscow, 19 February. At www.mid.ru/ru/foreign_policy/news/-/asset_publisher/UdAzvXr89FbD/content/id/4048982 (accessed 4 May 2020, in Russian)

Lavrov, S. (2020d). Remarks at the High-Level Segment of the 43rd Regular Session of the UN Human Rights Council. Geneva, 25 February. At www.mid.ru/ru/foreign_policy/news/-/asset_publisher/cKNonkJE02Bw/content/id/4058794 (accessed 4 May 2020, in Russian)

Lavrov, S. (2020e). Remarks and at a news conference on Russia's diplomatic performance in 2019. Moscow, 17 January. At www.mid.ru/ru/foreign_policy/news/-/asset_publisher/cKNonkJE02Bw/content/id/4001740 (accessed 4 May 2020, in Russian)

Lavrov, S. (2020f). Interview with radio stations 'Sputnik', 'Komsomol'skaya Pravda' and 'Govorit Moskva'. Moscow, 14 October. At www.mid.ru/ru/foreign_policy/news/-/asset_publisher/cKNonkJE02Bw/content/id/4381977 (accessed 10 November 2020, in Russian)

Lavrov, S. (2020g). Answers to questions on the 'Great Game' programme on Channel One, Moscow, 25 April. At www.mid.ru/ru/foreign_policy/news/-/asset_publisher/cKNonkJE02Bw/content/id/4105593 (accessed 27 July 2021, in Russian)

Lavrov, S. (2021). Answers to questions during a special session of the 'Valdai' International Discussion Club's panel on the Middle East. Moscow, 31 March. At www.mid.ru/ru/foreign_policy/news/-/asset_publisher/cKNonkJE02Bw/content/id/4660109 (accessed 7 June 2021, in Russian)

Lavrov, S. (2022a). Foreign Minister Sergey Lavrov's remarks and answers to questions following a meeting of the Gulf Cooperation Council. Riyadh, 1 June. At https://mid.ru/ru/foreign_policy/news/1815613 (accessed 25 July 2022)

Lavrov, S. (2022b). Foreign Minister Sergey Lavrov's interview with the programme 60 Minutes, Moscow, 11 October. At https://mid.ru/ru/foreign_policy/news/1833291 (accessed 29 November 2022, in Russian)

Leech, P. and Gaskarth, J. (2015). British foreign policy and the Arab Spring. *Diplomacy & Statecraft*, 26(1), 139–160

Legvold, R. (ed.) (2007). *Russian Foreign Policy in the Twenty-First Century and the Shadow of the Past*. New York: Columbia University Press

Levada Center (n/d). At www.levada.ru/en/ratings/ (accessed 15 July 2021)

Levada Center (2015a). Survey carried out between 23 and 26 October 2015. Published 6 November 2015. At www.levada.ru/en/2015/11/06/russian-participation-in-the-syrian-military-conflict/ (accessed 15 July 2021)

Levada Center (2015b). Survey carried out between 2 and 5 October 2015. Published 13 October 2015. At www.levada.ru/en/2015/10/13/russian-participation-syrian-conflict (accessed 15 July 2021)

Levada Center (2016a). Survey carried out between 11 and 14 March 2016. Published 10 June 2016. At www.levada.ru/en/2016/06/10/syria-2/ (accessed 15 July 2021)

Levada Center (2016b). The results of year. 11 January. At www.levada.ru/en/2016/01/11/the-results-of-year/ (accessed 15 July 2021)

Leverett, F. (2005). *Inheriting Syria: Bashar's Trial by Fire*. Washington, DC: Brookings Institution Press.

Lewis, D. (2022). Contesting liberal peace: Russia's emerging model of conflict management. *International Affairs*, 98(2), 653–673.

Lewis, D., Heathershaw, J. and Megoran, N. (2018). Illiberal peace? Authoritarian modes of conflict management. *Cooperation and Conflict*, 53(4), 486–506

Liangxiang, J. (2020). *China and Middle East Security Issues: Challenges, Perceptions and Positions*. Istituto Affari Internazionali paper 20/23, 8 August. At www.iai.it/en/pubblicazioni/china-and-middle-east-security-issues-challenges-perceptions-and-positions (accessed 29 April 2021)

Lieven, A. (2018). The dance of the ghosts: A new Cold War with Russia will not serve Western interests. *Survival*, 60(5), 115–140

Lister, C.R. (2017). *The Syrian Jihad: The Evolution of an Insurgency*. 2nd edition. London: Hurst & Co

Lo, B. (2015). *Russia and the New World Disorder*. Baltimore, MD: Brookings Institution Press/Royal Institute of International Affairs

Lomagin, N. (2012). Interest groups in Russian foreign policy: The invisible hand of the Russian Orthodox Church. *International Politics*, 49(4), 498–516

Lons, C., Fulton, J., Sun, D. and Al-Tamini, N. (2019). *China's Great Game in the Middle East*. European Council on Foreign Relations policy brief, October. At www.ecfr.eu/publications/summary/china_great_game_middle_east (accessed 21 April 2020)

Lopes da Silva, D., Tian Nan, Béraud-Sudreau, L., Marksteiner, A. and Xiao Liang (2022). *Trends in World Military Expenditure 2021*. Stockholm International Peace Research Institute Fact Sheet, April. At www.sipri.org/sites/default/files/2022-04/fs_2204_milex_2021_0.pdf (accessed 4 May 2022)

Lounnas, D. (2018a). *Jihadist Groups in North Africa and the Sahel: Between Disintegration, Reconfiguration and Resilience*. MENARA working paper No. 16, 4 October, at www.iai.it/sites/default/files/menara_wp_16.pdf (accessed 23 November 2018)

Lounnas, D. (2018b). *The Libyan Security Continuum: The Impact of the Libyan Crisis on the North African/Sahelian Regional System*. MENARA working paper 11, October, at www.iai.it/sites/default/files/menara_wp_15.pdf (accessed 23 November 2018)

Lounnas, D. (2020). The Libyan crisis: A case of failed collective security. *Middle East Policy*, 27(2), 34–52

Lovotti, C. and Ambrosetti, E.T. (2019). How does the European Union perceive Russia's role in the MENA region? In Talbot, V. and Lovotti, C. (eds), *The Role of Russia in the Middle East and North Africa Region: Strategy or Opportunism?* Euromesco Joint Policy Study 12, April, 70–88. At www.euromesco.net/publication/the-role-of-russia-in-the-middle-east-and-north-africa-region-strategy-or-opportunism-4/ (accessed 15 April 2021)

Lucas, S., Yakinthou, C. and Wolff, S. (2016). Syria: Laying the foundations for a credible and sustainable transition. *The RUSI Journal*, 161(3) 22–32

Luck, E.C. (2015). R2P at ten: A new mindset for a new era? *Global Governance: A Review of Multilateralism and International Organizations*, 21(4), 499–504

Lukyanov, G. and Mamedov, R. (2016). *Playing Pick-Up-Sticks in Libya*. Russian International Affairs Council, 6 June. At https://russiancouncil.ru/en/analytics-and-comments/analytics/playing-pick-up-sticks-in-libya/ (accessed 22 June 2017)

Lukyanov, G. and Mamedov, R. (2017). *The Fifth Assault Corps. Back to Order in Syria?* Russian International Affairs Council, 16 June. At https://russiancouncil.ru/en/analytics-and-comments/analytics/the-fifth-assault-corps-back-to-order-in-syria-/ (accessed 11 August 2019)

Lund, A. (2019). *Russia in the Middle East*. Stockholm: The Swedish Institute of International Affairs

Lynch, A.C. (2016). The influence of regime type on Russian foreign policy toward 'the West', 1992–2015. *Communist and Post-Communist Studies*, 49(1), 101–111

Lynch, M. (2021). The Arab uprisings never ended: The enduring struggle to remake the Middle East. *Foreign Affairs*, 100(1), 111–122

Lynch, M. (2022). The end of the Middle East: How an old map distorts a new reality. *Foreign Affairs*, 101(2), 58

MacFarlane, S. Neil (2003). Russian perspectives on order and justice. In Foot, R., Gaddis, J. and Hurrell, A. (eds), *Order and Justice in International Relations*. Oxford and New York: Oxford University Press, 176–206

MacMillan, J. (2013). Intervention and the Ordering of the Modern World. *Review of International Studies*, 39(5), 1039–1056

Maier, C.S. (2000). International associationalism: The social and political premises of peacemaking after 1917 and 1945. In Kennedy, P. and Hitchcock, W.I. (eds), *From War to Peace: Altered Strategic Landscapes in the Twentieth Century*. New Haven, CT and London: Yale University Press

Makarychev, A.S. (2008). Rebranding Russia: Norms, politics and power. In Tocci, N. (ed.), (2008). *Who Is a Normative Foreign Policy Actor?* Brussels: Centre for European Policy Studies, 156–210, at http://aei.pitt.edu/32609/1/48._Who_is_a_Normative_Foreign_Policy_Actor.pdf (accessed 25 July 2017)

Makdisi, K. (2017). From transformation to maintenance of regional order. In Boserup, R.A., Hazbun, W., Makdisi, K. and Malmvig, H. (eds), *New Conflict Dynamics: Between Regional Autonomy and Intervention in the Middle East and North Africa*. Copenhagen: Danish Institute for International Studies, 93–106

Makhmutov, T. and Mamedov, R. (2017). *Proposals on Building a Regional Security System in West Asia and North Africa*. Russian International Affairs Council working paper 38, Moscow

Malashenko, A. (2020). Russia's Muslim community in the world *Ummah* (Rossiiskaya musul'manskaya obshchina v mirovoi umme). *Mirovaya ekonomika I mezhdunarodnye otnosheniya*, 64(3), 98–104 (in Russian)

Malashenko, A. V. (2013). *Russia and the Arab Spring*. Moscow: Carnegie Moscow Center, October, at https://carnegieendowment.org/files/russia_arab_spring2013.pdf (accessed 13 November 2018)

Mälksoo, L. (2015). *Russian Approaches to International Law*. Oxford: Oxford University Press

Malley, R. and Pomper, S. (2021). Accomplice to carnage: How America enables war in Yemen. *Foreign Affairs*, 100(2), 73–88

Malmlöf, T and Engvall, J. (2019). Russian armament deliveries. In Westerlund, F. and Oxenstierna, S. (eds), *Russian Military Capability in a Ten-Year Perspective – 2019*. Swedish Defence Research Agency, FOI-R--4758--SE, December, 115–136. At www.researchgate.net/publication/337948965_Russian_Military_Capability_in_a_Ten-Year_Perspective_-_2019 (accessed 17 February 2021)

Malmvig, H. (2017). Wars within wars: Regional actors' involvement in the battle for Syria. In Boserup, R.A., Hazbun, W., Makdisi, K. and Malmvig, H. (eds), *New Conflict Dynamics: Between Regional Autonomy and Intervention in the Middle East and North Africa*. Copenhagen: Danish Institute for International Studies, 67–78

Mamedov, R. (2019). *After the Caliphate: The Prospects of Russia–Iraq Relations*. Russian International Affairs Council working paper 46, Moscow

Mammadov, R. (2018). *Russia in the Middle East: Energy Forever?* The Jamestown Foundation, 8 March. At https://jamestown.org/program/russia-middle-east-energy-forever/#_ednref11 (accessed 24 February)

Marchetti, R. and Al Zahrani, Y. (2017). Hybrid partnerships in Middle East turbulence. In Kamel, L. (ed.), *The Frailty of Authority: Borders, Non-State Actors and Power Vacuums in a Changing Middle East*. Istituto Affari Internazionali. Rome: Edizioni Nuova Cultura, 107–121

Markedonov, S. (2013). *The Rise of Radical and Nonofficial Islamic Groups in Russia's Volga Region*. Washington, DC: Center for Strategic and International Studies, January

Markedonov, S. (2017). *Myanmar, Russia's Muslims, and a New Foreign Policy*. Moscow: Carnegie Moscow Center, 12 September. At https://carnegie.ru/commentary/73070 (accessed 16 August 2019)

Marochkin, S.Y. (2009). On the recent development of international law: Some Russian perspectives. *Chinese Journal of International Law*, 8(3), 695–714

Martin, I. (2022). *All Necessary Measures? The United Nations and International Intervention in Libya*. London: Hurst & Company

Martínez, J.C. and Eng, B. (2018). Stifling stateness: The Assad regime's campaign against rebel governance. *Security Dialogue*, 49(4), 235–253

Martini, A. (2020). The Syrian wars of words: International and local instrumentalisations of the war on terror. *Third World Quarterly*, 41(4), 725–743

Martini, A. (2022). Debating Syria in the Security Council: The discursive processes of legitimisation and delegitimisation of actors involved in the Syrian War. *The International Spectator*, 57(2), 18–35

McFaul, M. (2014). Moscow's choice. *Foreign Affairs*, 93(6), 167–71

McFaul, M. (2020). Putin, Putinism, and the domestic determinants of Russian foreign policy. *International Security*, 45(2), 95–139

Mead, W.M. (2014). The return of geopolitics: The revenge of the revisionist powers. *Foreign Affairs*, 93(3), 69–79

Mearsheimer, J.J. (2019). Bound to fail: The rise and fall of the liberal international order. *International Security*, 43(4), 7–50

Meddeb, H., Colombo, S. Dalacoura, K., Kamel, L. and Roy, O. (2019). Religion and politics: Religious diversity, political fragmentation and geopolitical tensions in the MENA region. In Quero, J. and Sala, C. (eds), *The MENARA Booklet for Academia*. Barcelona: CIDOB, 49–59

Mehchy, Z, Haid Haid and Khatib, L. (2020). *Assessing Control and Power Dynamics in Syria: De Facto Authorities and State Institutions*. Chatham House Research Paper Middle East and North Africa Programme, November

MEMRI (2017). *Russia In Syria: All Pain and No Gain*. The Middle East Media Research Institute, Special Dispatch No. 6880, 18 April. At www.memri.org/reports/russia-syria-all-pain-and-no-gain (accessed 12 December 2019)

Menkiszak, M, Strachota, K. and Żochowski, P. (2018). Russian losses near Deir ez-Zor – A problem for the Kremlin. OSW Commentary, 21 February, at www.osw.waw.pl/en/publikacje/analyses/2018-02-21/russian-losses-near-deir-ez-zor-a-problem-kremlin (accessed 16 April 2018)

Middle East Monitor (2022). Putin calls on Arab league summit to help establish a multipolar world order, 2 November. At www.middleeastmonitor.com/20221102-putin-calls-on-arab-league-summit-to-help-establish-multipolar-world-order (accessed 23 December 2022)

Milosevich, M. (2019). The 2010s: 'Grand strategy' or tactical opportunism? In Talbot, V. and Lovotti, C. (eds), *The Role of Russia in the Middle East and North Africa Region: Strategy or Opportunism?* Euromesco Joint Policy Study 12, European Institute of the Mediterranean (IEMed), April, 30–53. At www.euromesco.net/publication/the-role-of-russia-in-the-middle-east-and-north-africa-region-strategy-or-opportunism-4/ (accessed 15 April 2021)

MFA (Ministry of Foreign Affairs) (2012). Answers by Russian foreign minister S.V. Lavrov to media questions on the results of the Russia-EU summit, Brussels, 21 December. At www.mid.ru/ru/foreign_policy/news/-/asset_publisher/cKNonkJE02Bw/content/id/128518 (accessed 30 October 2019, in Russian)

MFA (Ministry of Foreign Affairs) (2013a). Interview of deputy minister of foreign affairs G.M. Gatilov to RIA Novosti, 13 December. At www.mid.ru/ru/foreign_policy/news/-/asset_publisher/cKNonkJE02Bw/content/id/84018 (accessed 30 October 2019, in Russian)

MFA (Ministry of Foreign Affairs) (2013b). Comment by information and press department of the Russian MFA concerning possible US coercive action against Syria, 4 September. At www.mid.ru/ru/foreign_policy/news/-/asset_publisher/cKNonkJE02Bw/content/id/98022 (accessed 6 January 2020, in Russian)

MFA (Ministry of Foreign Affairs) (2014). Interview of Russia's Permanent Representative at the United Nations department in Geneva A.N. Borodavkin to ITAR-TASS Agency, 26 September. At www.mid.ru/ru/foreign_policy/news/-/asset_publisher/cKNonkJE02Bw/content/id/669020 (accessed 7 January 2020, in Russian)

MFA (Ministry of Foreign Affairs) (2015a). Speech by moderator of intra-Syrian consultative meeting in the 'Moscow platform' V.V. Naumkin, Moscow, 29 January. At www.mid.ru/ru/foreign_policy/news/-/asset_publisher/cKNonkJE02Bw/content/id/916441 (accessed 30 October 2019, in Russian)

MFA (Ministry of Foreign Affairs) (2015b). Moscow platform. Positions on which mutual agreement reached at second intra-Syrian consultative meeting, Moscow, 9 April. At www.mid.ru/ru/foreign_policy/news/-/asset_publisher/cKNonkJE02Bw/content/id/1157887 (accessed 30 October 2019, in Russian)

MFA (Ministry of Foreign Affairs) (2015c). Statement by official representative of the Russian MFA M.V. Zakharova on coordinating efforts to fight Islamic State, 7 October. At www.mid.ru/ru/foreign_policy/news/-/asset_publisher/cKNonkJE02Bw/content/id/1831095 (accessed 30 October 2019, in Russian)

MFA (Ministry of Foreign Affairs) (2016a). Comment by information and press department of the Russian MFA in connection with a decision of the OPCW on Syria, 12 November. At www.mid.ru/ru/foreign_policy/news/-/asset_publisher/cKNonkJE02Bw/content/id/2520020 (accessed 25 November 2019, in Russian)

MFA (Ministry of Foreign Affairs) (2016b). Statement and answers to media questions by official representative of the Russian MFA M.V. Zakharova in connection with air strikes on the Syrian army in the town of Deir-ez-Zor on 17 September 2016 by a coalition headed by the US, 18 September. At www.mid.ru/ru/foreign_policy/news/-/asset_publisher/cKNonkJE02Bw/content/id/2444387 (accessed 28 November 2019, in Russian)

MFA (Ministry of Foreign Affairs) (2016c). Joint declaration of the foreign ministers of the Islamic Republic of Iran, the Russian Federation and the Republic of Turkey on agreed measures to revitalise the political process with the aim of ending the Syria conflict, Moscow, 20 December. At www.mid.ru/ru/foreign_policy/news/-/asset_publisher/cKNonkJE02Bw/content/id/2573489 (accessed 28 November 2019, in Russian)

MFA (Ministry of Foreign Affairs) (2016d). Foreign policy concept of the Russian Federation (approved by President of the Russian Federation Vladimir Putin on November 30, 2016), 1 December. At www.mid.ru/en/foreign_policy/official_documents/-/asset_publisher/CptICkB6BZ29/content/id/2542248 (accessed 5 January 2020)

MFA (Ministry of Foreign Affairs) (2016e). Remarks by Deputy Foreign Minister Gennadii Gatilov at the High-Level Meeting on Global Responsibility Sharing for Syrian Refugees, Geneva, 30 March. At www.mid.ru/ru/foreign_policy/news/-/asset_publisher/cKNonkJE02Bw/content/id/2193224 (accessed 12 February 2021, in Russian)

MFA (Ministry of Foreign Affairs) (2017a). Briefing by official representative of the Russian MFA M.V. Zakharova, Moscow, 5 April. At www.mid.ru/ru/foreign_policy/news/-/asset_publisher/cKNonkJE02Bw/content/id/2717014 (accessed 25 November 2019, in Russian)

MFA (Ministry of Foreign Affairs) (2017b). Briefing by official representative of the Russian MFA M.V. Zakharova, Vladivostok, 8 June. At www.mid.ru/ru/foreign_policy/news/-/asset_publisher/cKNonkJE02Bw/content/id/2778888 (accessed 29 November 2019, in Russian)

MFA (Ministry of Foreign Affairs) (2017c). Joint statement of Iran, Russia and Turkey on the results of the international meeting on Syria in Astana on 23–24 January 2017, 26 January. At www.mid.ru/ru/foreign_policy/news/-/asset

_publisher/cKNonkJE02Bw/content/id/2610777 (accessed 29 November 2019, in Russian)

MFA (Ministry of Foreign Affairs) (2017d). Concept paper on the joint group (agreed as a result of the international meeting on Syria in Astana on 16 February 2017), 17 February. At www.mid.ru/ru/foreign_policy/news/-/asset_publisher/cKNonkJE02Bw/content/id/2647737 (accessed 29 November 2019, in Russian)

MFA (Ministry of Foreign Affairs) (2017e). Memorandum of the creation of de-escalation zones in the Syrian Arab Republic, 6 May. At www.mid.ru/ru/foreign_policy/news/-/asset_publisher/cKNonkJE02Bw/content/id/2746041 (accessed 29 November 2019, in Russian)

MFA (Ministry of Foreign Affairs) (2018a). Interview of Russian deputy foreign minister S.V. Vershinin, 8 October. At www.mid.ru/ru/foreign_policy/news/-/asset_publisher/cKNonkJE02Bw/content/id/3369410 (accessed 29 November 2019, in Russian)

MFA (Ministry of Foreign Affairs) (2018b). Briefing by official representative of the Russian MFA M.V. Zakharova, Moscow, 17 October. At www.mid.ru/ru/foreign_policy/news/-/asset_publisher/cKNonkJE02Bw/content/id/3377309 (accessed 2 December 2019, in Russian)

MFA (Ministry of Foreign Affairs) (2018c). Final statement of the Congress of the Syrian National Dialogue, Sochi, 30 January. At www.mid.ru/ru/foreign_policy/news/-/asset_publisher/cKNonkJE02Bw/content/id/3046246 (accessed 29 November 2019, in Russian)

MFA (Ministry of Foreign Affairs) (2019a). Comment by information and press department of the Russian MFA on the situation at the OPCW, 26 March. At www.mid.ru/ru/foreign_policy/news/-/asset_publisher/cKNonkJE02Bw/content/id/3591569 (accessed 25 November 2019, in Russian)

MFA (Ministry of Foreign Affairs) (2019b). Briefing by official representative of the Russian MFA M.V. Zakharova, Moscow, 8 May. At www.mid.ru/ru/foreign_policy/news/-/asset_publisher/cKNonkJE02Bw/content/id/3639606#6 (accessed 2 December 2019, in Russian)

MFA (Ministry of Foreign Affairs) (2019c). Comment by the Information and Press Department on the mechanism for the cross-border delivery of humanitarian aid to the Syrian Arab Republic, 23 December. At www.mid.ru/ru/foreign_policy/news/-/asset_publisher/cKNonkJE02Bw/content/id/3975548 (accessed 4 May 2020, in Russian)

MFA (Ministry of Foreign Affairs) (2019d). Briefing by official representative of the Russian MFA M.V. Zakharova, Moscow, 28 February. At www.mid.ru/ru/foreign_policy/news/-/asset_publisher/cKNonkJE02Bw/content/id/3549162 (accessed 2 December 2019, in Russian)

MFA (Ministry of Foreign Affairs) (2019e). Briefing by official representative of the Russian MFA M.V. Zakharova, Yalta, 18 April. At www.mid.ru/ru/foreign_policy/news/-/asset_publisher/cKNonkJE02Bw/content/id/3619482 (accessed 2 December 2019, in Russian)

MFA (Ministry of Foreign Affairs) (2020a). On Russia's position at the 75th session of the UN General Assembly, 23 July. At www.mid.ru/ru/foreign_policy/news/-/

asset_publisher/cKNonkJE02Bw/content/id/4252717 (accessed 27 July 2021, in Russian)

MFA (Ministry of Foreign Affairs) (2020b). On the cross-border delivery mechanism for humanitarian aid to the Syrian Arab Republic, 15 July. At www.mid.ru/ru /foreign_policy/news/-/asset_publisher/cKNonkJE02Bw/content/id/4232110 (accessed 27 July 2021)

MFA (Ministry of Foreign Affairs) (2020c). Briefing by official representative of the Russian MFA M.V. Zakharova, Moscow, 20 February. At www.mid.ru/ru /foreign_policy/news/-/asset_publisher/cKNonkJE02Bw/content/id/4050747 (accessed 4 May 2020, in Russian)

Miskimmon, A. and O'Loughlin, B. (2017). Russia's narratives of global order: Great power legacies in a polycentric world. *Politics and Governance*, 5(3), 111–120

Miskimmon, A., O'Loughlin, B. and Roselle, L. (2014). *Strategic Narratives: Communication Power and the New World Order*. New York: Routledge

Mokhova, I.M. (2013). *Obraz Rossii v arabskom mire: Ot sovetsko-arabskoi druzhby do problem poiska novogo obraza* (Russia's image in the Arab world: from Soviet-Arab friendship to the problematic search for a new image). Middle East Institute, 1 February. At www.iimes.ru/?tag=%D0%B8-%D0%BC%D0 %BE%D1%85%D0%BE%D0%B2%D0%B0 (accessed 10 August 2020, in Russian)

Monaghan, A. (2016). *Russian State Mobilization: Moving the Country on to a War Footing*. Chatham House Russia and Eurasia Programme Research Paper, May. At www.chathamhouse.org/sites/default/files/publications/research/2016-05-20 -russian-state-mobilization-monaghan-2.pdf (accessed 23 February 2021)

Monaghan, A. (2018). From plans to strategy: Mobilization as Russian Grand Strategy. In Deni, J. (ed.), *Current Russian Military Affairs: Assessing and Countering Russian Strategy, Operational Planning, and Modernization*. U.S. Army War College Strategic Studies Institute, July

Monaghan, A. (2019). *Dealing with the Russians*. Cambridge and Medford, MA: Polity Press

Monier, E. (2015). Introduction: Narratives of (in)security and (in)stability in the Middle East. In Monier, E. (ed.), *Regional Insecurity After the Arab Uprisings: Narratives of Security and Threat*. New York and Basingstoke: Palgrave Macmillan, 1–15

Moore, C. (2015). Foreign bodies: Transnational activism, the insurgency in the North Caucasus and 'beyond'. *Terrorism and Political Violence*, 27(3), 395–415

Moore, C. and Tumelty, P. (2008). Foreign fighters and the case of Chechnya: A critical assessment. *Studies in Conflict & Terrorism*, 31(5), 412–433

Moore, C. and Youngman, M. (2017). 'Russian-Speaking' Fighters in Syria, Iraq and at Home: Consequences and Context. Centre for Research and Evidence on Security Threats policy brief, 20 November, at https://crestresearch.ac.uk/ resources/russian-speaking-fighters-full-report/ (accessed 13 August 2019)

Moran, J. (2017). *No Longer a New Kid on the Block: China in the Middle East*. Brussels: Centre for European Policy Studies Commentary, 29 November, at www.ceps.eu/system/files/JM_ChinaMiddleEast.pdf (accessed 16 February 2018)

Bibliography 247

Morris, J. (2005). Normative innovation and the great powers. In Bellamy, A.J. (ed.), *International Society and Its Critics*. Oxford: Oxford University Press, 265–281

Morris, J. (2017). The Responsibility to Protect: A long view. In Hehir, A. and Murray, R.W. (eds), *Protecting Human Rights in the 21st Century*. Abingdon and New York: Routledge

Morozova, N. (2015). *Particularism and Universalism in Russian Post-Soviet Foreign Policy: Russia's Discourse on Humanitarian Cooperation in the CIS*. Higher School of Economics Research Paper No. WP BRP, 24

Morozova, N. (2018). Resisting the West, forging regional consensus: Russia's discourse on humanitarian cooperation in the commonwealth of independent states. *Geopolitics*, 23(2), 354–377

Mueller, K.P., Wasser, B., Martini, J. and Watt, S. (2017). *U.S. Strategic Interests in the Middle East and Implications for the Army*. Rand Corporation Perspective

Mukhin, V. (2020). V Krasnom more gotovyat platsdarm dly atomnykh submarine Rossii (Base for Russian nuclear submarines under preparation in the Red Sea). *Nezavisimaya gazeta*, 13 November, 2

Münster, A. (2014). *Transnational Islam in Russia and Crimea*. London: Chatham House Russia and Eurasia Programme, November

Murray, R.W. (2017). Humanitarian intervention in post-American international society. In Hehir, A. and Murray, R.W. (eds), *Protecting Human Rights in the 21st Century*. Abingdon and New York: Routledge

Nakhle, C. (2018). Russia's energy diplomacy in the Middle East. In Popescu, N. and Secrieru, S. (eds), *Russia's Return to the Middle East: Building Sandcastles?* Chaillot paper No. 146, July. Paris: EU Institute for Security Studies, 29–36

Naumkin, V. (2014). Tsivilizatsii i krizis natsii-gosudarstv (Civilisations and the crisis of nation-states). *Rossiya v Global'noi Politike*, 12(1), 41–58. At https://globalaffairs.ru/number/Tcivilizatcii-i-krizis-natcii-gosudarstv-16393 (accessed 26 January 2020, in Russian)

Naumkin, V. (2017a). *Qatar Crisis: What's Next?* Russian International Affairs Council, 13 June. At https://russiancouncil.ru/en/analytics-and-comments/analytics/qatar-srisis-what-s-next-/ (accessed 22 June 2017)

Naumkin, V. (2017b). Real'nost i teoriya (Reality and theory). *Mezhdunarodnye protsessy*, 15(2), 27–43 (retrieved from EastView database, in Russian)

Naumkin, V. (2018). *U Rossii ogromnyi opyt raboty s konfliktuyushchimi storonami* (Moscow has a huge experience of working with conflicting parties). Russian International Affairs Council, 16 February. At https://russiancouncil.ru/analytics-and-comments/comments/u-rossii-ogromnyy-opyt-raboty-s-konfliktuyushchimi-storonami/?sphrase_id=90745215 (in Russian)

Naumkin V., Kuznetsov V., Soukhov N. and Zvyagelskaya I. (2016). *The Middle East in a Time of Troubles: Traumas of the Past and Challenges of the Future*. Valdai Discussion Club, August, at http://valdaiclub.com/files/11592/ (accessed 10 September 2017)

Naumkin, V., Aksenenok, A., Dolgov, B., Zvyagelskaya, I., Kuznetsov, V. and Popov, V. (2013). *Islam in Politics: Ideology or Pragmatism?* Valdai Discussion Club analytical report, August. At http://valdaiclub.com/files/11450/ (accessed 13 November 2018)

Negrón-Gonzales, M. and Contarino, M. (2014). Local norms matter: Understanding national responses to the Responsibility to Protect. *Global Governance: A Review of Multilateralism and International Organizations*, 20(2), 255–276

Newman, E. and Stefan, C.G. (2020). Normative power Europe? The EU's embrace of the responsibility to protect in a transitional international order. *Journal of Common Market Studies*, 58(2), 472–490.

Newman, E. and Zala, B. (2018). Rising powers and order contestation: Disaggregating the normative from the representational. *Third World Quarterly*, 39(5), 871–888

Neyaskin, G. (2012). *Stat'ya Putina o vneshnei politike: 'Ne mogu ponyat', otkuda takoi voinstvennyi zud'* (I can't understand why they have this itch to go to war). Republic.ru, 27 February. At https://republic.ru/posts/l/756601 (accessed 29 November 2020, in Russian)

Nizameddin, T. (2013). *Putin's New Order in the Middle East*. London: Hurst

Notte, H. (2015). *New 'Axis of Resistance'? Why Russia Avoids Full Identification with the Syrian-Iranian Alliance*. Russian International Affairs Council, 15 December. At https://russiancouncil.ru/en/analytics-and-comments/columns/digest/new-axis-of-resistance-why-russia-avoids-full-identification/?sphrase_id=210262 (accessed 11 August 2019)

Notte, H. (2020). The United States, Russia, and Syria's chemical weapons: A tale of cooperation and its unravelling. *The Nonproliferation Review*, 27(1–3), 201–224

Novye Izvestiya (2017). *Eksperty –o Sirii: Voina konchaetsia, no ugroza ostalas'* (Experts on Syria: the war is coming to an end but the threat remains), 21 November (retrieved from EastView database 12 December 2019, in Russian)

The Observer (2021). Assad needs to pay for his decade of butchery. 21 March, 44

Oeter, S. (2019). Conflicting norms, values, and interests: A perspective from legal academia. *Ethics & International Affairs*, 33(1), 57–66

O'Hagan, J. (2005). The question of culture. In Bellamy, A.J. (ed.), *International Society and Its Critics*. Oxford: Oxford University Press, 209–228

OIC (Organisation of Islamic Cooperation) (2020). *Al-Othaimeen: 'We Cooperate with Russia on Issues of Interreligious and Intercultural Dialogue and on Counter-Terrorism'*. At www.oic-oci.org/topic/?t_id=23582&ref=14068&lan=en (accessed 16 August 2021)

Okyay, A.S. (2017). Turkey's post-2011 approach to its Syrian border and its implications for domestic politics. *International Affairs*, 93(4), 829–846

Öniş, Z. and Yılmaz, Ş. (2016). Turkey and Russia in a shifting global order: Cooperation, conflict and asymmetric interdependence in a turbulent region. *Third World Quarterly*, 37(1), 71–95

OPCW (Organisation for the Prohibition of Chemical Weapons) (2020). *First Report by the OPCW Investigation and Identification Team 'Addressing the Threat from Chemical Weapons Use'*, OPCW Technical Secretariat, S/1867/2020, 8 April. At www.opcw.org/iit (accessed 4 May 2020)

Orlov, P. (2012). *Za veskh, kto protiv* (For all who are against). *Trud*, No. 109, 3 August, 2 (retrieved from EastView database, in Russian)

Ottaway, M. and Carothers, T. (2004). *The Greater Middle East Initiative: Off to a False Start*. Washington, DC: Carnegie Endowment for International Peace, 29 March. At https://carnegieendowment.org/files/Policybrief29.pdf (accessed 20 November 2019)

Owen, C., Heathershaw, J. and Savin, I. (2018). How postcolonial is post-Western IR? Mimicry and mētis in the international politics of Russia and Central Asia. *Review of International Studies*, 44(2), 279–300

Oxenstierna, S. (2019). The economy and military expenditure. In Westerlund, F. and Oxenstierna, S. (eds), *Russian Military Capability in a Ten-Year Perspective–2019*. Swedish Defence Research Agency, FOI-R--4758--SE, December, 97–114. At www.researchgate.net/publication/337948965_Russian_Military_Capability_in_a_Ten-Year_Perspective_-_2019 (accessed 17 February 2021)

Oxenstierna, S. and Westerlund, F. (2019). Introduction. In Westerlund, F. and Oxenstierna, S. (eds), *Russian Military Capability in a Ten-Year Perspective – 2019*. Swedish Defence Research Agency, FOI-R--4758--SE, December, 17–22. At www.researchgate.net/publication/337948965_Russian_Military_Capability_in_a_Ten-Year_Perspective_-_2019 (accessed 17 February 2021)

Özçelik, A.O. (2019). A litmus test for Europe: EU Mediterranean politics after the Arab Spring. In Çakmak, C. and Özçelik, A.O. (eds), *The World Community and the Arab Spring*. Cham: Palgrave Macmillan, 41–62

Ozerov, O. (2016). Rossiya i budushchee Blizhnego Vostoka (Russia and the future of the Middle East). *Mezhdunarodnaya zhizn'*, 4, 74–89 (in Russian)

Paphiti, A. and Bachmann, S.D. (2018). Syria: A legacy of Western foreign-policy failure. *Middle East Policy*, 25(2), 136–162

Parasiliti, A., Reedy, K. and Wasser, B. (2017). *Preventing State Collapse in Syria*. Santa Monica: RAND National Defense Research Institute. At www.rand.org/pubs/perspectives/PE219.html (accessed 20 November 2019)

Pearson, W.R., Tol, G., Stein, A. and Hintz, L. (2018). Turkey's emerging role in the Middle East. *Middle East Policy*, 25(2), 5–26

Petrov, E. (2000). Doktrina Putina? (The Putin doctrine?). *Nezavisimaya voennoe obozrenie*, 2 February

Petrov, N. (2017). The elite. New wine into old bottles? *Russian Politics & Law*, 55(2), 115–132

Petrov, N. and Gel'man, V. (2019). Do elites matter in Russian foreign policy? The gap between self-perception and influence. *Post-Soviet Affairs*, 35(5–6), 450–460

Phillips, C. (2015). Sectarianism and conflict in Syria. *Third World Quarterly*, 36(2), 357–376

Phillips, C. (2016). *The Battle for Syria: International Rivalry in the New Middle East*. New Haven and London: Yale University Press

Phillips, C. (2019). Structure, agency and external involvement in the Syria conflict. In *Shifting Global Politics and the Middle East*, Project on Middle East Political Science Studies 34, March

Phillips, C. (2021). Syria: Is Biden's withdrawal the next move? *Middle East Eye*, 23 September. At www.middleeasteye.net/opinion/syria-us-troops-withdrawal-biden-next-move (accessed 10 November 2021)

Physicians for Human Rights (2021). At http://syriamap.phr.org/#/en/findings (accessed 6 July 2021)

Pieper, M. (2014). Chinese, Russian, and Turkish policies in the Iranian nuclear dossier: Between resistance to hegemony and hegemonic accommodation. *Asian Journal of Peacebuilding*, 2(1), 17–36

Pieper, M. (2019) 'Rising power' status and the evolution of international order: Conceptualising Russia's Syria policies. *Europe-Asia Studies*, 71(3), 365–387

Pierini, M. (2019). *Four Game Changers in Europe's South*. Carnegie Europe, 26 February, at https://carnegieeurope.eu/strategiceurope/78447 (accessed 7 July 2019)

Popescu, N. and Secrieru, S. (eds) (2018). *Russia's Return to the Middle East: Building Sandcastles?* Chaillot paper No. 146, July. Paris: EU Institute for Security Studies

Posch, W. (2017). Ideology and strategy in the Middle East: The case of Iran. *Survival*, 59(5), 69–98

Posch, W. (2019). Iran's Islamic Revolution at 40: On the Way to a Post-Revolutionary Society. Istituto Affari Internazionali commentary 19/22, March. At www.iai.it/en/pubblicazioni/irans-islamic-revolution-40-way-post-revolutionary-society (accessed 13 May 2019)

Poti, L. (2018). *Russian Policies Towards the MENA Region*. MENARA working papers, No. 9, July

Pravda (2013). *Protiv Sirii – i terroristy, i 'bortsy s terrorizmom'* (Terrorists and 'fighters against terrorism' are both lining up against Syria). No. 35, 2 April, 1 (retrieved from EastView database 12 December 2019, in Russian)

President of Russia (2011). Statement by the President of Russia on the situation in Libya. 25 February. At http://en.kremlin.ru/events/president/news/10439 (accessed 4 May 2018)

President of Russia (2013). Draft Federal law 'On introducing changes in certain legislative acts of the Russian Federation. PR-2242, 26 September

President of Russia (2016). Expanded meeting of the Defence Ministry Board, Moscow, 22 December. At http://en.kremlin.ru/events/president/news/53571 22.12.2016 (accessed 28 November 2019)

President of the Russian Federation (2022). Decree of the President of the Russian Federation dated September 5, 2022 No. 611 'On Approval of the Concept of Humanitarian Policy of the Russian Federation Abroad'. At http://publication.pravo.gov.ru/Document/View/0001202209050019 (accessed 29 November 2022, in Russian).

Primakov, E. (2011). 'Arabskaya vesna' i teoriya stolknoveniya tsivilizatsii (The 'Arab Spring' and the clash of civilisations). *Rossiiskaya gazeta*, 27 July, 6 (in Russian)

Pukhov, R. (2017). Moscow-based think tank director: Russia's unexpected military victory in Syria. *Defense News*, 11 December. At https://eng.globalaffairs.ru/articles/moscow-based-think-tank-director-russias-unexpected-military-victory-in-syria/ (accessed 6 August 2020)

Putin, V. (2012a). Being strong: Why Russia needs to rebuild its military. *Foreign Policy*, 21 February. At https://foreignpolicy.com/2012/02/21/being-strong/ (accessed 29 January 2020)
Putin, V. (2012b). Address to the Federal Assembly. Moscow, 12 December. At http://en.kremlin.ru/events/president/news/17118 (accessed 29 January 2020)
Putin, V. (2013a). Interview to Channel One and Associated Press news agency. 4 September. At https://genius.com/Vladimir-putin-interview-to-channel-one-and-associated-press-09-03-2013-annotated (accessed 18 August 2023)
Putin, V. (2013b). Speech at a meeting with muftis from Russia's Muslim spiritual administrations. 22 October. At http://en.kremlin.ru/events/president/transcripts/19474 (accessed 20 January 2020)
Putin, V. (2013c). Presidential Address to the Federal Assembly. Moscow, 12 December. At http://en.kremlin.ru/events/president/news/19825 (accessed 28 May 2015)
Putin, V. (2014). Meeting of the Valdai International Discussion Club. Sochi, 24 October. At http://en.kremlin.ru/events/president/news/46860 (accessed 20 November 2014)
Putin, V. (2015a). Address at 70th session of the UN General Assembly, New York. 28 September. At http://en.kremlin.ru/events/president/news/50385 (accessed 5 January 2016)
Putin, V. (2015b). Presidential address to the Federal Assembly. At http://en.kremlin.ru/events/president/news/50864 (accessed 20 January 2020)
Putin, V. (2016a). Vladimir Putin answered questions from Russian journalists, 16 October. At http://en.kremlin.ru/events/president/news/53103 (accessed 28 November 2019)
Putin, V. (2016b). Vladimir Putin's annual news conference, Moscow, 23 December. At http://en.kremlin.ru/events/president/news/53573 (accessed 28 November 2019)
Putin, V. (2018). Direct line with Vladimir Putin. Moscow, 7 June. At http://en.kremlin.ru/events/president/news/57692 (accessed 17 November 2020)
Putin, V. (2019). Interview with *The Financial Times*. Moscow, 27 June. At http://en.kremlin.ru/events/president/news/60836 (accessed 4 May 2020)
Pynnöniemi, K. (2018). Russia's national security strategy: Analysis of conceptual evolution. *The Journal of Slavic Military Studies*, 31(2), 240–256
Pynnöniemi, K. (2019). Information-psychological warfare in Russian strategic thinking. In Kanet, R.E. (ed.), *Routledge Handbook of Russian Security*. Abingdon and New York: Routledge, 214–226
Quandt, W.B. (2014). U.S. Policy and the Arab Revolutions of 2011. In Gerges, F.A. (ed.), *The New Middle East: Protest and Revolution in the Arab World*. New York: Cambridge University Press, 418–428
Quero, J. and Sala, C. (eds) (2019). *The MENARA Booklet for Academia*. Barcelona: CIDOB
Radio Free Europe (2012). *Kadyrov's 'Chechen Sufism' Accommodates Christmas Trees, 'Holy Water'*. RFE/RL Caucasus report, 16 January. At www.rferl.org/a/kadyrovs_chechen_sufism_accomodates_christmas_trees_holy_water/24453480.html (accessed 17 February 2021)

Ralph, J., Holland, J. and Zhekova, K. (2017). Before the vote: UK foreign policy discourse on Syria 2011–13. *Review of International Studies*, 43(5), 875–897

Ramani, S. (2019a). *Sada: Moscow's Hand in Sudan's Future*. Carnegie Endowment for International Peace, 11 July, at https://carnegieendowment.org/sada/79488 (accessed 16 July 2019)

Ramani, S. (2019b). *Russia's Cautious Calculus in Algeria*. Carnegie Endowment for International Peace, 22 March, at https://carnegieendowment.org/sada/78667 (accessed 21 June 2019)

Ramani, S. (2020). Russia and the UAE: An ideational partnership. *Middle East Policy*, 27(1), 125–140

Rashed, D. (2019). Geography, resources and the geopolitics of Middle East conflicts. In Koch, B. and Stivachtis, Y.A. (eds), *Regional Security in the Middle East: Sectors, Variables and Issues*. Bristol: E-International Relations Publishing, 131–145

Ratelle, J.F. (2016). North Caucasian foreign fighters in Syria and Iraq: Assessing the threat of returnees to the Russian Federation. *Caucasus Survey*, 4(3), 218–238

Renz, B. (2018). *Russia's Military Revival*. Cambridge and Medford MA: Polity Press

Renz, B. (2019). Russian responses to the changing character of war. *International Affairs*, 95(4), 817–834

Reus-Smit, C. (2001). Human rights and the social construction of sovereignty. *Review of International Studies*, 27(4), 519–538

Reus-Smit, C. (2005a). Liberal hierarchy and the licence to use force. *Review of International Studies*, 31(S1), 71–92

Reus-Smit, C. (2005b). The constructivist challenge after September 11. In Bellamy, A.J. (ed.), *International Society and Its Critics*. Oxford: Oxford University Press, 81–94

Reus-Smit, C. (2018). *On Cultural Diversity: International Theory in a World of Difference*. Cambridge: Cambridge University Press

Reuters (2018). U.N. says Astana meeting on Syria a missed opportunity, no progress. *Reuters World News*, 29 November. At www.reuters.com/article/uk-mideast-crisis-syria-talks/u-n-says-astana-meeting-on-syria-a-missed-opportunity-no-progress-idUSKCN1NY0VS (accessed 29 November 2019)

RIA Novosti (2016). *Dogovor o razmeshchenii aviagruppy v SAR zaklyuchen na bessrochnyi period* (Agreement on deployment of aviation group in Syria concluded for an indefinite period). 14 January. At https://ria.ru/20160114/1359734984.html (accessed 27 November 2019, in Russian)

Richmond, O.P. and Tellidis, I. (2014). Emerging actors in international peacebuilding and statebuilding: Status quo or critical states? *Global Governance: A Review of Multilateralism and International Organizations*, 20(4), 563–584

Richter, J. (2008). Integration from below? The disappointing effort to promote civil society in Russia. In Blum, D.W. (ed.), *Russia and Globalization: Identity, Security and Society in an Era of Change*. Washington, DC: Woodrow Wilson Center Press and Baltimore, MD: The Johns Hopkins University Press, 181–203

Risse-Kappen,T. (1994). Ideas do not float freely: Transnational coalitions, domestic structures, and the end of the Cold War. *International Organization*, 48(2), 185–214

Robinson, N. (2017). Russian neo-patrimonialism and Putin's 'cultural turn'. *Europe-Asia Studies*, 69(2), 348–366

Rodkiewicz, W. (2019). *Russia vis-à-vis Iran*. OSW Commentary, 31 January, at www.osw.waw.pl/en/publikacje/osw-commentary/2019-01-31/russia-vis-a-vis-iran (accessed 21 June 2019)

Romanova, T. (2018). Russia's neorevisionist challenge to the liberal international order. *The International Spectator*, 53(1), 76–91

Rosatom (2021). *Projects*. At https://rosatom.ru/en/investors/projects/ (accessed 29 November 2021)

Roth, A. (2019). 'We aren't dangerous': Why Chechnya has welcomed women who joined caliphate. *The Guardian*, 2 March, 41

Roth, A. and Sauer, P. (2022). Who has Putin's ear? *The Observer*, 3 April, 31–34

Rouhi, M. (2018). US–Iran tensions and the oil factor. *Survival*, 60(5), 33–40

Rüma, İ. and Çelikpala, M. (2019). Russian and Turkish foreign policy activism in the Syrian theater. *Uluslararasi Iliskiler*, 16(62), 65–84

Russell, J. (2009). The geopolitics of terrorism: Russia's conflict with Islamic extremism. *Eurasian Geography and Economics*, 50(2), 184–196

Russell, M. (2016). *Russia's Humanitarian Aid Policy*. European Parliamentary Research Service, PE 582.039, May, at www.europarl.europa.eu/RegData/etudes/ATAG/2016/582039/EPRS_ATA(2016)582039_EN.pdf (accessed 5 July 2017)

Russian Direct Investment Fund (2021). *RDIF Partnerships*. At https://rdif.ru/Eng_Partnership/ (accessed 10 September 2021)

Russian Foreign Trade (2020). At https://en.russian-trade.com (accessed 24 February 2021)

Russian NGOs (Russian Non-Governmental Organisations and Human Rights Defenders) (2021). *A Devastating Decade: Violations of Human Rights and Humanitarian Law in the Syrian War* (accessed 11 October 2021)

Sadiki, L. (ed.) (2015). *Routledge Handbook of the Arab Spring: Rethinking Democratization*. Abingdon and New York: Routledge

Safi, M. (2020). Life has got worse since Arab spring, say people across Middle East. *The Guardian*, 17 December. At www.theguardian.com/global-development/2020/dec/17/arab-spring-people-middle-east-poll (accessed 15 March 2021)

Sakwa, R. (2011). Russia's identity: Between the 'domestic' and the 'international'. *Europe-Asia Studies*, 63(6), 957–975

Sakwa, R. (2015). Dualism at home and abroad: Russian foreign policy neo-revisionism and bicontinentalism. In Cadier, D. and Light, M. (ed.), *Russia's Foreign Policy: Ideas, Domestic Politics and External Relations*. Basingstoke and New York: Palgrave Macmillan, 65–79

Sakwa, R. (2017). *Russia Against the Rest: The Post-Cold War Crisis of World Order*. Cambridge: Cambridge University Press

Salahi, A. (2020). Is Assad now a liability? The mysterious Russian media campaign against Syria's dictator. *The New Arab*, 1 May. At https://english.alaraby.co.uk

/english/indepth/2020/5/1/is-syrias-assad-now-a-liability-to-russia (accessed 9 July 2020)

Salamey, I. (2015). Post-Arab Spring: Changes and challenges. *Third World Quarterly*, 36(1), 111–129

Salisbury, P. (2016). *Yemen: Stemming the Rise of a Chaos State*. Chatham House Middle East and North Africa Programme research paper, May. At www.chathamhouse.org/sites/default/files/publications/research/2016-05-25-yemen-stemming-rise-of-chaos-state-salisbury.pdf (accessed 5 July 2017)

Salisbury, P. (2018). *Yemen's Southern Powder Keg*. Chatham House Middle East and North Africa Programme research paper, March. At www.chathamhouse.org/sites/default/files/publications/research/2018-03-27-yemen-southern-powder-keg-salisbury-final.pdf (accessed 22 October 2019)

Samaha, N. (2019). *Can Assad Win the Peace?* European Council on Foreign Relations policy brief, 15 May, at www.ecfr.eu/page/-/can_assad_win_the_peace_syria.pdf (accessed 30 June 2019)

Santini, R.H. (2008). Policies towards Syria, 2003–07: Realpolitik Unintended. In Tocci, N. (ed.), *Who Is a Normative Foreign Policy Actor?* Brussels: Centre for European Policy Studies, at http://aei.pitt.edu/32609/1/48._Who_is_a_Normative_Foreign_Policy_Actor.pdf (accessed 25 July 2017)

Schmitt, O. (2018). When are strategic narratives effective? The shaping of political discourse through the interaction between political myths and strategic narratives. *Contemporary Security Policy*, 39(4), 1–25

Schmitt, O. (2020). How to challenge an international order: Russian diplomatic practices in multilateral security organisations. *European Journal of International Relations*, 26(3), 922–946

Schumacher, T. (2015). The European Union and democracy promotion: Reacting to the Arab Spring. In Sadiki, L. (ed.), *Routledge Handbook of the Arab Spring: Rethinking Democratization*. Abingdon and New York: Routledge, 559–573

Schumacher, T. (2020). The EU and its neighbourhood: The politics of muddling through. *JCMS: Journal of Common Market Studies*, 58, 187–201

Schumacher, T. and Nitoiu, C. (2015). Russia's foreign policy towards North Africa in the wake of the Arab Spring. *Mediterranean Politics*, 20(1), 97–104

Senyücel, S. and Dark, G. (2019). Turkey's response to and management of the Syrian refugee crisis. In Quero, J. and Sala, C. (eds), *The MENARA Booklet for the Humanitarian Sector*. Barcelona: CIDOB, 68–74

Serebrov, S. (2017). *Yemen Crisis: Causes, Threats and Resolution Scenarios*. Moscow: Russian International Affairs Council policy brief 14, October, at http://russiancouncil.ru/papers/Yemen-Policybrief14-en.pdf (accessed 23 September 2018)

Shaikh, S. and Notte H. (2018). *The Sochi Congress Under a Magnifying Glass: A Constructive Critique of Russia's Initiative for a Syrian-Syrian Dialogue*, Valdai Discussion Club, 22 February. At http://valdaiclub.com/a/highlights/the-sochi-congress-under-a-magnifying-glass/ (accessed 11 July 2019)

Shestakov, E. (2016). Chto zhdet Blizhnii Vostok? (What awaits the Middle East?) *Nezavisimaya gazeta*, 29 February, 6 (in Russian)

Shumilin, A. (2018). *Posle Khel'sinki: Perspektivy siriiskogo uregulirovaniya* (After Helsinki: prospect for a Syrian settlement). Moscow: Russian Academy of Sciences Institute of Europe analysis no 33, 9 August, at www.instituteofeurope.ru/images/uploads/analitika/2018/an129.pdf (accessed 10 September 2018, in Russian)

Shumilin, A. (2021). Blizhnevostochnye konflikty segodnya: Mezhdu religiei i geopolitikoi (The Middle East conflicts today: between religion and geopolitics). *Mirovaya ekonomika i mezhdunarodnye otnosheniya*, 65(1), 50–60

Shumilin, A. and Shumilina, I. (2017). Russia as a gravity pole of the GCC's new foreign policy pragmatism. *The International Spectator*, 52(2), 115–129

Siddi, M. (2020). The Mediterranean dimension of West-Russia security relations. In Futter, A. (ed.), *Threats to Euro-Atlantic Security. New Security Challenges*. Cham: Palgrave Macmillan, 165–177

Sidło, K.W. (2020). China's economic engagement in the MENA region. In Sidło, K.W. (ed.), *The Role of China in the Middle East and North Africa (MENA): Beyond Economic Interests?* Euromesco Joint Policy Study 16, European Institute of the Mediterranean (IEMed), July, 32–57. At www.euromesco.net/publication/the-role-of-china-in-the-middle-east-and-north-africa-beyond-economic-interests/ (accessed 30 June 2021)

Sil, R. and Katzenstein, P. J. (2010). Analytic eclecticism in the study of world politics: Reconfiguring problems and mechanisms across research traditions. *Perspectives on Politics*, 8(2), 411–431

Silitski, V. (2010). Survival of the fittest: Domestic and international dimensions of the authoritarian reaction in the former Soviet Union following the colored revolutions. *Communist and Post-Communist Studies*, 43(4), 339–350

Sladden, J., Wasser, B., Connable, B. and Grand-Clement, S. (2017). *Russian Strategy in the Middle East*. Rand Corporation Perspective

Smith, M. (2018). The EU, the US and the crisis of contemporary multilateralism. *Journal of European Integration*, 40(5), 539–553

Soler i Lecha, E., Colombo, S., Kamel, L. and Quero, J. (2019). Re-conceptualizing orders in the MENA region. In Quero, J. and Sala, C. (eds), *The MENARA Booklet for Academia*. Barcelona: CIDOB, 7–25

Sosnowski, M. and Hastings, P. (2019). Exploring Russia's humanitarian intervention in Syria. The Washington Institute, 25 June. At www.washingtoninstitute.org/fikraforum/view/exploring-russias-humanitarian-intervention-in-syria (accessed 13 April 2020)

Sosnowski, M. and Robinson, J. (2020). Mapping Russia's soft power efforts in Syria through humanitarian aid. Atlantic Council, 25 June, at www.atlanticcouncil.org/blogs/menasource/mapping-russias-soft-power-efforts-in-syria-through-humanitarian-aid/ (accessed 29 November 2021).

Souleimanov, E.A. (2014). Globalizing jihad? North Caucasians in the Syrian Civil War. *Middle East Policy*, 21(3), 154–162

Souleimanov, E.A. (2016). Mission accomplished? Russia's withdrawal from Syria. *Middle East Policy*, 23(2), 108–118

Souleimanov, E.A. and Abbasov, N. (2020). Why Russia has not (yet) won over Syria and Libya. *Middle East Policy*, 27(2), 81–93

Souleimanov, E.A. and Dzutsati, V. (2018). Russia's Syria war: A strategic trap? *Middle East Policy*, 25(2), 42–50

Souleimanov, E.A. and Petrylova, K. (2015). Russia's policy toward the Islamic State. *Middle East Policy*, 22(3), 66–78

Statista (2021). Russia's share of total imports of major arms in countries where it is one of top three suppliers from 2016 to 2020. At www.statista.com/statistics/1102702/countries-where-russia-is-a-major-arms-supplier/ (accessed 29 November 2021)

Stent, A. (2016). Putin's power play in Syria: How to respond to Russia's intervention. *Foreign Affairs*, 95(1), 106–113

Stent, A. (2022). The West vs. the rest. *Foreign Policy*, 2 May. At https://foreignpolicy.com/2022/05/02/ukraine-russia-war-un-vote-condemn-global-response (accessed 25 July 2022)

Stepanova, E. (2016). Russia in the Middle East: Back to a 'grand strategy' – or enforcing multilateralism? *IFRI Politique étrangère*, 2, 23–35. At www.ifri.org/sites/default/files/atoms/files/pe2_stepanova_ok.pdf (accessed 17 February 2018)

Stepanova, E. (2018a). Russia and conflicts in the Middle East: Regionalisation and implications for the West. *The International Spectator. Italian Journal of International Affairs*, 53(4), 35–57

Stepanova, E. (2018b). *Russia's Syria Policy: The Hard Path of Military Disengagement*. PONARS Eurasia Policy Memo no. 511, February

Stepanova, E. (2019). Regionalization as the key trend of Russia's policy on Syria and the Middle East. In *Russia's Policy in the Middle East: Determination, Delight, and Disappointment*. Central Asia Program CAP paper No. 212, Institute for European, Russian and Eurasian Studies, George Washington University, January, 8–12

Stivachtis, Y.A. (2018). The EU and the Middle East: The European Neighbourhood Policy. In Stivachtis, Y. (ed.), *Conflict and Diplomacy in the Middle East: External Actors and Regional Rivalries*. Bristol: E-International Relations, at www.e-ir.info/wp-content/uploads/2018/11/Conflict-and-Diplomacy-in-the-Middle-East-E-IR.pdf (accessed 23 September 2018, 110–127)

Stivachtis, Y.A. (2019). Political (in)security in the Middle East. In Koch, B. and Stivachtis, Y.A. (eds), *Regional Security in the Middle East: Sectors, Variables and Issues*. Bristol: E-International Relations Publishing, 23–44

Stoeckl, K. (2012). The human rights debate in the external relations of the Russian Orthodox Church. *Religion, State and Society*, 40(2), 212–232

Stoeckl, K. (2016). The Russian Orthodox Church as moral norm entrepreneur. *Religion, State and Society*, 44(2), 132–151

Stoner, K. and McFaul, M. (2015). Who lost Russia (this time)? Vladimir Putin. *Washington Quarterly*, 38(2), 167–187

Suny, R.G. (2007). Living in the hood: Russia, empire, and old and new neighbors. In Legvold, R. (ed.), *Russian Foreign Policy in the Twenty-First Century and the Shadow of the Past*. New York: Columbia University Press

Sychov, V. (2015). Iz pushki po vorob'yam. Zachem Rossii ponadobilos' zapuskat' rakety s Kaspiya (Shooting sparrows with a cannon. Why Russia had to launch missiles from the Caspian). Slon.ru, 8 October. At https://republic.ru/posts/57688 (accessed 4 May 2021)

Szostek, J. (2017). Defence and promotion of desired state identity in Russia's strategic narrative, *Geopolitics*, 22(3), 571–593

Tajbakhsh, K. (2018). Who wants what from Iran now? The post-nuclear deal US policy debate. *The Washington Quarterly*, 41(3), 41–61

Thakur, R. (2019). Global justice and national interests: How R2P reconciles the two agendas on atrocity crimes. *Global Responsibility to Protect*, 11(4), 411–434

Thomas, T. (2020). *Russian Lessons Learned in Syria: An Assessment*. MITRE Center for Technology and National Security, June. At www.mitre.org/sites/default/files/publications/pr-19-3483-russian-lessons-learned-in-syria.pdf (accessed 8 August 2020)

Thomson, A. and Shah, S. (2020). *Europe, Iran and the United States: A Roadmap for 2020*. European Leadership Network Global Security Report, 27 January. At www.europeanleadershipnetwork.org/report/europe-iran-and-the-united-states-a-roadmap-for-2020/ (accessed 4 May 2020)

Thornton, R. (2019) Countering prompt global strike: The Russian military presence in Syria and the Eastern Mediterranean and its strategic deterrence role. *The Journal of Slavic Military Studies*, 32(1), 1–24

Tocci, N. (ed.) (2008). *Who Is a Normative Foreign Policy Actor?* Brussels: Centre for European Policy Studies, at http://aei.pitt.edu/32609/1/48._Who_is_a_Normative_Foreign_Policy_Actor.pdf (accessed 25 July 2017)

Tocci, N. (2014). *On Power and Norms: Libya, Syria, and the Responsibility to Protect*. Washington, DC: Transatlantic Academy Paper Series, 2

Trading Economics (2020). At https://tradingeconomics.com/russia/ (accessed 24 February 2021)

Trenin, D. (2012). Why Russia Supports Assad. *The New York Times*, 9 February. At www.nytimes.com/2012/02/10/opinion/why-russia-supports-assad.html?_r=1&emc=eta1 (accessed 5 August 2018)

Trenin, D. (2013). *The Mythical Alliance: Russia's Syria Policy*. The Carnegie papers, Carnegie Moscow Center, February, at https://carnegieendowment.org/files/mythical_alliance.pdf (accessed 22 June 2017)

Trenin, D. (2016). *Russia and Iran: Historic Mistrust and Contemporary Partnership*. Carnegie Moscow Center, 18 August, at http://carnegie.ru/2016/08/18/russia-and-iran-historic-mistrust-and-contemporary-partnership-pub-64365 (accessed 4 May 2017)

Trenin, D. (2017a). *Looking out Five Years: Who Will Decide Russian Foreign Policy?* Carnegie Moscow Center, 17 August, at https://carnegie.ru/commentary/72811 (accessed 15 October 2018)

Trenin, D. (2017b). *Transformation of Power in the Middle East and the Implications for UK Foreign Policy*. Testimony: International Relations Committee of the House of Lords, Carnegie Moscow Center, 18 January, at https://carnegie.ru/2017/01/18/transformation-of-power-in-middle-east-and-implications-for-uk-foreign-policy-pub-67927 (accessed 15 October 2018)

Trenin, D. (2018a). What drives Russia's policy in the Middle East? In Popescu, N. and Secrieru, S. (eds), *Russia's Return to the Middle East: Building Sandcastles?* Chaillot paper No. 146, July. Paris: EU Institute for Security Studies, 21–28

Trenin, D. (2018b). *What Is Russia up to in the Middle East?* Cambridge and Medford MA: Polity Press

Tsygankov, A.P. (2012). Assessing cultural and regime-based explanations of Russia's foreign policy: Authoritarian at heart and expansionist by habit? *Europe-Asia Studies*, 64(4), 695–713

Tsygankov, A. (2016). Crafting the state-civilization: Vladimir Putin's turn to distinct values. *Problems of Post-Communism*, 63(3), 146–158

Ucko, D.H. (2018). Preventing violent extremism through the United Nations: The rise and fall of a good idea. *International Affairs*, 94(2), 251–270

UK Government (2013). Friends of Syria Core Group – Final Communique Joint Statement, press release, 22 June. At www.gov.uk/government/news/friends-of-syria-core-group-final-communique (accessed 5 January 2016)

Ülgen, S. and Kasapoğlu, C. (2021). *Russia's Ambitious Military-Geostrategic Posture in the Mediterranean*. Carnegie Europe, 10 June. At https://carnegieeurope.eu/2021/06/10/ussia-s-ambitious-military-geostrategic-posture-in-mediterranean-pub-84695 (accessed 10 November 2021)

UNGA (United Nations General Assembly) (2012). *Final Communiqué of the Action Group for Syria*. A/66/865–S/2012/522, 30 June. At https://peacemaker.un.org/sites/peacemaker.un.org/files/SY_120630_Final%20Communique%20of%20the%20Action%20Group%20for%20Syria.pdf (accessed 22 June 2017)

UNGA (United Nations General Assembly) (2014). *Report of the Independent International Commission of Inquiry on the Syrian Arab Republic*. Human Rights Council A/HRC/25/65, 12 February. At www.ohchr.org/en/hrbodies/hrc/iicisyria/pages/documentation.aspx (accessed 25 April 2020)

UNGA (United Nations General Assembly) (2017). *Report of the Independent International Commission of Inquiry on the Syrian Arab Republic*. Human Rights Council A/HRC/34/64, 2 February. At https://undocs.org/A/HRC/34/64 (accessed 25 April 2020)

UNHRC (United Nations Human Rights Council) (2016). *Out of Sight, Out of Mind: Deaths in Detention in the Syrian Arab Republic*. A/HRC/31/CRP.1 (Advance Version), 3 February

UNHRC (United Nations Human Rights Council) (2022). *Refugee Data Finder*. At www.unhcr.org/refugee-statistics/ (accessed 26 October 2022)

UNOCHA (United Nations Office for the Coordination of Humanitarian Affairs) (2020). Annual Report 2020. N/d. At www.unocha.org/sites/unocha/files/2020%20OCHA%20annual%20report.pdf (accessed 27 July 2021)

UNSC (United Nations Security Council) (2011a). 6528th meeting, S/PV.6528, 4 May. At www.un.org/en/ga/search/view_doc.asp?symbol=S/PV.6528 (accessed 19 November 2019)

UNSC (United Nations Security Council) (2011b). 6627th meeting, S/PV.6627, 4 October. At www.un.org/en/ga/search/view_doc.asp?symbol=S/PV.6627 (accessed 19 November 2019)

Bibliography

UNSC (United Nations Security Council) (2011c). 6524th meeting, S/PV.6524, 27 April. At www.un.org/en/ga/search/view_doc.asp?symbol=S/PV.6524 (accessed 22 November 2019)

UNSC (United Nations Security Council) (2011d). 6647th meeting, S/PV.6647, 2 November. At www.un.org/en/ga/search/view_doc.asp?symbol=S/PV.6647 (accessed 22 November 2019)

UNSC (United Nations Security Council) (2011e). 6598th meeting, S/PV.6598, 3 August. At www.un.org/en/ga/search/view_doc.asp?symbol=S/PV.6598 (accessed 22 November 2019)

UNSC (United Nations Security Council) (2011f). 6491st meeting, S/PV.6491, 26 February. At www.un.org/en/ga/search/view_doc.asp?symbol=S/PV.6491 (accessed 5 January 2020)

UNSC (United Nations Security Council) (2011g). 6498th meeting, S/PV.6498, 17 March. At www.un.org/en/ga/search/view_doc.asp?symbol=S/PV.6498 (accessed 5 January 2020)

UNSC (United Nations Security Council) (2012a). 6734th meeting, S/PV.6734, 12 March. At www.un.org/en/ga/search/view_doc.asp?symbol=S/PV.6734 (accessed 19 November 2019)

UNSC (United Nations Security Council) (2012b). 6711st meeting, S/PV.6711, 4 February. At https://undocs.org/en/S/PV.6711 (accessed 22 November 2019)

UNSC (United Nations Security Council) (2012c). 6810th meeting, S/PV.6810, 19 July. At https://undocs.org/en/S/PV.6810 (accessed 22 November 2019)

UNSC (United Nations Security Council) (2012d). 6841st meeting, S/PV.6841, 26 September. At https://undocs.org/en/S/PV.6841 (accessed 25 November 2019)

UNSC (United Nations Security Council) (2012e). 6731st meeting, S/PV.6731, 7 March. At https://undocs.org/en/S/PV.6731 (accessed 5 January 2020)

UNSC (United Nations Security Council) (2014a). 7116th meeting, S/PV.7116, 22 February. At https://undocs.org/en/S/PV.7116 (accessed 27 November 2019)

UNSC (United Nations Security Council) (2014b). 7180th meeting, S/PV.7180, 22 May. At https://undocs.org/en/S/PV.7180 (accessed 27 November 2019)

UNSC (United Nations Security Council) (2014c). *Report of the Secretary-General on the Implementation of Security Council Resolutions 2139 (2014) and 2165 (2014)*. S/2014/840, 21 November. At www.securitycouncilreport.org/atf/cf/%7B65BFCF9B-6D27-4E9C-8CD3-CF6E4FF96FF9%7D/s_2014_840.pdf (accessed 27 November 2019)

UNSC (United Nations Security Council) (2015a). 7419th meeting, S/PV.7419, 27 March. At www.securitycouncilreport.org/atf/cf/%7B65BFCF9B-6D27-4E9C-8CD3-CF6E4FF96FF9%7D/s_pv_7419.pdf (accessed 27 November 2019)

UNSC (United Nations Security Council) (2015b). 7401st meeting, S/PV.7401, 6 March. At www.securitycouncilreport.org/atf/cf/%7B65BFCF9B-6D27-4E9C-8CD3-CF6E4FF96FF9%7D/s_pv_7401.pdf (accessed 25 November 2019)

UNSC (United Nations Security Council) (2015c). 7588th meeting, S/PV.7588, 18 December. At https://undocs.org/S/PV.7588 (accessed 27 November 2019)

UNSC (United Nations Security Council) (2015d). *Report of the Secretary-General on the implementation of Security Council resolutions 2139 (2014), 2165 (2014) and 2191 (2014)*. S/2015/962, 11 December. At www.securitycouncilreport.org/atf/cf/%7B65BFCF9B-6D27-4E9C-8CD3-CF6E4FF96FF9%7D/s_2015_962.pdf (accessed 27 November 2019)

UNSC (United Nations Security Council) (2016a). Letter dated 12 February 2016 from the Secretary-General addressed to the President of the Security Council. S/2016/142, 12 February. At www.securitycouncilreport.org/atf/cf/%7B65BFCF9B-6D27-4E9C-8CD3-CF6E4FF96FF9%7D/s_2016_142.pdf (accessed 25 November 2019)

UNSC (United Nations Security Council) (2016b). Letter dated 24 August 2016 from the Secretary-General addressed to the President of the Security Council. S/2016/738, 24 August. At www.un.org/ga/search/view_doc.asp?symbol=S/2016/738 (accessed 25 November 2019)

UNSC (United Nations Security Council) (2016c). *Report of the Secretary-General Pursuant to Resolution 2299 (2016)*. S/2016/897, 25 October. At https://undocs.org/S/2016/897 (accessed 27 November 2019)

UNSC (United Nations Security Council) (2016d). 7687th meeting, S/PV.7687, 4 May. At www.securitycouncilreport.org/atf/cf/%7B65BFCF9B-6D27-4E9C-8CD3-CF6E4FF96FF9%7D/s_pv_7687.pdf (accessed 28 November 2019)

UNSC (United Nations Security Council) (2016e). 7774th meeting, S/PV.7774, 21 September. At https://undocs.org/S/PV.7774 (accessed 28 November 2019)

UNSC (United Nations Security Council) (2016f). 7795th meeting, S/PV.7795, 26 October. At https://undocs.org/S/PV.7795 (accessed 28 November 2019)

UNSC (United Nations Security Council) (2016g). 7777th meeting, S/PV.7777, 25 September. At https://undocs.org/S/PV.7777 (accessed 28 November 2019)

UNSC (United Nations Security Council) (2016h). 7757th meeting, S/PV.7757, 22 August. At www.securitycouncilreport.org/atf/cf/%7B65BFCF9B-6D27-4E9C-8CD3-CF6E4FF96FF9%7D/s_pv_7757.pdf (accessed 28 November 2019)

UNSC (United Nations Security Council) (2017a). Letter dated 30 June 2017 from the Secretary-General addressed to the President of the Security Council. S/2017/567, 30 June. At www.securitycouncilreport.org/atf/cf/%7B65BFCF9B-6D27-4E9C-8CD3-CF6E4FF96FF9%7D/s_2017_567.pdf (accessed 25 November 2019)

UNSC (United Nations Security Council) (2017b). *Implementation of Security Council Resolutions 2139 (2014), 2165 (2014), 2191 (2014), 2258 (2015) and 2332 (2016)*. S/2017/339, 19 April. At www.securitycouncilreport.org/atf/cf/%7B65BFCF9B-6D27-4E9C-8CD3-CF6E4FF96FF9%7D/s_2017_339.pdf (accessed 25 November 2019)

UNSC (United Nations Security Council) (2018a). *Security Council Demands 30-Day Cessation of Hostilities in Syria to Enable Humanitarian Aid Delivery, Unanimously Adopting Resolution 2401 (2018)*. SC13221, 24 February. At www.un.org/press/en/2018/sc13221.doc.htm (accessed 29 November 2019)

UNSC (United Nations Security Council) (2018b). *General Assembly Endorses Landmark Global Compact on Refugees, Adopting 53 Third Committee Resolutions, 6 Decisions Covering Range of Human Rights*, GA/12107, 17 December. At www.un.org/press/en/2018/ga12107.doc.htm (accessed 29 November 2019)

UNSC (United Nations Security Council) (2018c). *The Situation in the Middle East*. S/PV.8434, 20 December. At www.securitycouncilreport.org/un-documents/document/spv-8434.php (accessed 4 May 2022)

UNSC (United Nations Security Council) (2021). *Security Council Extends Use of Border Crossing for Humanitarian Aid into Syria, Unanimously Adopting Resolution 2585 (2021)*. SC/14577, 9 July. At www.un.org/press/en/2021/sc14577.doc.htm (accessed 10 September 2021)

UNSC (United Nations Security Council) (2022a). *The Situation in the Middle East*. S/PV.9163, 25 October. At https://documents-dds-ny.un.org/doc/UNDOC/PRO/N22/651/73/PDF/N2265173.pdf?OpenElement (accessed 29 November 2022)

UNSC (United Nations Security Council) (2022b). *Humanitarian Needs in the Syrian Arab Republic*. S/2022/933, 12 December. At https://documents-dds-ny.un.org/doc/UNDOC/GEN/N22/742/88/PDF/N2274288.pdf?OpenElement (accessed 23 December 2022)

US DoD (United States Department of Defense) (2018). *Summary of the 2018 National Defense Strategy of the United States of America*. At https://dod.defense.gov/Portals/1/Documents/pubs/2018-National-Defense-Strategy-Summary.pdf (accessed 4 June 2020)

US Mission (2013). *Secretary of State John Kerry and Russian Foreign Minister Sergey Lavrov Joint Statements*. U.S. Mission to International Organizations in Geneva, 2013/T14–01, 12 September. At https://geneva.usmission.gov/2013/09/12/secretary-of-state-john-kerry-and-russian-foreign-minister-sergey-lavrov-joint-statements%E2%80%8F/ (accessed 26 January 2021)

Vakil, S. and Quilliam, N. (2021). *Steps to Enable a Middle East Regional Security Process*. Chatham House Middle East and North Africa research programme, April. At www.chathamhouse.org/2021/04/steps-enable-middle-east-regional-security-process (accessed 4 May 2021)

Vasil'ev, A.M. (2011). Tsunami revolyutsii (A tsunami of revolutions). *Aziya i Afrika Segodnya*, 3, 2–18 (in Russian)

Vasiliev, A. (2018). *Russia's Middle East Policy: From Lenin to Putin*. London: Routledge

Wastnidge, E. (2017). Iran and Syria: An enduring axis. *Middle East Policy*, 24(2), 148–159

Weiss, A.S. and Ng, N. (2019). *Collision avoidance: The Lessons of U.S. and Russian Operations in Syria*. Carnegie Endowment for International Peace, 20 March, at https://carnegieendowment.org/2019/03/20/collision-avoidance-lessons-of-u.s.-and-russian-operations-in-syria-pub-78571 (accessed 15 April 2019)

Weldes, J. (1996). Constructing national interests. *European Journal of International Relations*, 2(3), 275–318

Welsh, J.M. (2010). Implementing the 'Responsibility to Protect': Where expectations meet reality. *Ethics & International Affairs*, 24(4), 415–430

Welsh, J.M. (2021). The Security Council's role in fulfilling the Responsibility to Protect. *Ethics & International Affairs*, 35(2), 227–243

Wezeman, P.D., Fleurant, A., Kuimova, A., Lopes da Silva, D., Tian Nan and Wezeman, S.T. (2020). *SIPRI Fact Sheet: Trends in International Arms Transfers*,

2019. Stockholm International Peace Research Institute, March. At www.sipri.org/sites/default/files/2020-03/fs_2003_at_2019.pdf (accessed 6 August 2020)

Wezeman, P.D., Kuimova, A. and Wezeman, S.T. (2021). *SIPRI Fact Sheet: Trends in International Arms Transfers, 2020*. Stockholm International Peace Research Institute, March. At https://sipri.org/sites/default/files/2021-03/fs_2103_at_2020.pdf (accessed 29 November 2021)

Whitehead, L. (2015). On the Arab Spring: Democratization and related political seasons. In Sadiki, L. (ed.), *Routledge Handbook of the Arab Spring: Rethinking Democratization*. Abingdon and New York: Routledge

The White House (2011). Remarks by the President on the Middle East and North Africa, 19 May. At https://obamawhitehouse.archives.gov/the-press-office/2011/05/19/remarks-president-middle-east-and-north-africa (accessed 19 November 2019)

The White House (2012). Remarks by the President to the White House Press Corps, 20 August. At https://obamawhitehouse.archives.gov/the-press-office/2012/08/20/remarks-president-white-house-press-corps (accessed 25 November 2019)

The White House (2013). Statement by the President on Syria 31 August. At https://obamawhitehouse.archives.gov/the-press-office/2013/08/31/statement-president-syria (accessed 25 November 2019)

The White House (2015). U.S.-Gulf Cooperation Council Camp David Joint Statement, 14 May. At https://obamawhitehouse.archives.gov/the-press-office/2015/05/14/us-gulf-cooperation-council-camp-david-joint-statement (accessed 19 November 2019)

Whittall, J. (2014). The 'new humanitarian aid landscape': Case study: MSF interaction with non-traditional and emerging aid actors in Syria 2013–14, Médecins Sans Frontières, July. At www.almendron.com/tribuna/wp-content/uploads/2019/08/the-new-humanitarian-aid-landscape.pdf (accessed 12 February 2021)

Wilhelmsen, J. (2017). *Russia's Securitization of Chechnya: How War Became Acceptable*. Abingdon and New York: Routledge

Wilhelmsen, J. (2018). Inside Russia's imperial relations: The social constitution of Putin-Kadyrov patronage. *Slavic Review*, 77(4), 919–936

Wilhelmsen, J. (2019). Putin's power revisited: How identity positions and great power interaction condition strategic cooperation on Syria. *Europe-Asia Studies*, 71(7), 1091–1121

Wilhelmsen, J. and Youngman, M. (2020). Violent mobilization and non-mobilization in the North Caucasus. *Perspectives on Terrorism*, 14(2), 2–10

Williams, B.G. and Souza, R. (2016). Operation 'Retribution': Putin's military campaign in Syria, 2015–16. *Middle East Policy*, 23(4), 42–60

Wintour, P. (2020). 'Anything goes'. First Syria, then Covid-19. Is global cooperation dead? *The Guardian*, 23 July, 30

Wintour, P. (2022). Hopes rising in Kyiv for Nuremberg-style tribunal over Russian war crimes. *The Guardian*, 5 December, 24

Wood, D.L. (ed.) (2019). *2019 Index of U.S. Military Strength*. Washington: The Heritage Foundation. At www.heritage.org/sites/default/files/2018-09/2019_IndexOfUSMilitaryStrength_WEB.pdf (accessed 1 October 2019)

World Bank (2021a). World Integrated Trade Solution data 2019. At https://wits.worldbank.org/CountryProfile/en/Country/MEA/Year/2019/TradeFlow/EXPIMP/Partner/by-country (accessed 29 November 2021)
World Bank (2021b). Foreign direct investment, net inflows – Russian Federation (2019). At https://data.worldbank.org/indicator/BX.KLT.DINV.CD.WD?locations=RU (accessed 29 November 2021)
World Bank (2021c). Foreign direct investment, net outflows – Russian Federation (2020). At https://data.worldbank.org/indicator/BM.KLT.DINV.CD.WD?locations=RU (accessed 29 November 2021)
World Bank (2021d). The World Bank in Syrian Arab Republic. Overview. 21 October update. At www.worldbank.org/en/country/syria/overview#1 (accessed 29 November 2021)
World Nuclear Association (2021). *Nuclear Power in Russia*. October 2021 update. At www.world-nuclear.org/information-library/country-profiles/countries-o-s/russia-nuclear-power.aspx (accessed 29 November 2021)
Xinhua (2018). China, Arab states to forge strategic partnership. 11 July. At http://english.www.gov.cn/news/top_news/2018/07/11/content_281476217762580.htm (accessed 29 November 2019)
Yablokov, I. (2015). Conspiracy theories as a Russian public diplomacy tool: The case of Russia Today (RT). *Politics*, 35(3–4), 301–315
Yakovenko, A.V. (2019). Article by Rector of the Diplomatic Academy of the Russian Foreign Ministry 'Russia and the Islamic World: Looking into the Future'. Interfax News Agency, 27 November. At www.mid.ru/ru/foreign_policy/news/-/asset_publisher/cKNonkJE02Bw/content/id/3922592 (accessed 4 May 2020, in Russian)
Youngman, M. (2016). Between Caucasus and caliphate: The splintering of the North Caucasus insurgency. *Caucasus Survey*, 4(3), 194–217
Youngs, R. (2018). *Bolstering Europe's Localist Approach to Syria*. Carnegie Europe, 4 April at https://carnegieeurope.eu/2018/04/04/bolstering-europe-s-localist-approach-to-syria-pub-75914 (accessed 4 May 2018)
Youngs, R. (2022). *The Awakening of Geopolitical Europe?* Carnegie Europe, 28 July. At https://carnegieeurope.eu/2022/07/28/awakening-of-geopolitical-europe-pub-87580 (accessed 10 September 2022)
Youngs, R. and Gutman, J. (2015). *Is the EU Tackling the Root Causes of Middle Eastern Conflict?* Carnegie Europe, 1 December. At https://carnegieeurope.eu/2015/12/01/is-eu-tackling-root-causes-of-middle-eastern-conflict-pub-62138 (accessed 20 November 2019)
Zagorski, A. (2009). The limits of a global consensus on security: The case of Russia. In Peral, L. (ed.), *Global Security in a Multipolar World*. Chaillot paper No. 118, October. Paris: EU Institute for Security Studies
Zamirirad, A. (2017). *Iran und Russland: Perspektiven der bilateralen Beziehungen aus Sicht der Islamischen Republik*. SWP-Studie 7, April. Berlin: Stiftung Wissenschaft und Politik (in German, all translations by the present author)
Zevelev, I. (2016). *Russian National Identity and Foreign Policy*. Center for Strategic and International Studies, December, at www.csis.org/analysis/russian-national-identity-and-foreign-policy (accessed 4 May 2017)

Zhekova, K. (2018). *Russian Discourses of Intervention 2011–2014: Constructing the Western Other*. PhD thesis, December. The University of Leeds. At http://etheses.whiterose.ac.uk/22298/

Ziegler, C.E. (2012). Conceptualizing sovereignty in Russian foreign policy: Realist and constructivist perspectives. *International Politics*, 49(4), 400–417

Zvyagel'skaya, I.D. (2014). *Blizhnevostochnyi klinch. Konflikty na Blizhnem Vostoke i politika Rossii* (In the Middle Eastern embrace: The conflicts in the Middle East and Russia's policy). Moscow: Aspekt-press (in Russian)

Zvyagel'skaya, I.D. (2015). Arkhaizatsiya v arabskom mire: Posle i vmesto revolyutsii (Archaisation in the Arab world: After and instead of revolution). *Vostok. Afroaziatskie obshchestva: Istoriya i sovremennost'*, 4, 104–113 (in Russian)

Zvyagelskaya, I. (2016). Russia, the new protagonist in the Middle East. In Ferrari, A. (ed.), *Putin's Russia*. Milano: Ledizioni, July, 73–91, at https://www.ispionline.it/sites/default/files/pubblicazioni/putins.russia_ebook.pdf (accessed 26 March 2019)

Zvyagelskaya, I. and Surkov, N. (2019). *Russian Policy in the Middle East: Dividends and Costs of the Big Game*. Russian International Affairs Council working paper No. 51, Moscow. At https://russiancouncil.ru/en/activity/workingpapers/russian-policy-in-the-middle-east-dividends-and-costs-of-the-big-game/ (accessed 4 May 2020)

Zvyagel'skaya, I., Svistunova, I. and Surkov, N. (2020). The Middle East in conditions of 'negative certainty' (Blizhnii vostok v usloviyakh 'negativnoi opredelennosti'). *Mirovaya ekonomika i mezhdunarodnye otnosheniya*, 64(6), 94–103

Zygar', M. (2015). 'Nash sukin syn'. Pochemu Vladimir Putin gotov voevat' za Bashara Assada ('Our son of a bitch'. Why Vladimir Putin is ready to fight for Bashar Assad). Republic (Slon), 22 September

Index

9/11 22, 44, 48, 150
   see also war on terror

Abraham Accords 37
Admiral Gorshkov (ship) 175
Admiral Kuznetsov (ship) 175
Afghanistan 44, 118, 154
Afrin (Syria) 35, 83, 88, 90
agile diplomacy 7, 29, 192
Ahrar al-Sham 60
aid, humanitarian *see* humanitarian
air defence systems 34, 35, 42, 174, 175, 177, 182, 186
Akhmat Kadyrov Public Foundation 144, 164
al-Assad, Bashar
   Assad's forces 14, 21, 33, 36, 45, 52, 60, 73, 75, 77, 78, 79, 83, 89, 93, 97, 129, 138, 141, 154, 164
   and China 53, 62, 137
   and the European Union (EU) 49, 51
   and France 66
   and Hezbollah 31
   and Iran 31, 32, 67, 133, 203
   and Israel 37
   and Qatar 38
   removal of Assad 2, 48, 49, 51, 53, 57, 58, 59, 61, 62, 63, 64, 65, 70, 71, 72, 76, 87, 92, 93, 96, 137, 138
   and Russia 13, 15, 25, 27, 31, 32, 37, 51, 53, 61, 62, 63, 67, 70, 73, 74, 75, 77, 80, 83, 86, 91, 92, 93, 94, 95, 98, 103, 104, 108, 113, 116, 127, 129, 130, 133, 137, 138, 141, 143, 144, 146, 156, 158, 171, 174, 185, 199, 203
   and Saudi Arabia 38
   Syrian protestors 2, 6, 21, 57, 59, 60, 61

   and Turkey 33, 38, 81, 88
   and the United Kingdom (UK) 52, 58, 66
   and the United States (US) 45, 62, 66, 76, 77, 88
al-Assad, Hafez 107
Alawite leadership (Syria) 58, 59, 60, 93
Aleppo (Syria) 35, 59, 69, 71, 74, 75, 76, 77, 78, 79, 82, 93, 95, 111, 142, 146, 164
al-Gaddafi, Muammar 1, 2, 6, 26, 28, 40, 41, 49, 58, 61, 92, 93, 95, 104, 136, 137, 181, 194, 201
   see also Libya
Algeria 21, 23, 42, 43, 108, 178, 180, 181, 182, 201, 206
al-Islam, Saif 41
Allison, Roy 9, 104, 118, 121, 170, 194
al-Nusra front 65, 66, 68, 71, 77
   see also Jabhat al-Nusra
Al-Qaeda 23, 28, 39, 44, 148, 152, 155
Al-Qaryatayn 79
al-Sarraj, Fayez 40, 41
al-Sisi, Abdel Fatteh 25, 42, 49, 108, 182
Al-Tanf military base (Syria) 88
Amnesty International 11
Ankara (Turkey) 29, 33, 34, 35, 36, 79, 81, 83, 88, 89, 183
Annan, Kofi 63, 64, 65, 66
anti-access area denial (A2AD) strategy 175, 177
Arab Awakening 20, 147, 166, 167
Arab League 62, 71, 206, 207, 209
Arab Libyan Forces (ALF) 40
Arab Policy Paper 2016 (China) 53, 183
Arab Spring (Arab uprisings) 1–12 passim, 14, 16–18 passim, 19–26 passim, 30, 33, 36, 42, 44, 50, 53,

55, 59, 70, 95–99 passim, 101, 103, 104, 106, 107–108, 109, 115–118 passim, 120–123 passim, 129, 131, 132, 134, 144, 145, 147, 151, 152, 154, 158, 161, 163, 166, 173, 178, 185, 190, 192, 194, 196–199 passim, 201, 205, 206, 207, 209
armaments 32, 40, 43, 111, 182, 183, 188
  see also disarmament programmes
armed conflict 24, 112, 135, 148, 189, 199, 204
armed forces *see* Russian armed forces; Syrian armed forces
Armenia 35
arms supply 1, 29, 41, 42, 49, 54, 60, 62, 72, 171, 178, 182, 183, 200
Asian Infrastructure Investment Bank 53
Asia-Pacific Economic Cooperation summit (2017) 86
Astana process 15, 29, 34, 35, 59, 79, 80, 81, 82, 83, 86, 88, 90, 91, 92, 140, 192
Atlantic Council 77
authoritarianism 23, 59, 107, 155, 208
Azerbaijan 35

Bab al-Hawa 142
Badia region 91
Baghdad 40, 71
Bahrain 2, 25, 28, 37, 38, 53, 179, 180, 206
Barcelona Process Euro-Mediterranean Partnership (EMP) 48
Barnes-Dacey, J. 81
Bashagha, Fathi 41
Bedford, S. 160
Beijing (China) 53, 54, 55, 137, 183, 205
Benghazi 136
Berlin Conference on Libya (2020) 41
Beslan school massacre (Russia, 2004) 150
Biden, Joe 31, 38, 46, 89, 202
Black Sea 173, 175
Bogdanov, Mikhail 2, 110
Bolotnaya protests (2011–2012) 103, 104, 105, 108, 195
Bouazizi, Mohammed 1
Bouteflika, Abdelaziz 43

Brahimi, Lakhdar 65, 67, 68, 69, 94
Brazil 64
Breedlove, Philip 46
BRICS group 64, 77, 131
Brussels 49, 50, 51, 81
Bush, George W. 44, 128
Bushehr nuclear plant 51, 181

Caesar Syria Civil Protection Act (US) 89, 202
Cairo 42
Cameron, David 52, 53, 66, 202
Canada 60
Carnegie Moscow Center 110
Carter, Ashton 45, 46, 47
Caspian Sea 171, 172, 173
Caucasus Emirate 155, 156, 159
Ceasefire Task Force (ISSG) 72
Centre for Reconciliation of Opposing Sides and Refugee Migration Monitoring 143
Chapter VII (UN Charter) 62, 67, 68, 84, 129, 135, 136
Chechnya 17, 75, 112, 113, 140, 147, 148, 149, 150, 154, 155, 156, 163, 164, 165, 166, 167, 207
  see also Kadyrov, Ramzan
chemical weapons (CW) 14, 45, 52, 53, 59, 66, 67, 70, 83, 84, 85, 93, 97, 110, 116, 129, 138
Chemical Weapons Convention (CWC) 66, 67, 83
China 11, 15, 20, 24, 32, 40, 47, 51, 53–55 passim, 56, 60, 61, 62, 63, 64, 68, 116, 137, 138, 139, 142, 146, 182, 183, 205
  see also Beijing (China)
China-GCC Strategic Dialogue 53
chlorine 84, 86
Christians 59, 60, 102, 158, 161, 162, 163, 167
Churkin, Vitalii 25, 61, 62, 63, 68, 69, 74, 75, 76, 84
Clinton, Hillary 63
Clunan, A.L. 99
Cold War 3, 7, 13, 27, 91, 95, 100, 121, 122, 127, 130, 134, 141, 169, 170, 187, 191, 207, 208
Collective Security Treaty Organisation 108, 131
colour revolutions 9, 79, 103, 104, 106, 117, 197, 207

Common Security and Defence Policy (EU) 49
Commonwealth of Independent States Anti-Terrorism Centre 157
Communist Party *see* Russian Federation Communist Party
Conference on Security and Cooperation in Europe 91
Congress of the Syrian National Dialogue 86
conservatism 106, 159, 160
constitutional committee 86, 87, 88, 90, 96
corruption 2, 21, 40, 55, 57, 124, 146, 159, 198, 201
cosmopolitan moralists 130, 131
Council of Muftis of Russia 161
counter-terrorism 26, 29, 42
Covington, S.R. 169, 172, 186
Crimea annexation 3, 77, 94, 103, 104, 110, 113, 124, 175, 178, 183
crimes against humanity 60, 62, 68, 141
Criminal Code *see* Russian Federation Criminal Code
cruise missiles 172, 174, 175, 182
Cyprus 35

Dagestan 151, 154, 156, 157
Damascus 33, 59, 62, 63, 76, 79, 84, 88, 142, 180, 185, 199, 206
Dannreuther, Roland 3, 9, 103, 106, 150, 166
Dara'a 57
Darayya 84
Dbeibeh, Abdul Hamid 41, 206
Deir ez-Zor 79–80, 90, 114, 199
de Mistura, Staffan 69, 71, 73, 75, 78, 81, 86, 87, 88
Democratic Union Party (PYD) (Syria) 33, 81, 86
democratisation 23, 26, 44, 106
Den'gov, Lev 165
disarmament programmes 31, 45, 67, 110
    see also Russian State Armament Programme to 2027 (SAP 2027)
diversity
    civilisational 9, 101, 102, 103
    cultural 101, 102, 103, 107, 120
    ethnic 159
    global 102
Djibouti 54

Douma 85
Dozhd (television channel) 116
drones 32, 129, 171, 207
Druze 59, 60
Dubrovka theatre attack (Russia, 2002) 150

Eastern Mediterranean 20, 175, 180, 181, 187, 188
Egypt 2, 21, 24, 25, 33, 40, 42, 49, 53, 54, 57, 59, 82, 87, 96, 108, 151, 156, 164, 175, 178, 179, 180, 181, 182, 184, 196, 201, 202
    see also al-Sisi, Abdel Fatteh; Morsi, Mohamed; Mubarak, Hosni
El Dabaa nuclear power plant 181
electronic warfare 174, 175
equality, sovereign *see* sovereign equality
Erdoğan, Recep Tayyip 33, 34, 86, 88, 89, 90, 155
ethnic cleansing 135
ethno-confessional divisions 20, 22, 43, 151, 166, 191
EUBAM Libya 49
EUFOR Libya 49
Euphrates 89, 90, 91
Eurasian Group on Combating Money-Laundering and the Financing of Terrorism 157
European Civil Protection and Humanitarian Aid Operations 141
European Parliamentary Research Service 144
European Union (EU) 1, 11, 12, 20, 24, 32, 34, 48, 49, 50, 51, 52, 54, 60, 67, 71, 81, 91, 94, 144, 202, 203, 204
EU–Turkey migration agreement (2016) 50
extremism 21, 68, 149, 151, 163, 166, 195
    see also Islamism
extremists 3, 36, 61, 73, 81, 147, 151, 153, 155, 161
    see also Islamism

Federal Assembly, Moscow 153, 172
Fethullah Gülen, M. 34
fight against terrorism narrative 17, 64, 91, 94, 96, 147, 152, 153, 167, 194

fighter jets 35, 41, 42, 71
Final Communiqué of the Action Group for Syria 64, 65, 66, 69, 72, 92
force, use of 2, 4, 16, 45, 57, 61, 62, 76, 100, 112, 121, 122, 123, 127–132 passim, 134, 135, 138, 139, 144, 145, 146, 174, 201, 205, 209
foreign fighters 17, 29, 49, 68, 148, 149, 152, 153, 154, 155, 156, 157, 166, 167
Foreign Policy Concept *see* Russian Foreign Policy Concept
formal institutions 24, 106, 113, 119, 197
Fradkov, Mikhail 62
France 11, 40, 48, 49, 51, 52, 53, 60, 61, 63, 66, 85, 87, 203
 see also Hollande, François; Macron, Emmanuel; Paris terrorist attacks (France, 2015); Sarkozy, Nicolas
Freedman, Lawrence 119, 123–124, 128, 145
Free Syrian Army 33, 57, 73, 77, 116
Friends of Syria 62, 65
Fund for Islamic Culture and Education 151

G7 developed economies 184
G8 Lough Erne (2013) 65, 66
G8 summit (2011) 2
G20 157, 184
G20 summit (2017) 82
Gaddafi *see* al-Gaddafi, Muammar
gas 35, 40, 42, 84, 112, 176, 178, 179, 180, 182, 183, 186
Gas Exporting Countries Forum (GECF) 179
Gaza Strip 36
Gazprom 180, 183
Gel'man, Vladimir 110, 115
Geneva Communiqué *see* Final Communiqué of the Action Group for Syria
Geneva I–III conferences 63, 66, 68, 69, 73, 75, 92
Geneva process 58, 60, 80, 86, 87, 93, 96, 192, 203
genocide 69, 88, 135
Georgia 1, 139, 154, 171

Gerasimov, Valerii 70, 76, 112, 173, 174, 177
Germany 48, 49, 51, 60, 61, 63, 87
 see also Merkel, Angela
Ghouta chemical attack (Syria, 2013) 45, 52, 53, 66, 84, 138
global financial crisis 1, 188
GLONASS satellite navigation system 178
Golan Heights (Israel) 36, 37
Goldstein, J. 8, 99
Gol'ts, Aleksandr 113
Government of National Accord (GNA) 40, 41, 151
Government of National Unity 41
grain 36, 42, 178, 209
Greater Middle East 44, 201
Grozny (Russia) 75, 149, 164
GRU *see* Russian Federation Main Intelligence Directorate (GRU)
Gulf Cooperation Council (GCC) 28, 38, 39, 45, 53, 86, 136, 183, 206
Gulf (Arab Gulf) states 21, 28, 29, 30, 32, 38, 45, 46, 52, 54, 64, 113, 179–180, 182, 183, 184, 185, 202, 206
Guterres, António 201

Hadi, Abdrabbuh Mansur 38, 39
Haftar, Khalifa 35, 40, 41
Hague, William 63
Halbach, U. 163, 164, 165
Hama (Syria) 76, 79, 82, 83, 84
Hamas 36, 151
Hammarskjöld, Dag 121, 125, 146
Hay'at Tahrir al-Sham 89, 91, 94, 155
helicopters 42, 70, 84, 86, 171, 174
Herrmann, R.K. 7
Hezbollah 28, 31, 34, 36, 37, 54, 68, 151
High Negotiations Committee (HNC) 74, 86
Hinnebusch, R. 56, 58, 60, 64, 65
Hollande, François 73
Homs 76, 79, 80, 82, 83, 84, 164
Houthis 30, 36, 38, 39, 202
humanitarian
 access 63, 65, 67, 72, 74, 78, 80, 81, 82, 86, 206
 agencies 61, 68, 90
 aid 49, 68, 72, 86, 140–144 passim, 164

Index

assistance 17, 56, 78, 88, 89, 117, 122, 138, 141, 142, 143, 144, 146, 198, 202, 204
corridors 75, 76, 146, 207
costs 14, 45, 143
intervention 16, 61, 66, 128, 130, 131, 132, 137, 138, 139, 189
issues 49, 50, 146, 162
law 2, 25, 51, 65, 118, 130, 134, 135, 143, 199
offences 78, 131, 135
Humanitarian Task Force (ISSG) 72
Human Rights Council *see* UN Human Rights Council (UNHRC)
Human Rights Watch 11, 70, 77, 143
Hurrell, Andrew 4, 5, 121, 122–123, 124, 130, 131, 189, 193
hydrocarbon production 179, 180

identity
Chechen 163
civilisational 99, 101, 118, 162
cultural 8, 100, 101, 118, 120, 193
ethnic 17, 21
Islamic 148, 159
national 16, 17, 22, 30, 99, 100, 101, 120, 148, 158, 160, 166, 195
religious 17, 21, 123, 133, 148, 158, 160, 161, 166
Russian 5, 8, 9, 16, 17, 100, 101, 102, 119, 148, 158, 159, 160, 161, 172
sectarian 21, 23, 60
social 123, 133
subnational 165
tribal 21
Idlib (Syria) 35, 76, 80, 82, 83, 84, 86, 88, 89, 93, 96, 133, 142, 146, 157
Imperial Orthodox Palestine Society 162
Independent International Commission of Inquiry (IICI) *see* UN Independent International Commission of Inquiry (IICI)
India 64, 182, 183
information war (Russia) 14, 87, 94, 208
Institute for the Study of War 77
insurgents 21, 60, 133, 148, 149, 150, 152, 154, 155, 156, 157, 158, 159
integrity, territorial 33, 61, 68, 69, 132, 143

International Commission on Intervention and State Strategy (ICISS) 135
International Committee of the Red Cross 141
International Criminal Court (ICC) 1, 58, 68, 69, 139, 140
International Crisis Group 11, 199
International Syria Support Group (ISSG) 49, 51, 71, 72, 74, 78, 80
see also Ceasefire Task Force (ISSG); Humanitarian Task Force (ISSG)
inter-state rivalries 20, 24, 96, 147, 204, 209
Investigation and Identification Team (IIT) 85, 86
Iran
and China 32, 54, 183
domestic pressures 30
and the European Union (EU) 51–52
and France 52
and Iraq 71
Islamic Awakening 30
Islamic Revolutionary Guard Corps 37
and Israel 29, 30, 32, 36, 37, 46, 90, 202
nuclear programme 30, 31, 37, 44, 47, 48, 51, 52, 54, 73, 110, 129, 202, 203
and Russia 13, 15, 29, 30, 31, 32, 34, 36, 37, 39, 40, 47, 51, 52, 54, 59, 67, 71, 80, 81, 82, 83, 86, 87, 91, 93, 113, 129, 139, 178, 179, 180, 181, 182, 184, 206, 207, 209
and Saudi Arabia 22, 28, 30, 38, 39, 46, 179, 202, 204
security threats against Iran 30
and Syria 30, 31, 32, 34, 36, 37, 60, 67, 71, 80, 81, 82, 83, 86, 87, 92, 114, 116, 133, 171, 203
and Turkey 29, 33, 35, 59, 80, 81, 82, 86, 91
and Ukraine 32, 206
and the United States (US) 4, 22, 31, 32, 35, 36, 40, 44, 45, 46, 47, 51, 52, 87, 89, 129, 183
West Asia 30, 31
and Yemen 30, 33, 38, 139, 202
see also Astana process; Khamenei, Ayatollah; Raisi, Ebrahim;

Rouhani, Hassan; Soleimani, Qassem; Tehran
Iraq 1, 13, 17, 22, 24, 28, 30, 31, 32, 33, 37, 39, 40, 44, 48, 49, 52, 54, 55, 60, 61, 69, 71, 85, 92, 108, 128, 129, 134, 142, 148, 153, 154, 155, 156, 157, 158, 180, 182, 183, 184, 198, 199, 201, 202
Islam
  non-traditional 149, 150, 152
  political 17, 21, 22, 147, 148, 152, 160, 166, 189
  traditional 150, 161
Islamic Awakening 30
Islamic Revolutionary Guard Corps 37
Islamic State 17, 20, 22, 23, 26, 28, 33, 34, 35, 39, 40, 45, 46, 47, 52, 60, 61, 65, 68, 69, 70, 71, 73, 75, 76, 77, 81, 84, 89, 91, 94, 117, 129, 131, 147, 148, 152, 154, 155, 156, 157, 158, 163, 164, 167
Islamism
  extremist 4, 8, 17, 19, 21, 22, 30, 33, 36, 44, 52, 65, 68, 79, 94, 104, 117, 149, 151, 152, 154, 155, 158, 162, 167, 202
  jihadi 165, 166
  militant 4, 15, 17, 21, 23, 26, 27, 29, 33, 45, 48, 69, 70, 95, 147, 149, 150, 155, 161, 163, 166
  Sunni 26, 28, 30, 33, 36, 58, 152, 163
Islamist terrorism 6, 47, 58, 73, 77, 127
Israel 15, 20, 28, 29, 30, 32, 36–37 passim, 44, 45, 46, 52, 54, 82, 83, 90, 178, 202, 206
  see also Netanyahu, Binyamin
Istanbul 72, 88
Italy 48

Jabhat al-Nusra 60, 76, 82, 89, 155
  see also al-Nusra front
Jarabulus (Syria) 81
jihadi
  activity 156
  forces 60, 93, 198
  groups 75, 76, 78, 82, 83, 89, 94
  movements 94, 200
  see also Islamism; Salafist jihadism
Joint Comprehensive Plan of Action (JCPOA) 31, 32, 51, 52, 53

Jordan 21, 23, 37, 82, 87, 96, 142, 164, 181, 198, 201

Kabardino-Balkaria (Russia) 156
Kadyrov, Ramzan 17, 112, 148, 156, 163, 164, 165, 168, 207
Kalibr missiles 173, 175
Kazakhstan 80
Keohane, R.O. 8, 99
Kerry, John 46, 67, 69, 72, 73, 75, 78, 111
Khamenei, Ayatollah 71
Khan Sheikhun 84, 85
Khasavyurt accords 149
Khmeimim air base (Syria) 70, 71, 74, 79, 84, 143, 173, 175
Khomeinism 30
Ki-moon, Ban 72, 153
Kinshchak, Aleksandr 110
Kortunov, A. 19
Krasner, S.D. 100
Kurdish forces 34, 88, 90, 129
Kurdish region 32, 33, 34, 80, 83
Kurdistan Workers' Party (PKK) 33, 34, 83, 90
Kurds 29, 32, 33, 34, 35, 39, 60, 90, 91
Kuwait 179, 180, 181
Kyiv (Ukraine) 36, 119, 207

Latakia (Syria) 34, 70, 71, 79, 82, 157
Lavrent'ev, Aleksandr 110
Lavrov, Sergei 1–4 passim, 13, 25, 26, 27, 31, 35, 46, 60–64 passim, 67, 69, 70, 72, 75, 76, 80, 81, 85–89 passim, 95, 98, 101, 102, 110, 111, 113, 121–127 passim, 132, 133, 134, 136, 137, 138, 146, 147, 157, 162, 184, 187, 190, 193, 195, 208
law
  enforcement 152, 156, 159, 165
  international 1, 12, 14, 16, 27, 31, 39, 52, 67, 77, 84, 93, 100, 102, 117, 124, 126, 127, 128, 129, 130, 131, 133, 134, 136, 137, 138, 145, 172, 193, 204
  international humanitarian 2, 25, 51, 65, 118, 130, 134, 135, 143, 199
  international human rights 11, 135, 136, 139
  sharia 163, 164
  of war 131, 201, 209

see also rule of law
League of Arab States (LAS) 28, 62, 63, 67, 136, 161
League of Nations 132
Lebanon 37, 54, 162, 180, 198, 199, 201
see also Hezbollah; Salamé, Ghassan
Levada Center *see* Yuri Levada Analytical Center
Levant, the 20, 28, 60
liberal constitutionalists 130, 131
liberal democracies 7, 8, 26, 43, 44, 108, 130, 131, 192, 196, 205
Liberal Democratic Party of Russia 116
liberalism *see* Western liberalism
Libya
  arms embargo 41
  EU policy in Libya 50
  and France 52
  Libya model 92, 136
  Misrata militias 151
  NATO intervention 28, 44, 52, 69, 109, 129, 139
  post-Gaddafi era 40, 41, 49, 58, 61, 95, 104, 146, 200, 201
  and Russia 1, 2, 6, 10, 26, 35, 41, 42, 43, 47–48, 104, 108, 115, 126, 136, 137, 139, 141, 145, 165, 175, 181, 184, 199, 206, 207
  and Turkey 35
  and the United Kingdom (UK) 52, 53, 202
  and the United States (US) 23, 44, 45, 46, 48, 201
  Western intervention 1, 13, 23, 25, 28, 52, 55, 61, 136, 137, 138, 189, 207
  see also al-Gaddafi, Muammar; al-Sarraj, Fayez; Bashagha, Fathi; Haftar, Khalifa
liquefied natural gas (LNG) 180
Lough Erne (2013) *see* G8 Lough Erne (2013)
Ltamenah (Syria) 85
Lukoil 183

Macron, Emmanuel 52, 88
Maier, Charles 9
Mali 115
Mälksoo, L. 126
Marea (Syria) 84
McFaul, Michael 10, 105–106

Mearsheimer, John 200
Médecins Sans Frontières 142, 143
Mediterranean area 20, 28, 31, 50, 171, 173, 175, 177
  see also Eastern Mediterranean
Medvedev, Dmitrii 1, 109, 151, 156
MENARA research consortium 12, 20
mercenaries 41, 116, 207
Merkel, Angela 88
migration 49, 50, 143, 149, 202
Mikheev, Aleksandr 182
military hardware 32, 36
militias 22, 23, 28, 32, 39, 57, 60, 68, 77, 82, 91, 114, 133, 151, 171, 198, 199, 207
Ministry of Economic Development 186
Moore, C. 154, 155, 157, 158
Morgenthau, Hans 169
Morocco 21, 23, 37, 42, 43, 178, 206
Morsi, Mohamed 25, 38
Moscow Declaration 80
Moscow platform 69
Mubarak, Hosni 25
multilateralism 102, 131, 205
Muslim Brotherhood 24, 25, 33, 38, 42, 59, 151, 152
mustard gas 84

national beliefs 8, 99–103 passim, 119, 196
National Coalition of Syrian Revolutionary and Opposition Forces 64–65, 67, 69
National Defense Strategy 2018 (US) 46–47
national interests 7, 10, 36, 79, 86, 99, 100, 107, 135, 173, 174, 187, 193, 195, 196, 197, 210
National Oil Corporation (Libya) 180
national security 22, 36, 50, 52, 152, 176, 177, 185, 190, 191
NATO 2, 28, 36, 44, 45, 52, 69, 71, 109, 128, 129, 131, 136, 137, 139, 177
Naumkin, Vitalii 43, 158, 159, 162
Ned Lebow, R. 7
Netanyahu, Binyamin 36, 37
non-aligned movement 207, 208
non-intervention 93, 102, 103, 115, 124, 126, 132, 134, 136, 137, 194

normative regionalism 132
North Caucasus region 4, 17, 26, 29, 147–152 passim, 154–159 passim, 161, 163–168 passim, 173
nuclear power 35, 42, 53, 112, 174, 178, 181

Obama, Barack 3, 10, 31, 44, 45, 46, 47, 52, 66, 67, 73, 92
OECD Development Assistance Committee 141
Office of the UN High Commissioner for Refugees 141
Office of the United Nations High Commissioner for Human Rights 198
oil 38, 40, 41, 53, 112, 176, 178, 179, 180, 182, 183, 186, 188
oil-for-goods programme 180
Oman 180
OPCW-UN Joint Investigative Mechanism (JIM) 84, 85
Operation Allied Force 128
Operation Decisive Storm 38
Operation Euphrates Shield 35
Operation Olive Branch 83
Operation Peace Spring 89
Organisation for the Prohibition of Chemical Weapons (OPCW) 11, 66, 67, 77, 83, 84, 85, 204
 see also OPCW-UN Joint Investigative Mechanism (JIM)
Organisation of Islamic Cooperation (OIC) 28, 38, 67, 136, 161
Organisation of the Islamic Conference (2005) 151, 161
Organization for Security and Co-operation in Europe 209
Organization of the Petroleum Exporting Countries (OPEC) 179
Orthodox Church see Russian Orthodox Church
Oxfam 143, 144

P5 members 51, 68, 75, 87, 97, 127, 134, 135, 136, 139, 140, 205
Pakistan 154
Palestine 28, 37, 42, 44, 46, 141, 202
Paris terrorist attacks (France, 2015) 52, 73
Partnership and Strategic Cooperation Agreement (Russia–Egypt) 42

Partnership for Democracy and Shared Prosperity 48
Partnerships for Modernisation 1
Pedersen, Geir 90, 200
People's Protection Units (YPG) 33, 35, 83, 88, 90
Physicians for Human Rights 77, 199
Pinheiro, Paulo Sérgio 200
PKK see Kurdistan Workers' Party (PKK)
Plan of Action for Preventing Violent Extremism 153
pluralist systems 9, 21, 64, 93, 108, 109, 112, 123, 124, 125, 132, 134, 145, 151, 166, 193, 194, 196, 200, 205, 208
Portugal 61, 63
poverty 24, 55, 198
Prigozhin, Evgenii 114
Primakov, Evgenii 25–26, 149, 152, 161
private military contractors (PMC) 35, 40, 114, 171, 177, 187, 199, 207
Prokhanov, Aleksandr 116
protests 1, 2, 6, 17, 21, 23, 25, 26, 38, 42, 43, 44, 45, 57, 59, 60, 61, 62, 94, 95, 103, 104, 105, 107, 108, 136, 149, 166, 189, 195, 201
Putin, Vladimir
 agency 196–197
 and Angela Merkel 88
 approval ratings 104, 110
 authoritarian regime 10, 16, 110, 113
 autocratic regime 9
 and Bashar al-Assad 86, 92
 and Binyamin Netanyahu 36, 37
 cultural code 101
 domestic state order 98, 100, 106
 and Donald Trump 82, 86
 and Emmanuel Macron 88
 fight against terrorism 153
 and Hassan Rouhani 86
 humanitarian assistance 141
 international security system 100
 and Israel 36
 legitimacy of Putin's leadership 9, 10
 militancy 151, 156
 national identity 16, 100, 101
 personal world view 10
 political methods 10
 and Ramzan Kadyrov 164, 165

and Recep Tayyip Erdoğan 86, 88, 89, 90
and the Russian elite 9
Russia's economic interests 178
state-of-the-nation address (March 2018) 172
and Syrian civil war 3, 5, 6, 9, 10, 16, 70, 71, 74, 77, 79, 82, 86, 88, 89, 90, 92, 95, 103, 104, 106, 110, 118, 156, 162, 174–175
third presidency 3, 65, 103, 104
traditional values 102
and Turkey 34, 90
Western leadership 124, 125
Western threats to Russia 105
world view 10, 106, 110, 172, 189
Putin government, the 10, 16, 42, 98, 106, 108, 117, 150, 151, 167, 178
Putin leadership, the 3, 5, 7, 10, 11, 18, 34, 70, 74, 94, 97, 103, 104, 105, 106, 109, 119, 161, 170, 184, 187, 188, 190, 192, 208
PYD *see* Democratic Union Party (PYD) (Syria)

Qatar 28, 38, 40, 60, 82, 179, 181, 182
Qmenas (Syria) 84

radicalisation 149, 152, 158, 159, 165, 166, 167, 200
Raisi, Ebrahim 31, 32, 202
rally round the flag effect 103, 104
Raqqah (Syria) 80
Red Cross *see* International Committee of the Red Cross
Red Sea 175
refugee flows 34, 202, 207, 209
refugees 2, 33, 47, 49, 50, 61, 70, 73, 81, 83, 88, 90, 91, 142, 143, 164, 198, 203
regime change 2, 3, 9, 25, 26, 27, 46, 49, 52, 61, 62, 67, 70, 75, 87, 92, 96, 104, 105, 108, 115, 116, 118, 125, 127, 128, 129, 137, 141, 194, 201, 202, 203
repression 21, 22, 26, 45, 50, 58, 61, 103, 107, 123, 124, 150, 152, 153, 163, 166, 200, 201, 204, 207
Responsibility to Protect doctrine 12, 122, 126, 134–140 passim, 205
Reus-Smit, C. 101, 120, 130, 132
Richmond, O.P. 141

Rif Dimashq (Syria) 80
Riyadh (Saudi Arabia) 38, 39, 72, 86
Rohingya Muslims 164
Rosatom 181
Rosneft 180
Rosoboronexport 182
Rossotrudnichestvo federal agency 117
Rouhani, Hassan 86
RT (television channel) 117
rule of law 125, 200, 202
rules-based order 17, 50, 125, 132, 145, 190, 193, 204
Russia-Arab Business Council 179
Russia-GCC Strategic Dialogue 28
Russia-Islamic World Strategic Vision Group 38, 161
Russian-Arab Cooperation Forum 28, 64
Russian armed forces 79, 95, 171, 172, 173, 177, 186
Russian Direct Investment Fund 178, 179
Russian Federation Communist Party 116
Russian Federation Criminal Code 156
Russian Federation Main Intelligence Directorate (GRU) 114
Russian Federation Maritime Doctrine 173
Russian Federation Military Doctrine (2014) 173
Russian Federation Security Council 110, 112, 113
Russian Foreign Policy Concept 101, 134, 173
Russian Humanitarian Mission 144
Russian International Affairs Council 12
Russian National Anti-Terrorism Committee 156
Russian Orthodox Church 17, 112, 148, 158, 160, 161, 162, 163, 167
Russian State Armament Programme to 2027 (SAP 2027) 171, 174, 176, 188
Russia-Saudi Economic Council 180
Ryabkov, Sergei 110

S-300 missile defence system 30, 51
S-400 missile defence system 34, 35
Safronkov, Vladimir 110
Sakwa, Richard 99, 122

Salafism 151, 163, 164
Salafist jihadism 94, 150, 151
Salafists 58, 94, 150, 151, 154, 155, 156
Salamé, Ghassan 41, 200
Saleh, Ali Abdullah 25, 38
Samaha, N. 185, 203
Sana'a (Yemen) 38, 39
Saraqib (Syria) 86
sarin 66, 84, 85
Sarkozy, Nicolas 202
Sarmin (Syria) 84
Saudi Arabia 13, 22, 27, 28, 30, 32, 33, 38, 39, 40, 46, 49, 54, 59, 60, 62, 82, 86, 87, 139, 165, 178, 179, 180, 181, 182, 183, 202, 204, 209
    see also Riyadh (Saudi Arabia)
sectarian conflict 26, 28, 61
sectarian identity 21, 23, 60
sectarianism 19, 22, 33, 60
sectarian tensions 33, 38, 45, 73, 96, 151, 158, 165
sectarian violence 39, 55, 65, 191
Shabiha 60
Shaimiev, Mintimer 161
Shanghai Cooperation Organisation 31, 108, 131, 157
Shia forces 30, 32, 33, 38, 39, 60, 158, 167, 199
Shoigu, Sergei 79, 95, 103, 111, 197
Skripal, Sergei 85
Small Group on Syria 87
Sochi (Russia) 35, 86, 89, 157
social cohesion 24, 55
soft power 29, 54, 117, 144
Soleimani, Qassem 71, 129
Souleimanov, E.A. 76, 160
South Africa 64
Southern Transitional Council 39
sovereign equality 76, 122, 124, 125, 126, 132–134 passim, 139, 145
sovereignty 3, 4, 8, 9, 16, 23, 34, 36, 37, 39, 54, 61, 68, 69, 88, 91, 93, 97, 98, 100–104 passim, 118, 122, 124, 127, 130–136 passim, 138–146 passim, 152, 160, 164, 173, 193, 194, 200, 205, 206, 207, 209
State Armament Programme see Russian State Armament Programme to 2027 (SAP 2027)
State Duma (Russia) 115, 165

statehood 8, 15, 23, 95, 96, 100, 133, 160, 165, 193
Steiner, George 189
Stepanova, E. 6, 82, 105, 185, 187
Strategy on Syria (EU) 50–51
submarines 174, 175
Sudan 37, 115, 175
Sufism 151, 163, 164, 165
Sunnis 22, 26, 28, 30, 33, 34, 36, 39, 58, 59, 60, 83, 93, 94, 152, 155, 158, 159, 163, 164, 167, 199
surrender or starve tactics 142
Syrian Arab Red Crescent 142, 144
Syrian armed forces 84, 85, 87, 174
Syrian de-escalation agreement 69, 82, 87, 192
Syrian de-escalation zones 82, 89, 192
Syrian Democratic Forces 88, 89, 90
Syrian National Council 33, 59, 65, 67
Syrian Observatory for Human Rights 77
Syrian refugees see refugees
Syria Trust for Development 142

Talmenes 84
Tartus naval base (Syria) 79, 173, 174, 175, 176
Tatarstan 161
Tehran 29, 30, 31, 32, 34, 36, 37, 38, 46, 48, 51, 52, 54, 71, 79, 81, 83, 129, 180, 202, 206
Tellidis, I. 141
territorial integrity see integrity, territorial
terrorist attacks 34, 39, 52, 73, 94, 118, 157, 202
terrorists 36, 47, 68, 71, 72, 74, 75, 80, 88, 90, 96, 116, 123, 130, 140, 148, 153, 157
    see also Islamist terrorism
terrorist threats 50, 73, 149, 152, 177
Third World 121, 169
Tocci, N. 66, 139, 145
trade relations 17, 32, 34, 35, 38, 43, 51, 52, 53, 54, 55, 56, 109, 170, 173, 175, 178, 179, 180, 182, 183, 184, 185, 186, 188, 191, 192, 202, 206, 209
Trenin, Dmitri 110, 118, 169, 184
Tripoli 35, 40, 41
Trump, Donald 3, 31, 36, 45, 46, 50, 51, 80, 82, 86, 88, 89, 131

Tunisia 1, 2, 21, 23, 25, 42, 43, 53, 57, 201
Turkey 4, 13, 15, 20, 28, 29, 32, 33–36 passim, 37, 38, 40, 41, 50, 52, 54, 59, 60, 64, 70, 78, 80, 81, 82, 83, 88, 89, 90, 91, 142, 155, 178, 179, 180, 181, 183, 184, 198, 202, 206, 209
   see also Ankara (Turkey); Erdoğan, Recep Tayyip; Fethullah Gülen, M.
Turkstream gas project 178

Uighur fighters 54
Ukraine–Russia war
   annexation 35, 103, 113
   civilian casualties 207
   condemnation of Russia 39, 41, 42, 43
   consequences for Russia 6, 16, 18, 56, 119, 140, 170, 183, 186, 188, 197, 206, 208
   criticism of Russia 32, 36
   Donbas region 3
   drones 32
   implications for MENA countries 208, 209, 210
   private military contractors (PMC) 114, 207
   Revolution of Dignity 2014 3
   Russia and Western relations 143
   Russia's finances 176, 183, 192
   Russia's 'information war' 14
   Russia's military overextension 116, 176, 186
   Russia's military power 97
   Ukrainian sovereignty 36, 97, 146, 194, 206, 207
   Western sanctions 35, 36, 38, 48
   Western unity 52, 56, 77
   see also Crimea annexation; Kyiv (Ukraine)
UN Charter 61, 84, 94, 121, 124, 125, 129, 131, 134, 135, 137, 145, 193
   see also Chapter VII (UN Charter)
UN Development Program 141
UN Disengagement Observer Force 36
UN General Assembly (UNGA) 3, 11, 36, 42, 43, 63, 64, 87, 125, 126, 130, 143, 153, 206
UN Human Rights Council (UNHRC) 11, 60, 62, 126, 161, 204, 206

UN Independent International Commission of Inquiry (IICI) 11, 62, 70, 77, 85, 93, 200, 202
Union for the Mediterranean 48
United Arab Emirates (UAE) 28, 37, 38, 39, 40, 96, 178, 179, 180, 181, 182, 206, 209
United Kingdom (UK) 11, 39, 48, 49, 52–53, 58, 60, 61, 63, 66, 85, 87, 129, 202
   see also Cameron, David; Hague, William
United States (US)
   and Egypt 42, 182
   inconsistent policymaking 3, 4, 13, 22
   influence across the Middle East 32
   and Iran 4, 22, 31, 32, 35, 36, 40, 44, 45, 46, 47, 51, 52, 87, 89, 129, 183
   and Iraq 1, 22, 24, 39, 48, 61, 128, 202
   and Israel 36, 37
   and Libya 23, 44, 45, 46, 48, 201
   Middle East trade 54
   Muammar al-Gaddafi arrest warrant 1
   multilateral disarmament agreements 31
   National Security Strategy (2022) 202
   and Russia 1, 2, 5, 7, 8, 20, 32, 38, 44–48 passim, 51, 53, 56, 65, 67, 72, 74, 78, 80, 84, 90, 94, 95, 105, 114, 115, 116, 127, 129, 183, 187
   and Saudi Arabia 202
   and Syria 34, 53, 57, 58, 60, 62, 63, 65, 66, 68, 70, 71, 72, 74, 76, 77, 78, 79, 80, 82, 84, 85, 88, 89, 91, 92, 95, 108, 110, 114, 117, 129, 133, 138, 143, 177, 202
   and Turkey 35
   and Ukraine 42, 56
   US–Egypt Strategic Dialogue 42
   war on terror 22, 128
   and Yemen 39
   see also Biden, Joe; Kerry, John; Obama, Barack; Trump, Donald; Washington
Universal Declaration of Human Rights 126

UN Office for the Coordination of Humanitarian Affairs (UNOCHA) 142, 143
UN Office of Counter-Terrorism 153, 157
UN Secretary-General 11, 41, 67, 71, 72, 85, 125, 129, 142, 153, 201
UN Security Council (UNSC)
  resolution 1674 135
  resolution 1929 51
  resolution 1970 1, 68, 136, 139
  resolution 1973 1, 2, 6, 25, 104, 109, 115, 129, 136, 137, 201
  resolution 2014 38
  resolution 2042 63
  resolution 2043 63
  resolution 2118 66, 67, 84
  resolution 2139 68, 77, 199
  resolution 2165 68, 142, 199
  resolution 2170 68
  resolution 2201 39
  resolution 2209 84
  resolution 2216 38
  resolution 2231 51
  resolution 2235 84
  resolution 2254 51, 71, 72, 73, 75, 80, 87, 92, 203
  resolution 2258 72
  resolution 2268 72
  resolution 2336 78
  resolution 2401 86
  resolution 2510 41
  resolution 2585 142
  resolution 2624 39
UN Supervision Mission in Syria (UNSMIS) 63
UN Support Mission in Libya 48
uranium 51, 181

Valdai Discussion Club 12
Vershinin, Sergei 110
vessels, surface 174, 175
Vienna meetings (2015) 71, 72, 73
Violations Documentation Center 198

violent non-state actors 147, 148, 150
Voronkov, Vladimir 153

Wagner Group 40, 114
Wahhabism 163, 164
war crimes 41, 68, 75, 85, 86, 90, 130, 135, 208
war on terror 22, 128, 150, 156
  see also 9/11
Washington 6, 22, 34, 35, 42, 44, 46, 47, 87, 103, 115, 129, 131, 201, 202
weapon of mass destruction 85, 128, 129
West Asia 30, 31
Western liberalism 7, 8, 106, 130, 131, 160, 162, 163, 192, 196
Westphalian norms 124, 145
Women's Protection Units 33
World Health Organization 66
World Summit (2005) 129, 135, 138, 139, 205

Yang Jiechi 63
Yavlinskii, Grigorii 116
Yeltsin, Boris 149
Yemen 2, 13, 21, 22, 25, 28, 30, 33, 38, 39, 45, 46, 49, 53, 55, 57, 134, 139, 200, 201, 202, 206, 207
  see also Hadi, Abdrabbuh Mansur; Houthis; Saleh, Ali Abdullah
YPG see People's Protection Units (YPG)
Yuri Levada Analytical Center 104, 117, 118

Zakharova, Maria 57, 76, 84, 85, 88, 111
Zartman, I.W. 64, 65
Zavtra (newspaper) 116
Zhirinovsky, Vladimir 116
Zohr natural gas field (Egypt) 180
Zygar', Mikhail 116
Zyuganov, Gennadii 116